D1373286

Provincial Offences for Paralegals

Jennifer Zubick & Steve Weir

2013
Emond Montgomery Publications
Toronto, Canada

Copyright © 2013 Emond Montgomery Publications Limited.

NOTICE & DISCLAIMER: All rights reserved. No part of this publication may be reproduced in any form by any means without the written consent of Emond Montgomery Publications. Emond Montgomery Publications and all persons involved in the creation of this publication disclaim any warranty as to the accuracy of this publication and shall not be responsible for any action taken in reliance on the publication, or for any errors or omissions contained in the publication. Nothing in this publication constitutes legal or other professional advice. If such advice is required, the services of the appropriate professional should be obtained.

Emond Montgomery Publications Limited
60 Shaftesbury Avenue
Toronto ON M4T 1A3
http://www.emp.ca/highered

Printed in Canada.
Reprinted January 2015.

We acknowledge the financial support of the Government of Canada through the Canada Book Fund for our publishing activities.

Acquisitions editor: Bernard Sandler
Developmental editor: Sarah Gleadow
Marketing manager: Christine Davidson
Director, sales and marketing, higher education: Kevin Smulan
Supervising editor: Jim Lyons
Copy editor: Paula Kulig
Production editor: Cindy Fujimoto
Proofreader and indexer: Paula Pike
Designers: Shani Sohn and Tara Wells
Cover image: Bernard Sandler

Library and Archives Canada Cataloguing in Publication

Zubick, Jennifer, 1969-
    Provincial offences for paralegals / Jennifer Zubick, Steve Weir.

ISBN 978-1-55239-328-4
Includes index.

    1. Contraventions (Criminal law) — Ontario — Textbooks.   2. Summary proceedings — Ontario — Textbooks.   I. Weir, Steve   II. Title.

KEO1175.Z83 2012   345.713'02   C2012-900788-9
KF9620.ZB3Z83 2012

Contents

1 An Overview of the Provincial Offences Act

Preface

Provincial Offences for Paralegals is a text that is both foundational and advanced in its approach. Our goal was to write this text in a straightforward and engaging manner. You will be guided through the different procedural streams and charging documents; the classification of offences and available defences; and the anatomy of a trial. Practice tips throughout the text complement the subject-specific knowledge you will gain, offering invaluable advice that will help you to build and maintain your reputation as a professional in your future career.

Beginning with an overview of the *Provincial Offences Act* and a discussion of the roles and responsibilities of the key parties involved in the provincial offences system, *Provincial Offences for Paralegals* traces the process of a client being charged, arrested, and tried. It outlines the choices available to a paralegal at each stage, and describes the processes and techniques for entering pleas; filing motions, applications, and appeals; and interviewing and questioning witnesses. The principles of sentencing are discussed, and the steps that a paralegal should take following a satisfactory or an unsatisfactory outcome at trial are set out.

The text also offers coverage of common offences under the *Highway Traffic Act*, and provides an overview of selected sections from other key provincial legislation, including the *Liquor Licence Act*, *Environmental Protection Act*, *Occupational Health and Safety Act*, *Trespass to Property Act*, *Blind Persons' Rights Act*, *Dog Owners' Liability Act*, and relevant municipal legislation. In order to provide insight into some proposed changes and possible future directions of the POA, Appendix E to the text includes the executive summary from the final report by the Law Commission of Ontario on the modernization of the *Provincial Offences Act*, released in August 2011.

This text reflects the law and related forms as of March 31, 2012. You are advised to consult the relevant court websites to access the current versions of the forms included here.

Acknowledgments

The authors would like to thank the team at Emond Montgomery Publications who helped us through every step of the development and completion of this text—specifically, Sarah Gleadow and Bernard Sandler, publishers; Paula Kulig, copy editor; Jim Lyons, supervising editor; and Cindy Fujimoto, production editor.

Anyone who has ever been involved in a project like this knows that you cannot get from there to here without the support and assistance of many people. I would like to thank my colleagues on the Board of Directors of the Prosecutors' Association of Ontario, my employers (Mary Proc, Matt Holland) for their support and encouragement, and, most importantly, my family. My wife, Daina, and my children, Madison, Cameron, and Zaira, showed immense patience as I burrowed away writing in a locked room during summer holidays in Muskoka. Without your love and support, I could not have undertaken this project.

— Steve Weir

This text would not have been possible if not for the support and understanding of friends and family. I would like to thank my students, past and present, from the Paralegal Education program at Humber College for helping me to realize the need for a text geared toward paralegals and for appreciating the work that I do. I would also like to thank my colleagues at Humber College, including Samantha Callow, Mark Hanna, Tracy Ryder, Alvina Cassiani, and all of the law faculty who inspire me on a daily basis. As well, I would like to thank Carla Mariuz, Peggy Buchan, and Michelle Roy McSpurren, who helped me to envision and commence this project. Last but not least, I extend a very special thank you to my family for their ongoing support, patience, encouragement, and love. Thank you to my mom, José, Gabe, and Zack—you are the inspiration and the motivation for everything that I do.

— Jennifer Zubick

An Overview of the Provincial Offences Act

1

OVERVIEW

LEARNING OUTCOMES

After reading this chapter, you will understand

- when and how the *Provincial Offences Act* is used;

- the proper citation for the *Provincial Offences Act*;

- which legislation is covered by the *Provincial Offences Act*;

- the types of matters that are heard before the provincial offences court;

- how the *Provincial Offences Act* is administered;

- the difference between criminal and provincial offences; and

- the breakdown of the *Provincial Offences Act* and regulations.

INTRODUCTION

The *Provincial Offences Act*, R.S.O. 1990, c. P.33 (POA) is an Ontario statute that sets out the procedures for the administration and prosecution of charges laid under provincial statutes, municipal bylaws, and certain federal statutes. The POA is reproduced in Appendix A to this text. The offences covered by the Act are considered to be **regulatory offences**—meaning that laws have been enacted to regulate behaviour in society. For example, a stop sign regulates when drivers must bring vehicles to a halt. Committing a regulatory offence is typically considered to be a minor infraction or a social wrongdoing and is penalized accordingly.

An act under which a person is charged is known as the **charging act**. The POA is seldom used to initiate charges and it is typically considered to be more of a procedural act than a charging act. For example, a driver may be charged with speeding under the *Highway Traffic Act*, R.S.O. 1990, c. H.8 (the charging act) but would follow the procedures for responding to the speeding charge as set out in the *Provincial Offences Act* (the procedural act). The POA does include some offences, but they relate to procedural matters (e.g., fail to appear in court, contempt of court). It is much more common for paralegals to defend clients charged under various other statutes and bylaws than to defend clients charged with one of the offences created by the POA.

regulatory offences
laws that have been enacted to regulate behaviour in society (also known as provincial offences)

charging act
a piece of legislation under which a person is charged (e.g., the *Highway Traffic Act*)

PROPER STATUTORY CITATION

As a primary source of law, the *Provincial Offences Act* must be cited using the proper statutory citation. The proper citation for the POA is:

Provincial Offences Act, R.S.O. 1990, c. P.33

- *Provincial Offences Act* = name of the statute
- R.S.O. = the name of the statute series in which the Act appears (Revised Statutes of Ontario)
- 1990 = the year in which the statute was last published in a revised volume
- P.33 = Chapter "P.33" (Note: the letter "P" makes reference to the first letter of the name of the Act—"*Provincial Offences Act*"—not the page, paragraph, or part)

STATUTES GOVERNED BY THE PROVINCIAL OFFENCES ACT

The offences under provincial statutes are administered and prosecuted using the procedures set out in the POA. Examples of commonly prosecuted provincial statutes include: the *Highway Traffic Act, Compulsory Automobile Insurance Act*, R.S.O. 1990, c. C.25, *Liquor Licence Act*, R.S.O. 1990, c. L.19, *Occupational Health and Safety Act*, R.S.O. 1990, c. O.1, and *Environmental Protection Act*, R.S.O. 1990, c. E.19.

The *Municipal Act, 2001*, S.O. 2001, c. 25, a provincial statute, creates the authority for municipalities (e.g., regions, cities, towns, townships) to enact bylaws that apply within their municipal boundaries. Infractions of these bylaws are also subject to the procedures set out in the POA.

A limited number of federal statutes are also governed by the procedures of the POA. Examples include: the *Canadian Environmental Protection Act*, S.C. 1999, c. 33, *Canada Shipping Act, 2001*, S.C. 2001, c. 26, and *Fisheries Act*, R.S.C. 1985, c. F-14.

PRACTICE TIP

When preparing to represent your clients, it is important to consult the procedures set out in the charging act as well as in the *Provincial Offences Act* (the procedural act). The charging act may contain provisions that override the procedures of the POA. For example, although the POA specifies that the general limitation period for laying charges is six months, one of the provisions in the *Compulsory Automobile Insurance Act* overrides this limitation period. Specifically, under the *Compulsory Automobile Insurance Act*, proceedings may be commenced at any time within three years after the date of the offence if a driver was found operating a motor vehicle without insurance. The POA provides standard procedural information that applies in most situations to most offences. However, if the charging act contains procedural information specific to the offence, the charging act provisions should be followed. If the charging act does not contain the required procedural information, look to the POA for the necessary information.

COMMON CHARGES

Traffic violations appear to be the most commonly disputed charges in the provincial offences system. Of those traffic violations, a large proportion is related to speeding offences. Other common traffic violations include: improper stop at stop sign, fail to surrender insurance, failure to wear complete seat belt assembly, and careless driving.

Parking offences are also subject to the procedures set out in the POA. Examples include: parking in reserved spaces, failing to display parking permits, and parking at an expired meter.

Bylaws vary from municipality to municipality. Behaviours that are regulated in one municipality might not be regulated in a neighbouring municipality. However, some of the bylaw charges common in most municipalities include: noise violations, non-compliance with a business licence, and building permit violations.

Most environmental infractions, whether covered by municipal, provincial, or federal legislation, follow the procedures as set out in the POA.

> **PRACTICE TIP**
>
> Always review the actual wording of the charge(s) against each client. Reviewing the appropriate section(s) of the charging act will provide you with information you will need in preparing your defence and will help you to anticipate the prosecutor's case.

Comparison with Criminal Charges

Section 2 of the POA indicates that one of the purposes of the Act is to distinguish between provincial and criminal offences. In order to make such a distinction, when creating the POA it was necessary to establish a set of procedures that were separate from the procedures used for criminal matters. The procedures that have been established for provincial offences are less restrictive and complex than criminal procedures, while still providing the opportunity for defendants to have their day in court.

quasi-criminal offences offences that bear a resemblance to criminal matters because the procedure for dealing with them is similar to the criminal process (also known as provincial offences)

Although provincial offences are sometimes called **quasi-criminal offences**, the offences are not considered to be criminal in nature. Provincial offences are often less serious than criminal offences and a conviction does not result in a criminal record. The offences are referred to as quasi-criminal because they do bear a resemblance to criminal matters (e.g., a defendant is charged for breaking a law) and because the procedure for dealing with some of the matters is similar to the criminal process (e.g., the defendant has the right to a trial and will be penalized if convicted).

Many people who consider themselves to be law-abiding citizens will find themselves in provincial offences court one day. For example, a driver could unintentionally make an improper turn while driving in an unfamiliar area. If a provincial offences officer witnesses this driving infraction, the driver may be charged. Theoretically, while the driver should be punished in some way for the wrongfulness of the act, he or she should not be punished to the same extent that criminal acts are punished. While there are some severe penalties under the POA, most are less severe than those under the *Criminal Code,* R.S.C. 1985, c. C-46, and the defendant will not receive a criminal record if convicted.

ADMINISTRATION OF THE PROVINCIAL OFFENCES ACT

Over the past decade, the attorney general has transferred most of the responsibility for administering the POA to the municipal level. Municipalities now have the responsibility for prosecuting all Part I and Part II matters, while the province has retained responsibility for the prosecution of Part III matters. Municipalities are also responsible for administering all of the provincial offences courts and collecting all fines under the Act.

PRACTICE TIP

When preparing to represent your clients, it will be important to consider the municipality that has jurisdiction over each matter. Different municipalities may have slightly different administrative procedures. For example, smaller municipalities may run their provincial offences courts only on specified days, while large municipalities have several courtrooms running at various locations every day. As well, different options may be available in different municipalities. For example, municipalities may have different forms and practices for obtaining disclosure requirements.

BREAKDOWN OF THE PROVINCIAL OFFENCES ACT

The POA is divided into ten parts. Parts I, II, and III set out the procedures to commence proceedings for the different classifications of offences. Specifically, Part I deals with minor offences that are commenced using a Certificate of Offence, Part II focuses on the initiation of parking charges using a Certificate of Parking Infraction, and Part III involves commencing proceedings for more serious infractions by way of a document called an Information.

Parts IV through VIII contain general provisions that are applicable to Part I, Part II, and Part III hearings. Part IV deals with trials and sentencing, while Part V provides miscellaneous additional information entitled "General Provisions." Part VI contains the special rules that apply if the defendant is a young person, Part VII discusses appeals and reviews, and Part VIII sets out the rules and procedures relating to arrest, bail, and search warrants.

Part IX and Part X each deal with a specific issue that relates to the application and administration of the POA. Part IX deals with situations where another statute has authorized taking a proceeding before the Ontario Court of Justice or a justice for an order. Part X is specific to the municipal transfer agreements that provide municipalities with the authority to administer and prosecute under the Act.

The full text of the POA is reproduced in Appendix A.

PROVINCIAL OFFENCES ACT REGULATIONS

Regulations are the principles or rules that are enacted under the authority of a statute. At present, nine regulations have been made under the authority of the *Provincial Offences Act*.

regulations
legislation that contains the rules or principles that are enacted under the authority of a statute

1. Costs, R.R.O. 1990, Reg. 945—Sets out, in chart format, the costs that may be applicable under ss. 60(2) and 60(1).
2. Electronic Documents, O. Reg. 67/12—Defines and sets out procedures for the use of electronic documents.
3. Extensions of Prescribed Times, R.R.O. 1990, Reg. 946—Permits the courts to extend time periods in the event of a mail strike.

4. Fee for Late Payment of Fines, O. Reg. 679/92—Establishes the administrative fee payable for fines in default.
5. Fine Option Program, R.R.O. 1990, Reg. 948—Establishes a program to permit the payment of fines in default by means of credit for work performed.
6. Forms, O. Reg. 108/11—Provides information about provincial offences forms and sets out, in chart format, a table of forms.
7. Parking Infractions, R.R.O. 1990, Reg. 949—Provides specific information and designated forms to be used for parking infractions.
8. Proceedings Commenced by Certificate of Offence, R.R.O. 1990, Reg. 950—Format to be used for Certificates of Offence and other court forms, and provides the short-form wording that can be used on the Certificate of Offence.
9. Victim Fine Surcharges, O. Reg. 161/00—Sets out, in chart format, the victim fine surcharges that are added to every offence.

PRACTICE TIP

It is important to learn the content of the regulations as well as the content of the Act because the regulations will provide more specific information about designated topics. For example, the Act does not provide specific information about additional costs that are payable on conviction, but Regulation 945 sets out the various costs that may be added to a fine when there is a conviction.

COURTS OF JUSTICE ACT

The *Courts of Justice Act*, R.S.O. 1990, c. C.43 (CJA) is an Ontario statute. Together with its associated regulations, the CJA sets out the rules used for Ontario courts. Because provincial offences are dealt with in the Ontario Court of Justice and the Superior Court of Justice, it is important to understand the rules that apply to these courts.

Two of the sections that apply to provincial offences matters are ss. 38 and 39. These sections create the authority for the court and the justices. Specifically, s. 38(2) of the *Courts of Justice Act* indicates that the Ontario Court of Justice has jurisdiction to perform any function assigned to it by or under the POA. Section 39 of the CJA grants power for a judge to preside in the Ontario Court of Justice and for a justice of the peace to preside in the Ontario Court of Justice in a proceeding under the POA.

In addition, the regulations to the CJA provide copies of the proper forms for provincial offences matters (e.g., O. Reg. 721/94, Form 4 is used for the Notice of Appeal).

KEY TERMS

charging act
quasi-criminal offences

regulations
regulatory offences

REVIEW QUESTIONS

True/False

_____ 1. The *Provincial Offences Act* is considered to be a procedural act.

_____ 2. A conviction on a regulatory offence will result in a criminal record for the defendant.

_____ 3. In the statutory citation *Provincial Offences Act*, R.S.O. 1990, c. P.33, "P.33" refers to page 33.

_____ 4. Most environmental infractions follow the procedures as set out in the *Provincial Offences Act*.

_____ 5. Part VI of the *Provincial Offences Act* contains the special rules that apply if the defendant is a young person.

_____ 6. The *Highway Traffic Act* outlines the proper procedures for defending a client charged with a traffic offence.

_____ 7. The *Courts of Justice Act* provides the authority for a justice of the peace to preside over provincial offences matters.

_____ 8. The regulation pertaining to electronic documents, O. Reg. 67/12, provides the short-form wording that can be used on the Certificate of Offence.

Short Answer

1. Would the *Provincial Offences Act*, R.S.O. 1990, c. P.33, apply to a person charged with speeding in British Columbia? Why or why not?

2. Explain why provincial offences are sometimes referred to as "quasi-criminal" offences.

3. Explain whether you would follow the provisions in the charging act or the procedural act (the POA) if they contain different procedural information.

4. Section 61 of the POA states that the maximum fine for a Part III offence is $5,000. However, the *Highway Traffic Act* indicates that the penalty for stunt driving, a Part III offence, can range from $2,000 to $10,000. Which maximum amount would apply and why?

5. When preparing for trial, which types of legislation should a paralegal consult?

Roles and Responsibilities

2

OVERVIEW

LEARNING OUTCOMES

After reading this chapter, you will understand

- the various parties involved with provincial offences matters; and

- the duties and responsibilities of each of the parties.

INTRODUCTION

In order to understand how the provincial offences system works, it is necessary to understand the roles and responsibilities of the people who are involved with the administration and prosecution of provincial offences. This chapter will define and discuss the key players who are employed in the provincial offences field and provide a general overview of the functions they perform.

DEFENDANT (CLIENT)

There are several terms that refer to a person who has been charged with an offence under a statute that is governed by the *Provincial Offences Act*. The person charged is most commonly referred to as the **defendant** but may also be called the accused or the offender. If the defendant decides to hire a paralegal, the defendant becomes a "client" to the paralegal.

defendant
has been charged with an offence under a statute governed by the *Provincial Offences Act*

A properly retained paralegal is able to negotiate on a client's behalf and represent a client in provincial offences court proceedings. While in many cases a client does not need to be present for negotiations or the proceedings, it is crucial that the client remains involved throughout the process. A client must provide instructions to the paralegal to authorize settlement offers. In addition, he or she may be required to attend court as a witness in order to give evidence, and must assume all responsibility for paying court-imposed fines, surcharges, and costs.

The defendant may decide to represent himself or herself in court. In cases of self-representation, the justice is obliged to offer guidance to the defendant. Specifically, the justice has a duty to provide the required information and assistance to allow the defendant to make a full and proper defence to the charges before the court.

PROVINCIAL OFFENCES OFFICER/POLICE OFFICER

Provincial offences officers and police officers have the authority to lay charges against a defendant. Section 1(1) of the POA provides definitions for a **police officer** and for a **provincial offences officer**:

police officer
has the authority to lay charges against a defendant

provincial offences officer
has the authority to lay charges against a defendant for specific types of provincial offences (includes a police officer)

> "Police Officer" means a chief of police or other police officer but does not include a special constable or by-law enforcement officer.
>
> "Provincial Offences Officer" means,
>> (a) a police officer;
>> (b) a constable appointed pursuant to any Act;
>> (c) a municipal law enforcement officer referred to in subsection of 101(4) of the *Municipal Act, 2001* or in subsection 79(1) of the *City of Toronto Act, 2006* while in the discharge of his or her duties;
>> (d) a by-law enforcement officer of any municipality or of any local board of any municipality, while in the discharge of his or her duties;
>> (e) an officer, employee or agent of any municipality or of any local board of any municipality, whose responsibilities include the enforcement of a by-law, an Act or a regulation under an Act, while in the discharge of his or her duties; or
>> (f) a person designated under subsection (3).

On the basis of these definitions, a "provincial offences officer" is a broad term that includes a police officer, municipal law enforcement officer, bylaw enforcement officer, parking enforcement officer, and other designated individuals (e.g., fire prevention inspectors, environmental protection officers, animal control officers). By contrast, the term "police officer" is a very specific term that does not include other provincial offences officers. If a statute intends that an action be carried out only by a police officer, it will specifically use the term "police officer."

The officer is the person who charges the defendant with an offence. If the defendant requests the officer's attendance at trial, the officer will be notified to attend court. The officer is at court to provide support and information to the prosecutor, but it is not the officer's duty to negotiate a settlement with the defendant—negotiations are left to the prosecutor's discretion. If the matter proceeds to a trial, the officer can be called as a witness for the prosecution in order to provide evidence to support a conviction against the defendant.

REPRESENTATIVE (PARALEGAL/LAWYER)

A **representative** is a lawyer or a paralegal who is authorized to represent a defendant in a proceeding under the POA. In accordance with s. 1(1) of the POA, the definition of a representative is as follows:

> "Representative" means, in respect of a proceeding to which this Act applies, a person authorized under the *Law Society Act* to represent a person in that proceeding.

The *Law Society Act*, R.S.O. 1990, c. L.8 authorizes both lawyers and paralegals to represent clients in legal proceedings. Lawyers and paralegals are required to meet educational requirements and complete an exam or exams in order to become a licensee of the Law Society of Upper Canada. The terms "barrister" and "solicitor" are sometimes used to refer to a lawyer. Terms that have been used to describe paralegals include "agent" or "court and tribunal agent."

A legal representative is often hired to defend someone who has been charged with an offence. It is more common to see paralegals representing clients in provincial offences court than it is to see lawyers. However, lawyers will typically be retained if a client wants to appeal to the Court of Appeal or the Supreme Court of Canada because paralegals are only permitted to handle appeals in the Ontario Court of Justice. Both paralegals and clients must abide by rules of conduct that are enforced by the Law Society of Upper Canada.

representative
a lawyer or a paralegal who is authorized to represent a defendant in a proceeding under the POA

COURT ADMINISTRATION STAFF

Court administration staff work in the courthouse providing information and performing various administrative duties. They serve an important role within provincial offences court. Their duties include: accepting payment of fines, scheduling trials, providing intake services, arranging for an officer's attendance at trial, requesting interpreters, and answering general inquiries about provincial offences.

court administration staff
work within the courthouse providing information and performing various administrative duties

While the court administration staff can provide information to defendants and their representatives, they are not in a position to provide legal advice or make court appearances on a defendant's behalf.

COURT CLERK

court clerk
ensures POA proceedings run smoothly by providing assistance to the judge or justice

The **court clerk** ensures that POA proceedings run smoothly by providing assistance to the judge or justice. The clerk sits directly in front of the justice and faces the seating area of the courtroom. He or she wears a black robe, but does not wear a sash. A court clerk should be referred to as "Mister/Madam Clerk."

The court clerk will announce the justice's arrival in the courtroom and will commence and close the court proceedings. The clerk will also call the names of the defendants, administer oaths, arraign the defendants, record court proceedings, collect and itemize all exhibits used during a trial, and complete the necessary paperwork. As well, the clerk will ensure that courtroom protocol is followed at all times, often having to remind defendants and representatives of appropriate etiquette.

COURT SECURITY OFFICER

court security officer
special constables who have been appointed to assist with courthouse security and attend to specific incidents that may arise

Some provincial offences court locations employ **court security officers**. Court security officers are civilian members of a police services board who are appointed as "special constables" under s. 53(2) of the *Police Services Act*, R.S.O. 1990, c. P.15. Upon appointment, the powers of a police officer are conferred upon a special constable as is necessary to carry out the responsibilities of the job. Court security officers continually monitor all areas of the courthouse and attend to specific incidents when called into a courtroom.

In some larger municipalities, court security officers screen everyone entering the courthouse using a metal detector, and search all bags and belongings being brought into court facilities.

PROSECUTOR (CROWN)

prosecutor
an agent of the attorney general who prosecutes the charges against the defendant

A **prosecutor** is an agent of the attorney general who prosecutes the charges against the defendant, and is sometimes referred to as "the Crown." According to s. 1(1) of the POA, the definition of a prosecutor is as follows:

> "Prosecutor" means the Attorney General or, where the Attorney General does not intervene, means the person who issues a certificate or lays an information and includes an agent acting on behalf of either of them.

While most prosecutors are agents of the Ministry of the Attorney General, some prosecutors will be employed by a municipality and others will be employed by the province. Municipal prosecutors are responsible for Part I and Part II provincial offences charges, while provincial prosecutors conduct the prosecution for Part III matters. The majority of prosecutors in provincial offences court are not lawyers; most are graduates from a paralegal diploma program at a community college.

The prosecutor's office duties include: preparing cases, evaluating charges, reviewing statements, interviewing witnesses, assessing the admissibility of evidence, researching case law, ensuring evidence has been collected, and providing disclosure to defendants (e.g., officer's notes, accident report).

At court, a prosecutor will participate in plea negotiations and resolution discussions with the defendant, and, if necessary, present a case to the justice as to why there is sufficient evidence to support a conviction.

According to Rule 4.01(5.1) of the *Paralegal Rules of Conduct* (Toronto: Law Society of Upper Canada, 2007):

> When acting as a prosecutor, a paralegal shall act for the public and the administration of justice resolutely and honourably within the limits of the law while treating the tribunal with candour, fairness, courtesy, and respect.

As such, the prosecutor's role is to assist with the administration of justice, act as an agent of the court, and ensure that proceedings are fair and ethical. A prosecutor should not be concerned about "winning" or "losing," but with ensuring that justice is served.

THE JUSTICE

A justice presides over provincial offences proceedings. The Ontario Court of Justice is composed of provincially appointed judges and justices of the peace. Section 1(1) of the POA provides definitions for a judge and for a justice:

"Judge" means a provincial judge.
"Justice" means a provincial judge or a justice of the peace.

On the basis of these definitions, a "justice" is a broad term that includes a provincial judge or a justice of the peace. By contrast, "judge" is a very specific term that refers only to a judge.

PRACTICE TIP

It is important to look at the wording in the statute. If it is intended to apply to only a judge, the statute will specify "judge." If the section could also apply to a justice of the peace, the term "justice" will be used.

Justice of the Peace

A justice of the peace is sometimes referred to as a JP. However, JP is an informal term that should never be used in a professional setting. A justice of the peace, who wears a black robe with white neck tabs and a green sash across the chest, should be addressed as "Your Worship."

A **justice of the peace** is part of a lay bench whose members are not required to have legal training or experience in the justice system. Historically, there were no formal requirements to become a justice of the peace because such appointments were political. However, the *Access to Justice Act, 2006*, S.O. 2006, c. 21—Bill 14 changed the appointment process to include an application and interview, leading

justice of the peace
a magistrate who presides over proceedings in provincial offences court

to an appointment by an advisory committee. Applicants for a justice of the peace position must have completed a degree or diploma, and have at least 10 years of full-time work experience, not necessarily related to the law. As a result, justices of the peace have varied backgrounds, including a wide range of educational, business, and volunteer experiences.

The powers, duties, and jurisdiction of a justice of the peace are established in case law and by statute. The two main areas of jurisdiction for justices of the peace are criminal law pursuant to the *Criminal Code* and provincial offences under the POA. A justice of the peace deals with virtually all trial-level provincial offences decisions, including municipal bylaw prosecutions. Justices of the peace are also responsible for denying or issuing an information and applications (e.g., summons or warrant), accepting guilty pleas, and presiding at trials.

In the criminal courts, justices of the peace have jurisdiction to hold bail hearings, grant search warrants, and preside over some criminal hearings. They are responsible for issuing or denying information documents, summonses, warrants (including search warrants), and other matters of the criminal process.

Provincial Court Judge

provincial court judge
a lawyer who has been appointed a judge and typically presides over more serious provincial offences cases and appeals

A **provincial court judge** also wears a black robe, but can be distinguished by a red sash across the chest. A judge should be referred to as "Your Honour."

Provincial judges decide some of the more serious provincial offences cases. The charging act would specify if a judge is to preside over the matter. As well, provincial judges hear all provincial offences appeals. Provincial judges are appointed by the lieutenant governor in council on the recommendation of the attorney general. The qualifications of a provincial court judge are set out in s. 42(2) of the *Courts of Justice Act*. Specifically, provincial court judges must have been a member of the bar (i.e., a lawyer) of one of the provinces or territories of Canada for at least 10 years.

COURT INTERPRETER

In accordance with s. 14 of the *Canadian Charter of Rights and Freedoms*, part I of the *Constitution Act, 1982*, RSC 1985, app. II, no. 44:

> A party or witness in any proceedings who does not understand or speak the language in which the proceedings are conducted or who is deaf has the right to the assistance of an interpreter.

And with s. 125(2)(a) of the *Courts of Justice Act*:

> [H]earings in courts shall be conducted in the English language and evidence adduced in a language other than English shall be interpreted into the English language.

court interpreter
provides translation services to defendants who do not speak English

Therefore, if a defendant does not understand or speak English, a **court interpreter** can be provided if requested. Court interpreters provide translation services on a freelance basis but must apply to the Ministry of the Attorney General in order to appear on the roster of accredited court interpreters. Court interpreters must translate exactly what has been stated.

Court interpreters provide services in many different languages, including sign language. The defendant (or defendant's representative) must request the interpreter in advance, typically at least four weeks before the trial date. The defendant (or defendant's representative) must complete a Notice of Intention to Appear (NIA) and indicate the desired language of interpretation. Alternatively, an Interpreter Request form can be used after the Notice of Intention to Appear has been filed. The court administration staff will be responsible for ensuring an interpreter is present. The services of a court interpreter are provided at no cost to a defendant or witness.

Section 84 of the POA indicates that a judge or justice "may authorize a person to act as interpreter in a proceeding before the justice [judge] where the person swears the prescribed oath and, in the opinion of the justice [judge], is competent." This allows some discretion on the part of the justice to allow non-accredited individuals to act as interpreters.

WITNESSES

Witnesses have first-hand knowledge about the matter being prosecuted. The provincial offences officer who laid the charges against the defendant will typically be called as a witness by the prosecutor. There may also be civilian witnesses who are willing to testify at trial for the prosecution.

witness
has first-hand knowledge about the matter being prosecuted

The main witness for the defence is usually the defendant. Other defence witnesses may include individuals who were with the defendant at the time of the alleged offence or civilian witnesses.

If a witness refuses to attend the trial, he or she can be summoned for trial. The person wishing to summon the witness must appear before a justice of the peace and swear the summons. If the justice is satisfied that the witness will provide material evidence, the summons will be issued and it must be served by a provincial offences officer pursuant to s. 26 of the POA. Witnesses can recover minimal costs associated with attendance at court, as set out in Regulation 945, "Costs."

KEY TERMS

court administration staff
court clerk
court interpreter
court security officer
defendant
justice of the peace

police officer
prosecutor
provincial court judge
provincial offences officer
representative
witness

REVIEW QUESTIONS

True/False

_____ 1. Defendants must be represented by a paralegal or lawyer to have a trial.

_____ 2. All justices of the peace are lawyers.

_____ 3. All judges are lawyers.

_____ 4. All prosecutors are lawyers.

_____ 5. The term "provincial offences officer" includes a police officer.

_____ 6. The provincial offences officer has the responsibility of engaging in plea negotiations and resolution discussions with the defendant immediately prior to trial.

_____ 7. The court clerk wears a black robe, but no sash.

_____ 8. Municipal prosecutors have the jurisdiction to prosecute Part I and Part III matters.

_____ 9. The term "justice" includes a provincial court judge.

_____ 10. Defendants must provide their own interpreter in the provincial offences courts.

Short Answer

1. You walk into a courtroom and see a justice wearing a black gown and a red sash across the chest. What is this person's role and how will you address this individual?

2. Which forms can be used to request a court interpreter?

3. What are the two main areas of jurisdiction for a justice of the peace?

4. What is the procedure for compelling a witness to attend a trial?

5. Describe the duties of a court clerk.

Procedural Streams

3

OVERVIEW

LEARNING OUTCOMES

After reading this chapter, you will understand

- the different procedural streams and charging documents under parts I, II, and III of the *Provincial Offences Act*;

- the framework for fines, service, and limitation periods for each procedural stream; and

- where to find additional information about commencing proceedings and procedural requirements.

INTRODUCTION

The *Provincial Offences Act* (POA) is divided into three parts that govern the commencement of proceedings for various provincial offences. Part I of the POA deals with minor offences and Part II with parking offences, while Part III sets out the procedure for the more serious offences that are prosecuted under the POA.

PART I OFFENCES

Part I of the POA deals with the majority of minor offences, such as speeding, drinking in public, trespassing, and other infractions. Part I offences have a prescribed corresponding set fine. Only a provincial offences officer may commence a proceeding under Part I by completing, signing, and then filing a certificate of offence (see Figure 3.1).

Charging Document

certificate of offence
a certificate of a violation prepared by an officer under Part I of the POA

Officers are required to fill in the **certificate of offence** so that it is "complete and regular on its face." The certificates are included in a single book of usually no more than 25. They are sequentially numbered and a record is kept of which tickets have been issued to each officer. Carbon copies attached to each certificate are used for the police officer's records, for filing with the court, and for service on the defendant. The copy that is served on the defendant is a yellow slip called the **offence notice**, commonly referred to as a "ticket."

offence notice
a yellow copy attached to a certificate of offence that is served on the defendant, commonly called a "ticket"

Set Fines

set fine
the amount of monetary penalty determined by the chief justice of the Ontario Court of Justice for an offence under Part I or Part II

The term "set fine" refers to the amount of the predetermined out-of-court payment as established by the chief justice. The **set fine** is a fixed amount, and does not include costs, the victim fine surcharge, and added fees. The set fine amount for an **offence** under Part I is included on the certificate of offence in a box near the bottom labelled "set fine."

offence
a violation of a piece of legislation, or of a regulation or a bylaw made under a piece of legislation

For most offences, especially those under provincial statutes, the government ministry or other body that administers the legislation applies to the chief justice for approval on short-form wordings and a corresponding set fine for offences. Officers cannot issue a fine that is different than the set fine. If a higher fine is warranted, the defendant must receive a **summons** to appear in **court** to allow the justice to determine the appropriate fine.

summons
a document issued to a defendant requiring attendance in court

Municipalities have recently been given broad authority to enact their own fines, including escalating fines for bylaws. Traditionally, municipalities would apply to the regional senior justice for approval on short-form wordings and corresponding set fines for bylaw matters.

court
the Ontario Court of Justice, which includes the provincial offences court

If a matter proceeds to court for a trial, the set fine does not apply and the penalty provisions of the POA or the enabling statute prevail. The maximum fine for Part I matters is $1,000.

Figure 3.1 Certificate of Offence Under Part I of the POA

ICON Location Code *Code d'emplacement du RIII*	Offence number *Numéro d'infraction*

Form 1, *Provincial Offences Act*, Ontario Court of Justice, O. Reg. 108/11
Formulaire 1, Loi sur les infractions provinciales, Cour de justice de l'Ontario, Règl. de l'Ont. 108/11

Certificate of Offence
Procès-verbal d'infraction

I, _____ ,
Je soussigné(e)   (print name / *nom en lettres moulées*)

believe and certify that on the day of   Y / A   M / M   D / J   Time / *heure*
crois et atteste que le   2 0 | | | | | M

Name _____
Nom   (family / *nom de famille*)

_____
(given / *prénom*)   (initials / *initiales*)

Address _____
Adresse   (number and street / *numéro et nom de la rue*)

(municipality / *municipalité*)   (P.O. / C.P.)   (province)   (postal code / *code postal*)

Driver's licence no. / *N° de permis de conduire*   Juris / *Aut. Lég.*

Birth date / *Date de naissance* Y / A M / M D / J	Sex / *Sexe*	Motor vehicle involved / *Véhicule impliqué* ☐ N / N	Collision involved / *Collision* ☐ Y / O	Witnesses / *Témoins* ☐ Y / O

At _____
À   (municipality / *municipalité*)

Did commit the offence of _____
A commis l'infraction de

contrary to _____ sect. _____
contrairement à   *l'art.*

Plate no. *N° de la plaque d'immatriculation*	Juris *Aut. Lég.*	Commercial *Utilitaire* ☐ Y / O	CVOR *IUVU* ☐ Y / O	NSC *CNS* ☐ Y / O	Code
CVOR No. - NSC No. / *N° de l'IUVU - N° du CNS*					

And I further certify that I served an offence notice   ☐ Or other service date of:
personally upon the person charged on the offence date.   *Autre date de signification, le :*
J'atteste également qu'à la date de l'infraction, j'ai signifié, en
mains propres, un avis d'infraction à la personne accusée.

Signature of issuing Provincial Offences Officer *Signature de l'agent des infractions provinciale*	Officer No. *N° de l'agent*	Platoon *Peloton*	Unit *Unité*

Set fine of *Amende fixée de* $ $	Total payable *Montant total exigible* $ $	Total payable includes set fine, applicable victim fine surcharge and costs. / *Le montant total* *exigible comprend l'amende fixée, la suramende* *compensatoire applicable et les frais.*

Summons issued. You are   Y / A   M / M   D / J   Time / *heure*
required to appear in court on   2 0 | | | M
Assignation. *Vous êtes* | Ct. room / *Salle*
d'audience | at the Ontario Court of Justice POA Office at / *à la Cour*
tenu(e) de comparaître devant   *de justice de l'Ontario, Bureau des infractions provinciales au*
le tribunal le

Deemed not to dispute charge under s. 9(1)(a) of the *Provincial Offences Act*. Set fine imposed. / *Réputé ne pas*
contester l'accusation aux termes de l'alinéa 9 (1) (a) de la Loi sur les infractions provinciales. *Amende fixée imposée.*
                            Y / A   M / M   D / J
                        2 0 | | |

_____
Justice / *Juge*

Short-Form Wordings

certificate of parking infraction
a notice of a violation issued by an officer under Part II of the POA

The term "short-form wordings" refers to approved language used to describe an offence on a certificate of offence or **certificate of parking infraction**. Short-form wordings provide the defendant with notice of which offence they are alleged to have committed, usually referring to the statute and section.

PRACTICE TIP

Approved set fines and short-form wordings can be found on the Ontario Court of Justice website (www.ontariocourts.on.ca/ocj/en/setfines) and are updated when the chief justice approves changes.

Proper Service

In the majority of cases under Part I, a provincial offences officer will personally serve the defendant with an offence notice or ticket, or a summons by handing it to the defendant. Under s. 3 of the POA, when an officer believes that someone has committed an offence, the officer has up to 30 days from the date of the offence to issue and serve an offence notice or summons on the defendant.

Service is usually simple. The issuing officer who completed the certificate of offence gives the offence notice to the defendant and signs the certification area on the certificate to indicate when and how service was completed. The POA also has provisions that allow an officer to serve an offence notice that was completed by another officer. In such cases, the serving officer must complete the affidavit of service on the back of the certificate of offence.

It is sufficient under Part I for an officer to certify that service has taken place, and he or she would not normally be asked to testify in court to establish proper service.

PRACTICE TIP

It is important for paralegals to ensure that service of an offence notice or summons on a client complied with the POA. An officer may not leave the charging document with someone other than the defendant. As an exception to the general rule, in *City of London v. (Leslie) Erdesz*, [2009] O.J. No. 1008, the Superior Court of Justice ruled that an officer was able to leave an offence notice in the defendant's mailbox because the defendant refused to answer the door to be served.

PRACTICE TIP

If your client is a young person, the special provisions in Part VI of the POA apply. A young person must receive a summons to appear in court. An offence notice cannot be used.

Limitation Periods

The **limitation period** is the time within which an officer is allowed to lay a charge against a defendant. For Part I offences, this is a two-stage calculation. Under s. 3(3) of the POA, the officer is required to serve the defendant with the offence notice or summons within 30 days of the date of the alleged offence. As well, the officer must file the certificate of offence in court as soon as possible, but no later than seven days after service has taken place. Service of the offence notice alone is not sufficient to commence a proceeding.

limitation period
the time allowed for an officer to lay a charge against a defendant

---

PRACTICE TIP

Regulation 200 of the *Courts of Justice Act*, R.S.O. 1990, c. C.43 provides the framework for calculating the limitation period. To calculate the service time frame, add 30 days to the date of the offence (in other words, for an offence that occurs on March 1, the officer must serve the defendant by March 31). To calculate the filing time frame, exclude the date of service, and if the last day for filing is a holiday (Saturday, Sunday, or a statutory holiday), it is extended to the first business day following the holiday.

PART II OFFENCES

Part II of the *Provincial Offences Act* deals with parking infractions. Most drivers who run afoul of regulatory requirements and are charged as a result have improperly used a motor vehicle, violating rules for stopping, standing, or parking.

Charging Document

The charging document for Part II is a certificate of parking infraction. The copy served to the defendant (or owner of the motor vehicle) is called the parking infraction notice (PIN). Like Part I, traditionally the PIN was a carbon copy of the certificate of parking infraction. However, in recent years most municipalities and other bodies have adopted technology to aid in the administration of parking enforcement. Many tickets are now computer-generated and printed by a mobile printer before being served on a driver—usually by being placed on a vehicle's windshield (see Figure 3.2).

Set Fines

Part II offences have approved set fines, similar to Part I. There is no provision to issue a summons to an individual under Part II; the amount of the fine is indicated on the certificate of parking infraction. Some municipalities or other bodies have implemented early payment amounts and set fine amounts.

Most set fines for Part II offences are established through municipalities' bylaws or the regional senior judge. The process of applying to the chief justice is used for very few parking infraction set fines, but the exceptions are found on the Ontario Court of Justice website.

Figure 3.2 Certificate of Parking Infraction Under Part II of the POA

Form 11, *Provincial Offences Act*, Ontario Court of Justice
Formulaire 11, Loi sur les infractions provinciales, Cour de justice de l'Ontario

Certificate of Parking Infraction
Procès-verbal d'infraction de stationnement

I, _____ ,
Je soussigné(e)   (Print name / *Nom en lettres moulées*)

believe from my personal knowledge and certify that on the _____ day of
crois, en me fondant sur me connaissance directe de faits, et atteste que le   *jour de*

_____ , 20 _____ , Time
                              À (heure) | **M** |

the owner (or operator) of the vehicle upon which was displayed the number plate:
le propriétaire de (ou l'utilisateur) du véhicule portant la plaque d'immatriculation suivante :

Plate No. / *Nº de plaque d'immatriculation*	Province	Expiry Date *Date d'expiration* M / M Y / A

did commit the parking infraction of:
a commis l'infraction de stationnement de :

_____

_____

at _____
à

_____
(Municipality / *Municipalité*)

contrary to _____ sect. _____
contrairement à   *l'art.*

I further certify that I: ***J'atteste en outré j'ai :***

A. served a parking infraction notice on the owner of the vehicle identified herein by affixing it to the vehicle in a conspicuous place at the time of this alleged infraction or,   ☐   A. *signifié un avis d'infraction de stationnement au propriétaire de véhicule ci-identifié en apposant cet avis sur ce véhicule à un endroit bien en vue au moment d'infraction reprochée ou;*

B. served a parking infraction notice on the owner (or operator) of the vehicle identified herein by delivering it personally to the person having care and control (or operator) of the vehicle at the time of the alleged infraction.   ☐   B. *signifié un avis d'infraction de stationnement au propriétaire (ou à utilisateur) du véhicule ci-identifié en remettant cet avis en mains propres à la personne qui a la garde et le contrôle (ou à utilisateur) du véhicule au moment de l'infraction reprochée.*

Signature of issuing Provincial Offences Officer *Signature de l'agent des infractions provinciale*	SET FINE *AMENDE FIXÉE*
	$ $
Officer No. / *Nº de l'agent*	Unit / *Unité*

Complete only if operator Is charged / *Ne remplir que si l'utilisateur est inculpé*

Name of operator _____
Nom de l'utilisateur   (Last / *Nom*)   (First / *Prénom*)   (Middle / *Initiale*)

Address _____
Adresse

(Municipality / *Municipalité*)   (Province)   (Postal code / *Code postal*)

Driver's licence no. / *Nº de permis de conduire*			
Birth date / *Date de naissance* Y / A M / M D / J	Sex / *Sexe*		Province

Form / *Formulaire* 11 (March 17, 2011 / *17 mars 2011*)

PRACTICE TIP

In reviewing options with a client, it is important for paralegals to remember that the set fine for a Part I or Part II offence refers only to the out-of-court payment amount. If a trial takes place, the court may impose any fine in accordance with the POA; the set fine is only a guide, not a rule. As with Part I offences, Part II of the Act provides for a maximum fine of $1,000.

Proper Service

Service requirements for Part II are different from those for any other proceeding. Most parking offences are observed in the absence of the person who has care and control of the vehicle. Officers usually serve a parking infraction notice by leaving it in a conspicuous place—usually under a vehicle's windshield wiper blade. No one needs to be present at the vehicle for the PIN to be properly served, and once placed on the vehicle, the officer certifies service.

The provisions also allow for the operator of the motor vehicle to be served, but this is usually avoided to ensure officer safety in situations that can often become confrontational.

Unlike Part I, Part II requires immediate service of the PIN. There is no provision to serve a parking infraction notice at any time other than when the offence takes place. If service cannot comply with those requirements, officers may choose to lay a charge under Part III.

Limitation Periods

There is no limitation period for service under Part II—or, to put it another way, the limitation period is immediate. Parking infraction notices must be served at the time and place of the offence based on the personal knowledge of the officer.

Once served, however, several limitation periods or time calculations begin. The defendant or owner of the motor vehicle has 15 days to respond to the PIN. If no response is made, a notice of impending conviction may be mailed to the owner providing an additional 15 days to respond.

If the defendant pays the ticket, the matter is closed and no proceeding is commenced. If the defendant completes a Notice of Intention to Appear and requests a trial, the municipality or other body will have 75 days from the date of the offence to commence a proceeding by filing the certificate of parking infraction.

If the defendant still fails to respond to the ticket, the municipality or other body may file a certificate requesting a conviction, provided this is done within 75 days of the date of offence. As well, the municipality or other body must certify that no payment has been received and no request for a trial has been filed.

The 75-day limitation period cannot be extended without a court order.

PART III OFFENCES

The final procedural stream of the *Provincial Offences Act* is Part III, entitled Commencement of Proceeding by Information. The procedure of laying charges under Part III is very similar to the process of initiating a criminal proceeding.

Unlike simple and straightforward ticketing offences dealt with under Part I and Part II of the POA, Part III is commonly reserved for those offences that are complex or more serious in nature, or where the limitation periods under Part I or Part II have expired.

Charging Document

In most cases, defendants are made aware that a proceeding under Part III has been commenced against them by being served with a summons (Form 104) (see Figure 3.3) before an information is laid. The summons is similar to an appearance notice (Form 9) used in criminal proceedings, and allows a provincial offences officer to compel a defendant to attend court prior to swearing an information before a justice of the peace. However, there are times when the summons will be served after the information is laid. In these situations, Form 106 is used.

The summons is not the "charging" document, as it would be under Parts I and II. It simply advises the defendant that the officer has grounds to believe that an offence has been committed and that the defendant is required to attend court to answer to the charge.

A Form 104 summons must be served at or near the place of the offence, and on the same date and at the same time that it occurred. The procedure and service requirements for a summons before an information is laid are found in s. 22 of the POA.

> 22. Where a provincial offences officer believes, on reasonable and probable grounds, that an offence has been committed by a person whom the officer finds at or near the place where the offence was committed, he or she may, before an information is laid, serve the person with a summons in the prescribed form.

After a provincial offences officer has served a summons but before an information is laid, or if the officer decides to compel the defendant's attendance after the offence date, the officer must prepare and swear an information alleging the offence before a justice of the peace.

> 23(1) Any person who, on reasonable and probable grounds, believes that one or more persons have committed an offence, may lay an information in the prescribed form and under oath before a justice alleging the offence and the justice shall receive the information.

The information (Form 105) is the formal charging document for commencing proceedings under Part III of the POA (see Figure 3.4).

In many jurisdictions, the provincial offences officer who has investigated the offence and served the Form 104 summons is the same officer who completes and swears the information before a justice of the peace. However, the POA allows an information to be sworn by anyone. Some larger agencies rely on administrative staff to swear the formal information to keep officers free for service.

Figure 3.3 Summons to Defendant Before an Information Is Laid Under POA s. 22

Form 104 Courts of Justice Act
R.R.O. 1990 Reg. 200
Formule 104 Loi sur les tribunaux judiciaires
L.R.O. 1990, Régl. 200

SUMMONS TO DEFENDANT
SOMMATION ADRESSÉE AU DÉFENDEUR
Under Section 22 of the Provincial Offences Act
Aux termes de l'article 22 de la Loi sur les infractions provinciales

Ontario Court of Justice Province of Ontario
Cour de Justice de l'Ontario Province de l'Ontario

CD 000000

You are charged with the following offence
Vous êtes accusé(e) de l'infraction suivant

On the
Le _____ day of _____ yr *an* 20 _____ at *à* _____ | M

Name
Nom _____
Last/*Nom de famille* First/*Prénom* Middle/*Initiale*

Address
Adresse _____
Number and Street/*N° et rue*

At
À _____
Municipality/*Municipalité* P.O./*C.P.* Province Postal Code/*Code postal*

Did commit the offence of
Vous avez commis l'infraction suivante _____
Municipality/*Municipalité*

Contrary to
Par dérogation à _____
Section
Article _____

Therefore you are commanded in Her Majesty's name to appear before the Ontario Court of Justice

À ces causes, au nom de Sa Majesté, vous êtes sommé(e) de comparaître devant la Cour de Justice de l'Ontario

At
À _____

yr *an* 20 _____ at *à* _____ | M

and to appear thereafter as required by the court in order to be dealt with according to law.

On the
Le _____ day of _____

Courtroom/*Salle d'audience* _____

et de comparaître par la suite chaque fois que le tribunal l'exigera de façon à ce que vous soyez jugé(e) selon la Loi.

Issued - *Émis* this *ce* day of _____ yr *an* 20 _____

Signature of Provincial Offences Officer
Signature de l'agent d'infractions provinciales

Summons confirmed
Sommation confirmée ☐

Summons cancelled
Sommation annulée ☐

this _____ day of _____ yr 20 *an* _____ by *par* _____

A judge or justice of the peace in and for the Province of Ontario
Juge ou juge de paix dans et pour la province de l'Ontario

Driver's Licence No. *N° du permis de conduire* _____ Class *Catégorie* Cond *Restriction*

Sex *Sexe* | Birthdate *Date de naissance* D/J M Y/A | Registration No. *Numéro d'enregistrement* | Year *Année* | Province | Make *Marque*

Officer No. *Matricule de l'agent de police* | Unit *Groupe*

Defendant's Copy
Copie du défendeur

Note This summons is issued under Part III of the Provincial Offences Act.
Cette sommation est émise aux termes de la partie III de la Loi sur les infractions provinciales.

Figure 3.4 Information Under Part III of the POA

INFORMATION
DÉNONCIATION

ONTARIO COURT OF JUSTICE
COUR DE JUSTICE DE L'ONTARIO
PROVINCE OF ONTARIO
PROVINCE DE L'ONTARIO

Under Section 23 of the *Provincial Offences Act*
En vertu de l'article 23 de la Loi sur les infractions provinciales

Form / *Formule* **105**
Courts of Justice Act
Loi sur les tribunaux judiciaires
R.R.O / *R.R.O.* 1990 / O. Reg. / *Règl. de l'Ont.* 200

This is the information of
Dénonciation déposée par _____

of _____
de _____ , _____
(occupation / *profession*)

I have reasonable and probable grounds to believe and do believe that _____
J'ai des motifs raisonnables de croire et je crois effectivement que
(name / *nom*)

on or about the _____ day of _____ , yr. 20 _____
le ou vers le *jour de* *an*

at _____
à(au) (location / *lieu*)

did commit the offence of
a commis l'infraction suivante :

contrary to _____ section _____
contrairement à(au) *article*

_____
Signature of informant / *Signature du dénonciateur*

SUMMONS RETURNABLE / *SOMMATION À RAPPORTER*

Sworn before me
Déclaré sous serment devant moi

at _____   at _____
à(au)   *à(au)*

this _____ day of _____ , yr. 20 _____   on the _____ day of _____ , yr. 20 _____
ce *jour de* *an*   *le* *jour de* *an*

at _____ .m., at _____
à *h, dans* (courtroom / *salle d'audience*)

Judge or Justice of the Peace in and for the Province of Ontario
Juge ou juge de paix dans et pour la province de l'Ontario

(Sec. / Art. 24) ☐   Summons for _____ , yr. 20 _____   Confirmed on _____ , yr. 20 _____
Sommation pour *an*   *Confirmée le* *an*

Justice of the Peace
Juge de Paix

Date				

Pleads / *Plaidoyer* ☐ Guilty / *Coupable* ☐ Not Guilty / *Non coupable* ☐ Withdrawn / *Accusation(s) retirée(s)*

Found / *Décision* ☐ Guilty / *Coupable* ☐ Not Guilty / *Non coupable* ☐ In Absentia / *Défaut de comparution*

☐ Sentence Suspended
Condamnation avec sursis

Fined $ _____ & $ _____ costs. Time to pay _____
Amende de *$ et* *$ pour les frais. Délai de paiement*

Date of Birth _____
Date de naissance Day / *jour* Mo. / *mois* Yr. / *année*

Probation for _____
Période de probation de

Exhibits Filed
Pièces déposées

☐ Yes ☐ No
Oui Non

Sentenced to imprisonment for _____
Peine d'emprisonnement de

Judge or Justice of the Peace in and for the Province of Ontario
Juge ou juge de paix dans et pour la province de l'Ontario

FOR INFORMATION ON ACCESS
TO ONTARIO COURTS
FOR PERSONS WITH DISABILITIES, CALL
1-800-387-4456
TORONTO AREA **416-326-0111**

POUR PLUS DE RENSEIGNEMENTS SUR L'ACCÈS
DES PERSONNES HANDICAPÉES
AUX TRIBUNAUX DE L'ONTARIO, COMPOSEZ LE
1-800-387-4456
RÉGION DE TORONTO **416-326-0111**

POA 0001 CSD (rev. 11/03) (CD 001)

As part of receiving the information, a justice of the peace may hear and consider evidence in the absence of the defendant in order to determine whether the information alleging the offence is made out. Section 24 of the POA provides the procedure and framework for the laying and receiving of the information with respect to an offence.

> 24(1) A justice who receives an information laid under section 23 shall consider the information and, where he or she considers it desirable to do so, hear and consider in the absence of the defendant the allegations of the informant and the evidence of witnesses and,
>> (a) where he or she considers that a case for so doing is made out,
>>> (i) confirm the summons served under section 22, if any,
>>> (ii) issue a summons in the prescribed form, or
>>> (iii) where the arrest is authorized by statute and where the allegations of the informant or the evidence satisfy the justice on reasonable and probable grounds that it is necessary in the public interest to do so, issue a warrant for the arrest of the defendant; or
>> (b) where he or she considers that a case for issuing process is not made out,
>>> (i) so endorse the information, and
>>> (ii) where a summons was served under section 22, cancel it and cause the defendant to be so notified.

If a summons has not yet been served and if the justice is satisfied that the case has been made out, a Form 106 Summons will be issued and served on the defendant.

Fines

In Part I and Part II, fines are established through the set fine procedure, but in Part III, there is no set fine or out-of-court settlement. The defendant cannot settle the case by paying an out-of-court amount. Instead, the fine for all Part III proceedings must be determined by a justice.

When determining a fine amount for Part III proceedings, it is important to look to the enabling legislation for the offence. Many statutes provide their own penalty provisions (e.g., s. 2(b) of the *Trespass to Property Act*, R.S.O. 1990, c. T.21 provides a maximum fine of $2,000 for trespassing), but if a particular statute does not, the general penalty provisions found in s. 61 of the POA apply and the maximum fine is $5,000.

Proper Service

Unlike a Part I notice or summons, which must be served on the defendant, or a Part II parking infraction notice, which must be served on the operator/owner of the vehicle, s. 26(2) of the Act stipulates that a Part III summons can be served personally on the defendant, or can be left with someone at the defendant's usual or last known place of residence with someone who appears to be at least 16 years of age.

There are provisions in the POA for a provincial offences officer to serve the summons on persons who do not reside in Ontario:

26(3) Despite subsection (2), where the person to whom a summons is directed does not reside in Ontario, the summons shall be deemed to have been duly served seven days after it has been sent by registered mail to the person's last known or usual place of abode.

There are also provisions in the Act for service on corporations:

26(4) Service of a summons on a corporation may be effected,
  (a) in the case of a municipal corporation by,
    (i) delivering the summons personally to the mayor, warden, reeve or other chief officer of the corporation or to the clerk of the corporation, or
    (ii) mailing the summons by registered mail to the municipal corporation at an address held out by it to be its address;
  (b) in the case of any corporation, other than a municipal corporation, incorporated or continued by or under an Act by,
    (i) delivering the summons personally to the manager, secretary or other executive officer of the corporation or person apparently in charge of a branch office of the corporation, or
    (ii) mailing the summons by registered mail to the corporation at an address held out by it to be its address;
  (c) in the case of corporation not incorporated or continued by or under an Act by,
    (i) a method provided under clause (b),
    (ii) delivering the summons personally to the corporation's resident agent or agent for service or to any other representative of the corporation in Ontario, or
    (iii) mailing the summons by registered mail to a person referred to in subclause (ii) or to an address outside Ontario, including outside Canada, held out by the corporation to be its address.

The most common method of establishing proof of service is for the provincial offences officer who is serving the summons to complete and swear an affidavit of service.

Limitation Periods

When determining limitation periods, it is important to examine the enabling legislation, but if a specific reference cannot be found, the general provisions of the POA will apply. Section 76 of the POA provides for a limitation period for offences under the Part III procedural stream. If no limitation period is stipulated under the legislation pertaining to the offence, a general limitation period of six months applies:

76(1) A proceeding shall not be commenced after the expiration of any limitation period prescribed by or under any Act for the offence or, where no limitation period is prescribed, after six months after the date on which the offence was, or is alleged to have been, committed.

(2) A limitation period may be extended by a justice with the consent of the defendant.

A limitation period prevents charges from being laid if too much time has passed since an offence occurred. It is important to establish the correct limitation period before commencing a proceeding.

PRACTICE TIP

It is important to understand the statutory framework of the limitation period and at what point the computation of time starts. You must determine if time should be computed starting at when the offence is committed or when the offence comes to the attention of an official, or if it is an offence that continues until it is remedied. Suggested Reading: *R. v. Pickles* (2004), 237 D.L.R. (4th) 568, 2004 CanLII 60020 (Ont. C.A.).

KEY TERMS

certificate of offence	offence
certificate of parking infraction	offence notice
court	set fine
limitation period	summons

REVIEW QUESTIONS

True/False

_____ 1. Anyone may serve an offence notice if there is reason to believe an offence has been committed.

_____ 2. Anyone may lay an information alleging an offence before a justice of the peace.

_____ 3. A parking infraction notice may be served on the owner of a motor vehicle at his or her place of work or residence.

_____ 4. The maximum fine for a Part I offence is $500.

_____ 5. Once the offence notice is served, a certificate of offence must be filed with the court within seven days.

_____ 6. Only a provincial offences officer may serve a summons under Part III of the POA.

_____ 7. All Part I offence notices can be mailed to defendants to advise them of a charge.

_____ 8. If a matter proceeds to trial, the set fine is only a guide, not a rule, if the defendant is convicted.

Short Answer

1. What is the general limitation period for commencing a proceeding under Part III of the *Provincial Offences Act*? Include the statutory reference.

2. In reviewing a case with your client, you need to ensure that there are no errors in service. What are the service requirements under Part I of the POA?

3. A summons under Part III could be served on someone other than the defendant. What are the service options under Part III? What section of the POA outlines service options on a corporation?

4. If the statute under which your client has been charged has no limitation period provisions, where is the limitation period found for service of a summons under Part III?

5. If a defendant ignores a parking infraction notice, what steps must be taken by the municipality or other body to register a conviction?

Exercise

Justin is on his way home from work. He is driving along a city street at the rate of 85 km/h in a 50 km/h zone. He is using his cellphone when he loses control of his car and slams into a parked pickup truck on the side of the road. Justin is uninjured, so he gets out of his car and approaches the pickup truck. There appears to be no one else around. He takes a photo of the dent on the pickup truck and drives home. He then calls the non-emergency number for the police station, but only a voice mail messaging system is available. Justin does not leave a message and goes to bed, deciding he will drive to the station the next day. Justin did not realize that a neighbour heard the crash. The neighbour looked out the window, wrote down his licence plate number, and called the police. The police arrive at Justin's door at 8 a.m. the next day.

1. What document(s) will the police serve on Justin under Part I of the POA?

2. Speeding, careless driving, driving while operating a hand-held communications device, and failure to report could all be charges that apply in this case. Individually or in small groups, answer the following:

   a. In which statute and section can the offence be found?

   b. What is the penalty for the offence?

   c. Name the document that will be served on the defendant.

   d. How is the document served?

   e. What is the proof of service if the document is served by an officer?

   f. What is the maximum fine?

   g. What is the limitation period for the offence (provide the statutory reference)?

Classification of Offences

OVERVIEW

Introduction
Mens Rea **Offences**
Strict Liability Offences
Absolute Liability Offences
Charter Issues
Classification/Reclassifications of Offences
Key Terms
Review Questions

LEARNING OUTCOMES

After reading this chapter, you will understand

- the classification of regulatory offences (i.e., *mens rea*, strict liability, absolute liability); and

- how the classification of offences has an impact on the roles of the prosecution and the defence.

INTRODUCTION

In the significant decision *R. v. Sault Ste. Marie (City)*, [1978] 2 S.C.R. 1299, the Supreme Court of Canada held that all regulatory (provincial) offences can be classified as:

1. *mens rea* offences;
2. strict liability offences; or
3. absolute liability offences.

The classification of an offence as *mens rea*, strict liability, or absolute liability provides the framework for the prosecution's case. Specifically, an offence's classification dictates what the prosecution will have to prove in order for a defendant to be convicted. Understanding the classification process is also key to the defence because it provides insight into how the prosecution will likely be proceeding, and it assists a paralegal in determining how to best defend a client against charges.

It is important to carefully examine the actual wording of the offence in the charging act when determining how it should be classified. It is also necessary to review existing case law for each offence to determine whether the classification has already been established by a court. The court's classification takes precedence over any interpretations that are made based on the wording of the offence.

MENS REA OFFENCES

"*Mens rea*"—Latin for "guilty mind"—refers to the mental element of the offence or the defendant's state of mind at the time of the offence. The wording of the offence will not actually state that it is a ***mens rea* offence**, but will instead use specific terminology to refer to the defendant's state of mind. For instance, such words as "intentionally," "knowledge," and "wilfully" suggest that the defendant was aware of his or her actions when the offence was committed. Most criminal offences are *mens rea* offences, but only a few provincial offences are classified in this manner.

mens rea offence
an offence for which the prosecution must prove that the defendant committed the illegal act and had a guilty mind (i.e., the knowledge, intent, or willingness to commit the act)

beyond a reasonable doubt
a standard of proof where the prosecution must fully prove that the defendant committed the illegal act (to the extent that a reasonable person would not doubt that the act was committed)

When a charge is classified as a *mens rea* offence, the prosecutor must prove, **beyond a reasonable doubt**, that the defendant committed the illegal act and possessed the necessary mental element at the time of the offence.

Mens rea offences are considered to be more difficult for the prosecution to prove than either strict liability or absolute liability offences. The prosecution has to prove not only the defendant's wrongful actions, but also the defendant's thought process at the time of the infraction. It is not easy to prove what another person was thinking at any point in time. In an effort to prove the mental element of the offence, the prosecution may rely upon admissions from the defendant, inferences from the defendant's behaviour, and other evidence that may be relevant to the situation.

An example of a *mens rea* offence is s. 46(1)(a) of the *Gaming Control Act*, S.O. 1992, c. 24, which states:

46(1) Every person is guilty of an offence who,

   (a) knowingly furnishes false information in any application under this Act or in any statement or return required to be furnished under this Act or the regulations.

This is a *mens rea* offence because it refers to the defendant's knowledge at the time that the application was completed—specifically, the defendant's intent to provide false information on the application.

When dealing with a *mens rea* offence, the defence must either cast doubt on whether the defendant committed the illegal act or introduce evidence to raise a reasonable doubt about whether the actions were done intentionally, wilfully, or with knowledge. In the above example, the prosecution will attempt to prove that the defendant knew the information was false when he or she prepared the application but chose to include the false information anyway.

However, if the defendant had relied on information from another person and believed this information to be true, the defendant has not committed the mental element of the offence (i.e., it was not done knowingly). Although the prosecution may be able to prove that the defendant did complete the application with false information, there should not be a conviction because the action was not done knowingly.

STRICT LIABILITY OFFENCES

In accordance with the Supreme Court of Canada's decision in *Levis (Ville) v. Tetreault*, [2006] 1 S.C.R. 420, most regulatory (provincial) offences are classified as **strict liability offences**. In fact, it is presumed that an offence is a strict liability offence unless the wording suggests that it should be classified as a *mens rea* or an absolute liability offence, or a court has already decided how it is to be classified.

For a strict liability offence, the prosecutor must only prove, beyond a reasonable doubt, that the defendant committed the illegal act. Unlike *mens rea* offences, the defendant's state of mind at the time of the offence is irrelevant.

Once the prosecution has proven that the defendant committed the offence, the **onus** switches to the defendant to provide a **due diligence** defence for his or her actions—specifically, that the defendant took all reasonable care to avoid committing the offence or was operating under a reasonable misapprehension of the relevant facts (i.e., mistake of fact).

The defence must prove due diligence on a **balance of probabilities**—a lower standard of proof than those instances when the prosecution must prove allegations beyond a reasonable doubt. That means the court must find that it was more likely than not that a defendant exercised due diligence in the circumstances. If due diligence is proven, the charges against the defendant will be dismissed and there will not be a conviction.

An example of a strict liability offence is failing to remain at the scene of an accident, contrary to s. 200 of the *Highway Traffic Act*, R.S.O. 1990, c. H.8:

strict liability offence
an offence for which the prosecution must prove that the defendant committed the illegal act; the defendant then has an opportunity to prove reasonableness or due diligence

onus
the responsibility on the part of the prosecution for proving an allegation, or on the part of the defendant for bringing forward and proving a defence

due diligence
the standard of care that a reasonable person would be expected to apply to a specific situation

balance of probabilities
a standard of proof where an illegal act must be proven to be more likely than not to have occurred

200(1) Where an accident occurs on a highway, every person in charge of a vehicle or street car that is directly or indirectly involved in the accident shall,

(a) remain at or immediately return to the scene of the accident;

(b) render all possible assistance; and

(c) upon request, give in writing to anyone sustaining loss or injury or to any police officer or to any witness his or her name, address, driver's licence number and jurisdiction of issuance, motor vehicle liability insurance policy insurer and policy number, name and address of the registered owner of the vehicle and the vehicle permit number.

There is nothing in the wording of this offence to suggest that the prosecution must prove the defendant's state of mind (i.e., the words "intentionally," "wilfully," and "knowingly" are not included—see *mens rea* offences above). There is also no indication that due diligence cannot be used as a defence (see absolute liability offences below). Without such wording (and subject to a review of the case law), it can be presumed that it is a strict liability offence.

If the prosecution proves that the defendant left the scene of the accident, the defendant will have an opportunity to outline the steps that were taken to avoid leaving the scene or to explain how due diligence was exercised following the accident. The court will determine whether the defendant took all reasonable steps to remain at the scene.

ABSOLUTE LIABILITY OFFENCES

absolute liability offence
an offence for which the prosecution must prove that the defendant committed the illegal act; the defendant has no opportunity to argue reasonableness or due diligence

Absolute liability offences are those where the defendant is liable even if he or she was not at fault. The wording of the offence does not stipulate that it is an **absolute liability offence**, but it will often indicate that the defendant has no opportunity to demonstrate reasonableness or due diligence. For instance, the terminology will usually indicate that due diligence cannot be used as a defence, thereby making it an absolute liability offence.

The prosecutor must prove, beyond a reasonable doubt, that the defendant committed the illegal act, but there is no need for the prosecution to prove the defendant's state of mind at the time of the offence. As well, the defendant is not given an opportunity to demonstrate due diligence.

Speeding, for example, is classified as an absolute liability offence. If the defendant did not realize that he or she was speeding because other vehicles were travelling at the same rate of speed, a conviction will still be entered if the prosecutor can prove that the defendant was driving at a rate of speed above the posted limit. Therefore, the defendant is absolutely liable for the offence. The defendant's state of mind (e.g., intention to speed or knowledge of the rate of speed) is irrelevant because this infraction is not classified as a *mens rea* offence. And because this is not a strict liability offence, the defendant does not have an opportunity to demonstrate due diligence (i.e., that it was reasonable to drive at the same speed as the other vehicles on the road).

An example of an absolute liability offence is s. 84.1 of the *Highway Traffic Act*, which states:

84.1(1) Where a wheel becomes detached from a commercial motor vehicle, or from a vehicle being drawn by a commercial motor vehicle, while the commercial motor vehicle is on a highway, the operator of the commercial motor vehicle and the owner of the vehicle from which the wheel became detached are guilty of an offence. ...

84.1(5) It is not a defence to a charge under subsection (1) that the person exercised due diligence to avoid or prevent the detaching of the wheel.

In this example, subsection 5 clearly states that due diligence cannot be used as a defence. As a result, the defendant is absolutely liable even though reasonable steps may have been taken to prevent the wheel from detaching from the vehicle.

Absolute liability offences are generally considered the easiest for the prosecution to prove and the most difficult to defend against. Although due diligence cannot be argued by the defendant, some limited defences may apply in specific fact situations (i.e., involuntariness, causation, necessity).

For more information on defences, see the discussion in Chapter 11.

In *R. v. Sault Ste. Marie (City)*, [1978] 2 S.C.R. 1299, Dickson J. indicated that the following factors should be primary considerations in determining whether an offence is one of absolute liability:

1. The overall regulatory pattern adopted by the legislature.
2. The subject matter of the legislation.
3. The importance of the penalty.
4. The precision of the language used.

CHARTER ISSUES

An offence cannot be classified as absolute liability if a jail term is a possible penalty. In such cases, a jail sentence infringes on the defendant's life, liberty, and security of the person, contrary to s. 7 of the *Canadian Charter of Rights and Freedoms*, because some opportunities for a defence are not available for absolute liability offences. As such, the section of the charging act in question would be deemed unconstitutional and may be **quashed**. In cases where an absolute liability offence can result in a jail sentence, the court will often reclassify the offence as a strict liability offence, which gives the defendant the opportunity to demonstrate due diligence.

quash
to nullify or invalidate charges against a defendant

CLASSIFICATION/RECLASSIFICATIONS OF OFFENCES

The burden of proof rests with the party seeking to have the offence classified or reclassified. For instance, the defendant may want an offence to be classified as *mens rea* (because it is difficult for the prosecution to prove) or as strict liability (because it creates an opportunity to demonstrate due diligence). The defence would then be responsible for convincing the court that an offence should be classified/reclassified.

KEY TERMS

absolute liability offence	*mens rea* offence
balance of probabilities	onus
beyond a reasonable doubt	quash
due diligence	strict liability offence

REVIEW QUESTIONS

True/False

_____ 1. The majority of provincial offences are classified as *mens rea*.

_____ 2. Provincial offences are presumed to be strict liability offences.

_____ 3. When demonstrating due diligence, the defendant's standard of proof is "beyond a reasonable doubt."

_____ 4. The onus switches to the defendant to demonstrate due diligence for all types of offences.

_____ 5. The defence must prove the defendant's mental state for *mens rea* offences.

Short Answer

1. What does the prosecution have to prove to secure a conviction for an absolute liability offence?

2. What does the defendant have to prove to successfully defend against a strict liability offence?

3. What type of offence is "wilfully avoiding a police officer while being pursued"? How do you know?

4. For which type of offence must the prosecution prove that the defendant committed the illegal act beyond a reasonable doubt?

5. What does it mean if the description of an offence states that "anyone who knowingly falsifies a document is guilty of an offence ..."?

Exercise

Section 104 of the *Highway Traffic Act* reads:

104(2.1) No person shall ride on or operate a bicycle on a highway unless the person is wearing a bicycle helmet that complies with the regulations and the chin strap of the helmet is securely fastened under the chin.

104(2.2) No parent or guardian of a person under sixteen years of age shall authorize or knowingly permit that person to ride on or operate a bicycle ... on a highway unless the person is wearing a bicycle helmet as required by subsection (2.1).

1. If Zack was charged under s. 104(2.1), which type of offence would he face?
    a. *mens rea*
    b. strict liability
    c. absolute liability
    d. none of the above

2. If Zack's mother was charged under s. 104(2.2), which type of offence would she face?
    a. *mens rea*
    b. strict liability
    c. absolute liability
    d. none of the above

Your Client Has Been Charged 5

OVERVIEW

LEARNING OUTCOMES

After reading this chapter, you will understand

- some of the concerns and considerations for defendants charged with an offence;

- a paralegal's role in advising clients and making decisions about how to proceed;

- practical considerations for the intake interview and for dealing with your client throughout the process;

- the requirements for arrest, with or without a warrant; and

- the requirements for interim release (bail).

INTRODUCTION

As a paralegal, you will become accustomed to dealing with legal matters and making court appearances. After a few months of practice, you will likely start to lose the stress and anxiety that comes with appearing in court and will become more comfortable in the courtroom.

However, paralegals should keep in mind that for their clients, being charged with an offence can be difficult, stressful, or even embarrassing. It is important to try to see things from the client's perspective and make the process run as smoothly as possible for each and every client. You will need to take the time to explain all aspects of the charges and the process to your client, present options and recommendations, and ensure that the client provides full and complete instructions.

INTAKE INTERVIEW

The initial meeting with a client is an important step in understanding the case and building a defence. The information that you obtain during the intake interview will be critical in providing advice, conducting research, and representing your client's best interests.

Because many clients will be anxious about being charged with an offence, it is important that they feel comfortable in their discussions with a paralegal, and that they receive the guidance and support they need. You should assure clients that any information that is disclosed will remain confidential, and take the time to explain the process and their options.

When a client schedules an appointment to meet, ensure that copies of all relevant documentation are brought to the intake interview. When the client arrives for the meeting, you should verify the client's identity and make copies of the relevant documents for the file (i.e., driver's licence, proof of insurance, charging document, accident report). If the client comes to the office without an appointment, you may need to schedule a follow-up meeting to obtain the photocopies of relevant documents.

A defendant who consults a paralegal shortly after being charged should be instructed to make detailed notes of everything that occurred on the date that the charge was laid. This will help the defendant to collect his or her thoughts and recall some details that may otherwise have been forgotten. It will also provide the client with the option of using the notes to refresh his or her memory at trial—just as provincial offences officers can use their notes if they were made immediately after the incident.

Using notes at a trial may be helpful for those defendants who are nervous about testifying. However, the notes can only be used if they were made shortly after the incident because this is when the details will be recalled with the most accuracy. If there has been a delay before the notes were made, they will not be considered a reliable and accurate recollection of the incident.

PRACTICE TIP

When a client arrives at your office, he or she should be taken to a separate room and given a pen and paper. The client should then be asked to write down all of the details that he or she can remember from the day of the incident. You should not interrupt or coach the client because it is important that the client's own recollection be obtained. Spending a few minutes to collect his or her thoughts will help your client to remember some of the details and to recall the incident in the proper chronological order.

CHARGING DOCUMENTS

At the first meeting with a client, you should carefully review the **charging documents** and any other related documentation, clarifying anything that requires a further explanation and checking for errors. Very few errors are considered to be "fatal" and most can be amended in court with the justice's approval. However, even **non-fatal errors** on the charging document (i.e., a misspelled name or incorrect plate number) should be raised in court because they can undermine the officer's credibility and make it more difficult for the prosecution to prove the case beyond a reasonable doubt. If there is a **fatal error** on the charging document (i.e., if the certificate of offence was not signed by the officer), you can bring a motion to quash the certificate or information.

This is also an appropriate time to ensure that the proper charging document was used. As discussed in Chapter 3, to commence proceedings a defendant charged with a Part I offence must be personally served with an offence notice (or Part I summons); the owner/operator of a vehicle must be properly served with a notice of parking infraction for a Part II offence; and a defendant charged with a Part III offence must be personally served with an information and summons, or the information and summons must be left at the defendant's usual or last-known place of residence with someone who appears to be at least 16 years of age.

TIME FRAMES

Proper limitation periods and time frames must be followed by all parties dealing with provincial offences. For Part I matters, the offence notice or summons must be served within 30 days of the alleged offence, while for Part II matters, the parking infraction notice must be served at the time of the alleged infraction. The information and summons must be served within six months for alleged offences under Part III.

If service is to take place outside of these time frames, the defendant would have to consent to an extension of the limitation period. Most defendants would not agree to extend the limitation period for service because it means that they would be charged with an offence when the prescribed time for laying charges has expired.

charging documents
used to initiate charges against a defendant

non-fatal error
a mistake on a charging document that is not serious and will likely be amended in court

fatal error
a serious mistake on a charging document that will result in the charges being withdrawn, dismissed, or stayed

If there is an issue concerning proper service within the limitation period, the defence can challenge the jurisdiction of the court to hear the matter, and ask the prosecutor to withdraw the charges or bring a motion to quash the charging document.

If it is a Part I matter, the defendant must make a choice on how to respond to the charges within 15 days of being served. For Part II matters, there is also a 15-day response time, but defendants are given an additional 15 days to respond.

Regulation 200, s. 11(1) of the *Courts of Justice Act* states: "The clerk of the court shall not accept for filing a certificate of offence more than seven days after the day on which the offence notice or summons was served unless the time is extended by the court."

Therefore, provincial offences officers must ensure that their notices are filed within seven days or the matter will be considered abandoned. If a defendant pays the set fine listed on the offence notice and the certificate is not subsequently filed with the court, Regulation 200, s. 19 of the *Courts of Justice Act* requires the money to be refunded to the defendant.

The time it takes for a matter to get to court will vary depending on whether the charge falls under Part I, Part II, or Part III, and where the jurisdiction is located in the province (i.e., some courts may experience a backlog, causing a longer wait for trial dates). In accordance with s. 11(b) of the *Canadian Charter of Rights and Freedoms*, a trial must be held without unreasonable delay. A trial scheduled within 11 or 12 months is typically seen as a reasonable time frame. The time the defendant takes to select an option for a Part I offence is subtracted from the total time it takes for a case to go to trial. Any further delays by the defendant (e.g., requesting an adjournment) are not factored into the length of time it takes for a trial to be scheduled.

All days referred to in the POA are calendar days, not business days, as specified in Regulation 200, s. 4 of the *Courts of Justice Act*. The regulation further specifies that:

1. The time shall be calculated by excluding the first day and including the last day of the period.
2. Where a period of less than six days is prescribed, a Saturday or holiday shall not be reckoned.
3. Where the last day of the period of time falls on a Saturday or a holiday, the day next following that is not a Saturday or a holiday shall be deemed to be the last day of the period.
4. Where the days are expressed to be clear days or where the term "at least" is added, the time shall be calculated by excluding both the first day and the last day of the period.

OPTIONS/POSSIBLE OUTCOMES/RISKS

As a paralegal, you should present each client with the options, explain the possible outcomes and risks associated with each option, and make recommendations.

However, your client will make the final decision on how to respond to a charge. Although a paralegal will know the law and procedure, only the client will fully appreciate the personal and/or professional impact that such a decision will have, and is therefore in the best position to make a decision.

This is not to suggest that the client will dictate every decision on the file. Although the client will be responsible for significant decisions, the paralegal should be entrusted to make any decisions that are necessary to meet the client's goals.

The duty to present options, outcomes, and risks to your client is set out in Rule 3.02(1) of the *Paralegal Rules of Conduct*, which states, "A paralegal shall be honest and candid when advising clients." This is further explained within Guideline 7.1 of the *Paralegal Professional Conduct Guidelines*:

> A paralegal must honestly and candidly advise the client regarding the law and the client's options, possible outcomes and risks of his or her matter, so that the client is able to make informed decisions and give the paralegal appropriate instructions regarding the case. Fulfillment of this professional responsibility may require a difficult but necessary conversation with a client and/or delivery of bad news. It can be helpful for advice that is not well-received by the client to be given or confirmed by the paralegal in writing.

All clients should be fully informed of their options. It is easy to share good news and desirable outcomes with a client, but there may be a reluctance to share bad news. Guideline 7.1 explains the importance of documenting any advice given to a client, especially if the advice is not likely to be well received. You should confirm all advice in writing so that there is a paper trail in the file in case your actions are ever investigated.

Options for Part I: Offence Notice

A defendant who has been served with an offence notice has several options under the POA:

- *Option 1—Payment Out of Court:* In accordance with s. 8, a defendant who does not wish to dispute the charge may plead guilty by paying the set fine (plus costs and surcharges). This is considered to be the payment out-of-court option because it does not require a court appearance. Payment can be made by mail, and over the telephone or Internet.

For more information on the options, outcomes, and risks associated with pleading guilty and making a payment out of court, see the discussion in Chapter 6.

- *Option 2—Plea of Guilty with Submissions:* Section 7 provides the authority for a plea of **guilty with submissions**. A defendant who does not wish to dispute the charge can enter a guilty plea and still have the opportunity to make submissions to the court (i.e., statements about the penalty or the amount of time to pay the fine). There is a common misconception that providing submissions means providing an explanation that could lead to the charge being dismissed or withdrawn, but that is not the case. A plea of

guilty with submissions
pleading guilty, but providing additional information on why the penalty should be reduced or the time for payment should be extended

guilty with submissions results in a finding of guilt by the court, but the submissions may bring a lower fine or additional time in which to pay.

For more information on the options, outcomes, and risks associated with pleading guilty with submissions, see the discussion in Chapter 6.

- *Option 3—Intention to Appear:* Sections 5 and 5.1 set out the procedure for a defendant to give notice of an intention to appear in court to enter a plea and have a trial. In accordance with s. 5, notification can be given by completing the notice of intention to appear, found on the offence notice, or by completing the Notice of Intention to Appear (NIA) form (Form 8 under the POA—see Appendix B where this form is reproduced). If a defendant may want to challenge the officer's evidence at trial, he or she must indicate so at this time. Otherwise, the officer will not be notified of the trial date and the prosecution can rely on the officer's sworn statements, which means the defence will not have an opportunity to cross-examine the officer's evidence. The NIA form can be signed by either the defendant or the defendant's representative.
- *Option 4—Failure to Respond:* A defendant who does not select an option within the 15-day time period has failed to respond. It is not usually considered to be an appropriate option and is not listed on the back of the offence notice, but some defendants will opt not to respond.

A defendant who fails to respond will be deemed to have not disputed the charge. In accordance with s. 9, the justice is required to examine the certificate of offence to ensure that it is complete and regular on its face. If the certificate is found to be complete and regular on its face, the justice will enter a conviction. In many cases, a failure to respond is equivalent to the defendant agreeing to plead guilty.

However, there is a potential benefit to failing to respond. If there is an error on the certificate, it will not be considered complete and regular on its face. The certificate will then be quashed and there will not be a conviction. If the justice overlooks the error, in many cases the conviction can be appealed. It is interesting to note that if a similar error on the certificate was brought to the court's attention at trial, the certificate would likely be amended instead of quashed.

Options for Part I: Summons

A defendant who has been served with a Part I summons does not have as many options as someone who has been served with an offence notice.

Options are limited to entering a guilty plea, negotiating with the prosecutor, or pleading not guilty and having a trial. A defendant who has been summoned to court does not need to request a court date because the summons will specify the courtroom, and the time and date of the trial. The officer has already decided that there will be a court date.

Attending court is mandatory if a summons has been issued. If a defendant does not appear for a court date after receiving a Part I summons, the court may issue an arrest warrant. Alternatively, the trial may proceed in the defendant's absence (***ex parte* trial**) and if the allegations are proven, a conviction will be entered.

***ex parte* trial**
a trial held without
the defendant or the
defendant's representative

Options for Part II: Parking Infraction Notice

A defendant who has been served with a parking infraction notice has several options under the POA:

- *Option 1—Payment Out of Court:* In accordance with s. 16, a defendant who does not wish to dispute the charge may plead guilty by delivering the parking infraction notice and the set fine to the court office. In some jurisdictions, there is an early-payment amount to encourage defendants to pay the fine instead of challenging the ticket.
- *Option 2—Intention to Appear:* Sections 17(1) and 18(1) allow a defendant who is served with a parking infraction notice or notice of impending conviction to give notice of intention to appear in court to enter a plea and have a trial by indicating this on the parking infraction notice and delivering the notice to a specified court.
- *Option 3—Informal Negotiations:* Although not listed as an option on the parking infraction notice, some municipalities will allow defendants to engage in informal negotiations at the municipal office. A bylaw officer or municipal employee may authorize a reduced payment (which amounts to a guilty plea and a conviction).
- *Option 4—Failure to Respond:* A defendant who does not make a choice within 15 days is not automatically considered to have failed to respond. Because parking infraction notices are often served by placing the document on the vehicle, there is no guarantee that the owner/operator of the vehicle actually received the notice on the date it was served, or that the owner/operator received it at all. Because of this, defendants are given a further 15 days to make a choice. Typically, the defendant will be sent a notice of impending conviction pursuant to s. 18.1(1) of the POA after the initial 15-day period has lapsed. If the defendant still does not respond to the notice within the additional 15 days, he or she will have failed to respond and a conviction will be entered.

Options for Part III: Information

A defendant who has been served with a Part III summons must appear in court on the date specified on the summons. In court, the defendant has the option of pleading guilty or not guilty to the offence described in the charging document, pursuant to s. 45. The prosecutor may also offer the defendant an opportunity to plead guilty to an included charge (i.e., an alternative charge that still fits with the facts of the offence but carries a lesser penalty). Therefore, the defendant also has the option of pleading guilty to the alternate offence with the consent of the prosecutor and acceptance by the justice.

Where the defendant pleads guilty, the court may accept the plea and register a conviction. However, the court will not accept the guilty plea unless it is satisfied that the plea was made voluntarily. The court must also be satisfied that the defendant understands that the plea is an admission of the essential elements of the offence, understands the nature and consequences of the plea, and understands that the court is not bound by any agreement between the defendant and the prosecutor.

The defendant can also plead not guilty and have a trial pursuant to s. 46(1), giving him or her the opportunity to make full answer and defence to the charges.

In most cases, a defendant does not need to appear in court to respond to a summons, but has the option of hiring a lawyer or paralegal to represent his or her interests in court. If the defendant or the defendant's representative fails to appear, the court can hear the case in the defendant's absence (an *ex parte* trial), or can adjourn the hearing and issue a summons or warrant.

FEES/RETAINER AGREEMENT

retainer agreement
an agreement for legal services between a licensee and a client

A **retainer agreement** is a contract between the paralegal and the client outlining the legal services that the paralegal will provide and the fees, disbursements, and HST to be paid by the client. Retainer agreements for lawyers and paralegals are not mandated by the Law Society of Upper Canada, but they are considered to be a "best practice." Guideline 5 of the *Paralegal Professional Conduct Guidelines* provides some guidance on setting up a retainer. Guideline 5.4 states that a paralegal should clearly identify the clients to whom legal services will be provided to ensure that the paralegal fulfills his or her duties to those clients.

Legal fees can add up quickly, and a client may become upset when presented with a final bill that is more than expected. Clients have been known to complain to the Law Society of Upper Canada about fees. Guideline 13.6 suggests that it is a good practice to discuss fees and disbursements at the outset of the retainer. To ensure that there is no misunderstanding, this information should be provided or confirmed in writing.

monetary retainer
a sum of money paid up front for legal services to be provided in the future

For provincial offences matters, it is common to charge a flat fee and to collect a monetary retainer before the paralegal begins to work on the file. Like any other type of **monetary retainer**, it must be deposited into the paralegal's trust account, and cannot be transferred to the general account until the work has been completed and a statement of account or bill has been sent to the client.

Collecting a monetary retainer is a good practice for paralegals because it means that the client will not have to be tracked down to pay fees when the case is over. Collecting payment could be problematic if the matter was not resolved in the client's favour and the client is reluctant to pay. It also means that there is no confusion for the client about the amount of money being charged for the services being provided.

PRACTICE TIP

Fees vary for representation in provincial offences court. It is worth investigating the accepted rate in your jurisdiction to ensure that your fees are not set too low or too high in terms of what is considered to be fair and reasonable.

SPECIAL CONSIDERATIONS FOR YOUNG PERSONS

Section 93 of the POA defines a young person as someone who appears to be 12 years of age or older, but under the age of 16. Notice that this definition has a different upper limit from the age commonly prescribed by societal standards and in other legislation. It is also important to note that no one can be convicted of an offence if it was committed while he or she was under the age of 12.

The POA gives special consideration to young persons. Section 95 indicates that for Part I matters, a summons, not an offence notice, must be served on a young person. In addition, a copy of the summons must be delivered to the parent of the young person, pursuant to s. 96. In many cases, this leads to the parent taking an interest in the proceedings against the young person.

When representing a young person, the paralegal must keep in mind that the young person is the client, not the person paying for legal services—often the parent. Because of this, special duties of confidentiality must be clarified. Fees can be discussed with the parent, but the retainer letter should establish who the client is, and therefore who will receive information about the case and who will provide instructions.

Because a young person is served with a summons instead of an offence notice, he or she does not have the option of making an out-of-court payment, even for a Part I offence. Under s. 98 of the POA, a young person must be present in court for an entire trial, unless otherwise permitted by the court. That means a young person cannot avoid appearing in court by simply hiring a paralegal to deal with the matter on their behalf.

Where a young person fails to appear for a hearing despite being issued a summons, the court may adjourn the hearing and issue a summons to appear or an arrest warrant, pursuant to s. 98(4) of the POA.

SPECIAL CONSIDERATIONS IF YOUR CLIENT HAS BEEN ARRESTED

Part VIII of the POA deals with arrest, bail, and warrants. Although the Act provides for the arrest of a defendant, with or without a warrant, most defendants charged with a provincial offence will not be arrested and will therefore not be attending a bail hearing.

Arrest with a Warrant

Section 24 of the POA gives a justice the authority to issue a warrant for the defendant's arrest at the time that the information is laid. Specifically, s. 24(1)(a)(iii) states that where a justice "considers that a case for doing so is made out":

> ... where the arrest is authorized by statute and where the allegations of the informant or the evidence satisfy the justice on reasonable and probable grounds that it is necessary in the public interest to do so, issue a warrant for the arrest of the defendant ... .

It is important to note that the POA does not provide a general power to arrest. Instead, it refers to authorization under the charging act, and the justice's reasonable and probable grounds to believe that it would be in the public interest to issue a warrant. After confirming such grounds through the allegations or evidence, the justice must complete Form 107 under Regulation 200 of the *Courts of Justice Act* in order to issue the warrant.

A warrant of arrest under s. 24 must include the name or description of the defendant, and the offence, and order that the defendant be arrested immediately and brought before a justice. The warrant remains in force until it is executed by an officer.

Section 144 of the POA further clarifies the procedure for executing the arrest warrant. A police officer carries out a warrant by arresting the defendant, and the warrant only applies to a defendant in Ontario. It should be noted that the Act specifies that a warrant must be executed by a police officer, which means a provincial offences officer cannot carry out this duty. Upon arrest, the police officer must inform the defendant of the reason for arrest and produce the warrant, where feasible.

Arrest Without a Warrant

A police officer may arrest someone without a warrant if the officer has reasonable and probable grounds to believe that a warrant is already in effect. Therefore, it is not always necessary for a police officer to possess a warrant.

It is possible in some situations for a person to be arrested without a warrant and by a civilian, not a police officer. In accordance with s. 145 of the POA:

> Any person may arrest without warrant a person who he or she has reasonable and probable grounds to believe has committed an offence and is escaping from and freshly pursued by a police officer who has lawful authority to arrest that person, and, where the person who makes the arrest is not a police officer, shall forthwith deliver the person arrested to a police officer.

A civilian arrest without a warrant is only authorized if a person is believed to have committed an offence and is trying to escape from a police officer. Because this type of situation requires the police officer to have lawful authority, the charging act must indicate that an arrest can be made without a warrant for specified offences.

Interim Release

In most cases, a defendant who has been arrested will be released once served with a summons or offence notice. In fact, s. 149 of the POA specifies that a defendant must be released by the arresting officer "as soon as is practicable." However, an officer does not have to release a defendant in cases where there are reasonable and probable grounds to believe that it is in the public interest to confirm the defendant's identity, to secure or preserve evidence, or to prevent an offence, and in cases where there is reason to believe that the defendant is not an Ontario resident, and so will not respond to a summons or offence notice.

If the defendant has been detained, the arresting officer is required under s. 149 to escort him or her to the officer in charge at the police station. The officer in charge may release the defendant at this point if it is determined that the reasons for detaining the defendant no longer exist. In the case of a non-resident, the officer in charge may require bail to ensure the defendant's response to the charging document.

Bail Hearing

If a defendant has not been released by the arresting officer or the officer in charge, he or she must be brought before a justice within 24 hours for a bail hearing. The defendant then has an opportunity to plead guilty or undertake to appear at trial. In accordance with s. 150 of the POA, the justice may release the defendant on an undertaking to appear at trial, unless the prosecutor can show cause as to why it is necessary to detain the defendant in order to ensure that he or she appears in court. A defendant who is being released may be required to enter into a **recognizance** to appear in court with or without a **surety**.

recognizance
an acknowledgment and agreement by the defendant that he or she will attend the next scheduled court appearance

surety
a person who agrees to be responsible for the defendant's appearance in court

---

PRACTICE TIP

Before a bail hearing, a paralegal should speak to the prosecutor in order to obtain disclosure about the offence, the reasons for detainment, and the possible need for a surety.

KEY TERMS

charging documents
ex parte trial
fatal error
guilty with submissions
monetary retainer

non-fatal error
recognizance
retainer agreement
surety

REVIEW QUESTIONS

True/False

_____ 1. The Notice of Intention to Appear form (NIA) can be signed by either the defendant or the defendant's representative.

_____ 2. If the defendant's last name is misspelled on the offence notice, it will be considered a fatal error and the charges will be withdrawn by the prosecutor as a result.

_____ 3. A motion to quash should be brought for fatal and non-fatal errors on the charging document.

_____ 4. For Part III matters, the defendant does not need to personally appear in court, but can instead hire a paralegal or a lawyer.

_____ 5. In some cases, a civilian can arrest someone who is believed to have committed a crime and is trying to escape from police.

Short Answer

1. What will happen if a defendant does not respond within 15 days of receiving a notice of parking infraction?

2. What will happen, in most cases, if a defendant does not respond within 15 days of receiving an offence notice?

3. What will happen, in most cases, if the defendant fails to appear at a trial after submitting a Notice of Intention to Appear?

4. What will happen, in most cases, if the defendant fails to appear at a trial after being served with a summons?

5. Under what circumstances will a defendant not be released on an undertaking during a bail hearing?

Exercise

Rebecca is a 15-year-old girl who was observed by a police officer to be consuming alcohol in a parking lot outside a movie theatre. The police issued a Part I summons pursuant to s. 31(2) of the _Liquor Licence Act_, R.S.O. 1990, c. L.19 for having/consuming alcohol in a place other than a residence, a licensed premises, or a private place.

1. Which of the following is an incorrect statement about the above scenario?
   a. Rebecca's parents must be notified.
   b. Rebecca cannot be convicted because she is younger than 16 years of age.
   c. Her identity cannot be published.
   d. All of the above are incorrect.
   e. None of the above are incorrect.

2. Rebecca's father retained a paralegal to represent her interests. Which of the following statements is correct?

   a. Rebecca will have to attend court because legal representation is not permitted for young persons.

   b. Her paralegal, but not Rebecca, must attend court.

   c. Both Rebecca and her paralegal will have to attend court.

   d. No one is required to attend court; Rebecca can just pay a fine.

   e. None of the above are correct.

3. When Rebecca's father retained the paralegal, he indicated that because he was paying the bill, he wants copies of all documents in the file. Does this raise any ethical issues for the paralegal?

   a. Yes, the paralegal's confidentiality requirements will not allow the disclosure of such information to anyone who is not a client.

   b. Yes, the paralegal cannot accept payment from anyone other than a client.

   c. No, a client is defined as the person who pays for services, so Rebecca's father is the client and is entitled to all documents.

   d. No, Rebecca and her father are joint clients and therefore are both entitled to all documents.

   e. None of the above.

Your Client Wants to Plead Guilty

6

OVERVIEW

LEARNING OUTCOMES

After reading this chapter, you will understand

- the options and outcomes in making a guilty plea;

- criteria that must be met in order for the court to accept a guilty plea; and

- consequences of a conviction.

INTRODUCTION

If your client is considering pleading guilty, options are available concerning when and how the guilty plea will take place. A guilty plea can occur either in or out of court, depending on the circumstances. After discussing these options, it is important to advise your client of the consequences of a conviction.

OPTIONS AND OUTCOMES

A guilty plea can take place at different stages of the proceedings.

Out-of-Court Payment

In accordance with s. 8 of the *Provincial Offences Act*, a defendant who does not wish to dispute the charge may plead guilty by paying the set fine (plus costs and a victim fine surcharge). This is called the payment out-of-court option because it does not require a court appearance. Most jurisdictions have several methods for paying a fine, including by mail, in person, or over the Internet.

Making an out-of-court payment is considered to be an admission of guilt and the defendant will be convicted of the offence. This option may be desirable for someone who is in need of closure or certainty, who wants to accept responsibility for their actions, or who does not want to invest additional time and money in the case. However, it is not always the best option because the defendant will have to pay the full set fine. By waiting until a later stage in the proceedings, the defendant may be able to request a reduced fine or even have the charge amended to a lesser offence.

Plea of Guilty with Submissions

Section 7 of the POA provides the authority for a plea of guilty with submissions. A defendant who does not wish to dispute the charge can enter a guilty plea and still have the opportunity to make submissions to a justice on the penalty. Although s. 7 states that the submissions concern the penalty, defendants are often under the misconception that if they provide an explanation as to why they committed the offence, the charges will be dismissed. A defendant's submissions may result in a lower fine or additional time to pay, but a guilty plea will result in a conviction.

Under s. 7, the justice has discretion to impose the set fine or a lesser fine, but cannot impose a fine that is higher than the set fine. A defendant will not risk having to pay more by pleading guilty with submissions than if he or she had made an out-of-court payment, and may actually end up paying less.

Defendants seeking a lesser fine often submit that their finances are strained as a result of unemployment, being in school, maternity leave, or child support payments, for example. Some defendants are willing to pay the full amount but are just not able to do so within the prescribed 15-day time limit, and are requesting an extension of time to pay the fine.

Because this option is also considered to be an admission of guilt, it will result in a conviction and carry the normal penalties that follow such an outcome. This option may be desirable for a defendant who is not interested in fighting the charges, but who hopes to receive a break on the penalty. It also provides a sense of closure and certainty, and allows a matter to be resolved quickly.

Meeting with the Prosecutor

A defendant who does not necessarily want to have a trial, but also does not want to plead guilty to the charges, can consider meeting with the prosecutor. In accordance with s. 5.1(2), a defendant may request a meeting with the prosecutor to discuss resolving the charges. This has been historically referred to as a first-attendance meeting and allows for out-of-court negotiations.

During the meeting, the prosecutor will sometimes offer to amend the charges in exchange for a guilty plea. The prosecutor may suggest a substituted offence, which would result in a lower fine or fewer **demerit points**, in the case of a driving offence. If a defendant accepts the prosecutor's offer, he or she will appear before a justice sitting in court and plead guilty to the amended charge. At this point, the defendant and the prosecutor will have the opportunity to give submissions regarding the penalty. The justice has discretion to impose the set fine or any other fine that is permitted by law.

It is important to note that, unlike in cases where a defendant pleads guilty with submissions, the justice is not limited to imposing the set fine or a lesser fine. This means that a defendant who chooses this option could end up paying a fine that is higher than the set fine, up to the maximum allowed under the POA or the charging act. However, in most cases, a guilty plea before a trial date is considered to be a **mitigating factor**, and it is unlikely that the justice would increase the fine.

If the defendant does not request a meeting with the prosecutor, there will typically be an opportunity to speak with the prosecutor immediately before the trial. At this point, it is still possible to see charges substituted in exchange for a guilty plea.

This option may be desirable for a defendant who is not interested in having a trial, but hopes to reach a more desirable outcome.

demerit points
a penalty administered by the Ministry of Transportation for driving offences

mitigating factor
information about a defendant that is presented to a justice after conviction and may lead to a lesser penalty

---

PRACTICE TIP

Before meeting with the prosecutor, review the charging act to get a sense of offences that could be considered included offences. Look for those that carry a lower fine or fewer demerit points. If you are not satisfied with the offer made by the prosecution, you might suggest alternate charges that may put your client in a better position.

Pleading Guilty at Trial

Sometimes a defendant who requested a trial date, intending to dispute the charges, changes his or her mind by the time the trial date arrives. At this point, the defendant is not required to follow through with a trial, and still has an opportunity to plead guilty to the original charges or to amended charges as negotiated with the prosecutor. The set fine is only considered to be persuasive, so the justice has discretion to impose another amount.

This option may be desirable to a defendant who was initially unsure of how to handle the matter, and needed more time to consider the options and make an appropriate decision.

PROCEDURE

The procedure for pleading guilty depends on the stage in the proceedings that the plea is entered. If the defendant makes an out-of-court payment of the set fine, it is considered to be a guilty plea and a conviction is registered as soon as the fine is paid.

In order to plead guilty with submissions, the defendant must attend court and appear before a justice. The guilty plea is put on the record and the defendant may then make submissions on the penalty. In this case, the defendant is usually given time to pay the fine (i.e., the statutory 15 days, or longer if specified by the justice).

Different jurisdictions have varied procedures concerning a meeting with the prosecutor. Some municipalities allow a defendant to meet with a prosecutor without an appointment (often referred to as "walk-in first attendance"), while others require a meeting to be scheduled. Inquiries should be made at individual court offices about procedures for meeting with the prosecutor.

To plead guilty at trial, the defendant must complete the Notice of Intention to Appear form (see this form in Appendix B), attend at the scheduled trial date, and enter a plea.

With the exception of cases where voluntary payment is made of the set fine, the justice can exercise discretion on whether to accept the defendant's guilty plea. Pursuant to s. 45 of the POA, the justice may only accept a guilty plea if he or she is satisfied that the defendant:

(a) is making the plea voluntarily;

(b) understands that the plea is an admission of the essential elements of the offence;

(c) understands the nature and consequences of the plea; and

(d) understands that the court is not bound by any agreement made between the defendant and the prosecutor.

CONSEQUENCES OF CONVICTION

Regardless of when the defendant pleads guilty, the result is the same: The defendant has admitted that he or she committed the offence, has given up the right to a trial, and is aware that there will be a finding of guilt and a conviction.

costs
a fee added to a court-imposed penalty

victim fine surcharge
a fee added to a court-imposed penalty that is then transferred to a special fund to assist victims of crime

A conviction means the defendant must pay a fine, plus **costs** and a **victim fine surcharge**. Other than in cases when the payment out-of-court option is chosen by the defendant or when the defendant pleads guilty with submissions, the set fine is only persuasive. The justice has discretion to impose a fine that is higher than the set fine.

For driving-related matters, a guilty plea means that the Ministry of Transportation will be notified and the conviction will be registered on the defendant's driving record for three years. If demerit points are associated with the offence, they will remain on the defendant's record for two years from the date of the offence. Demerit points are automatically imposed by the Ministry of Transportation, not by the court. It is beyond the jurisdiction of the officer, prosecutor, or justice to remove the points. The only way to decrease the number of demerit points is to plead guilty to an alternate offence that carries a lower number.

With any driving-related conviction, there is also a risk that the defendant's insurance premiums will increase, but that is a private matter for the defendant to discuss with an insurer. Each insurance company has its own policies and procedures for premium increases. Any insurance rate increase is determined by the insurer, not the court or the Ministry.

If the charges are related to a motor vehicle accident, there is a possibility that the conviction will be used against the defendant if a civil lawsuit is commenced. Because this can have serious implications for the defendant, it is advisable to seek legal advice.

KEY TERMS

costs
demerit points
mitigating factor
victim fine surcharge

REVIEW QUESTIONS

True/False

_____ 1. A guilty plea can take place at various stages of the proceedings.

_____ 2. A plea of guilty with submissions means that charges may be dismissed against a defendant if he or she provides a good explanation for committing the offence.

_____ 3. The justice has the authority to administer a fine higher than the set fine if the defendant pleads guilty with submissions.

_____ 4. The justice has the authority to administer a fine higher than the set fine if the defendant pleads guilty at trial.

_____ 5. The justice has the discretion to remove demerit points as a penalty.

_____ 6. Demerit points stay on a driver's record for two years from the date of the conviction.

Short Answer

1. What possible submissions may a defendant make when requesting a lesser fine?

2. How are demerit points imposed?

3. How does a conviction affect a defendant's driving record?

4. How does a driving conviction affect what a defendant pays for auto insurance?

Exercise

Luke, a self-represented defendant, indicates that he would like to plead guilty with submissions. In his submissions to the court, he explains that he should not be convicted of a speeding charge because he was hurrying to get to the hospital after receiving a phone call from his son's school that his son had been injured on the playground.

1. Why is it proper for the justice to convict Luke in this case?

2. Luke tells the justice that he is willing to pay the fine, but he would like the demerit points associated with the offence to be removed. Do you think the justice will remove the points in this case?

3. What should Luke do in this case?

Your Client Wants to Request a Trial Date

7

OVERVIEW

LEARNING OUTCOMES

After reading this chapter, you will understand

- the process of requesting a trial; and
- the defendant's options, risks, and outcomes once a trial has been requested.

INTRODUCTION

Requesting a trial date is only an option for Part I matters (without a summons) and those that fall under Part II. A Part I or Part III summons already includes a date and time for trial, so the defendant does not have the option or the responsibility of making such a request.

A defendant who does not want to plead guilty or guilty with submissions can give notice of his or her intention to appear in court to enter a plea and have a trial, and this procedure is set out in ss. 5 and 5.1 of the POA. In accordance with s. 5, the proper indication can be made on the back of the offence notice, while, under s. 5.1, indication can also be given by completing Form 8, a **Notice of Intention to Appear** (NIA) (see Appendix B).

Notice of Intention to Appear
Form 8, used for the defendant to request a trial

A defendant who may want to challenge the officer's evidence at trial must indicate so at this time. Otherwise, the officer will not be notified of the trial date and the prosecution can rely on his or her sworn statements—providing no opportunity for the defence to cross-examine the officer's evidence. The court clerk will then set a trial date and give notice of the date to the defendant.

NOTICE OF INTENTION TO APPEAR

The Notice of Intention to Appear, or Form 8, can be used for Part I or Part II matters to allow the defendant to request a trial date.

In many jurisdictions, this form is copied on yellow paper and is available from court offices. However, a growing number of municipalities are posting the forms online, and so not all of the NIA forms will be copied on yellow paper.

The NIA can be completed by either the defendant or the defendant's representative. It must include the defendant's correct name and address, even if the offence notice contained an error. The form allows the defendant to indicate whether he or she would like to challenge the officer's evidence and request that the officer attend the trial. If the appropriate box is checked, the officer will be notified of the trial date. If it is not checked, the officer will be able to provide certified statements as sworn evidence, instead of making a personal appearance. The defendant may also use this form to request a trial in English or an interpreter who can provide services in another language.

In accordance with s. 125(2) of the *Courts of Justice Act*, evidence presented in a language other than English must be interpreted into English. Therefore, if your client or a witness does not speak or understand English adequately, an interpreter should be considered. For Part I and Part II matters, the interpreter can be requested by checking the appropriate box on the NIA.

Once an interpreter has been requested, the court administrative staff will make the arrangements for a qualified interpreter to attend court and to translate as needed, at no charge to the defendant or witnesses. Family members do not typically act as interpreters. If the interpreter fails to attend court, the prosecutor may withdraw the charges or request an adjournment to another date.

NOTICE OF TRIAL

For Part I matters, s. 5.1(11) states that the court clerk shall, as soon as is practicable, give notice to the defendant and prosecutor of the time and place of the trial. The authority for the requirement to give notice for parking infractions under Part II is contained in s. 17(4).

The notice will be sent to the address listed on the NIA or the offence notice. It is important to ensure that the address is correct and that the court is notified if there is an address change.

Notice of trial is not necessary for a Part I or Part III summons because the defendant received the details of the trial, such as the date, time, and courtroom, when served with the summons.

OPTIONS, OUTCOMES, AND RISKS

A defendant who requests a trial date may take further steps and has additional options beyond having a trial.

Seek Disclosure

Because the defendant's decision must be made within 15 days of being served, there is not enough time to obtain **disclosure** from the prosecution and make an informed choice on how to proceed with the matter. By giving notice of an intention to appear, the defendant has an opportunity to request and obtain disclosure from the prosecution. After reviewing any documents that are disclosed, the defendant may be able to determine whether the case is strong enough to proceed to trial. If disclosure is not requested by the trial date, the defendant may want to ask for an adjournment in order to obtain disclosure. However, such a request is subject to the justice's approval and is not always granted.

disclosure
documentation that the prosecutor will be relying on to prove the charges against the defendant

Negotiate with the Prosecutor

The defendant will typically have an opportunity to negotiate with the prosecutor or show required documentation to the prosecutor either immediately before trial or at a scheduled meeting with the prosecutor. The negotiations may lead to the charges being withdrawn, a lesser charge being offered in exchange for a guilty plea, or an agreement with the prosecutor regarding submissions on the penalty. A lesser charge is considered to be an included offence pursuant to s. 55 of the POA.

The best-case scenario for the defendant would be to have the charges withdrawn. This may occur if they are considered to be "paper charges"—for example, if the defendant was a licensed driver at the time of the offence, but had unintentionally left his or her driver's licence at home. The prosecutor has the discretion to withdraw the charge if proof is shown that the driver has a licence. Another example is a charge that stems from the need for an auto repair, such as a broken headlight. If the defendant has a receipt from a mechanic showing that the repair was carried out within a reasonable time, the prosecutor may withdraw the charge.

PRACTICE TIP

Arrive at court 20 to 30 minutes before the scheduled time in order to speak to the prosecutor. This will ensure that the prosecutor has sufficient time to consider your client's charges before court commences.

Plead Guilty

A defendant who has changed his or her mind and decided to plead guilty can still do so at this stage.

For more information on guilty pleas, see the discussion in Chapter 6.

Ensure Officer's Attendance

Requesting a trial date gives the defendant a chance to ensure that the officer attends the trial. Occasionally, there may be a reason for an officer not to attend court, such as being called to another police matter, or scheduled for annual leave or training. In such situations, the prosecution will often withdraw the charges because the case would be difficult to prove without the officer's evidence. It is worth noting that the prosecutor has the option of requesting an adjournment. However, s. 49(3) states that the court shall not adjourn a Part I or Part II trial to allow the provincial offences officer who completed the certificate to attend court, unless the court is satisfied that it is required by the interests of justice.

PRACTICE TIP

Do not assume that an officer will not be attending court just because you do not see him or her in the courtroom. Some officers will arrive after court has already started. When you check in with the prosecutor, ask whether the officer has already checked in and, if not, whether the prosecutor is anticipating the officer's attendance.

Unreasonable Delay

institutional delay
the amount of time it takes for a matter to get to trial, minus any delay that was caused by the defendant

staying the proceedings
the prosecution of the offence has been halted and a conviction will not be entered against the defendant

Requesting a trial date allows the defendant to ensure that the trial is scheduled without unreasonable delay. Case law has established that an **institutional delay** of more than 11 to 12 months has been held to be unreasonable and is contrary to s. 11(b) of the *Canadian Charter of Rights and Freedoms*. If a motion for unreasonable delay is successful, the proper remedy is for the proceedings to be stayed by the justice. **Staying the proceedings** means that the prosecution of the offence has been halted and there will not be a conviction entered against the defendant.

For more information on motions brought under the *Canadian Charter of Rights and Freedoms*, see the discussion in Chapter 9.

Seek an Adjournment

A defendant who has been given a court date can attempt to **adjourn** the matter to a new date. The motion to adjourn can be brought with or without notice. However, it can be risky to request an adjournment without notice because there is no guarantee that the motion will be granted and the defendant may have to proceed on the original court date.

adjourn
put the trial over to a new date

Adjournments are often sought in order to retain a lawyer or paralegal. They are also commonly requested in order to allow a defendant to ask for and review disclosure materials.

For more information on motions for adjournment, see the discussion in Chapter 9.

Trial

Requesting a trial date provides the option of having a trial. Sometimes the defence will opt not to call witnesses or enter evidence at trial, but will instead use the proceedings to ensure that the prosecution proves all elements of the offence. Other times, both the prosecution and defence will call witnesses, and the justice will consider the evidence and render a decision.

A trial brings the possibility that the defendant will be successful and charges will be dismissed, which means there will not be a conviction. However, there is also the possibility that the defendant will be convicted. Upon conviction at trial, the justice has the opportunity to determine the sentence. It is worth noting that at this point, the set fine is only persuasive, and the justice has discretion to raise or lower the fine. If it is a driving-related offence, a conviction also leads to a driving record with the Ministry of Transportation, the possibility of demerit points, and a potential increase in insurance premiums.

Choosing a trial may be appropriate for someone who wants to keep his or her options open but does not necessarily need to resolve the matter quickly.

Failure to Appear

A defendant who requests a trial date and has been given notice of the trial but does not attend court on that date will be deemed not to dispute the charge. This is considered a failure to appear at trial, as set out in s. 9.1 of the POA. The justice is still required to examine the certificate of offence to ensure that it is complete and regular on its face. If the certificate is complete and regular on its face, the justice will enter a conviction in the defendant's absence and impose the set fine for the offence. In most cases, failing to appear is equivalent to a defendant indicating a desire to plead guilty.

However, there is a unique situation where a paralegal may intentionally decide not to appear on a Part I or Part II matter. If the justice finds an error on the certificate, it will not be considered complete and regular on its face. In this case, the certificate will be quashed and there will not be a conviction. It is interesting to note that if a similar error on the certificate were raised at trial, the document would likely be amended. Although there is a risk that the justice may miss the error, failing to appear at trial is an option if there is an obvious error on the certificate.

In cases where a defendant fails to appear for a Part III matter, an *ex parte* trial will take place, where the court will hear the prosecution's case. If the prosecutor is able to prove all elements of the offence, a conviction will be entered. Alternatively, instead of an *ex parte* trial, the justice has the discretion to adjourn the hearing and issue a summons to appear, or issue an arrest warrant for the defendant.

SPECIAL CONSIDERATIONS FOR OUT-OF-JURISDICTION MATTERS

Provincial offences matters are heard and determined by the Ontario Court of Justice in the county or district in which the offence occurred.

As a paralegal, if a defendant wants to retain you to defend a matter that is out of your local jurisdiction, or possibly even out of the province or country, you should consider several factors, including whether it would be cost effective for the defendant. Travel and accommodations, plus the fee for representation, may exceed any fines and consequences from a conviction. As well, Ontario is presently the only place in Canada or the United States that permits a paralegal to act as a paid legal representative in court.

It may be more appropriate to refer the matter to a legal representative who practises in the jurisdiction where the charges were laid.

KEY TERMS

adjourn	Notice of Intention to Appear
disclosure	staying the proceedings
institutional delay	

REVIEW QUESTIONS

True/False

_____ 1. A motion for an adjournment is always granted to a defendant at his or her first court appearance if it is for the purpose of requesting and reviewing disclosure.

_____ 2. At the trial stage, the set fine for an offence is only persuasive.

_____ 3. An error on the certificate of offence means that it is not complete and regular on its face.

_____ 4. The Notice of Intention to Appear (NIA) can only be filled out by the defendant.

_____ 5. The prosecutor will always be granted an adjournment if the officer is not present at trial.

Short Answer

1. What are two ways to request a trial date for a Part I matter?

2. Why is an NIA not used for Part III matters?

3. How are "paper charges" usually handled by the prosecutor?

4. What will happen if the defendant or the defendant's representative fails to appear at trial for a Part III matter?

Exercise

Sean did not attend his careless driving trial because his paralegal told him the wrong date. Although neither Sean nor his paralegal attended court, Sean was not convicted and the certificate was quashed.

1. Explain how it is possible that the certificate was quashed and Sean was not convicted.

2. A careless driving charge can be brought under Part I or Part III. How do we know that Sean was charged under Part I?

3. Assume that the certificate was complete and regular on its face. What would happen if Sean did not attend his trial?

Preparing for Court

OVERVIEW

LEARNING OUTCOMES

After reading this chapter, you will understand

- the steps that should be taken to prepare for court;

- the purpose of and procedure for requesting disclosure;

- how to summon a witness to court; and

- how to request an interpreter if your client or witness does not speak or understand English.

INTRODUCTION

Once a Notice of Intention to Appear has been filed with the court, you should immediately start preparing for the upcoming trial—even before a trial date has been assigned by the court.

NETWORK

If you have not handled a particular type of offence in the past, it can be worthwhile to speak to other paralegals who have experience with such a case or who have seen the charge defended in court. Your contacts may have ideas, information, and expertise to offer, so send a message to all of your paralegal contacts and see whether any of them are willing to share information.

PRACTICE TIP

Always try to share your ideas, information, and expertise with your network of contacts when asked. Other paralegals may be more willing to return the favour when you need assistance.

Becoming a member of a paralegal association, such as the Paralegal Society of Ontario and the Licensed Paralegals Association of Ontario, provides networking opportunities and mentoring for newly licensed paralegals. Whether the networking is through conferences, meetings, or online discussions, you will have a chance to meet and communicate with other paralegals throughout Ontario.

At the time of writing, the Law Society of Upper Canada requires paralegals to complete at least 12 hours of continuing professional development each year. Programs, seminars, and conferences offered by the Law Society of Upper Canada and other organizations bring paralegals together to learn as well as network with one another.

One of the best ways to meet new paralegals and learn how to handle offences is to sit in court and observe. This cannot be emphasized enough. Watching other paralegals in court will allow you to pick up some helpful tips and techniques, and gain an understanding of effective defence strategies. You will also have an opportunity to talk to other paralegals during breaks in the proceedings.

REVIEW THE CHARGING ACT

The charging act—the act under which your client has been charged—can provide important guidance on how to dispute a charge in court. Although it is critical to review the section under which your client has been charged, it is also beneficial to review related sections and subsections of the act that may describe penalties, possible defences, and exceptions to the charge.

Penalty provisions are typically found near the charging sections in any act, although the exact placement of these provisions varies from act to act and section to section. In some cases, the penalties are in the same section as the charge, while in others, the provisions are listed in a section or subsection that follows the charging section. In still other cases, the penalties are included at the end of a part to the act or, possibly, at the end of the entire act. Because the penalties are not listed in a consistent place for all charges in all acts, it is especially important to seek out the penalty provisions by reviewing all related sections and subsections.

The charging act also contains important information about the classification of an offence. It is a good idea to refer to the actual charge order to examine the wording of the offence. This will help to establish whether the offence is *mens rea*, strict liability, or absolute liability. It is necessary to understand the classification in order to prepare a full answer and defence to the charges. However, you cannot rely on the wording of the offence alone because the court may have considered the classification of the offence and decided it should be reclassified. Therefore, you should also review the relevant case law to determine the offence's current classification.

In some cases, the related sections and subsections of an act will describe which defences will or will not be accepted for that particular charge. For example, s. 2(2) of the *Trespass to Property Act* indicates, "It is a defence to a charge under subsection (1) in respect of premises that is land that the person charged reasonably believed that he or she had title to or an interest in the land that entitled him or her to do the act complained of." This subsection explains that a possible defence to a trespassing charge is a belief by the defendant that he or she owned the land. On the other hand, s. 84.1(5) of the *Highway Traffic Act* removes a potential defence, stating that "due diligence cannot be used as a defence to this charge."

Information about exceptions can also be found in the related sections and subsections. There are often exceptions or situations where an act that is usually prohibited is actually permitted. If one of these exceptions is relevant, the burden of proof is on the paralegal or defendant to show that the exception applies to the defendant on a balance of probabilities. For example, under s. 106 of the *Highway Traffic Act*, it is an offence to drive a vehicle while not wearing a seat belt. However, subsection (6) provides a list of several situations when a driver is not required to wear a seat belt, such as when he or she has a medical certificate. If your client recently had an injury or surgery, his or her doctor may have provided a medical certificate verifying the situation and eliminating the need for a seat belt. In such a case, producing the medical certificate in court should result in the charges being withdrawn or dismissed.

A thorough review of the charging act will also help to prepare you for any negotiations that may take place with the prosecutor, such as in a scheduled meeting before the trial. When reviewing the charging act, you should search for alternate charges—specifically, consider whether your client's fact situation could fit with any of the other offences listed in the act. Make a list of all other offences that could apply and then conduct further research regarding the applicable penalties for each of the alternate charges. With your client's approval, you may want to suggest a guilty plea to one of the alternate charges when meeting with the prosecutor.

A review of the regulations accompanying the charging act may provide additional information that is relevant to your client's situation. For example, Regulation 339/94 of the *Highway Traffic Act* lists the number of demerit points for various driving offences. This will help you to understand the impact that a conviction will have on your client. Be sure to ask your client about his or her driving record, the number of points that are registered on the record, and when the points will be removed. Knowing this information in advance allows you to be fully prepared and able to represent your client's best interests when entering into negotiations with the prosecutor.

PRACTICE TIP

Not all clients will be entirely truthful about their driving record or they may not remember specific details about previous convictions. Consider ordering a Driver's Abstract from the Ministry of Transportation so that you will have a full and detailed statement of your client's driving record. The abstract may be obtained for $18 (at the time of publication).

DETERMINE THE ELEMENTS OF THE OFFENCE

elements of the offence
the items that have to be proven by the prosecutor to secure a conviction

The **elements of the offence** are the items that have to be proven by the prosecutor to secure a conviction. In order to determine the elements of the offence, you will look to the actual wording of the charging section of the charging act, and consider each and every word in the section.

For example, s. 144(15) of the *Highway Traffic Act* states, "Every driver approaching a traffic control signal showing a circular amber indication and facing the indication shall stop his or her vehicle if he or she can do so safely, otherwise he or she may proceed with caution."

The elements of the offence that must be proven by the prosecutor (i.e., the evidence that the prosecutor's witnesses will have to provide) include:

- the defendant was the driver;
- the defendant was driving a vehicle;
- there was a traffic control signal showing an amber indication;
- the defendant approached the traffic control signal;
- the defendant did not stop at the traffic control signal; and
- it would have been safe for the defendant to stop, or that the defendant did not proceed through the intersection with caution.

When preparing for trial, making a list of the elements of the offence will help you to anticipate the prosecutor's evidence. If the prosecutor does not prove all elements of the offence, the defendant can bring a motion for a non-suit or can raise the elements that were not proven during closing statements.

LOOK FOR ERRORS ON THE CHARGING DOCUMENT

A paralegal should always review the charging document for errors. A common misconception is that if there is an error on the charging document, the charges will be withdrawn. However, that is rarely the case. In fact, there would have to be a fatal error on the charging document for the charges to be withdrawn or quashed. Most errors are not considered fatal, and in many cases the court will amend the charges at trial. Section 34 of the POA gives the court the authority to amend the information or certificate at any stage in the proceeding if there has been an error.

Minor errors on a charging document are quite common, so it is worthwhile to review the document for errors and to consider the effect that this will have in court. Minor mistakes, such as a misspelled name or address, or an incorrect digit in the licence plate, will be considered non-fatal errors. However, even minor errors on a charging document can raise a reasonable doubt as to whether there should be a conviction. If you find errors that interfere with your client's ability to prepare full answer and defence to the charge, you will want to consider bringing a motion to quash the charging document. However, be prepared for the prosecutor to request an amendment pursuant to s. 34.

For more information on quashing the charging document, see the discussion in Chapter 9.

Section 34(4) of the POA sets out what the court must consider when deciding whether to amend the charging document. Specifically, the court will consider the evidence that has been given, the circumstances of the case, whether the defendant has been misled or prejudiced, and whether the amendment can be made without causing injustice. If your client has been misled to the extent that he or she was unable to prepare a full answer and defence to the charges, or if you feel that there has been prejudice or injustice to your client, you may want to consider arguing against the prosecutor's amendment request.

If the court agrees to amend the charging document, the existence of the errors will still undermine the officer's credibility, raising questions about the overall investigation. You will want to summarize the errors in your closing statement so that the court can consider whether there is reasonable doubt about your client's guilt in the charges before the court.

As stated earlier, very few errors are considered to be "fatal," but there are a few that will justify quashing the charging document. Some examples include:

- The proper offence date and date of service must be written on the charging document. A document that contains an incomplete or incorrect date, or where the date is missing altogether, will likely be quashed. The correct dates are important because certain timelines take effect on these dates. For example, a notice must be served on the defendant within 30 days of the offence date for a Part I offence, and the defendant has 15 days from the date of service to respond. If the charging document contains incorrect dates, the timelines will be affected.

- Although a spelling error in the defendant's name is not fatal, that would not be the case if the name is missing altogether. The prosecution would have difficulty proving that the person before the court is the same person who committed the offence because the document does not specify who committed the offence.
- The charging document must specify where the offence took place to ensure that it was properly filed in the court that has jurisdiction for that location.
- The officer's signature is necessary—verifying, for example, that an offence notice was served upon the defendant for a Part I offence. Without the signature, there is no proof of service. However, it is essential that the certificate of offence is signed by the officer, but it is not essential that the offence notice copy is signed. If you notice that the officer's signature is missing from the defendant's copy, request to see the court's copy and verify that it was signed by the officer.

CONDUCT RESEARCH

Changes to the law and new interpretations of statutes occur every day in our courts, which means paralegals must continually research the law for updates and binding precedents. This can be a challenge for a busy paralegal who is trying to run an office and make court appearances. Fortunately, resources are available that allow paralegals to stay up to date with any changes to the law that affect provincial offences matters.

Belonging to a paralegal organization can be invaluable for sharing information and discussing new cases. Some organizations have regular meetings that allow for discussions, while others post relevant information on their websites or provide an online discussion area for their members. Electronic mailing lists are available for discussing case law and asking questions.

The annual volumes of the *Annotated Ontario Provincial Offences Act* and the *Annotated Ontario Highway Traffic Act* are indispensable because they list the leading cases for every section of the legislation. The amount of time saved is certainly worth the cost of purchasing a new volume each year.

Legal encyclopedias, textbooks, and articles can refer you to the leading cases on a topic. Electronic finding tools, such as Quicklaw and the Canadian Abridgment Case Digests, can help you to search for relevant case law. Other resources that may be useful in finding and updating cases include CanLII, LawSource, and BestCase.

REQUEST DISCLOSURE

When a defendant intends to plead not guilty, s. 46(2) of the POA indicates that he or she is entitled to make full answer and defence to the charges that have been laid. In order to do this, the paralegal should request and review copies of the evidence that the prosecutor will be using in the case. When the defence makes a request for disclosure, the prosecutor must provide any information that is in his or her possession and that will be relied on to prosecute the defendant. It is worth noting that the disclosure obligations are one-sided: While the prosecutor must give the defendant all relevant documents, the defendant does not have a reciprocal duty to disclose information to the prosecutor that will be used to defend against the charges.

Paralegals should submit a request for disclosure as soon as they are retained. It may take several weeks, or even months, for full compliance. The sooner that you request disclosure, the more likely you will receive the relevant documents before the trial date. A form used for disclosure requests is available at the court office. It is not a standardized form. Each court office will provide its own version of the disclosure request form. After the form is completed, it can be faxed or delivered to the office. Requests for disclosure can also be submitted at a scheduled meeting with a prosecutor (for Part I and Part II matters) or at the first court appearance when the trial date is set (for Part III matters) because the defendant or representative is already at court.

PRACTICE TIP

Obtain confirmation that your disclosure request has been received. If sending it by fax, print off the confirmation page to verify that it has been sent. If dropping it off in person, bring a second copy to the court office, and ensure that it is stamped and initialled by the court administration staff. If the disclosure request is not honoured, you will be able to prove that it was submitted and be in a good position to request an appropriate remedy, such as a stay of the proceedings, an adjournment, and/or an order for the production of the disclosure documents.

Each court has its own procedure for forwarding the disclosure documents. Some courts will fax the documents, while others will request that the documents be picked up. When you receive disclosure, arrange to meet with your client so that you will be able to review the documents together, and discuss and interpret the contents.

You can expect the disclosure to include a copy of the notes that the police officer made at the time of the alleged offence. It is useful for the defendant to see the notes because the officer may use them to refresh his or her memory at the trial. The amount of detail in the notes varies from officer to officer: Some provide specific details, while others write only one or two lines. Other documents in the disclosure package may include a copy of an accident report or witness statements.

When reviewing the documents, consider whether anything may be missing. If you think that is the case, submit another written request for disclosure. If you have made repeated requests and still not received disclosure by the trial date, you will have an opportunity to pursue a remedy.

When disclosure has been requested but not provided, the defence often seeks an adjournment and an order for production of the disclosure documents as a remedy. But it is difficult to justify a remedy if the defendant or the defendant's legal representative is partly responsible for the non-disclosure. Examples include if disclosure was not requested in a timely fashion before the trial date, or if the disclosure request form was incorrectly filled out or missing important information.

A stay of proceedings is another remedy that is used in exceptional circumstances. If there have been repeated requests for disclosure and the disclosure has not been provided, a stay of proceedings may be appropriate.

CONSIDER WITNESSES

When preparing for trial, you need to consider who your witnesses will be. They could include people who were present at the scene and involved in some way with the defendant, such as passengers in a car, or someone who witnessed the incident but was not directly involved. Some witnesses will volunteer to attend court, but others will need to be compelled to testify.

Section 39 of the POA provides the authority to issue a summons to witnesses to attend the trial. In order to compel a witness to attend court, the person requiring the witness must appear before a justice and swear the "summons to witness." The justice may ask for detailed reasons as to why this witness should be compelled to attend court. The summons will be granted if the justice is satisfied that the witness has material evidence to offer at trial. The summons will require the witness to attend court to give evidence, and can also specify that the witness bring anything that has been itemized in the summons. The summons is to be served on the witness by a provincial offences officer, in accordance with s. 26(2) of the POA.

PRACTICE TIP

Issuing a summons for a witness to appear in court is always a good practice. In addition to compelling the witness's attendance at court, a summons could assist the witness in getting time off work or school because it provides a documented reason for absence. As well, if for any reason the witness fails to attend court, you will be in a better position to request an adjournment because proper procedures were followed to compel the witness's attendance at court.

CONSIDER THE NEED FOR AN INTERPRETER

In accordance with s. 125(2)(a) of the *Courts of Justice Act*, evidence given in a language other than English must be interpreted into English. Therefore, if your client or one of your witnesses does not speak or understand English adequately, you should consider the need for an interpreter. For Part I and Part II matters, an interpreter can be requested by checking the appropriate box on the Notice of Intention to Appear. For Part III matters, an interpreter can be requested at the first court appearance when the trial date is set.

If the need for an interpreter arises after the Notice of Intention to Appear has been filed or after the first court appearance, an Interpreter Request form is available from the court and can still be completed. Once an interpreter has been requested, the court administrative staff will make the arrangements for an interpreter to attend court and to translate as needed. If the interpreter has been properly requested yet does not attend court, the justice may decide to adjourn the matter or to dismiss the charges.

CONSIDER ANY NECESSARY MOTIONS

As you prepare for trial, you should consider whether it is necessary to bring any motions, either with or without notice.

For more information on the types of motions and the procedure for bringing such motions, see the discussion in Chapter 9.

CONSULT WITH CLIENT

The most important person in any proceeding is your client. Clients often complain about a lack of communication or poor communication from their legal representatives, so be sure to update your client on a regular basis about the work that has been done on his or her file. No matter how busy your practice becomes, it is essential to take the time to consult with your client. It is also important to remember that your client is the ultimate decision-maker for any significant decisions on a file, so you must obtain their instructions and consent before taking any steps on the case.

Consider whether your client should testify at the trial. Some of your clients will likely want to take the stand, but others may not feel comfortable. You may also have clients who would not make a good witness. If your client is going to testify, you can assist by reviewing the evidence and preparing him or her for cross-examination. If your client is not going to take the stand, explain how this will limit your ability to defend the matter.

As a paralegal, you will become accustomed to going to court and you will start to feel comfortable in this environment. However, most of your clients will never feel comfortable going to court, and may rely on you for additional support and guidance.

KEY TERM

elements of the offence

REVIEW QUESTIONS

True/False

_____ 1. The penalty provisions in legislation are always contained in the same section as the offence.

_____ 2. The prosecutor has the burden of proof that an exception applies to a charge.

_____ 3. Both the offence notice and the certificate of offence must be signed by the officer.

_____ 4. The offence notice must be served on the defendant within 15 days of the offence.

_____ 5. The summons to witness will be granted if the justice is satisfied that the witness has material evidence to offer at trial.

Short Answer

1. Explain how to request an interpreter for Part I and Part II matters; and for Part III matters.

2. Outline some examples of fatal errors.

3. What will the court consider if the prosecution has requested an amendment to the charging document?

Exercise

Alison has a very busy paralegal practice. In preparing her client's case, she requested disclosure from the prosecution in a timely fashion, but it was never provided. Unfortunately, a key defence witness, who had guaranteed his attendance, did not show up for the trial.

1. How should Alison deal with this situation?

2. What remedy should Alison seek if the adjournment is granted but disclosure is still not provided by the new trial date?

3. What will Alison have to prove to the court in order to get the summons to witness?

Motions and Applications 9

OVERVIEW

LEARNING OUTCOMES

After reading this chapter, you will understand

- the procedures and process involved in motions and applications under the *Provincial Offences Act*;

- the framework for pretrial motions, motions without notice, and Charter applications; and

- where to find additional information about motions and applications.

INTRODUCTION

While the POA is meant to provide a streamlined process and allow matters to proceed on their merits by limiting technical challenges or objections, it is still important to understand the rules and procedures, and when it is best to introduce a motion or application—and when to avoid doing so. Knowing when it is not a good time to bring a motion or application comes with experience and practice, and there are some general suggestions to guide your judgment.

PRETRIAL MOTIONS

Pretrial motions are fairly uncommon in the provincial offences context, but the more serious the offence being prosecuted, the greater the likelihood that a pretrial motion will be necessary.

Some of the more common pretrial motions, even for minor offences, deal with procedural requirements or adjournments.

Notice of Motion

In order to bring an application through a notice of motion, an approved form must be used. This form is available from the provincial offences court. It should then be served on the prosecution and a copy should be filed in the court. The notice must be served at least three days before the motion is to be heard and filed at least two days before the motion hearing. Given the time requirements, filing a motion as soon as is practicable is the best approach.

A notice of motion (reproduced in Appendix B) allows all parties to understand the issue and adequately prepare a response, and gives the court the opportunity to properly exercise its jurisdiction.

Motion to Adjourn

It is not uncommon for a motion to adjourn to be dealt with orally and without notice on the day scheduled for a trial. However, if you know in advance that you or your client will not be able to proceed with the case on the trial date, you should follow the rules and complete a notice of motion. A defendant does not have a right to an adjournment, so he or she must be made aware that it is not uncommon for adjournments to be denied.

PRACTICE TIP

It is advisable to bring a motion to adjourn with notice before the trial date. If the motion is not granted, you and your client will know to be ready to proceed on the scheduled trial date. If you were to bring a motion to adjourn without notice, you run the risk of being forced to proceed unprepared if the motion is not granted.

Motion for Disclosure

Another common pretrial motion is for disclosure. While most prosecutors recognize that providing timely and full disclosure improves procedural efficiency, sometimes further disclosure through a court order is required.

When reviewing your client's case and the materials provided by the prosecution, it may be necessary to bring a motion for further disclosure if you believe the prosecution has withheld documents that you feel are relevant.

In order to make full answer and defence to the charge, a defendant is entitled to know the evidence to be used by the prosecution at trial.

The defendant's right to make full answer and defence under ss. 7 and 11(d) of the *Canadian Charter of Rights and Freedoms* is further stated in s. 46(2) of the POA.

The issue of bringing a motion before the court over disputed disclosure is not without jurisprudence in the provincial offences context.

The issue was before the Ontario Court of Appeal in *R. v. 1353837 Ontario Inc. et al.* (2005), 74 O.R. (3d) 401, 2005 CanLII 4189. The court found that where disclosure disputes arise, trial justices have the right to control the disclosure process. In this case, the defence brought a pretrial motion for further disclosure of 18 items. In response, the prosecution filed an affidavit by the chief building inspector, who alleged that all elements of the request for further disclosure were either irrelevant or had already been satisfied. The final determination was left to the justice. Most of the defence motions brought before the justice at trial ultimately failed, and those decisions where upheld by the Ontario Court of Appeal. But this case provides useful precedent on pretrial motions for disclosure.

Motion to Amend

A motion to amend a certificate or information may be brought at any stage of a proceeding. Although bringing a motion to amend is largely a procedure carried out by the prosecution, having a good understanding of the jurisprudence and statutory requirements is key to ensuring that your client's rights are protected. Most of the precedent cases have favoured the POA's broad curative provisions and granted amendments as long as there was no prejudice to the defendant.

Section 34 of the POA provides the framework for motions to amend:

> 34(1) The court may, at any stage of the proceeding, amend the information or certificate as may be necessary if it appears that the information or certificate,
>> (a) fails to state or states defectively anything that is requisite to charge the offence;
>> (b) does not negative an exception that should be negatived; or
>> (c) is in any way defective in substance or in form.
>
> (2) The court may, during the trial, amend the information or certificate as may be necessary if the matters to be alleged in the proposed amendment are disclosed by the evidence taken at the trial.

(3) A variance between the information or certificate and the evidence taken on the trial is not material with respect to,

>(a) the time when the offence is alleged to have been committed, if it is proved that the information was laid or certificate issued within the prescribed period of limitation; or

>(b) the place where the subject-matter of the proceeding is alleged to have arisen, except in an issue as to the jurisdiction of the court.

(4) The court shall, in considering whether or not an amendment should be made, consider,

>(a) the evidence taken on the trial, if any;

>(b) the circumstances of the case;

>(c) whether the defendant has been misled or prejudiced in the defendant's defence by a variance, error or omission; and

>(d) whether, having regard to the merits of the case, the proposed amendment can be made without injustice being done.

(5) The question whether an order to amend an information or certificate should be granted or refused is a question of law.

(6) An order to amend an information or certificate shall be endorsed on the information or certificate as part of the record and the trial shall proceed as if the information or certificate had been originally laid as amended.

Motion for Particulars

With the vast array of agencies, police departments, and other bodies that can commence proceedings under the POA, occasionally the circumstances of the case are unclear in the charging documents. It may be necessary in some circumstances to bring a motion for particulars with respect to the charge your client is facing. The essential elements of the offence and the allegations concerning your client's conduct may not be clear from the charging document. Section 35 of the POA provides the framework for a motion for particulars:

> 35. The court may, before or during trial, if it is satisfied that it is necessary for a fair trial, order that a particular, further describing any matter relevant to the proceeding, be furnished to the defendant.

Motion to Quash

If you find that the charging document has serious defects apparent on its face, and you can successfully argue that an amendment or further particulars would not be appropriate in your case, you can bring a motion to quash under s. 36(1), prior to entering a plea to the charge. Once the trial has begun, you may only bring a motion to quash with permission of the court.

Motions to quash can be successful when the officer has failed to properly complete the charging document or has committed serious jurisdictional errors in service or process. These motions are by no means guaranteed, and proper preparation and oral argument are the keys to a successful outcome for the defence.

MOTIONS WITHOUT NOTICE

While s. 7 of Regulation 200 under the *Courts of Justice Act* allows for any motion or application to be heard without notice, on consent, or where the court determines doing so would not be unjust, it is best to follow the proper procedure and bring your motion or application with notice.

There are some circumstances where notice is simply not practical—for example, when you learn the day before or the day of trial that your client will not be available for court. In such a case, it may be appropriate and necessary to bring your motion for adjournment without notice.

PRACTICE TIP

One of the best ways to ensure efficient advocacy for your client is to bring civility into your practice. Developing a rapport with court administrative staff and the prosecution will prove to be valuable when bringing motions and applications. It is also wise to consider consenting to prosecution motions without notice when doing so does not prejudice your client.

Motion for Non-Suit

A motion for non-suit—an example of a motion without notice—can only be brought by the defence at the conclusion of the prosecution's case. This is a rare motion and the test for success is high. If the prosecution fails, through error or omission, to present evidence on all of the essential elements in the case, you should be prepared to immediately introduce a motion for non-suit.

The test for non-suit is rarely at issue. The test is simply: Is there some evidence on each of the essential elements that could lead the trier of fact to properly convict? If the answer is yes, a motion for non-suit would not succeed. There is no weighing of the evidence at this stage. Although there is no risk to your client's case—unlike in the civil court system, where you would be prohibited from calling evidence if the motion failed—a motion for non-suit should be used only in the clearest of cases.

Motion to Amend or Divide a Count

You may also bring a motion without notice if your client is facing several counts or charges. Section 33 of the POA provides the framework:

33(1) A defendant may at any stage of the proceeding make a motion to the court to amend or to divide a count that,

(a) charges in the alternative different matters, acts or omissions that are stated in the alternative in the enactment that creates or describes the offence; or

(b) is double or multifarious,

on the ground that, as framed, it prejudices the defendant in the defendant's defence.

LEGAL FRAMEWORK FOR MOTIONS

The rules governing applications and motions for provincial offences proceedings are set out in s. 7 of Regulation 200 under the *Courts of Justice Act*:

7(1) An application provided for by the Act or these rules shall be commenced by notice of application.

(2) A motion provided for by the Act or these rules shall be commenced by notice of motion.

(3) There shall be at least three days between the giving of notice of application or notice of motion and the day for hearing the application or motion.

(4) An applicant or moving party shall file notice of application or notice of motion at least two days before the day for hearing the application or motion.

(5) Evidence on an application or motion may be given,

(a) by affidavit;

(b) with the permission of the court, orally; or

(c) in the form of a transcript of the examination of a witness.

(6) Upon the hearing of an application or motion and whether or not other evidence is given on the application or motion, the justice may receive and base his or her decision upon information the justice considers credible or trustworthy in the circumstances.

(7) An application or motion may be heard without notice,

(a) on consent; or

(b) where, having regard to the subject-matter or the circumstances of the application or motion, it would not be unjust to hear the application or motion without notice.

(8) Subrules (2) to (5) do not apply in respect of a motion under section 66 of the Act.

If you are the party bringing the motion (the "moving party"), particularly when requesting direction from the court or seeking an adjournment, it is to your advantage to demonstrate compliance with the rules.

Often a court will refuse to hear the merits of a motion when the rules have not been followed. Bringing a motion is a relatively straightforward process and only requires that a notice of motion be completed, usually with a corresponding affidavit sworn by your client. There are times it may be advisable to prepare a factum or book of authorities if the issue is complicated.

CHARTER MOTIONS

The *Canadian Charter of Rights and Freedoms* provides the framework for almost all of the legal procedures you will face in your career as a paralegal. The most common Charter motion in the provincial offences setting involves delay and the protections afforded under s. 11(b) of the Charter. Less frequent are motions to determine whether a statute or regulation violates the *Constitution Act, 1982*, R.S.C. 1985, app. II, no. 44.

From a practical standpoint, you need to be mindful of the time and effort needed to successfully bring a Charter motion and the evidence that is required. Bringing such a motion alleging a breach of your client's rights may be a strategic decision.

Proper research is essential in determining whether an actual breach has occurred, and even if one has, you still must weigh whether bringing a formal application to seek a remedy is appropriate. As a professional paralegal, you should avoid bringing "boilerplate" Charter motions for all cases that have taken an excessive amount of time to reach the trial stage. The majority of Charter issues have already been litigated, most before the Supreme Court of Canada, so searching for precedents prior to starting a Charter challenge is always in your client's best interest.

The legal framework for bringing a Charter motion is set out in s. 109 of the *Courts of Justice Act*:

> 109(1) Notice of a constitutional question shall be served on the Attorney General of Canada and the Attorney General of Ontario in the following circumstances:
> 1. The constitutional validity or constitutional applicability of an Act of the Parliament of Canada or the Legislature, of a regulation or by-law made under such an Act or of a rule of common law is in question.
> 2. A remedy is claimed under subsection 24(1) of the *Canadian Charter of Rights and Freedoms* in relation to an act or omission of the Government of Canada or the Government of Ontario.

In addition to serving the Attorney General of Canada and the Attorney General of Ontario, the notice of constitutional question (see Appendix B) must be served on the prosecution office at least 15 days before the trial date and it must be filed with the court.

As a legal representative, you are expected to know the requirements for notice. The likelihood of the court considering a Charter motion without proper notice under s. 109 is almost non-existent. If the Charter breach only comes to your attention after the proceeding has commenced, it may be necessary to adjourn the matter to allow for notice to be served and a proper application to be brought forward to the court.

If you proceed with a Charter motion, it is advisable—in addition to the documentation for the notice of constitutional question—to prepare and file a proper factum setting out the legal issues, the precedent(s) on which you are relying, and affidavits from your client and any other witnesses, as applicable.

Some justices prefer to reserve their decision on a Charter motion until the case has been completed to allow them time to assess the evidentiary issues and the context of the prejudice against the defendant.

REVIEW QUESTIONS

True/False

_____ 1. A motion is the proper method when first requesting disclosure from the prosecutor.

_____ 2. The provincial offences court has jurisdiction to hear Charter motions/applications.

_____ 3. It is extremely uncommon for a motion to adjourn to be heard orally.

_____ 4. There is no requirement to serve a notice of motion on the prosecution.

_____ 5. A notice of motion must be filed with the court.

_____ 6. A motion for non-suit is brought when the prosecution wishes to withdraw the charge.

_____ 7. A justice of the peace cannot grant a motion to amend a charge if evidence has already been introduced at trial.

_____ 8. Any party to a proceeding may bring a motion, and the rules apply equally to both sides.

Short Answer

1. How many days before a hearing must a notice of motion be served?

2. In addition to the prosecutor, who else needs to be served with a notice of constitutional question?

3. What must a justice consider before determining whether to grant a motion to amend?

4. What should you look for when determining whether to bring a motion to quash in your client's case?

5. What options are available if the prosecution is refusing to provide the disclosure you have requested?

Exercise

You have been hired to represent Peter Blossoms on a speeding offence. He was charged with travelling 90 km/h in a posted 50 km/h zone in Toronto two months prior to today's date. Before hiring you, he had already requested a trial and disclosure. He was told by the prosecution that no disclosure would be provided. In order to properly prepare for your client's case, you need to bring a motion for disclosure before the provincial offences court.

1. Go to the Court Services page of the City of Toronto website. Locate the notice of motion in the "Forms" section and prepare the form for your client. Briefly set out the disclosure required.

2. Prepare a one-page accompanying "cheat sheet" identifying key points to raise during the motion hearing. Make short-form points that you can easily refer to during your oral submissions.

3. Once completed, practise making your oral arguments with a partner.

What to Expect in the Courtroom

10

OVERVIEW

LEARNING OUTCOMES

After reading this chapter, you will understand

- rules and etiquette in provincial offences courtrooms;

- the layout of provincial offences courtrooms;

- provincial offences procedures and sequence of events; and

- what is involved in the arraignment of the defendant and entering a plea for your client.

INTRODUCTION

Rule 2.01(1) of the *Paralegal Rules of Conduct* states: "A paralegal shall conduct himself or herself in such a way as to maintain the integrity of the paralegal profession." This rule applies to a paralegal's conduct both outside and inside the courtroom. In court, maintaining the integrity of the profession means demonstrating appropriate behaviour, following all rules, displaying appropriate etiquette, showing respect for everyone within the justice system, and acting as a role model for everyone else in attendance. As such, this chapter will discuss appropriate behaviour in the courtroom.

Attending court can be intimidating and overwhelming for a newly licensed paralegal, who may not be aware of how a provincial offences courtroom is organized, as well as the procedures and the sequence of events that will take place. In order to make those initial court appearances less stressful, this chapter will also provide an overview of what to expect upon entering the courtroom.

RULES AND ETIQUETTE

Paralegals and everyone else attending court—from defendants and their representatives to witnesses and observers—are expected to abide by the rules and follow the norms of behaviour by displaying appropriate etiquette in the courtroom. Signs are typically posted at courtroom entrances to serve as a reminder of the rules.

Quiet in the Courtroom

While court is in session, everyone in the courtroom is expected to be quiet. Even whispering can be a distraction and is considered to be disrespectful. It is important to refrain from engaging in all side conversations, even with a client. If it is necessary to speak to a client, it would be more appropriate to leave the courtroom and have the conversation in the hallway.

Quiet in the courtroom also refers to turning off cellphones. Turning off a cellphone, rather than just using "vibrate" mode, is expected by the court. If vibrate mode is used, incoming calls can interfere with the court's intercom system, and the vibration signal may be amplified through the speaker system. Pagers or smartphone alert systems, such as text notification, should also be turned off while court is in session. You can be sure that the court clerk or the justice will remind or reprimand anyone who is not quiet in the courtroom, which can be embarrassing for a paralegal.

Recording Devices Prohibited

All recording devices are prohibited in the courtroom. While the courts are open to the public, the proceedings cannot be recorded in any way. This prohibition includes cameras, video cameras, tape recorders, photo phones, and all other recording devices. Unlike in the United States, television cameras and web cameras are rarely permitted to record Canadian court proceedings. With limited exceptions, s. 136(1) of the *Courts of Justice Act* prohibits anyone from producing visual or aural representations of a court hearing.

In addition to the ban on recording devices in the courtroom, the *Paralegal Rules of Conduct* and the *Rules of Professional Conduct* for lawyers indicate that paralegals and lawyers cannot record a conversation with a client or other members of the profession without disclosing an intention to do so.

No Food and Beverages Allowed

Food and beverages may not be brought into the courtroom, and in some cases, you may be asked to refrain from chewing gum. In some instances, a pitcher of water and glasses may be set up at the front of the court. You are permitted to fill a glass and have a drink of water, but you may not come to court with your own beverage.

Pay Attention to the Proceedings

Provincial offences courts are open to the public, so there may be observers in the courtroom for any number of reasons. However, everyone in the courtroom is expected to pay attention to the proceedings. Disrespectful conduct, such as reading a magazine or newspaper, texting, or checking phone messages, will not be tolerated. Attention should always be focused on the matters at hand.

Dress Appropriately

Appropriate attire in expected in the courtroom. Although the courts do not specify what is considered appropriate, paralegals should be professionally dressed. In provincial offences court, most paralegals wear a business suit, with males also wearing a tie.

Although clients do not have to be dressed professionally, they should be encouraged to dress in a tidy, conservative, and respectful manner, and avoid wearing jeans or printed T-shirts.

Everyone entering the courtroom will be required to remove sunglasses and hats (unless the hat is a religious head covering).

Show Respect for the Justice

It is customary to show respect for the justice by standing when he or she enters or leaves the courtroom. You will be expected to remain standing until the justice sits down or the court clerk advises everyone to be seated. If it is necessary to leave the courtroom while court is in session, the appropriate practice is to wait until the justice is not speaking (ideally in between matters) before leaving. When entering or exiting the courtroom while court is in session, paralegals and lawyers are expected to stop at the door, pause, turn toward the justice, and bow slightly.

COURTROOM LAYOUT

Most provincial offences courts are laid out in a very similar manner. The justice's bench is at the front and centre of the courtroom, slightly higher than the rest of the seating. The court clerk sits at a desk immediately in front of the justice. When a witness is called to testify, he or she is directed to the witness stand beside the justice's bench. All of these parties are facing the courtroom entrance.

The prosecution and defence tables are side by side, in front of the clerk's desk facing the justice. Typically, the prosecutor will be at the table on the right and the defence will at the table on the left (viewed from the back of the courtroom). Both tables have additional seating for witnesses, including provincial offences officers. Behind these tables is the public seating area for observers and for defendants, representatives, and witnesses who are waiting for their matters to proceed.

Provincial offences officers may sit in the public seating area, beside the prosecutor, or sometimes in additional seating provided around the perimeter of the courtroom.

Figure 10.1 shows a typical courtroom layout as found in provincial offences court.

Figure 10.1 Typical Provincial Offences Courtroom Layout

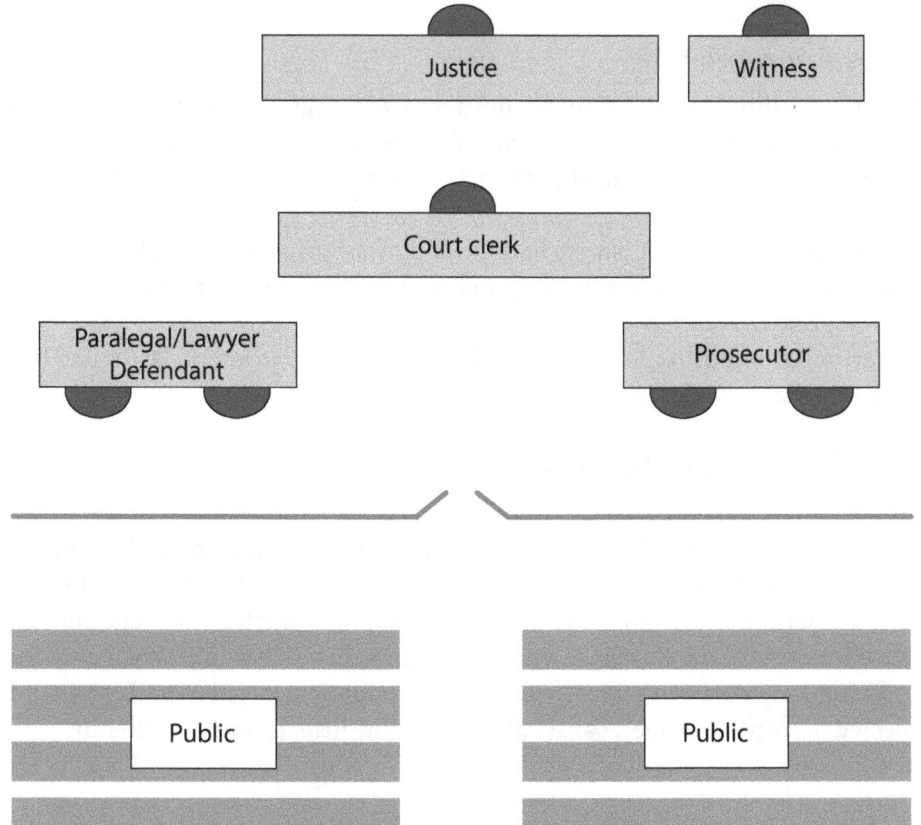

CHECKING IN WITH THE PROSECUTOR

The **docket** for all matters being heard in each **tier** will usually be posted just outside of the courtroom door. Before entering the courtroom, it is advisable to look at the docket to ensure your matters are listed for that courtroom on that date. By checking the docket, you will also be able to identify your client's case by line number. This will allow you to quickly and easily identify your matter when speaking to the prosecutor.

On arrival at the courtroom, paralegals should check in with the prosecutor. Legal representatives and defendants will typically do this by forming a line leading to the prosecutor's table. This process takes place on a first-come, first-served basis. It is advisable that you arrive early to ensure that there is sufficient time to speak to the prosecutor.

The prosecutor will expect you to identify the matter for which you have been retained (e.g., "Smith, line 14 on the docket") and will then ask how you would like to proceed. It is essential that you follow your client's instructions and inform the prosecutor if your client wishes to plead guilty or not guilty, or if an adjournment is being sought.

Recognizing that there will usually be a substantial number of matters on the docket, it is not possible for each and every defendant to have a trial. (For example, in the Greater Toronto Area, it is not unusual to have 40 to 50 Part I matters scheduled within a 90-minute tier). The prosecutor realizes this and will often suggest a resolution to the matter, such as an amended charge in exchange for a guilty plea—which will typically result in a lesser fine and/or fewer demerit points. This is usually a desirable outcome for defendants, but it is important to ensure that clients consent to amended charges.

docket
the list of defendants scheduled for trial

tier
a court session over a specific period of time

> **PRACTICE TIP**
>
> Always be prepared for court. Thoroughly review your client's charge and the facts surrounding the offence, as well as the relevant charging act for any other charges that may be consistent with your client's fact situation. If any of these charges carry a lesser fine and/or fewer demerit points, it may be appropriate to suggest the alternate charges to the prosecutor.

TYPICAL SEQUENCE

Prosecutors are in charge of the docket and have the authority to call matters in any order. They do not usually follow the order listed on the docket. One commonly used method of managing the docket is to first call matters that can be resolved quickly. This allows the courtroom to empty out somewhat and does not keep defendants waiting for any longer than is necessary. For example, it is common for a prosecutor to call **uncontested adjournments** or guilty pleas at the beginning of the court session because they can be dealt with quickly.

uncontested adjournment
moving a trial to a new date after a request by either the prosecution or the defence is agreed to by the other side

Most prosecutors will try not to needlessly inconvenience interpreters and civilian witnesses. Matters for which an interpreter is present will usually be called before other cases within the same resolution category. For example, guilty pleas with an interpreter would usually be called before guilty pleas with no interpreter, and trials with a civilian witness would commonly be called before trials that have only a police witness.

Some prosecutors will extend a professional courtesy to paralegals or lawyers in attendance. Recognizing that they may have matters in other courtrooms or other courthouses, prosecutors will sometimes be willing to call represented defendants before unrepresented defendants.

PRACTICE TIP

If you find yourself in a situation where you are needed in two different courtrooms during the same court tier, mention this to the prosecutor. Some prosecutors may be willing to deal with your matter early in the proceedings, while others may be willing to have your matter **held down** until later in the tier or even to a different court tier. Most prosecutors will be willing to accommodate in some way.

held down
hearing a matter at a later time

WHEN YOUR CLIENT IS CALLED

When the prosecutor calls your client's name, you will stand up, move to the front of the courtroom, and stand at the defence table facing the clerk and the justice. You should then identify yourself as the paralegal who has been retained to represent the defendant. It is customary in provincial offences court to state your last name, your first initial and your status—for example: "Good morning, Your Worship. My name is Jones, first initial B. I am a licensed paralegal retained to represent the defendant Smith in the matter before the court."

In most cases, the prosecutor will then inform the justice of the anticipated plea, request, or action. Specifically, the prosecutor may inform the justice of a request for an adjournment, a guilty plea (to the original or to an amended charge), a plea of not guilty, a withdrawal of the charge, or a stay of the proceedings. If the request or action is an adjournment, withdrawal, or stay, the court clerk will collect the necessary information and complete the appropriate paperwork. In the event of a guilty or not guilty plea, the defendant will be arraigned.

arraignment
the formal reading of the charges to the defendant or the defendant's representative in anticipation of a plea

THE ARRAIGNMENT AND PLEA

The **arraignment** takes place when the court clerk formally informs the defendant of the charges before the court. A paralegal can be arraigned in place of a client, or a paralegal may choose to **waive arraignment**. By waiving arraignment, a paralegal is advising the court that it is not necessary to read out the charges.

waive arraignment
a legal representative tells the court clerk that it is not necessary to read the charges

Under the arraignment procedure, the clerk asks the defendant to state his or her name; reads out the charges; asks whether the defendant understands the charges; and asks how the defendant would like to plead to the charges. The defendant can choose to plead:

- guilty (conviction entered and sentence passed);
- guilty with submissions (conviction entered and sentence passed, but defendant has an opportunity to request a lesser fine or more time to pay);
- guilty to an amended charge as specified by the prosecutor (conviction entered for amended charge and sentence passed); or
- not guilty (a trial will be held).

Pleas must be made voluntarily. The clerk or the justice will often check to ensure that the defendant has made an informed choice and is aware of the consequences that will arise from the plea.

KEY TERMS

arraignment	tier
docket	uncontested adjournment
held down	waive arraignment

REVIEW QUESTIONS

True/False

_____ 1. The arraignment of the defendant occurs immediately after the trial and is handled by the same justice who presided over the trial.

_____ 2. You should remain seated when a judge or justice enters the courtroom.

_____ 3. Cellphones should be turned off in the courtroom; it is not appropriate to just turn the cellphone to "vibrate" mode.

_____ 4. When you enter or leave the courtroom, you should recite the paralegal's oath.

_____ 5. It is permissible to tape-record provincial offences proceedings.

Short Answer

1. What is considered appropriate attire for a paralegal appearing in provincial offences court?

2. Where are you likely to find provincial offences officers sitting in the courtroom?

3. Explain the arraignment procedure?

4. Where can you find the docket for all matters in a specific court tier?

5. How do paralegals introduce themselves in court?

Exercise

Carol, an unrepresented defendant, arrived at the courtroom approximately 30 minutes after the court session had begun. She rushed in the door and loudly apologized to everyone in the courtroom. As she hurried to find a seat, she spilled her coffee all over her Bon Jovi T-shirt. She finally took a seat beside the provincial offences officer, who was sitting beside the prosecutor. Carol started chatting with the officer to find out what she had missed. When she looked around the room, Carol recognized her neighbour in the witness box and started waving. She then took out her cellphone to send text messages to all of her friends about the neighbour's charges. Carol then played around with her phone in order to find the app that she could use to videotape her neighbour's evidence.

1. List the rules and appropriate etiquette practices that were breached by Carol.

2. If Carol does not speak English and her interpreter is present so that she can enter a not guilty plea, when would the prosecution likely call her case?

   a. before guilty pleas are heard

   b. before other not guilty pleas are heard when no interpreter is present

   c. after other not guilty pleas are heard when no interpreter is present

   d. before uncontested adjournments

   e. none of the above; Carol cannot use an interpreter to plead not guilty

The Trial

11

OVERVIEW

LEARNING OUTCOMES

After reading this chapter, you will understand

- the components of a *Provincial Offences Act* trial;

- the framework for motions, evidentiary issues, and standards of proof;

- witness considerations, questioning techniques, and evidence; and

- closing statements and the verdict.

INTRODUCTION

Although it may seem that the trial is the most important part of the legal process, it is often the least likely outcome for the vast majority of offences. The other outcomes include agreements reached between the prosecution and defence that lead to guilty pleas, and numerous post-charge and pretrial issues that can prevent a matter from ever reaching trial.

As a professional paralegal, it is crucial that you have the skills to advocate on behalf of your client. This means properly preparing yourself by reviewing every aspect of the case to ensure the best possible outcome for your client. Your client is depending on you to provide candid and accurate advice, and sometimes that means achieving the best possible resolution without taking a case to a trial. But if a trial is in your client's best interest, the best chance he or she will have for a positive outcome is for you to be thoroughly prepared.

MOTIONS

As discussed in Chapter 9, several types of pretrial motions may apply. Either the prosecution or the defence may bring a motion before the arraignment of the defendant. Among other motions, the prosecution may seek a motion to adjourn and a motion to amend.

Motion to Adjourn

If the prosecution is seeking a motion to adjourn, you need to consider several factors as you prepare to respond (likely orally):

1. Did the prosecution provide you with prior notice?
2. Is the provincial offences officer present in court?
3. Is your client present?
4. Are there any witnesses?
5. Is the charge serious or straightforward?

There may be instances when it is in your client's best interest to consent to an adjournment request made by the prosecution, even when notice was not given. But if you are ready to proceed with the trial, in many cases the court will turn down the prosecution's request for an adjournment.

PRACTICE TIP

While the court will rarely grant an adjournment simply because a party is not prepared, consenting can go a long way to building your reputation as a fair and professional legal representative—as long as there is no prejudice to your client. Establishing a good reputation with the justices, court staff, and the prosecution will not only serve you as a professional, but will improve your effectiveness when representing your clients.

Motion to Amend

If the prosecution is seeking a motion to amend the certificate or information, you need to be prepared to respond by considering the following factors:

1. Did the prosecution provide you with prior notice?
2. Is the amendment designed to cure a defect in the certificate or information, or does it change the substance of the charge?
3. Is an adjournment necessary if the amendment is granted?
4. Is your client prejudiced by the requested amendment?
5. Is the amendment consistent with the administration of justice and the POA?

Several other types of motions that, if applicable, must be presented prior to the trial commencing, including Charter applications, change of venue motions, and bias motions. It is important to be familiar with the relevant jurisprudence and procedural sections of the Act.

STANDARD OF PROOF

The **standard of proof** for provincial offences is usually proof beyond a reasonable doubt. This standard of proof certainly applies to facts at issue, such as:

- the identity of the defendant;
- essential elements of the offence as charged; and
- the guilt of the defendant.

A defendant cannot be convicted of a regulatory offence unless the justice is convinced beyond a reasonable doubt that the prosecution has proven all of the essential elements of the offence.

Some other considerations for standards of proof are not directly related to the defendant's guilt or innocence. For example, when a defendant is charged with a strict liability offence, the prosecution must only prove the essential elements beyond a reasonable doubt. The defendant may then exonerate himself or herself by establishing mistake of fact or due diligence on a balance of probabilities.

The simplest way to describe the standard of a balance of probabilities is to imagine a measuring scale: Whichever side tips the scale with the evidence establishes the case in their favour.

standard of proof
the level of certainty needed for the prosecution to convict, or for a defendant to exonerate himself or herself; can be beyond a reasonable doubt or on a balance of probabilities

BURDEN OF PROOF

The **burden of proof** for establishing the defendant's guilt beyond a reasonable doubt always rests with the prosecution. The prosecution must establish all of the essential elements of the offence as charged.

There are a few occasions when the burden of proof shifts to the defendant, who must prove that he or she did not commit the offence. They include reverse-onus provisions in statutes, such as the "colour of right" defence in the *Trespass to Prop-*

burden of proof
the responsibility for proving guilt or innocence; rests with either the prosecution or the defence, depending on the circumstances

erty Act, and Charter applications to establish prejudice, such as unreasonable delay under s. 11(b).

The Ontario legislature has codified several examples in which the burden of proof lies with the defendant, as prescribed in s. 47(3) of the POA:

> The burden of proving that an authorization, exception, exemption or qualification prescribed by law operates in favour of the defendant is on the defendant, and the prosecutor is not required, except by way of rebuttal, to prove that the authorization, exception, exemption or qualification does not operate in favour of the defendant, whether or not it is set out in the information.

DEFENCES

In order to provide proper legal representation and identify any possible defences, you must first interview your client. During the interview, be sure to challenge your client's recollection and evidence after recording his or her account of the situation. If you believe you will be able to prove that your client did not commit the offence, the best defence may be to put your client on the stand to dispute the charges.

For some regulatory offences, the issue is not whether the client did or did not commit the act in question, but whether the client knew that he or she was prohibited from committing the act (i.e., a *mens rea* offence). Regulatory law is far more complicated and nuanced than criminal law, which has clear lines of societal and moral boundaries.

For absolute liability offences, knowledge of the defendant's mental state is not required. The prosecution must prove only that the act was committed for the court to register a conviction.

Defences designed to question the act itself—for example, raising reasonable doubt as to whether the act occurred at all—are used. It is important to pay attention to the fault element for all types of offences, ensuring that the prosecution has proven each element beyond a reasonable doubt. If it fails to do so, the best defence for your client may be to bring a motion for non-suit.

Possible defences to regulatory offences can include the defence of due diligence and the defence of necessity.

Defence of Due Diligence

defence of due diligence
the defendant must show that he or she took all reasonable steps to avoid committing the act in question

In the classic **defence of due diligence** or "reasonable precautions," the test laid out by the Supreme Court of Canada in *R. v. Sault Ste Marie (City)*, [1978] 2 S.C.R. 1299, 85 D.L.R. (3d) 161 is still used today. The defence is available to an accused if, on a balance of probabilities, it is established that:

- the accused believed in a mistaken set of facts that, if true, would render the act or omission innocent; or
- the accused took all reasonable steps to avoid the particular event.

Under this test, the burden of establishing that due diligence was exercised falls on the defendant. In *R. v. Chapin* (1979), 45 C.C.C. (2d) 333 (S.C.C.), a case often cited in tandem with *R. v. Sault Ste Marie (City)*, Dickson J. of the Supreme Court of Canada described the defence of due diligence as follows:

> An accused may absolve himself on proof that he took all the care which a reasonable man may have been expected to take in all the circumstances or, in other words, that he was in no way negligent.

There are many factors to consider when assessing the defence of due diligence. It is important to remember that due diligence is only open for the defendant in strict liability offences.

Defence of Necessity

To use the **defence of necessity**, the defendant must satisfy all of the following requirements, as described in *Perka v. The Queen*, [1984] 2 S.C.R. 232 at 259, 14 C.C.C. (3d) 385 at 404-5. The defendant must prove that:

- he or she needed to commit the act to avoid immediate peril;
- no other reasonable alternative existed;
- the harm caused by the defendant was less than the harm avoided; and
- he or she could not have foreseen the emergency.

defence of necessity
the defendant must show that it was necessary to commit the act in question, that no reasonable alternative existed, and that the harm caused by the act was outweighed by the harm that was avoided

As an example, a driver speeding on the highway to take his pregnant wife to the hospital would not likely meet the test for necessity. Most pregnancies do not result in immediate peril and are not viewed as emergencies. However, even if those requirements were met (e.g., a high-risk pregnancy and pre-term labour), there likely would have been reasonable alternatives, such as calling 911.

However, if, for example, a defendant was camping in a remote area and a friend suffered an unexpected serious injury (e.g., fell into the fire, was attacked by a bear), the necessity defence may apply if there was no other way to get the friend to the hospital.

TECHNICAL ERRORS ON THE OFFENCE NOTICE

The defence can object to a defect found on the certificate or information during trial. It is important to note that the justice of the peace may amend the document to correct the defects, because s. 34 of the POA provides broad curative powers to the court.

Technical errors that have resulted in the dismissal or quashing of charges include:

- the date of the offence is incorrect or missing;
- the defendant's name is missing;
- the charging officer's name is missing;
- the location of the offence is missing;
- a description of the offence is missing;
- the offence indicated is unknown to law; and
- the offence notice was not given to the defendant within 30 days of the offence date or not filed with the court within seven days.

As a paralegal, it is important to rely on technical error arguments only when necessary and appropriate, given the nature of the case and the facts. Bringing motions to quash or dismiss charges based on frivolous technical errors will diminish your reputation and effectiveness. There is a time and a place for such motions, and knowing this comes with experience.

PREPARING WITNESSES FOR COURT

Many cases before the provincial offences court will have independent witnesses, outside of the charging officer. It is important that you review disclosure materials for witness statements.

In preparing for the trial, you need to decide which witnesses you will require, and whether a witness will testify for the prosecution or the defence. Neither party "owns" a witness. As a defence representative, you are allowed to interview any witness, including prosecution witnesses, and the prosecution may do the same.

If you are going to rely on the evidence of a defence witness, it is important to interview the witness before trial. This is an opportunity to assess the witness's evidence and prepare him or her for court. You must ensure that the witness is able to recall his or her evidence and that it is consistent. You cannot coach the witness or suggest what the evidence should be.

PRACTICE TIP

Proper witness preparation is crucial for a successful trial. But even with the best preparation, most witnesses are not experts, and they are nervous and anxious. Never ask a question if you do not know the answer or cannot adequately anticipate the response. Even with the best of intentions, a witness can become lost in the process, which can be very detrimental to your case.

EXAMINATION-IN-CHIEF

examination-in-chief
the prosecution or defence questions its own witnesses at the trial

During the trial, the prosecution will present and question its witnesses first. This is known as **examination-in-chief**, which occurs when each side calls and questions its own witnesses. It is recommended that you make notes during the prosecution's examination-in-chief, pay attention to the witness's body language, and look for inconsistencies between the oral evidence and the disclosure provided by the prosecution.

It is equally important to challenge the prosecution witness's evidence, where appropriate, and to persuade the witness to agree with your theory and statements in order to establish your client's defence.

When questioning your own witnesses, including your client, you should only inquire into areas that will advance your client's interest. Being concise and clear will also be beneficial. Avoid asking questions that give the prosecution an opportunity to follow up with questions that result in evidence detrimental to your client's position. For example, if you do not want the prosecution to ask questions about your client's past driving record, avoid raising the issue through your own questions.

PRACTICE TIP

Establishing a rapport with a witness—even one who is hostile or unsympathetic—is also important. Avoid the appearance of harassing or getting upset with a witness, even if the evidence obtained is useful, because you may lose credibility and the message could be lost on the justice of the peace.

CROSS-EXAMINATION

At the conclusion of the examination-in-chief of each prosecution witness, you will have an opportunity to cross-examine. Cross-examination occurs when each side questions the opposing side's witnesses. Cross-examining witnesses is one of the most important skills you need to acquire and perfect. You must always be mindful of the goals of **cross-examination**. If you are not asking questions to achieve one of the following goals, you should stop asking questions and move on.

> **cross-examination**
> the prosecution or defence questions the opposing side's witnesses, following examination-in-chief

1. *Clarification:* After listening to the witness's testimony, it may be appropriate to clarify some of the evidence by asking questions that are beneficial to your client's position.

2. *Commitment to the evidence:* A witness must be committed to the evidence he or she provides to the court. Sometimes witnesses, knowingly or unknowingly, make contradictory statements that are vague on a question or fact. A paralegal must pursue an inconsistency in cases where the answer can be established in the client's favour. However, there will be times when it is best not to pursue an inconsistency with a witness if the answer may not serve your client's interest,

3. *Expose inadequate evidence:* Sometimes a witness's recollections may be less than perfect or an officer's notes may lack detail. This is an opportunity to persuade the justice to reduce the weight that should be applied to the evidence.

4. *Confront false evidence:* There are rare times when it is apparent that a witness may be lying. If you strongly believe that the evidence is false, you should not shy away from confronting the witness on the stand. However, there is a distinction between lack of credibility and outright lying. If uncertain, it may be enough to leave the trier of fact in doubt about the witness's credibility and move on.

EVIDENCE

Although courts rarely concern themselves with the question "What is evidence?" it is important for you, as part of your trial practice, to develop such an understanding. The law of evidence is vast, and this section provides only a primer on the areas you should consider when preparing for trial. Most courts adopt the definitions found in evidentiary texts when dealing with the question of evidence.

For example, *Phipson on Evidence*, 13th ed., by Sidney Lovell Phipson, J.H. Buzzard, R. May, and M.N. Howard, eds. (London: Sweet & Maxwell, 1982), at para. 1-03, states:

> Evidence, as used in judicial proceedings, has several meanings. The two main senses of the word are: first, the means, apart from argument and inference, whereby the court is informed as to the issues of fact as ascertained by the pleadings; secondly, the subject-matter of such means. The word is also used to denote that some fact may be admitted as proof and also in some cases that some fact has relevance to the issue of fact. In a real sense evidence is that which may be placed before the court in order that it may decide the issues of fact.

A simpler, less formal, and generally accepted definition of the term can be found in the introductory paragraph of *Cross on Evidence*, 6th ed., by Sir Rupert Cross and Colin Tapper (London: Butterworths, 1985):

> The evidence of a fact is that which tends to prove it—something which may satisfy an inquirer of the fact's existence.

As a paralegal, there are several types of evidence that you will either tender or respond to during a trial:

1. *Real evidence:* This is something that is tangible. Examples include videos or photographs, and items seized by the police, such as beer bottles or a weapon. The court can rely on this evidence to draw direct conclusions.
2. *Documentary evidence:* This is a very common form of evidence in regulatory trials. Examples include government records, corporate search records, municipal tax records, and building permits.
3. *Testimony:* This is the most common form of evidence in provincial offences trials, and takes the form of oral (*viva voce*) evidence of a witness. Examples include the observations of the charging officer, an independent witness, or your client. It is often through oral testimony that the other types of evidence are adduced and then admitted.

PRACTICE TIP

The various formats that evidence can take are extensive. At a minimum, you should review the rules outlined in the *Provincial Offences Act*, the *Evidence Act*, R.S.O. 1990, c. E.23, and the *Courts of Justice Act*. If the prosecution attempts to introduce evidence that has not been previously disclosed, be prepared to object.

VOIR DIRE

In some cases, it will be necessary to have a *voir dire*, which is a trial within a trial, in order to determine the admissibility of evidence. If there is a need for a *voir dire*, the trial is halted, the party seeking to tender the evidence calls its witnesses first, and the witnesses are sworn in again. There is also be an opportunity for cross-examination. The justice will make a decision on the *voir dire* and will apply the decision to the evidence in the original trial.

CLOSING STATEMENTS

The closing statement provides the best opportunity to persuade the court to rule in favour of your client. If you decided to call witnesses in your client's defence, you will be required to make your closing statement first, giving the prosecution the final word. However, there are times when the justice of the peace will call on the prosecution first to sum up its case.

Preparing the closing statement begins as soon as you start working on a case. From the very beginning, you should be formulating ideas for structuring a persuasive and legally sound defence. Those ideas are refined throughout the interview and case preparation (disclosure) phases of the case, as well as during the trial itself. The closing statement is perhaps the most important aspect of the trial, and, if done properly, can be an advocate's finest hour.

First, the closing statement allows you to explain the significance of the evidence, and to offer reasons that support conclusions and inferences. It also gives you a chance to discuss credibility and the law, and to advocate on behalf of your client.

Second, an effective closing statement presents a positive theory of the case in a clear, logical, and understandable fashion. It should incorporate the same theories that have been put forward throughout the trial.

Third, the closing argument must not only engage the justice intellectually but have emotional appeal as well, because your goal is a dismissal of the charges.

Fourth, you must emphasize why the court should rule in favour of your client. State the law and the weakness in the prosecution's case, and highlight your client's positive attributes. Strike a balance between quantity and quality.

PRACTICE TIP

It is important that you not read verbatim the notes for your closing statement. The justice will be watching you, so it is important to establish eye contact. This is your last opportunity to sell your theory and version of the facts, and to convince the court of the soundness of your case. Be aware of the justice's body language and be prepared to adapt.

THE VERDICT

verdict
the decision or ruling
of the justice

After both parties have made their closing statements, the justice will review the evidence and provide a ruling, called the **verdict**. Depending on the complexity and length of the trial, the justice may give an oral ruling immediately or reserve judgment and provide written reasons at a later date.

There is not much of an opportunity to offer any feedback or clarification when the justice is issuing a verdict. At this point, advocacy has no place, and your role is to make proper notes on the reasons provided.

PRACTICE TIP

If it is appropriate to ask the justice for clarification or to provide reasons, you must do so in a way that does not offend the court. Avoid using the phrase "with all due respect" and instead try "with the greatest of respect."

In most cases, you will receive an oral ruling immediately. If your client is found guilty, do not debate the verdict but put your efforts toward advocating for the best possible sentence for your client.

Regardless of the ruling, thank the court for its time. Civility and courtesy are always appropriate and in the best interests of the administration of justice.

KEY TERMS

burden of proof

cross-examination

defence of due diligence

defence of necessity

examination-in-chief

standard of proof

verdict

REVIEW QUESTIONS

True/False

_____ 1. The standard of proof in a *Provincial Offences Act* trial is on a balance of probabilities.

_____ 2. The court will always grant a motion to adjourn if you are not prepared to proceed on the day of trial.

_____ 3. The prosecution always goes first in a provincial offences trial.

_____ 4. The defence of due diligence is available for strict liability offences.

_____ 5. You are not allowed to interview prosecution witnesses prior to trial.

_____ 6. It is acceptable and often prudent to ask questions at trial that you do not know the answer to.

_____ 7. Videotapes or photographs are examples of real evidence.

_____ 8. If your client is found guilty, it is appropriate to ask the court to reconsider its decision and hear submissions.

_____ 9. A justice must be satisfied that your client is guilty beyond a reasonable doubt before a conviction can be registered.

Short Answer

1. What elements must the defendant establish in order to make out the defence of necessity?

2. Review the goals of cross-examination and provide a practical example of how you would approach two of the following goals:

   a. Clarification
   b. Commitment
   c. Exposing inadequate evidence
   d. Confronting false evidence

3. In your own words, how would you describe evidence and its purpose at a trial?

4. You are representing your client at court on the day of trial and the prosecution brings a motion without notice to amend the certificate of offence. What factors should you consider before providing oral submissions in response?

Exercises

Working with a partner or independently, write a paragraph in response to the following trial scenarios (ensure that you include the appropriate statutory reference if appropriate):

1. You are representing your client on a charge of following too close under the _Highway Traffic Act_. At the outset of the trial, the prosecution advises you that it is bringing a motion to amend the charge to careless driving under the HTA.

2. You are representing a client who has received a parking ticket under a city bylaw. After listening to the prosecutor question the issuing officer, you review your notes and are certain that the officer never mentioned the bylaw number in question or the motor vehicle's licence plate.

3. Your client is on trial for a _Building Code_ offence, in violation of a city bylaw. On the same day, you are also dealing with three _Highway Traffic Act_ matters in an adjacent courtroom. The prosecutor advises you that the chief building official is ill and unable to attend court that day, and asks if you are willing to consent to an adjournment?

Sentencing

12

OVERVIEW

LEARNING OUTCOMES

After reading this chapter, you will understand

- the principles of sentencing;
- the powers and restrictions of the court;
- set fines, costs, and victim fine surcharges;
- aggravating and mitigating factors; and
- imprisonment and special court orders.

INTRODUCTION

Now that your client has been found guilty, it may seem that the sentencing process requires the least amount of preparation. In fact, the sentencing stage is where you must put forth some of your strongest arguments on behalf of your client, which will ultimately have the greatest impact on your client's life.

Some justices will conduct full sentencing hearings and may even allow evidence to be called, depending on the nature of the charge, while others will move directly to sentencing with little opportunity for you to provide input. There will be times when the range of sentence, and even the exact sentence, is prescribed by statute, so making arguments in such circumstances will often be of little value.

PURPOSE AND OBJECTIVE

Regulatory laws ensure, among other things, that buildings are constructed properly, that workplaces are safe, and that drivers obey the rules of the road. It is in society's interest that individuals comply with such laws.

There should be consequences for someone who has been found guilty of violating a regulatory law, and for most offences, a monetary fine is imposed. Several other options available to a justice are found in the *Provincial Offences Act* and the enabling legislation. Regardless of the sentencing options available, the court is guided by sentencing principles.

It is important to note that the court must give both the defendant, or his or her representative, and the prosecution an opportunity to make submissions on sentencing before rendering a decision. Section 57 of the POA provides the legal framework:

> 57(1) Where a defendant who appears is convicted of an offence, the court shall give the prosecutor and the defendant's representative an opportunity to make submissions as to sentence and, where the defendant has no representative, the court shall ask the defendant if he or she has anything to say before sentence is passed.
>
> (2) The omission to comply with subsection (1) does not affect the validity of the proceeding.
>
> (3) Where a defendant is convicted of an offence, the court may make such inquiries, on oath or otherwise, of and concerning the defendant as it considers desirable, including the defendant's economic circumstances, but the defendant shall not be compelled to answer.

PRINCIPLES OF SENTENCING

The same principles of sentencing apply to both provincial and criminal offences. Section 718 of the *Criminal Code* provides a guide to sentencing principles, and can be referred to for assistance.

> 718. The fundamental purpose of sentencing is to contribute, along with crime prevention initiatives, to respect for the law and the maintenance of a just, peaceful

and safe society by imposing just sanctions that have one or more of the following objectives:

    (a) to denounce unlawful conduct;

    (b) to deter the offender and other persons from committing offences;

    (c) to separate offenders from society, where necessary;

    (d) to assist in rehabilitating offenders;

    (e) to provide reparations for harm done to victims or to the community; and

    (f) to promote a sense of responsibility in offenders, and acknowledgement of the harm done to victims and to the community.

This general-purpose provision of sentencing is framed by s. 718.1 of the *Criminal Code*:

    718.1 A sentence must be proportionate to the gravity of the offence and the degree of responsibility of the offender.

For the most part, sentencing in provincial offences cases focuses on **deterrence**, of which there are two types: specific and general.

- Specific deterrence focuses on the individual defendant and aims to deter that particular person from offending again.
- General deterrence aims to discourage others in society from committing that type of offence.

Deterrence, whether specific or general, is based on the assumption that potential offenders will consider the consequences of their actions and refrain from committing an offence. The court will usually place a greater emphasis on specific deterrence and compliance going forward.

deterrence
a principle of sentencing intended to discourage a defendant from reoffending; specific and general are the two types of deterrence

POWERS AND RESTRICTIONS

To understand the powers and restrictions of the court, it is important to review the procedural stream under which the matter was commenced.

- *Part I—Certificate of Offence:* The court has the power to impose a fine of up to $1,000. A defendant may not be sent to jail or placed on probation.
- *Part II—Certificate of Parking Infraction:* The court has the power to impose a fine of up to $1,000. A defendant may not be sent to jail or placed on probation.
- *Part III—Information:* A broad range of sentencing options are available to the court, including imprisonment, substantial fines, probation, and restitution. The POA and the charging legislation outline the appropriate range and sentencing options.

SET FINE

The term "set fine" may seem misleading, suggesting that the stipulated amount is the fine that will always be imposed by the court. The set fine, however, is the amount a defendant will pay in an out-of-court settlement. If your client is convicted after a trial, the amount of the fine is prescribed by the maximum amounts specified in the POA or in the enabling legislation, whichever applies.

Although the court may be guided by the set fine when determining the penalty after a trial, it is not uncommon for a defendant to be ordered to pay an amount that is higher than the set fine. This should not be seen as punishment for having a trial, but as reflecting the fact that the justice was able to hear all of the evidence and more thoroughly assess the case. In cases where the set fine is imposed by statute, the justice may not always have jurisdiction to assess a fine other than what is prescribed.

PRACTICE TIP

While the prosecution will often argue after a trial that the fine should be raised, your job is to advocate on behalf of your client for a fine that is appropriate given the nature of the offence, the overall circumstances of the case, the conduct of your client, and your client's ability to pay.

COSTS AND VICTIM FINE SURCHARGE

Paying a fine may not be the only monetary penalty that your client will face upon conviction. Regulation 945 made under the POA provides for fixed costs upon conviction, payable for the purposes of s. 60(1):

1.	For service of offence notice or summons	$5.00
2.	Upon conviction under section 9 of the Act	$5.00
3.	Upon conviction under section 9.1 of the Act	$10.00
4.	Upon conviction under section 18 of the Act as it read on August 31, 1993	$3.75
5.	Upon conviction under subsection 18.2 (6) of the Act	$16.00
6.	Upon conviction under section 18.4 of the Act	$12.75
7.	Upon conviction under subsection 54(1) of the Act	$30.00
8.	For service of a parking infraction notice issued other than under a municipal by-law	$3.75

Regulation 945 also provides that costs may be awarded under s. 60(2) of the Act up to a maximum amount:

1.	Fee for each witness for each day necessarily in attendance when trial scheduled	$6.00
2.	Travel expenses for each witness, i. where witness resides in place where trial held ii. where witness does not reside in place where trial held, a kilometre allowance as set out in Regulation 11 of the Revised Regulations of Ontario, 1990 entitled "Kilometre Allowances."	$2.50

Costs upon conviction under s. 60(1) are fixed and are added to the fine by court administrative staff. Costs under s. 60(2) are discretionary and are only added if ordered by the presiding justice. Even if a fine is not ordered by the court, your client may still have to pay the s. 60(1) costs if found guilty.

In addition to fixed and discretionary costs, any defendant who is fined must pay a victim fine surcharge. Designed to assist victims of crime, the surcharge goes to a special fund, and the money is allocated to programs and services, such as SupportLink, Victim Support Line, Victim Crisis Assistance and Referral Services, and Victim/Witness Assistance Programs.

The fines and corresponding victim fine surcharges are listed in Regulation 161/00 to the POA.

Column 1			Column 2
Fine Range			Surcharge
$			$
0	–	50	10
51	–	75	15
76	–	100	20
101	–	150	25
151	–	200	35
201	–	250	50
251	–	300	60
301	–	350	75
351	–	400	85
401	–	450	95
451	–	500	110
501	–	1000	125
Over 1000			25% of actual fine

AGGRAVATING AND MITIGATING FACTORS

In support of a higher penalty for your client, the prosecution may ask the court to consider certain aggravating factors. They include:

- the conduct of your client during the offence and during the court proceeding;
- public safety considerations;
- prevalence of the offence in the community; and
- previous convictions of your client.

In arguing for a more lenient sentence for your client, you may want to bring certain mitigating factors to the court's attention. They include:

- your client's ability to pay a fine (i.e., financial hardship);
- the remorse that your client has shown for the offence, particularly for the impact it had on the victim;
- the seriousness of the offence;
- the likelihood that your client will not reoffend; and
- other information about your client that may be relevant—for example, whether he or she is a student, single parent, recent immigrant, and so on.

PRACTICE TIP

A good client interview is essential to gathering additional information that you may be able to use to argue for a more lenient sentence.

It is appropriate to provide the court with a concise depiction of your client's background and present circumstances, to persuade the court to impose a sentence in the minimum range of the appropriate sentencing precedents.

TIME TO PAY

Regardless of the amount of the fine your client is ordered to pay, the court is often willing to provide a reasonable amount of time in which to pay. It is important that you be aware of your client's ability to pay a fine so as to be able to suggest a reasonable time frame to the court.

In the absence of any request for an extension, fines are payable 15 days after the court imposes sentence. Section 66 of the POA provides the framework for the time to pay and extensions:

> 66(1) A fine becomes due and payable fifteen days after its imposition.
>
> (2) Where the court imposes a fine, the court shall ask the defendant if the defendant wishes an extension of the time for payment of the fine.
>
> (3) Where the defendant requests an extension of the time for payment of the fine, the court may make such inquiries, on oath or affirmation or otherwise, of and con-

cerning the defendant as the court considers desirable, but the defendant shall not be compelled to answer.

(4) Unless the court finds that the request for extension of time is not made in good faith or that the extension would likely be used to evade payment, the court shall extend the time for payment by ordering periodic payments or otherwise.

(5) Where a fine is imposed in the absence of the defendant, the clerk of the court shall give the defendant notice of the fine and its due date and of the defendant's right to make a motion for an extension of the time for payment under subsection (6).

(6) The defendant may, at any time by motion in the prescribed form filed in the office of the court, request an extension or further extension of time for payment of a fine and the motion shall be determined by a justice and the justice has the same powers in respect of the motion as the court has under subsections (3) and (4).

IMPRISONMENT

Imprisonment is only available as a sentencing option for cases that have been commenced by an information under Part III of the POA, and then only if the enabling legislation provides for incarceration upon conviction.

Several provincial statutes include imprisonment as a sentencing option, but a defendant is unlikely to be sentenced to jail for first-time regulatory offences.

From the beginning of case preparation, it is important that you determine whether the prosecution will be seeking a jail term upon conviction. If the court is considering a term of imprisonment, you may be well advised to request a pre-sentence report to assist the court in determining whether a jail sentence is appropriate in the circumstances.

Imprisonment provisions and conditions are found in ss. 63 and 64 of the POA:

> 63(1) The term of imprisonment imposed by sentence shall, unless otherwise directed in the sentence, commence on the day on which the convicted person is taken into custody thereunder, but no time during which the convicted person is imprisoned or out on bail before sentence shall be reckoned as part of the term of imprisonment to which he or she is sentenced.
>
> (2) Where the court imposes imprisonment, the court may order custody to commence on a day not later than thirty days after the day of sentencing.
>
> 64. Where a person is subject to more than one term of imprisonment at the same time, the terms shall be served consecutively except in so far as the court has ordered a term to be served concurrently with any other term of imprisonment.

SPECIAL COURT ORDERS

probation order
a court order that places conditions on a defendant after conviction, often to control the defendant's movements and require certain action

A **probation order** is the most common form of court order following a conviction. A court may also make a prohibition order.

Probation Orders

When placed on probation, a defendant must comply with certain terms and conditions. Sections 72, 73, and 74 of the POA govern probation orders:

72(1) Where a defendant is convicted of an offence in a proceeding commenced by information, the court may, having regard to the age, character and background of the defendant, the nature of the offence and the circumstances surrounding its commission,

(a) suspend the passing of sentence and direct that the defendant comply with the conditions prescribed in a probation order;

(b) in addition to fining the defendant or sentencing the defendant to imprisonment, whether in default of payment of a fine or otherwise, direct that the defendant comply with the conditions prescribed in a probation order; or

(c) where it imposes a sentence of imprisonment on the defendant, whether in default of payment of a fine or otherwise, that does not exceed ninety days, order that the sentence be served intermittently at such times as are specified in the order and direct that the defendant, at all times when he or she is not in confinement pursuant to such order, comply with the conditions prescribed in a probation order.

(2) A probation order shall be deemed to contain the conditions that,

(a) the defendant not commit the same or any related or similar offence, or any offence under a statute of Canada or Ontario or any other province of Canada that is punishable by imprisonment;

(b) the defendant appear before the court as and when required; and

(c) the defendant notify the court of any change in the defendant's address.

(3) In addition to the conditions set out in subsection (2), the court may prescribe as a condition in a probation order,

(a) that the defendant satisfy any compensation or restitution that is required or authorized by an Act;

(b) with the consent of the defendant and where the conviction is of an offence that is punishable by imprisonment, that the defendant perform a community service as set out in the order;

(c) where the conviction is of an offence punishable by imprisonment, such other conditions relating to the circumstances of the offence and of the defendant that contributed to the commission of the offence as the court considers appropriate to prevent similar unlawful conduct or to contribute to the rehabilitation of the defendant; or

(d) where considered necessary for the purpose of implementing the conditions of the probation order, that the defendant report to a responsible person designated by the court and, in addition, where the circumstances warrant it, that the defendant be under the supervision of the person to whom he or she is required to report.

(4) A probation order shall be in the prescribed form and the court shall specify therein the period for which it is to remain in force, which shall not be for more than two years from the date when the order takes effect.

(5) Where the court makes a probation order, it shall cause a copy of the order and a copy of section 75 to be given to the defendant.

(6) The Lieutenant Governor in Council may make regulations governing restitution, compensation and community service orders, including their terms and conditions.

(7) The court shall not make a probation order when an individual has been convicted of an absolute liability offence, unless the order is made in addition to a sentence of imprisonment imposed under section 69 in default of payment of a fine.

73(1) A probation order comes into force,

(a) on the date on which the order is made; or

(b) where the defendant is sentenced to imprisonment other than a sentence to be served intermittently, upon the expiration of that sentence.

(2) Subject to section 75, where a defendant who is bound by a probation order is convicted of an offence or is imprisoned in default of payment of a fine, the order continues in force except in so far as the sentence or imprisonment renders it impossible for the defendant to comply for the time being with the order.

74. The court may, at any time upon the application of the defendant or prosecutor with notice to the other, after a hearing or, with the consent of the parties, without a hearing,

(a) make any changes in or additions to the conditions prescribed in the order that in the opinion of the court are rendered desirable by a change in circumstances;

(b) relieve the defendant, either absolutely or upon such terms or for such period as the court considers desirable, of compliance with any condition described in any of the clauses in subsection 72(3) that is prescribed in the order; or

(c) terminate the order or decrease the period for which the probation order is to remain in force, and the court shall thereupon endorse the probation order accordingly and, if it changes or adds to the conditions prescribed in the order, inform the defendant of its action and give the defendant a copy of the order so endorsed.

If your client faces the possibility of a high fine and you are concerned about his or her ability to comply, it may be in your client's best interest to suggest a term of probation for the court's consideration.

It is important to note that probation is not available for absolute liability offences, and unless the underlying offence includes imprisonment as a sentencing option, only the statutory conditions apply to the order.

Prohibition Orders

Some statutes authorize municipalities to obtain a **prohibition order** that is intended to prevent the recurrence of the offence or to counteract the behaviour of a defendant who may regard being fined simply as the cost of doing business (in violation of a municipal bylaw). For example, s. 67(3) of the *Planning Act*, R.S.O. 1990, c. P.13 states:

prohibition order
a court order that prohibits a defendant from engaging in activities that could lead to a repetition of the offence

Where a conviction is entered under subsection (1), in addition to any other remedy or any penalty provided by law, the court in which the conviction has been entered, and any court of competent jurisdiction thereafter, may make an order prohibiting the continuation or repetition of the offence by the person convicted.

Similar provisions are found in sections of the *Municipal Act, 2001*, S.O. 2001, c. 25 and the *Building Code Act, 1992*, S.O. 1992, c. 23. Under a prohibition order, a defendant who further contravenes the bylaw in question may face not only another charge under the bylaw but also a contempt-of-court charge.

KEY TERMS

deterrence
probation order
prohibition order

REVIEW QUESTIONS

True/False

_____ 1. The court is not required to give the defendant an opportunity to be heard during the sentencing phase of a trial.

_____ 2. The court can ask about the defendant's economic circumstances during sentencing.

_____ 3. The defendant must answer any questions from the court about his or her financial situation.

_____ 4. A sentence should usually reflect the nature of the offence and the seriousness of the conduct.

_____ 5. Sentences in provincial offences court tend to focus on deterrence.

_____ 6. A set fine is the amount that will always be ordered by the court upon conviction.

_____ 7. If a fine is ordered by the court, it must always be paid immediately by the defendant.

_____ 8. The court may order a defendant to pay a higher fine because of previous convictions.

_____ 9. Imprisonment is an option available to the court for any provincial offence.

_____ 10. Depending on the enabling statute and offence, a probation order could be ordered by the court.

Short Answer

1. Identify the sentencing options available to the court for each procedural stream.

2. Sentencing for provincial offences generally focuses on deterrence. What are the two types of deterrence? Provide a brief example of each.

3. If convicted, a defendant will often be ordered to pay a fine. In addition to a fine, what costs could a defendant be ordered to pay? How are these amounts determined?

4. Outline the aggravating and mitigating factors that a court may be asked to consider before sentencing a defendant.

5. Can a defendant be sent to jail for committing a provincial offence? If so, under what circumstances?

Exercise

Working with a partner, follow the model on the Law Society of Upper Canada's website, entitled "How to Prepare to Defend a Provincial Offences Case." Conduct a client interview to obtain the relevant history and then role play, making oral submissions on behalf of your client using the facts obtained during the interview. (If you are working alone, prepare and present a written submission.)

Following Up with a Client

13

OVERVIEW

LEARNING OUTCOMES

After reading this chapter, you will understand

- how to deal with satisfactory and unsatisfactory results; and

- the steps to take when closing a file.

INTRODUCTION

After a court case is finished, a paralegal must still complete certain tasks and fulfill obligations to the client.

SATISFACTORY/UNSATISFACTORY RESULTS

There is some degree of risk associated with going to court. In many cases, paralegals will be able to obtain a satisfactory result through negotiation with the prosecution or at trial. However, there will also be cases that produce a result that the client will view as an unsatisfactory result, such as a **conviction**.

conviction
a final decision by a justice that there is proof that the defendant committed the offence for which he or she was charged

Satisfactory Results

If the charges against your client are **dismissed** or **withdrawn**, he or she should be satisfied with the outcome because there is no penalty and it is unlikely that further court action will take place (unless the prosecution files an appeal of the dismissal). Therefore, this would be an appropriate time to take steps to close the file.

dismissed
a final decision by a justice that there is not enough evidence to support a conviction against the defendant

If the charges against your client are stayed, this should also be considered a satisfactory result. But the client should be cautioned that, technically, a stay of proceedings means that they have been halted and could be recommenced by the prosecution. However, it is quite rare for stayed proceedings to be recommenced, and the file can now be closed.

withdrawn
a decision by the prosecution to remove the charges against the defendant

Negotiating a guilty plea to an amended (lesser) charge or agreeing with the prosecutor on sentencing submissions, such as a suspended sentence or a set fine, is also a satisfactory result. Clients who are most concerned about demerit points may be satisfied with an outcome that reduces or eliminates those points. Your client must provide instructions on what type of negotiated resolution would be suitable. If a resolution has been negotiated, the matter is complete and the file should be closed.

PRACTICE TIP

Whenever possible, try to turn a satisfied client into a source of referrals and repeat business. Think of ways to pass along your contact information (e.g., provide copies of your business card or a brochure) or to stay in touch with former clients (e.g., send out an email newsletter at regular intervals to advise of changes to relevant laws). You want to leave a good, lasting impression.

Unsatisfactory Results

Despite your preparation and strong advocacy skills, you may not always achieve a result that your client finds satisfactory. Nevertheless, do not delay in discussing the results with your client.

Clients should be informed of their appeal rights and whether an appeal is recommended in their case. For more information on appeals, see the discussion in Chapter 14.

If a client has already gone through the appeal process, he or she should be made aware of further appeal rights (e.g., to the Ontario Court of Appeal and the Supreme Court of Canada), even though paralegals are only permitted to appear on appeals in the Ontario Court of Justice.

If the unsatisfactory result was achieved because of an error or omission on the part of the paralegal, the *Paralegal Rules of Conduct* should be consulted for guidance. Specifically, Rule 3.02(12) and Rule 4.01(7) indicate that errors and omissions must be promptly disclosed and rectified whenever possible. Disclosure means that notice will have to be provided to your client and your insurer. As well, the client should be told to seek independent legal advice concerning any rights he or she may have arising from the error or omission (i.e., there may be grounds for a complaint or a claim against you). In some cases, there may be an opportunity to rectify an error. For example, if a paralegal missed a court date and the client was convicted as a result, he or she may be in a position to request a reopening of the case.

PRACTICE TIP

Many clients will be upset with a conviction. It is important that clients are made aware of the possibility of a conviction before the matter goes to trial so that they are not surprised.

CONSEQUENCES OF A CONVICTION

After sentencing, a client must be made aware of the consequences of a conviction. This includes informing the client of upcoming deadlines and time frames, such as when a fine is due or the duration of a licence suspension.

The consequences may vary depending on the penalties specified in the charging act. In some cases, the penalty may be a monetary fine, while in others, it may include demerit points, a licence suspension, and/or jail time. Some legislation authorizes additional penalties specifically related to the offence. For example, under the *Dog Owners' Liability Act*, R.S.O. 1990, c. D.16, if a dog has injured a person or animal, the court may prohibit the owner from owning another dog for a specified period of time.

CLOSING LETTER AND FINAL ACCOUNT

The Law Society of Upper Canada (LSUC) provides guidelines on closing a file and completing a retainer. As suggested by the LSUC's *Practice Management Guidelines*, when a matter has been completed, the following steps should be taken:

1. Return documents and property to the client. For *Provincial Offences Act* matters, this may include the original charging documents, the defendant's licence, photographs, and any other property in your possession.
2. Provide the client with a written report of the outcome. This is required regardless of whether the client attended court. The report should provide an overview of all work that was completed and everything that led to the outcome.

3. Explain or recommend any further action or future need for review. Clients will need to be informed of anything that they are required to do relating to the matter.

4. Send the final account, which includes all fees and disbursements, to the client before closing the file.

5. Settle the account with the client. For example, a client who was charged hourly and paid a monetary retainer up front may be entitled to a refund.

6. Advise the client about storage, retention and retrieval of file contents. In most cases, files must be kept for a minimum of seven years, so arrangements will have to be made for storing the files. However, the client needs to be assured that he or she can have access to the contents of the file if needed.

PRACTICE TIP

For practical reasons, consider collecting a flat fee or retainer at the outset of a case in order to avoid trying to collect money from a disgruntled client. Paying a paralegal's bill may not be a top priority for a client who has just received a large fine or been sent to jail.

KEY TERMS

conviction
dismissed
withdrawn

REVIEW QUESTIONS

True/False

_____ 1. If there is a stay of proceedings, the prosecution of the offence has been halted, but there is a possibility that the prosecution will be recommenced.

_____ 2. Some legislation authorizes additional penalties specifically related to the offence.

_____ 3. In most cases, files must be kept for a minimum of ten years.

Short Answer

1. What steps should be taken if a paralegal becomes aware of an error or omission on a file?

2. What steps does the Law Society of Upper Canada recommend that paralegals take when closing a file?

Reopenings and Appeals

14

LEARNING OUTCOMES

After reading this chapter, you will understand

- when a reopening is appropriate;

- the procedure for requesting a reopening;

- the difference between reopenings and appeals;

- when an appeal is appropriate; and

- the procedure for bringing an appeal.

INTRODUCTION

In cases where a defendant has been convicted, it may be appropriate to consider a reopening or an appeal of the decision, depending on the circumstances. A reopening can be requested for Part I and Part II matters where the defendant has been convicted without a hearing. Appeals can be brought for all procedural streams if there are sufficient grounds to do so.

REOPENINGS

If the defendant in a Part I or Part II matter has been convicted of an offence without a hearing, you as a paralegal can help your client to apply to strike the conviction and reopen the proceedings. A conviction without a hearing usually occurs when a Notice of Intention to Appear was filed and a court date was set, but the defendant did not attend court, and so was deemed not to dispute the charges and a conviction was entered in his or her absence.

Pursuant to ss. 11 and 19(1) of the *Provincial Offences Act*, a defendant who seeks a reopening may apply at the court office to have the conviction struck within 15 days of becoming aware of the conviction. Note that the time frame is within 15 days of when the defendant learned of the conviction, not within 15 days of the actual conviction. This is because a defendant convicted without a hearing would have been absent from court, so it might take some time before he or she learns of the conviction.

Most defendants will become aware of a conviction when they receive a notice from the court setting out the fine and the due date. However, there may be situations where the defendant does not receive notice of the conviction (e.g., if the defendant is having problems with mail delivery or has moved), and so might not become aware of the conviction until he or she tries to renew a driver's licence and discovers outstanding fines.

To apply for a reopening, the defendant must complete the Affidavit in Support of a Request for Reopening (Form 102 under Regulation 200 of the *Courts of Justice Act*) (see this form in Appendix B). Because this document takes the form of an affidavit, it must be in the name of the defendant, not the legal representative.

The defendant will have to provide a reason on the affidavit for not attending the hearing by choosing one of two options: explain why he or she was unable to appear at the hearing through no fault of the defendant's or identify a notice or document relating to the offence that was not delivered to him or her.

In the case of a defendant who was unable to appear through no fault of his or her own, a reason must be provided supporting that claim. For example, a defendant who had car trouble on the way to court may be successful in suggesting that the absence was not his or her fault. However, a defendant who simply states that he or she forgot about the court date may have difficulty obtaining the reopening.

Alternatively, a defendant can identify a notice or document relating to the offence that was not delivered, including the notice of trial. In such a case, the defendant would not have known about the court date. However, it is important to keep in mind that a defendant is obligated to provide the court with an updated address. A defendant who does not properly inform the court of a new address contributes to the non-receipt of the notice or document and may have difficulty obtaining the reopening.

The statements made on Form 102 must be truthful and sworn before a commissioner of oaths. A reference to s. 86 of the POA is included at the bottom of the form. It states:

> Every person who makes an assertion of fact in a statement or entry in a document or form for use under this Act knowing that the assertion is false is guilty of an offence and on conviction is liable to a fine of not more than $2,000.

This is included as a warning so that defendants are aware that there is a penalty for falsifying information or lying on the form.

A justice will consider whether to reopen the matter. If the defendant's request is denied, the conviction remains, but if the conviction is struck, the defendant will be given a Certificate of Striking Out Conviction signed by the justice (Form 103 under the *Courts of Justice Act*, Regulation 200). The defendant returns to the position he or she was in before the conviction, and has the option of pleading guilty with submissions or completing a new Notice of Intention to Appear to request a trial date. If a trial date is requested, the original options are still available to the defendant, including negotiating with the prosecutor, pleading guilty, or pleading not guilty.

While Part I and Part II matters can either be reopened or appealed, Part III matters cannot be reopened. Reopening is only available if the defendant has been convicted without a hearing. However, for Part III matters it is not possible to have a conviction without a hearing because the court holds an *ex parte* trial if the defendant does not attend court. Even though the defendant is not present at the trial, an *ex parte* trial is still classified as a hearing.

PRACTICE TIP

Paralegals should consider applying to become commissioners for taking affidavits so that they can provide a commissioning service to their clients, such as a Request for a Reopening. The application is available through the Ministry of the Attorney General's Legal Appointments Office website.

APPEALS

Part I, Part II, and Part III matters can all be appealed, but the process, procedure, and rules differ slightly in the case of Part III matters. In all cases, either the prosecution or the defence may consider whether it would be appropriate and permissible to bring an appeal if either party is dissatisfied with the verdict or the sentence.

Subsection 6(2) of the Law Society of Upper Canada's By-Law 4 sets out the permitted areas of practice for paralegals. Specifically, the bylaw allows paralegals to represent clients in proceedings before the Ontario Court of Justice under the POA. Because most appeals take place in the Ontario Court of Justice, paralegals are regularly able to represent clients on appeals.

Notice of Appeal

appellant
the party bringing an appeal, either the defence or the prosecution

Before filing a Notice of Appeal, the **appellant** must pay the fine in full. If the appeal is successful, the payment will be refunded. An appellant who is unable or unwilling to pay the fine in advance can apply for a recognizance to appear on the appeal, which is an acknowledgment that the appellant is obligated to appear at the appeal and will pay a specified amount of money if he or she does not appear. The judge has discretion to determine the amount of the recognizance and to order it with or without a surety (someone who guarantees the appellant's attendance at the appeal).

Upon filing the appeal, a conviction is not automatically stayed unless ordered by a judge, pursuant to s. 112 of the POA. Most clients would want the conviction to be stayed pending the outcome of the appeal, so it is good practice to request a stay of the conviction. An additional step is recommended for *Highway Traffic Act* convictions. Convictions, demerit points, and suspensions are not automatically stayed for driving offences unless the Registrar of Motor Vehicles is served with a copy of the Notice of Appeal. Under s. 5 of Regulation 339/94 to the *Highway Traffic Act*, if the Registrar is served with notice of the appeal, the conviction, demerit points, and suspension shall not be entered on the driver's record. If the conviction, demerit points, and suspension have already been entered when notice is served, they shall be removed.

Part I or Part II

A Notice of Appeal must be filed with the clerk of the court to commence an appeal for a Part I or Part II matter. The notice must state the reasons for the appeal and be filed within 30 days of the court's decision (note that it is within 30 days of the decision, not within 30 days of learning of the decision). If more time is required to prepare the appeal, the defendant may apply for an extension, pursuant to s. 85 of the POA.

When the Notice of Appeal is filed, the court clerk will set a time and place for hearing the appeal. The document that is used for an appellant to give notice is the Notice of Appeal, which is Form 1 under Regulation 722/94 of the *Courts of Justice Act* (see this form in Appendix B).

Part III

For Part III matters, s. 116(3) of the POA indicates that "the appellant shall give notice of appeal in such manner and within such period as is provided by the rules of court." The Notice of Appeal must be filed within 30 days of the decision for such matters. If more time is needed to prepare the appeal, the defendant can apply for an extension, again under s. 85 of the POA.

The required form for Part III appeals is Form 1, Notice of Appeal under Regulation 723/94 of the *Courts of Justice Act* (see this form in Appendix B). The appellant must order a transcript of the original trial, and most courts require that the transcript be ordered and paid for when the Notice of Appeal is filed.

Grounds for Appeal

The Notice of Appeal must state the grounds for appeal. The POA sets out the types of appeals that can be brought, as well as the grounds for appeal.

For Part I and Part II matters, the defendant or the prosecution can appeal an acquittal, a conviction, or a sentence. Part III matters provide broader opportunities of appeal, including appeals of a conviction; a dismissal; a finding as to the ability to conduct a defence because of mental disorder; a sentence; or an order for costs.

The POA provides further guidance for Part III appeals. A conviction or a finding of ability to conduct a defence can be appealed on the grounds that the verdict is unreasonable or cannot be supported by the evidence. This may include the justice's failure to provide sufficient reasons or an error in findings concerning the credibility of witnesses. A conviction can also be appealed if a wrong decision was made on a question of law (e.g., interpretation of a case or statute, or admissibility of evidence) or if there has been a miscarriage of justice.

An acquittal can be appealed by the prosecution if there are sufficient grounds to believe that the defendant was wrongly acquitted, and the sentence can be appealed on the grounds that it is clearly unfit or unreasonable.

Procedure for Part I and Part II Appeals

An acquittal, a conviction, or a sentence can be appealed for Part I and Part II matters. Although either the defence or the prosecution may decide to appeal the sentence (e.g., the prosecutor believes the sentence was too lenient; the defendant believes the sentence was too harsh), it would be the prosecutor who considers appealing an acquittal and the defence who decides to appeal a conviction.

Sections 135 to 139 of the POA set out the procedure for Part I and Part II appeals. With the exception of appeals by a young person, Part I and Part II appeals are heard by a provincial court judge in the Ontario Court of Justice. Appeals by a young person are heard in the Superior Court of Justice, but, in accordance with s. 105 of the Act, the procedures and the powers of the court and any appeal from the judgment of the court are the same as if the appeal were heard in the Ontario Court of Justice by a provincial judge.

While the court will give the parties an opportunity to be heard in order to determine the issues, the appeal is conducted by way of a review. In reviewing the original decision, the appeal judge can hear or rehear recorded evidence, require any party to provide a transcript or exhibit, receive evidence from any witness, and require the trial justice to provide a written report, or the appeal judge may make a decision based on agreed statements of fact or admissions.

When the review is complete, the court has the authority to uphold, reverse, or vary the original decision, or order a new trial. A new trial will only be ordered if it is necessary to satisfy the ends of justice. It would be held in the Ontario Court of Justice before a justice other than the trial justice, unless the parties consent otherwise.

If dissatisfied with the result of the appeal, either of the parties can seek leave to appeal to the Ontario Court of Appeal. Pursuant to s. 139(1) of the POA:

> An appeal lies from the judgment of the Ontario Court of Justice in an appeal under section 135 to the Court of Appeal, with leave of a judge of the Court of Appeal, on special grounds, upon any question of law alone.

However, the grounds for leave to appeal can be difficult to satisfy. Under s. 139(2):

> No leave to appeal shall be granted under subsection (1) unless the judge of the Court of Appeal considers that in the particular circumstances of the case, it is essential in the public interest or for the due administration of justice that leave be granted. Furthermore, paralegals are not permitted to appear on appeals before the Court of Appeal.

Procedure for Part III Appeals

For Part III matters, the POA allows a conviction; a dismissal; a finding as to the ability to conduct a defence because of mental disorder; a sentence; or an order for costs to be appealed.

Sections 116 to 134 of the Act set out the procedure for Part III appeals. The court that will hear the appeal depends on whether the original decision was made by a justice of the peace or a judge. If the appeal stems from a decision of a justice of the peace, it will be heard in the Ontario Court of Justice by a provincial judge. If a provincial judge's decision is being appealed, it goes before the Superior Court of Justice. Although some charging acts specify that a trial is to be conducted by a judge, most trials take place before justices of the peace and therefore most appeals will go to the Ontario Court of Justice.

The court's powers for a Part III appeal are set out in s. 117 of the POA. Specifically, the court has the ability to:

> (a) order the production of any writing, exhibit or other thing relevant to the appeal;
>
> (a.1) amend the information, unless it is of the opinion that the defendant has been misled or prejudiced in his or her defence or appeal;
>
> (b) order any witness who would have been a compellable witness at the trial, whether or not he or she was called at the trial,
>
> > (i) to attend and be examined before the court, or
> >
> > (ii) to be examined in the manner provided by the rules of court before a judge of the court, or before any officer of the court or justice of the peace or other person appointed by the court for the purpose;
>
> (c) admit, as evidence, an examination that is taken under subclause (b)(ii);
>
> (d) receive the evidence, if tendered, of any witness;

(e) order that any question arising on the appeal that,

    (i) involves prolonged examination of writings or accounts, or scientific investigation, and

    (ii) cannot in the opinion of the court conveniently be inquired into before the court, be referred for inquiry and report, in the manner provided by the rules of court, to a special commissioner appointed by the court; and

(f) act upon the report of a commissioner who is appointed under clause (e) in so far as the court thinks fit to do so.

It is important to note that either the defence or the prosecution may make appeal arguments in writing instead of orally.

The court's options on an appeal depend on the type of appeal that has been brought. Section 120(1) of the POA sets out the court's powers when dealing with an appeal of a conviction and of a finding of the ability to conduct a defence. The court can allow the appeal or dismiss the appeal based on several grounds.

The court will allow the appeal if the findings are unreasonable or cannot be supported by the evidence, a wrong decision was made on a question of law, or a miscarriage of justice took place. If the appeal is allowed, the court can direct an acquittal or order a new trial. If the appeal is related to a finding of ability, the proper remedy is to order a new trial. An appeal of the conviction can be dismissed if the court believes that the appellant was properly convicted.

Where the appeal is against an acquittal, s. 121 stipulates that the court may dismiss the appeal or set aside the acquittal. If the acquittal is set aside, the court can order a new trial or enter a finding of guilt and sentence the defendant.

The specifics of an appeal against a sentence are outlined in s. 122. The court is obligated to consider the fitness of the sentence that is being appealed. It can then decide to dismiss the appeal or vary the sentence within the limits of the original charging act.

If the appeal is based on a defect with the information, the certificate, or the process, the judgment will only be in the appellant's favour if it can be shown that an objection was made at trial. An appeal can also be brought if there was a variance between the information, the certificate, or the process and the evidence at trial. In this case, the appellant can obtain a favourable judgment only if there was an objection at trial and a refusal to adjourn the trial, despite the variance.

If either party is not satisfied with the outcome of the appeal, he or she may seek leave to appeal to the Ontario Court of Appeal. Pursuant to s. 131(1) of the POA:

> A defendant or the prosecutor or the Attorney General by way of intervention may appeal from the judgment of the court to the Court of Appeal, with leave of a judge of the Court of Appeal on special grounds, upon any question of law alone or as to sentence.

However, as with Part I and Part II appeals, the grounds for leave to appeal are difficult to satisfy under s. 139(2). A judge of the Court of Appeal will only grant leave to appeal if the case is considered to be essential in the public interest or important for the administration of justice. Paralegals are not permitted to appear on appeals before the Court of Appeal.

KEY TERM

appellant

REVIEW QUESTIONS

True/False

_____ 1. Part III matters can either be reopened or appealed.

_____ 2. The affidavit for a reopening can be in the name of a paralegal, if that paralegal was properly retained by the defendant.

_____ 3. A defendant who missed the deadline for filing an appeal can apply for an extension.

_____ 4. A Part III appeal must be filed within 30 days of learning of a conviction.

_____ 5. Appeal arguments can be made orally or in writing.

Short Answer

1. Gary was convicted on October 2 for "Improper Stop at Intersection." He had tried unsuccessfully to quash his offence notice for a spelling error. He believes a wrong decision was made on a question of law and plans to appeal. What is the deadline to file the appeal?

2. Who is allowed to appeal a defendant's sentence?

3. Which court, and which type of justice, would hear the appeal in a Part I or Part II adult proceeding originally heard by a justice of the peace?

4. For a Part I offence, how many days does a defendant have to request a reopening?

5. Dawn is 15 years old. She was convicted of trespassing and plans to appeal. Which court would hear the appeal?

Exercise

Your client was convicted in a trial before a justice of the peace of careless driving and fined $1,200. He has had a perfect driving record for 20 years and retains you to appeal the decision.

1. What is the appropriate court to hear this appeal?

   a. Ontario Court of Appeal

   b. Superior Court of Justice

   c. Ontario Court of Justice presided over by a provincial judge

   d. Ontario Court of Justice presided over by a justice of the peace

   e. none of the above

2. How much time do you have to file the appeal in this case?

    a. within 15 days of the conviction
    b. within 15 days of learning of the conviction
    c. within 30 days of the conviction
    d. within 30 day of learning of the conviction
    e. an appeal is not appropriate; your client should request a reopening

3. Assume that the appeal is successful and a new trial is ordered. Unless otherwise agreed, the trial will be held:

    a. before the original justice who tried the defendant in first instance
    b. before a Superior Court judge
    c. before a Court of Appeal judge
    d. before a justice, other than the original justice, who tried the defendant in the first instance
    e. none of the above

Common Highway Traffic Act Offences

15

LEARNING OUTCOMES

After reading this chapter, you will understand

- common offences under the *Highway Traffic Act*;

- penalties associated with common offences under the Act, including fines and demerit points; and

- recent legislation that bans drivers from viewing display screens and using hand-held communication devices.

INTRODUCTION

Most charges prosecuted in provincial offences court have been laid under the *Highway Traffic Act* (HTA). Because the HTA is provincial legislation, its provisions apply to drivers throughout Ontario. Each province has its own version of the HTA, which applies to drivers in those provinces. The charges and their wording vary from province to province. A slight change in the wording can alter how an offence is classified (*mens rea*, strict liability, or absolute liability) and can change the court's interpretation of an offence.

That slight change in wording or interpretation can also modify the defence(s) available for that charge. For example, in Ontario speeding is classified as an absolute liability offence, but in some of the other provinces it is a strict liability offence. Therefore, a driver in a province with a strict liability classification is able to justify his or her actions by arguing due diligence, but due diligence would be irrelevant in Ontario because of the absolute liability classification for speeding.

PRACTICE TIP

When conducting case research, be sure to check in which province the charges originated. You do not want to present an argument about an interpretation that is based on wording of a charge from a different province. If the case is from another province, it may be persuasive, but it would not be binding in Ontario.

TERMINOLOGY

In order to understand the HTA, it is important to first examine some of the definitions found in s. 1(1) of the Act.

Highway

> 1(1) ... "highway" includes a common and public highway, street, avenue, parkway, driveway, square, place, bridge, viaduct or trestle, any part of which is intended for or used by the general public for the passage of vehicles and includes the area between the lateral property lines thereof.

Although the common, everyday understanding of the word "highway" tends to be an expressway (e.g., a 400-series highway), the HTA broadens that definition to include all types of roads and some other areas commonly driven on. Case law helps to further define areas that are, and are not, classified as part of a highway.

The following is an example of an HTA section that specifies "highway":

> 130. Every person is guilty of the offence of driving carelessly who drives a vehicle or street car on a highway without due care and attention or without reasonable consideration for other persons using the highway ... .

If the charging section of the HTA specifies that the prohibited behaviour must take place on a highway, as above, the charge applies only to behaviour that occurs in areas that fall within the definition or interpretation of a highway. For example, s. 130 prohibits careless driving on a highway, but a charge could not be laid under this section if the motorist was driving carelessly in a parking lot, because a parking lot is not considered to be part of a highway. (Other charges might apply, but not a charge under s. 130.)

Roadway

> 1(1) ... "roadway" means the part of the highway that is improved, designed or ordinarily used for vehicular traffic, but does not include the shoulder, and, where a highway includes two or more separate roadways, the term "roadway" refers to any one roadway separately and not to all of the roadways collectively.

Notice that the definition of "roadway" does not include the shoulder of the highway; it only includes the part of the highway that is most commonly driven on. If "roadway" is used within a charging section, it means that the behaviour is not prohibited on the shoulder. If a section of the Act is intended to apply to motorists who drive on the shoulder, the charging section will specify "highway" instead of "roadway."

The following is an example of an HTA section that specifies "roadway":

> 147(1) Any vehicle travelling upon a roadway at less than the normal speed of traffic at that time and place shall, where practicable, be driven in the right-hand lane then available for traffic or as close as practicable to the right-hand curb or edge of the roadway.

This section prohibits a driver from travelling too slow in a "fast" lane of traffic (i.e., the left lane) and allows a slow-moving vehicle to travel in the right lane. By using the word "roadway," a motorist driving at below the normal speed of traffic on the shoulder would not be charged under s. 147(1).

Motor Vehicle

> 1(1) ... "motor vehicle" includes an automobile, a motorcycle, a motor-assisted bicycle unless otherwise indicated in this Act, and any other vehicle propelled or driven otherwise than by muscular power, but does not include a street car or other motor vehicle running only upon rails, a power-assisted bicycle, a motorized snow vehicle, a traction engine, a farm tractor, a self-propelled implement of husbandry or a road-building machine.

Based on the definition, a motor vehicle does not use muscular power. Therefore, charges in the Act that apply to motor vehicles would not apply to any vehicle that does use muscular power (e.g., a bicycle). Case law helps to determine which vehicles are, and are not, classified as motor vehicles.

The following is an example of an HTA section that specifies "motor vehicle":

> 165. No person shall,
> (a) open the door of a motor vehicle on a highway without first taking due precautions to ensure that his or her act will not interfere with the movement of or endanger any other person or vehicle; ... .

This section ensures the safety of approaching persons and vehicles. The term "motor vehicle" was likely used because vehicles propelled by muscular power do not typically have doors.

Vehicle

> 1(1) ... "vehicle" includes a motor vehicle, trailer, traction engine, farm tractor, road-building machine, bicycle and any vehicle drawn, propelled or driven by any kind of power, including muscular power, but does not include a motorized snow vehicle or a street car.

"Vehicle" encompasses more than "motor vehicle." It includes all vehicles that use any power, including motor and muscular power. Therefore, any sections in the Act that refer to "vehicle" are intended to apply to such things as bicycles and wheelchairs, as well as to motor vehicles.

If a section of the Act is intended to apply to one of the excluded vehicles, the definition will be amended within the Act (e.g., s. 144(1) specifies that a vehicle will include a street car for that section, even though street car was excluded in s. 1(1)).

The following is an example of an HTA section that specifies "vehicle":

> 163(1) When the driver of a vehicle is approaching a railway crossing at a time when a clearly visible electrical or mechanical signal device or a flagman is giving warning of the approach of a railway train, he or she shall stop the vehicle not less than 5 metres from the nearest rail of the railway and shall not proceed until he or she can do so safely.

This section ensures that all types of vehicles stop at a railway crossing. It is not limited to motor vehicles.

Driver

> 1(1) ... "driver" means a person who drives a vehicle on a highway.

While the definition is quite vague, case law has assisted with interpreting the term "driver." A commonly accepted definition would be someone exercising control over a vehicle, and substantially controlling the movement and direction of a vehicle.

The following is an example of an HTA section that specifies "driver":

> 144(5) A driver who is directed by a traffic control signal erected at an intersection to stop his or her vehicle shall stop ... .

This section places the responsibility to ensure that a vehicle properly comes to a stop on the person in control of the vehicle (i.e., the driver). Therefore, the driver can be charged under s. 144(5). Other sections in the Act may specifically apply to passengers, occupants, or owners of vehicles.

PENALTIES

Set Fines

Set fines have been established for Part I offences and are intended to be used as the amount payable for out-of-court settlement (i.e., paying the ticket). Once a defendant proceeds to trial, the set fine is only persuasive. The justice has full discretion to set the fine up to the $1,000 Part I maximum.

The set fines for HTA offences are set out in Schedule 43 to the HTA (see Appendix C, Set Fines from the Provincial Offences Act).

Demerit Points

An additional type of penalty, unique to highway traffic offences, is demerit points. Demerit points are administered by the Ministry of Transportation and not the courts. Therefore, the prosecutor and the justice cannot take away or lower any demerit points that correspond with an offence.

It is a common misconception that drivers lose demerit points. A defendant who has been convicted of an HTA offence that carries demerit points will have the points added to his or her **driving record**. The points will stay on the record with the Ministry of Transportation for two years from the date of the offence. Accumulation of points will typically increase the driver's insurance rates, and may lead to further penalties and involvement by the Ministry of Transportation. The following indicates what occurs as demerit points are accumulated:

driving record
a record of convictions against a driver maintained by the Ministry of Transportation

- 6 points: driver is advised of record
- 9 points: driver is required to attend an interview with the ministry
- 15 points: driver's licence will be suspended for 30 days

After a suspension, the number of demerit points will be reduced to 7. If the driver reaches 15 points again, his or her licence will be suspended for six months.

PRACTICE TIP

Many of your clients will be concerned about the points associated with an offence—especially if they rely upon a driver's licence for their job and a "clean driving record" may be a condition of employment. It is important to try to negotiate with the prosecutor in order to get a reduced charge that would result in fewer demerit points or no points for your client.

The demerit points that correspond with HTA offences are set out in Ontario Regulation 339/94 (see Appendix D, Highway Traffic Act Demerit Point System).

COMMON OFFENCES

Although it is beyond the scope of this text to discuss every possible charge listed in the HTA, the pages that follow are intended to provide an overview of some of the more common offences that paralegals are likely to defend in provincial offences court.

Speeding

Although "speeding" is not defined in the HTA, a commonly accepted definition is "driving a motor vehicle at a rate of speed in excess of that permitted on the specified highway." The Act sets out the rules pertaining to the offence of speeding:

> 128(1) No person shall drive a motor vehicle at a rate of speed greater than,
>
> (a) 50 kilometres per hour on a highway within a local municipality or within a built-up area;
>
> (b) despite clause (a), 80 kilometres per hour on a highway, not within a built-up area, that is within a local municipality that had the status of a township on December 31, 2002 and, but for the enactment of the *Municipal Act, 2001*, would have had the status of a township on January 1, 2003, if the municipality is prescribed by regulation;
>
> (c) 80 kilometres per hour on a highway designated by the Lieutenant Governor in Council as a controlled-access highway under the *Public Transportation and Highway Improvement Act*, whether or not the highway is within a local municipality or built-up area;
>
> (d) the rate of speed prescribed for motor vehicles on a highway in accordance with subsection (2), (5), (6), (6.1) or (7);
>
> (e) the maximum rate of speed set under subsection (10) and posted in a construction zone designated under subsection (8) or (8.1); or
>
> (f) the maximum rate of speed posted on a highway or portion of a highway pursuant to section 128.01.

Notice that in each of these paragraphs, the rate of speed applies to motor vehicles on highways (one exception: (e) applies to a construction zone). Therefore, someone driving a non-motorized vehicle, such as a bicycle, could not be charged with speeding under this section. Further, a police officer would not charge someone with speeding under s. 128 if he or she was driving in an area that is considered a non-highway, such as a parking lot—although other charges may apply for speeding in a parking lot.

In most cases, a speed limit sign is posted to advise drivers on how fast they are permitted to drive. However, paragraphs (a) to (c) set the default rate of speed for a highway even if a sign is not visible—making it difficult for a defendant to argue that he or she did not know the speed limit or did not see a sign. Drivers are expected to know the rules of the road and the default rates of speed.

PRACTICE TIP

Take a close look at the offence notice. If the letter "R" is written in the Code box, it is unlikely that the prosecutor will reduce the defendant's alleged rate of speed. The "R" stands for "reduced," meaning that the officer already reduced the speed when the defendant was pulled over. Some officers will use this as a signal to the prosecutor to avoid a further reduction.

Commentary

There are four primary ways for the police to detect and measure the rate of speed:

1. *Laser:* The officer uses a device that sends infrared light pulses, which take a measurement based on the speed of light. Because multiple readings are taken in a second, the device is considered to be very accurate. The laser ("light amplification by stimulated emission radiation") device allows the officer to pinpoint one particular vehicle in a specific lane of traffic because the laser beam is very narrow. Typically, the laser device is mounted on a tripod because movement of the device can cause an inaccurate reading.

2. *Radar:* The officer uses a device that sends a radio beam and takes a measurement based on the speed of sound. While it is considered to be quite accurate, radar technology does not allow an officer to pinpoint a specific vehicle within a cluster of vehicles. Radar devices can be used as a hand-held device or mounted on the police cruiser's dashboard to take readings while the officer is driving.

3. *Pacing:* The officer can follow directly behind a vehicle at the same speed, and measure the vehicle's speed by the reading on the police cruiser's speedometer. Pacing is considered to be accurate as long as the officer keeps the distance between the vehicles constant.

4. *Aircraft:* There are signs along many Ontario highways that indicate speed can be detected by aircraft (i.e., a helicopter). One officer will be in the helicopter, and use a stop watch to measure how long it takes a vehicle to travel a predetermined fixed distance. If the officer in the aircraft determines that a vehicle is speeding, he or she will radio an officer on the highway to pull over the vehicle and issue a ticket.

Penalties

The penalties for exceeding the speed limit are set out in s. 128(14):

128(14) Every person who contravenes this section or any by-law or regulation made under this section is guilty of an offence and on conviction is liable, where the rate of speed at which the motor vehicle was driven,

(a) is less than 20 kilometres per hour over the speed limit, to a fine of $3 for each kilometre per hour that the motor vehicle was driven over the speed limit;

(b) is 20 kilometres per hour or more but less than 30 kilometres per hour over the speed limit, to a fine of $4.50 for each kilometre per hour that the motor vehicle was driven over the speed limit;

(c) is 30 kilometres per hour or more but less than 50 kilometres per hour over the speed limit, to a fine of $7 for each kilometre per hour that the motor vehicle was driven over the speed limit; and

(d) is 50 kilometres per hour or more over the speed limit, to a fine of $9.75 for each kilometre per hour that the motor vehicle was driven over the speed limit.

A higher per-kilometre penalty is charged for higher rates of speed. The actual offence is speeding; the rate of speed only determines the fine. Technically, driving even one kilometre over the posted rate of speed is considered to be an offence and a driver can be charged with speeding.

PRACTICE TIP

Caution your client about providing an estimate in court as to how fast he or she was driving. Defendants will sometimes take the stand and state that they were only driving five kilometres over the speed limit. This is an admission to the charge, because the offence itself is speeding. Your client should be careful not to give evidence that supports a conviction.

Demerit points for speeding are based on the rate of speed, as set out in Ontario Regulation 339/94, as follows:

- 0 to 15 kilometres over the limit: 0 demerit points
- 16 to 29 kilometres over the limit: 3 demerit points
- 30 to 49 kilometres over the limit: 4 demerit points
- 50 and plus kilometres over the limit: 6 demerit points

For example, if a defendant had been driving 75 km/h in a 50 km/h zone, he or she would have been driving 25 kilometres over the posted speed limit, which results in 3 demerit points. For speeding charges, the points automatically correspond with the number of kilometres over the limit. Neither the prosecutor nor the justice have the discretion to reduce or eliminate the points. However, negotiations with the prosecutor could lead to an amended speed that may correspond with fewer demerit points.

PRACTICE TIP

For speeding charges, it is not possible to receive just one or two demerit points. The points jump from 0 to 3, which can make it difficult to negotiate a more desirable outcome for your client. A prosecutor may be willing to amend the charge and reduce the speed, but not always by an amount that would lower the demerit points to 0. However, there may be other offences within the HTA that correspond with the fact scenario and carry fewer demerit points. For example, a charge of "disobey sign" could be laid instead, because a driver who is speeding is also disobeying the sign that posts the speed limit. Therefore, when negotiating with the prosecutor, it is important to thoroughly review the HTA, looking for charges that fit your client's situation and carry fewer demerit points.

PRACTICE TIP

amending up
the practice of having the defendant tried on the actual rate of speed instead of the reduced rate of speed specified by the officer when the charges were laid

Caution your client that a decision to take a speeding charge to trial means that he or she could be faced with an "**amending up**" situation. This means that the trial would be based on the actual rate of speed instead of the reduced rate of speed specified by the officer when the charges were laid. The practice of amending-up is permitted, as long as there is no prejudice or injustice to the defendant and the requirements of the POA are met.

Racing, Contests, and Stunt Driving

Section 172(1) of the HTA states: "No person shall drive a motor vehicle on a highway in a race or contest, while performing a stunt or on a bet or wager."

The particulars of what constitutes racing and stunt driving are set out in Ontario Regulation 455/07, as follows:

Race and contest, under s. 2(1), include:

- one or more persons engaged in a competition, above the lawful rate of speed;
- chasing another vehicle;
- driving without due care or attention at a high rate of speed; or
- repeatedly changing lanes close to other vehicles in an effort to advance past these vehicles at a higher rate of speed.

While most people tend to think of stunt driving as behaviour related to speeding or racing, it actually encompasses a wide range of different driving behaviours.

Stunt, under s. 3, includes:

- lifting one or more of the vehicle's tires off the road surface;
- purposely spinning the vehicle's tires;
- causing the vehicle to spin in a circle;
- driving beside another vehicle, where one of the vehicles is in the lane used by oncoming traffic but is not passing;
- driving with a person in the trunk;
- driving while not sitting in the driver's seat;
- exceeding the speed limit by 50 km/h or more;
- driving without due care or attention to prevent another vehicle from passing;
- stopping or slowing down to impede the flow of traffic;
- driving too close to another vehicle, pedestrian, or fixed object; or
- executing a left turn at a green light before the vehicle coming from the opposite direction is able to proceed straight through the intersection.

Commentary

The courts have recently dealt with the classification of stunt driving. Because many of the charges under s. 172 of the HTA have been for stunt driving by speeding, some trial-level decisions initially viewed it as an absolute liability offence, like speeding. However, because a jail term is possible, an absolute liability classification is contrary to s. 7 of the *Canadian Charter of Rights and Freedoms*, which guarantees life, liberty, and security of the person. The possibility of being absolutely liable and going to jail without being able to thoroughly defend oneself is contrary to the Charter. The Ontario Court of Appeal has reclassified stunt driving by speeding, under s. 172 of the HTA, as a strict liability offence—which gives defendants an opportunity to raise a due diligence defence.

Penalties

The possible penalties for racing, contests, and stunt driving are set out in s. 172 of the HTA:

- an immediate seven-day driver's licence suspension;
- a seven-day vehicle impound;
- costs for towing and storage of the impounded vehicle;
- a minimum fine of $2,000 to a maximum of $10,000;
- jail for not more than six months; or
- a driver's licence suspension for not more than two years on a first conviction.

In addition, a conviction under s. 172 results in 6 demerit points.

Stop Signs

Section 136(1) of the HTA sets out the requirements for obeying stop signs:

> 136(1) Every driver or street car operator approaching a stop sign at an intersection,
>   (a) shall stop his or her vehicle or street car at a marked stop line or, if none, then immediately before entering the nearest crosswalk or, if none, then immediately before entering the intersection;
>   (b) shall yield the right of way to traffic in the intersection or approaching the intersection on another highway so closely that to proceed would constitute an immediate hazard and, having so yielded the right of way, may proceed.

This section states that drivers must stop their vehicles at a stop sign and also indicates where, physically, they must stop. It also specifies the requirement of yielding the right-of-way, when appropriate. Therefore, a charge under s. 136(1) is not necessarily laid because the defendant did not come to a stop; it could be for other prohibited driving behaviour at a stop sign.

Commentary

There is nothing in the wording of this section to indicate how long drivers must stop at a stop sign. It is a common misconception that drivers are required to stop their vehicle for a specified amount of time. The requirement is for drivers to come to a full and complete stop, not a "rolling stop."

Penalties

As set out in Schedule 43 to the HTA, the set fine for failing to stop, stopping at the wrong place, or failing to yield at a stop sign is $85. The schedule also includes the set fines if the offence takes place in a community safety zone. A driver who stops in the wrong place in such a zone will face a $120 set fine, while those who to fail to stop or to yield in a community safety zone face a set fine of $150.

Three demerit points are associated with this charge. Some prosecutors may consider negotiating a lesser and included offence with no demerit points, but it is discretionary.

Traffic Lights

Section 144 of the HTA deals with traffic control signals, otherwise known as stop lights or traffic lights. Within this section are many different subsections setting out the various behaviours that are prohibited at traffic lights, including charges that involve motor vehicles, pedestrians, and cyclists.

Much like the stop sign offence, this section sets out not only the need to come to a stop, but also where on the road the driver is expected to stop the vehicle. According to s. 144(5) of the HTA:

144(5) A driver who is directed by a traffic control signal erected at an intersection to stop his or her vehicle shall stop,
(a) at the sign or roadway marking indicating where the stop is to be made;
(b) if there is no sign or marking, immediately before entering the nearest crosswalk; or
(c) if there is no sign, marking or crosswalk, immediately before entering the intersection.

A driver must not only stop at a traffic control signal when the light is red, but according to the HTA, a driver must also stop when the light is amber (yellow) if it is safe to do so. As set out in s. 144(15):

144(15) Every driver approaching a traffic control signal showing a circular amber indication and facing the indication shall stop his or her vehicle if he or she can do so safely, otherwise he or she may proceed with caution.

If a driver is charged under s. 144(15), the officer must have believed that he or she could have stopped safely or did not proceed with caution through the intersection. An accident could be caused by not proceeding with caution.

Section 144(18) deals with actually coming to a stop for a red traffic light. This section states:

144(18) Every driver approaching a traffic control signal showing a circular red indication and facing the indication shall stop his or her vehicle and shall not proceed until a green indication is shown.

Commentary

A variety of charges can be laid for a violation at a traffic light. While drivers understand the need to stop at a red light, many seem to believe that an amber light means to slow down—not realizing that it also means to stop when it is safe to do so.

Penalties

The set fines under s. 144 vary across the different subsections. The common charge of failing to stop under s. 144(18) has a set fine of $260. But if the offence takes place in a community safety zone, the set fine rises to $400.

While some of the offences outlined in the subsections to s. 144 do not have demerit points, other subsections have 2 or 3 demerit points. For example, a charge under s. 144(18) carries 3 demerit points.

PRACTICE TIP

If your client has been charged under s. 144, carefully review all of the other subsections to determine whether a different subsection could apply. Recommending a subsection to the prosecutor that is worded in a slightly different manner could result in a lesser penalty for your client.

Red Light Cameras

The offence of failing to stop at a red light and being detected by a red light camera, instead of by a police officer, is set out in s. 144(18.1), which states:

> 144(18.1) A person who issues a certificate of offence and offence notice under subsection 3(2) of the *Provincial Offences Act* for a contravention of subsection (18) shall, despite that Act and the regulations under that Act, specify this subsection, instead of subsection (18), as the provision that was contravened, if,
>> (a) the person who issues the certificate of offence and offence notice believes that the offence was committed on the basis of evidence obtained through the use of a red light camera system; and
>> (b) the defendant is being charged as the owner of the vehicle.

If the red light camera photographs a driver who does not stop at an intersection, the owner of the vehicle will be served with an offence notice by mail, pursuant to s. 144(18.1) of the HTA. While s. 144(18.2) does allow for the driver to be charged, it is usually the owner who will be charged. This is because the owner of the vehicle can easily be identified through a Ministry of Transportation search, but it would be very difficult to identify who was driving the vehicle at the time of the offence.

The offence notice contains photographs of the vehicle as it crossed into and proceeded through the intersection. The unique rules and procedures for red light camera offences are set out in ss. 205.15 to 205.25 of the HTA and in Ontario Regulation 277/99.

Commentary

In response to an increase in "red light running" and in an effort to increase road safety, red light camera intersections were introduced in Ontario in 2000. Not all municipalities use cameras at their intersections, but they are used in Toronto, Hamilton, Ottawa, and Halton, Peel, and Waterloo regions.

Designated intersections have a posted sign to indicate that it is a red light camera intersection. The cameras are rotated throughout the designated intersections, so not all of the intersections will have an active camera at all times. Therefore, drivers can never really be certain whether there is an active camera at an intersection. An offence takes place if a vehicle enters the intersection after the traffic light has turned red. Entering the intersection on an amber light will not result in a charge. Similarly, a driver already in the intersection (e.g., waiting to turn left) when the light changed to red will not trigger the red light camera.

Penalty

Although the set fine of $260 is the same as when a red light charge is laid by a police officer, it would not be reasonable to penalize the owner with demerit points, because the owner has no direct control over or responsibility for how the driver operates the vehicle. Therefore, there are no demerit points for a red light camera offence.

Improper Turn

The offence of making an improper turn is addressed in s. 141 of the HTA. Under subsections (2) and (3), a driver who wants to turn right at an intersection must approach the intersection in the right lane and turn into the right lane. If there are multiple marked turn lanes, the driver must stay in the corresponding lane while making the turn.

For left turns, subsection (5) states: "No driver or operator of a vehicle in an intersection shall turn left across the path of a vehicle approaching from the opposite direction unless he or she has afforded a reasonable opportunity to the driver or operator of the approaching vehicle to avoid a collision." Subsection (6) sets out the proper lanes from which to make a turn, so that the driver approaches the intersection immediately to the right of the centre line of the highway and turns left into the corresponding lane.

Commentary

Improper turns usually fall under the HTA, while illegal turns often come under a municipal bylaw. For example, a municipality may prohibit left-hand turns during rush hour, making it an illegal turn and leading to a charge under a local bylaw. But if a driver turned into the wrong lane, it would likely be an improper turn and bring a charge under the HTA.

Penalties

The set fines vary for the type of improper turn. In many cases, the set fine is $85, but if the offence takes place in a community safety zone, the set fine is either $120 or $150, depending on the circumstances.

Most of the improper turn offences come with 2 demerit points. An exception is an improper turn that results in a collision, which carries 3 demerit points.

Following Too Closely

Provisions in the HTA that govern following too closely are found in s. 158, entitled "Headway of Motor Vehicles."

General Provisions

Section 158(1) sets out the general provisions:

> 158(1) The driver of a motor vehicle or street car shall not follow another vehicle or street car more closely than is reasonable and prudent having due regard for the speed of the vehicle and the traffic on and the conditions of the highway.

Commentary

Many drivers charged with this offence have been involved in a rear-end collision. The police officer who comes to the accident scene examines the position of the vehicles, the damage to the vehicles, and tire marks on the road, and then talks to witnesses. From there, the officer may deduce that a motor vehicle was following another vehicle too closely, because the driver was unable to stop in time. In most cases, the officer has not actually witnessed the accident, and the other driver and civilian witnesses will be asked to testify for the prosecution in court.

The wording of this subsection also allows an officer to lay charges if a motor vehicle was tailgating another vehicle. However, it can be difficult for a prosecutor to prove the elements of the offence because s. 158(1) does not specify what distance would be considered too close. Without a specified distance, the appropriate distance will vary from situation to situation.

Notice that this subsection refers to reasonableness and considers the conditions of the highway. There is substantial opportunity to defend this charge because it provides subjective standards.

Commercial Motor Vehicles

In accordance with s. 158(2), a different standard applies to commercial motor vehicles:

> 158(2) The driver of a commercial motor vehicle when driving on a highway at a speed exceeding 60 kilometres per hour shall not follow within 60 metres of another motor vehicle, but this shall not be construed to prevent a commercial motor vehicle overtaking and passing another motor vehicle.

Commentary

The wording of this subsection provides an objective standard for commercial motor vehicles by setting out a specific rate of speed and distance.

PRACTICE TIP

Be sure to listen to the officer's evidence as to how he or she determined that the distance between the vehicles was 60 metres or less.

Penalties

The set fine for both commercial and non-commercial motor vehicles is $85, or $120 if the offence takes place in a community safety zone. This offence also carries 4 demerit points.

Careless Driving

Section 130 of the HTA sets out careless driving as follows:

> 130. Every person is guilty of the offence of driving carelessly who drives a vehicle or street car on a highway without due care and attention or without reasonable consideration for other persons using the highway ... .

It is important to note that the offence of careless driving is for a "vehicle," not a "motor vehicle," so that a cyclist could be charged with careless driving. As well, note that the offence must take place on a highway.

Commentary

The broad wording of this section means that a wide range of behaviours could fall within the requirements of "without due care and attention" or "without reasonable consideration." Examples include shaving while driving, cutting off another driver, falling asleep at the wheel, and hitting a parked car.

Penalties

Careless driving is considered to be one of the more serious charges in the HTA. The officer has discretion to lay charges under Part I or Part III. The officer would likely opt for Part III charges if there is an accident or serious injury, if the officer wants to require a court appearance, or if the offence takes place in a community safety zone.

Defendants charged under Part I will face a set fine of $400 plus 6 demerit points. Most drivers will be more concerned about the points than the fine because the number of points for this offence is significant, especially for insurance purposes.

Defendants charged under Part III will be required to attend court and face a fine in the range of $400 to $2,000, at the justice's discretion. A conviction under Part III also brings 6 demerit points, plus the possibility of up to six months in jail and a driver's licence suspension of up to two years.

PRACTICE TIP

Because a careless driving conviction results in 6 demerit points and a significant increase in insurance rates, it is a good idea to try to negotiate with the prosecutor. You may be able to negotiate a guilty plea to an included offence that carries fewer points. Some of the commonly used included offences for careless driving are:

- follow too closely;
- improper lane change;
- turn not in safety;
- fail to yield; and
- fail to drive in marked lane.

Fail to Report

Section 199(1) sets out the duty to report an accident:

> 199(1) Every person in charge of a motor vehicle or street car who is directly or indirectly involved in an accident shall, if the accident results in personal injuries or in damage to property apparently exceeding an amount prescribed by regulation, report the accident forthwith to the nearest police officer and furnish him or her with the information concerning the accident as may be required by the officer under subsection (3).

This section places a special legal obligation on drivers involved in accidents. Not only must they report the accident to the police, but they must report it immediately and without delay.

Notice that there is no requirement that the accident take place on a highway. That means a driver could be charged under s. 199(1) even if the accident occurred in a parking lot. The duty to report also applies to drivers who are indirectly involved in an accident, such as a driver who cut off another vehicle, causing an accident.

Commentary

The amount of damage to property that triggers this duty is set out in Regulation 596, which states that "the prescribed amount for damage to property is $1,000."

Therefore, a reasonable inspection must take place and if the damage is more than $1,000, the accident must be reported. In many cases, drivers will report the accident to a collision reporting centre instead of calling an officer to the scene.

Penalties

Three demerit points accompany a charge under s. 199(1), as well as a set fine of $85.

Fail to Remain

Section 200(1) of the HTA deals with the duty to remain at the scene of an accident:

> 200(1) Where an accident occurs on a highway, every person in charge of a vehicle or street car that is directly or indirectly involved in the accident shall,
> (a) remain at or immediately return to the scene of the accident;
> (b) render all possible assistance; and
> (c) upon request, give in writing to anyone sustaining loss or injury or to any police officer or to any witness his or her name, address, driver's licence number and jurisdiction of issuance, motor vehicle liability insurance policy insurer and policy number, name and address of the registered owner of the vehicle and the vehicle permit number.

The duty to remain at the scene of an accident, under s. 200(1), applies only if the accident occurs on a highway. It pertains to all vehicles at the scene, whether directly or indirectly involved. Because there is no threshold amount, the duty to remain begins as soon as there is an accident and is not connected to the seriousness of the accident.

Commentary

Not only does the driver have a duty to remain, but he or she also has a duty to assist and to provide particulars. In defending this charge, a paralegal should consider why the defendant left the scene and the reasonableness of that decision.

Penalties

This is considered to be a very serious charge. The fine ranges from $400 to $2,000, but because there is no set fine available, the charges will be laid under Part III. A jail term of up to six months is also possible. The driver's licence may be suspended for up to two years and 7 demerit points will be added to the defendant's driving record.

Seat Belt Legislation

The rules regarding the use of seat belts are set out in s. 106 of the Act. Section 106(2), which is directed at drivers, states:

106(2) Every person who drives on a highway a motor vehicle in which a seat belt assembly is provided for the driver shall wear the complete seat belt assembly as required by subsection (5).

With regard to passengers, s. 106(3) indicates:

106(3) Every person who is at least 16 years old and is a passenger in a motor vehicle on a highway shall.

(a) occupy a seating position for which a seat belt assembly has been provided; and

(b) wear the complete seat belt assembly as required by subsection (5).

Section 106(5) sets out the manner in which the seat belt is to be worn so that both the pelvic restraint and the torso restraint are securely fastened.

Commentary

Sections 106(6) and 106(7) of the HTA set out exceptions to the seat belt requirements. Specifically, a seat belt is not required when driving in reverse, presumably to allow the driver to turn his or her body for the best rear view. In addition, with proper documentation from a medical practitioner, a person may be exempt from wearing a seat belt for medical reasons (e.g., abdominal surgery) or because of size, build, or other physical characteristics (e.g., the person is too tall for the seat belt to be an effective restraint). There is a further exemption for someone whose work requires frequent entry into and exit from a motor vehicle, such as a garbage truck driver.

For more information about seat belts and child restraints, review Regulation 613 under the HTA.

Penalties

There is a set fine of $200 for all seat belt-related charges. Two demerit points are applied against a driver who was not wearing a seat belt or who did not ensure that a passenger under the age of 16 was wearing a seat belt. Passengers can be charged for not wearing a seat belt, but demerit points will not be applied.

Display Screens and Hand-Held Devices

In Ontario, the ban on "display screens" and "hand-held devices" took effect on October 26, 2009. There are two primary charges: viewing a display screen while driving and using a hand-held device while driving.

Display Screens

Section 78(1) of the HTA, which concerns display screens, states:

> 78(1) No person shall drive a motor vehicle on a highway if the display screen of a television, computer or other device in the motor vehicle is visible to the driver.

Commentary

Sections 78(2) and 78(3) set out some of the exceptions to this provision (e.g., GPS devices; drivers of ambulance, fire, or police vehicles). Ontario Regulation 366/09 provides additional exceptions from the ban on display screens (e.g., couriers, taxis, and limousines).

Hand-Held Devices

Hand-held communication devices, such as cellphones, are also banned. Specifically, s. 78.1(1) states:

> 78.1(1) No person shall drive a motor vehicle on a highway while holding or using a hand-held wireless communication device or other prescribed device that is capable of receiving or transmitting telephone communications, electronic data, mail or text messages.

Section 78.1(2) bans hand-held entertainment devices, such as gaming devices:

> 78.1(2) No person shall drive a motor vehicle on a highway while holding or using a hand-held electronic entertainment device or other prescribed device the primary use of which is unrelated to the safe operation of the motor vehicle.

The wording of both of these subsections indicates that hand-held devices are not permitted while driving a motor vehicle on a highway. In addition to not using a hand-held device, a motorist cannot even be holding the device while driving.

Commentary

There are several exemptions to the ban on display screens and hand-held devices. Section 78.1(3) allows for a hands-free mode to be used, and s. 78.1(5) permits a hand-held communication device to be used to contact ambulance, police, or fire department emergency services. Additional exemptions are set out in s. 78.1(4) and in Ontario Regulation 366/09.

As well, s. 78.1(6) indicates that hand-held device charges will not apply if the vehicle is off the roadway, such as on the shoulder, is not in motion, and is not impeding traffic. This allows drivers to safely pull to the side of the road and stop their vehicle in order to make a phone call or check messages.

Penalties

The set fine for display screen and hand-held device charges is $125. Although there are no demerit points associated with this charge, the officer still has the option of laying charges under these specific sections or as a careless driving charge, which carries 6 demerit points.

KEY TERMS

amending up
driving record

REVIEW QUESTIONS

True/False

_____ 1. A laser speed gun measures the round-trip time for a beam of light to reach a car and reflect back.

_____ 2. The *Highway Traffic Act* is provincial legislation.

_____ 3. The *Highway Traffic Act* specifies that a driver must stop at a stop sign for three seconds.

_____ 4. A prosecutor has the discretion to amend a speeding charge to the included offence of "disobey sign."

_____ 5. It is illegal for a driver to use a cellphone when parked off the roadway if he or she is not impeding traffic.

_____ 6. A GPS device is exempt from the ban on display screens.

_____ 7. A conviction for failing to remain at the scene of an accident would cause a defendant to lose seven demerit points.

Short Answer

1. Outline four methods that are used to detect a vehicle's rate of speed.

2. List three situations in which a motorist is more likely to be charged with careless driving under Part III than under Part I.

3. Your client was charged with speeding. He tells you that no speed limit was posted, so he drove through a built-up area in his municipality at 60 km/h. What should your client have done?

4. List three situations in which the police will come to the scene of an accident, instead of sending the driver to a collision reporting centre.

Exercises

1. Your client has been charged with driving 80 km/h in a posted 50 km/h zone. After negotiating with the prosecutor, you were able to reduce the speeding charge to 65 km/h in a 50 km/h zone.

   a. How many demerit points are associated with this charge at the original rate of speed?

   b. What is the set fine for the original rate of speed?

   c. What is the victim fine surcharge for the original rate of speed?

   d. How many demerit points are associated with the reduced rate of speed?

   e. What is the set fine for the reduced rate of speed?

   f. What is the victim fine surcharge for the reduced rate of speed?

2. Review Regulation 339/94 (see Appendix D). How many demerit points would a defendant receive if convicted of the following offences?

   a. Driving at 35km/h over the speed limit.

   b. Driving the wrong way on a divided highway.

   c. Using a cellphone while driving.

   d. Detected by a provincial offences officer driving through a red light.

   e. Detected by a red light camera driving through a red light.

Other Common Acts

16

OVERVIEW

LEARNING OUTCOMES

After reading this chapter, you will understand

- the acts, and common charges, that are commonly prosecuted in Ontario;

- Charter applicability and notice requirements;

- the areas of responsibility for which municipalities may enact bylaws; and

- how federal statutes may be prosecuted under the *Provincial Offences Act*.

INTRODUCTION

Previous chapters focused on laying the groundwork for the various procedures and processes involved in the regulatory framework in Ontario. It is important to understand how the framework functions, but you also need to understand the provisions of the enabling, or offence-creating, legislation under which a proceeding is commenced.

This chapter will discuss some of the more common offences prosecuted in Ontario under provincial legislation.

PRACTICE TIP

When representing a client, it is essential that you review the enabling provisions of the statute or bylaw that created the offence as part of case preparation.

COMPULSORY AUTOMOBILE INSURANCE ACT

The *Compulsory Automobile Insurance Act* (CAIA), R.S.O. 1990, c. C.25 requires every owner or operator of a motor vehicle on an Ontario highway to have an automobile insurance contract. Under the CAIA, the term "motor vehicle" has the same meaning as under the HTA, and includes motorized snow vehicles, all-terrain vehicles, trailers, and accessories of a motor vehicle.

The CAIA creates several offences. Some, like other regulatory offences, are minor and relatively straightforward; however, others are quite serious and can have a significant impact on your client if he or she is found guilty.

Some minor offences under the CAIA are:

- failing or refusing to surrender a licence (s. 2(6))
- failing to carry or produce the insurance card for the motor vehicle being operated (s. 3(1))
- failing to carry or produce evidence that the operator is covered under a contract of insurance (s. 3(1))
- failing to disclose the particulars of an insurance contract when requested by an individual involved in the accident (s. 4(1)).

Section 4(2) defines which particulars or information should be disclosed at a collision scene. This information should include the name and address of the insured; the make, model and serial number of the insured vehicle; the effective date and expiry date of the insurance contract; the name of the insurer and insurer's agent (if any); and the policy number of the contract.

Some major offences under the CAIA are:

- operating a motor vehicle with no insurance (s. 2(1))
- vehicle owner permitting the operation of a motor vehicle without insurance (s. 2(1))

- possessing/using/selling/producing an insurance card that is known or ought to be known to be false or invalid (s. 13.1(1))
- making false statements with respect to any information provided for the purposes of the Act, including purporting to be insured when renewing validation permits with the Ministry of Transportation and knowing that to be false (s. 13(11)).

Outside of the insurance penalties in the CAIA, driving convictions will also affect your client's insurance rating and how insurance companies will bill your client. To receive preferred or discounted rates, drivers must have a clean record; that is, usually no more than two minor convictions within a three-year period. Additional convictions can have serious implications for your client's ability to obtain insurance. Insurance rates can rise as much as 250 percent for serious convictions or multiple offences.

PRACTICE TIP

As a value-added service, it is important that you review and are familiar with the Facility Association rules and guidelines so that you can offer this option to your client who might not have other insurance options. The Facility Association (www.facilityassociation.com) is an entity established by the automobile insurance industry to ensure that automobile insurance is available to all owners and licensed drivers of motor vehicles where such owners or drivers are unable to obtain automobile insurance from regular insurance companies because of prior accidents, a poor driving record, or numerous insurance policy cancellations.

The Facility Association is an unincorporated non-profit organization of all automobile insurers that serves the following provinces and territories: Alberta, New Brunswick, Newfoundland and Labrador, Northwest Territories, Nova Scotia, Nunavut, Ontario, Prince Edward Island, and the Yukon.

Insurance obtained through the Facility Association is substantially higher than that obtained through regular insurers.

Several offences are prosecuted under the CAIA, and one of the most common offences is operating a motor vehicle without insurance. Given the nature of the offence and the penalties that are prescribed, it is commenced under Part III of the POA.

The chief justice has prescribed short-form wording and a set fine for five minor offences, and so they may be commenced under Part I of the POA. The set fines can be found in the Ontario Court of Justice, Schedule 1 to the *Compulsory Automobile Insurance Act*:

	Short-Form Wording	Section	Set Fine
1.	Fail to surrender suspended driver's licence	2(6)	$25.00
2.	Refuse to surrender suspended driver's licence	2(6)	$25.00
3.	Fail to have insurance card	3(1)	$50.00
4.	Fail to surrender insurance card	3(1)	$50.00
5.	Fail to disclose particulars of insurance	4(1)	N.S.F.*
* No Set Fine: A proceeding may still be commenced under Part I, but a summons is required.			

The offences found in s. 2(1) of the CAIA are commonly commenced under Part III of the POA. They are:

1. operate a motor vehicle without insurance, or
2. permit the operation of a motor vehicle without insurance.

The consequences of being convicted of serious offences under the CAIA, such as failing to carry insurance, are significant and represent some of the most serious of the regulatory offences involving the general public. The legislature has enacted heavy penalty provisions to serve as a deterrent to those who would risk operating motor vehicles on Ontario's highways without valid insurance (s. 2(1)) or who make false statements when claiming to be insured (s. 13(11)).

Section 2(3) of the CAIA provides the statutory framework for the penalty provisions for offences under ss. 2(1) and 13(11) of the Act. An owner or lessee of a motor vehicle who operates or permits the vehicle to be operated without insurance or shows false insurance documents to a police officer is guilty of an offence and is liable on a first conviction to a fine of not less than $5,000 and not more than $25,000 and on a subsequent conviction to a fine of not less than $10,000 and not more than $50,000 and, in addition, his or her driver's licence may be suspended for up to one year.

The CAIA also provides for a lengthy limitation period. Proceedings may be commenced at any time within three years from the date after which the offence was, or is alleged to have been, committed.

PRACTICE TIP

Many of the minor offences under the CAIA are often laid in conjunction with other driving-related charges. If your client took steps to update his or her insurance—or had valid insurance but was unable to produce proof at the time of interaction with the police officer—coming to court with all the necessary documentation may provide persuasive arguments for the prosecutor to accept a favourable plea settlement.

LIQUOR LICENCE ACT

The *Liquor Licence Act* (LLA), R.S.O. 1990, c. L.19 is a robust and sophisticated piece of legislation that is primarily responsible for establishing licensing and the safe and responsible use of alcohol in Ontario.

The Act establishes legal requirements for the sale, purchase, brewing, and consumption of alcohol in Ontario. Licensing and brewing are highly regulated and compliance is largely achieved through orders and threats of revocation of permits. As such, most administrative or non-compliance matters are dealt with through administrative monetary fines.

The Alcohol and Gaming Commission of Ontario (AGCO) is responsible for administering the *Liquor Licence Act*. Although the Commission will often perform inspections to ensure compliance, it will also form partnerships with local and regional police services to ensure effective enforcement of the responsible-use provisions of the Act.

Some Common Offences Under the Act

The LLA creates a number of offences with regard to both the consumer and the server. Common offences include:

- liquor being sold or supplied to any person who is or appears to be intoxicated (s. 29)
- persons under the age of 19 purchasing liquor or otherwise obtaining liquor (s. 30(8)) and who enter or remain on licensed premises (s. 30(10))
- the use of fake ID to enter licensed premises to purchase alcohol (s. 30(12))
- consuming alcohol in areas other than licensed establishments and having open liquor outside of one's home, a private place, or a licensed establishment (s. 31(2))
- conveying open liquor in a motor vehicle (s. 32(1)).

Responsible Use of Alcohol Under Regulation 719

Regulation 719, Licences to Sell Liquor, describes some offences that involve the responsible use of alcohol by those holding liquor licences. Sections 25 and 29 cover the service of alcohol outside of prescribed hours and the licence holder's failure to clear away within a specified time all evidence that alcohol has been served and consumed on a premises. Sections 41 and 42 deal with serving minors and the failure to check ID. Section 43 deals with overcrowding in premises that are licensed to serve alcohol, and sections 45, 45.1, 45.2, and 46 prescribe that drunkenness, unlawful gambling, violence, and disorderly conduct are not permitted on the premises or in areas adjacent to the premises under the exclusive control of the licence holder.

Penalties

Anyone convicted of an offence under the LLA faces the possibility of a maximum fine of $100,000, up to a year in jail, or both. Corporations convicted under the Act face a maximum fine of $250,000. However, corporations involved in the sale of alcohol to a minor are liable to a fine of up to $500,000. Individuals convicted of selling alcohol to a minor may receive a fine of up to $200,000 or face imprisonment of up to one year, or both a fine and imprisonment.

PRACTICE TIP

There are over 130 charges prescribed for offences under the LLA and its corresponding regulations. To be able to effectively represent your client, review the responsible-use provisions and the requirements of operating a licensed establishment.

ENVIRONMENTAL REGULATION

A particularly important area of provincial regulation today is environmental protection. The *Environmental Protection Act* (EPA), R.S.O. 1990, c. E.19, the *Clean Water Act, 2006*, S.O. 2006, c. 22, and the *Pesticides Act*, R.S.O. 1990, c. P.11 are just some examples of provincial legislation that create obligations to protect the environment and establish offences when breached.

The EPA regulates the actions of those in charge of pollutants, creating offences in such areas as spillage and littering. A person in charge of a pollutant must develop a plan to reduce the risk of spillage and respond effectively if spillage occurs. Those convicted of littering are liable to a fine of up to $1,000 for a first offence and up to $2,000 for a subsequent offence.

The *Clean Water Act* stipulates a number of obligations with regard to safe drinking water. Under this Act, if a person with source protection authority becomes aware of a drinking-water hazard, he or she must alert the Ministry of the Environment. It is also an offence to continue to engage in an activity that endangers a water supply.

The *Pesticides Act* imposes penalties on those who release pesticides into the environment outside of an ordinary course of events, and injury to the environment, animals, or persons is likely to occur.

PRACTICE TIP

If the prosecution has a strong case, you may need to work with subject-matter experts to determine the best strategy for advancing the defence and mitigating the evidence of the prosecution. Experts on soil analysis, air analysis, environmental impacts, and best practices may form a key part of a due-diligence defence.

OCCUPATIONAL HEALTH AND SAFETY ACT

The *Occupational Health and Safety Act* (OHSA), R.S.O. 1990, c. O.1 imposes duties on both workers and employers with respect to equipment, material, and protective devices to ensure that workplaces are safe.

Requirements Under the OHSA

Under the OHSA, workers must wear the clothing and equipment specified by their employers, and report any defects with such clothing or equipment (ss. 27(1) and 28(1)). Workers are also required to report to their employer any contraventions of the OHSA of which they are aware (s. 28(1)(c) and (d)). Among other duties, employers are required to develop and implement a health and safety program (s. 25(2)(j)), and formulate a policy regarding workplace violence and harassment (s. 32.0.1(1)).

The OHSA establishes a positive duty on employers to:

- provide a safe work environment,
- educate and train workers,
- have an occupational health and safety policy,
- create a violence and harassment policy,
- appoint competent supervision,
- ensure that workers and supervisors comply with the Act,
- immediately report accidents causing critical injury or death.

PRACTICE TIP

In preparing to represent a client charged with an offence under the OHSA, you should review the client's policies, procedures, and training documents. Review them again with the client and ensure that you have a functional understanding of the client's operations.

It is a contravention of the Act for any person to interfere in any way with a Ministry of Labour inspector (ss. 62(1), (2), and (3)), and this interference includes giving false information, failing to give required information, or interfering with any monitoring equipment left in the workplace. The Ministry may prosecute any person for violating the Act or the regulations, or for failing to comply with an order issued by an inspector or director of the Ministry of Labour (s. 66(1)). In deciding whether or not to prosecute, the Ministry will take into account factors that include, but are not limited to, the seriousness of the offence and whether there have been repeated contraventions or ignored orders.

Penalties

Section 66 of the OHSA provides that any person who contravenes or fails to comply with a provision of the Act or the regulations, an order or requirement of an inspector or a Director, or an order of the Minister is guilty of an offence. Failure to comply with provisions in the OHSA can result in maximum fines of $25,000 or up to 12 months in jail for persons, and a maximum fine of $500,000 for corporations.

PRACTICE TIP

Your client's ability to demonstrate that he or she took every reasonable precaution in the circumstances may constitute a defence to some of the charges under the Act.

TRESPASS TO PROPERTY ACT

The *Trespass to Property Act* (TPA), R.S.O. 1990, c. T.21 is one of the more common acts enforced by peace officers, security guards, and private citizens. It gives ordinary citizens the authority to remove unwanted individuals from their property and to post signs restricting access. There are two important definitions found in s. 1 of the TPA:

1. "Occupier," which includes a person who is in physical possession of a premises or a person (this can include a security guard or ticket collector) who has responsibility for and control over the condition of premises or the activities there carried on, or control over persons allowed to enter the premises, even if there is more than one occupier of the same premises.

   This includes anyone who is responsible for a property at any given time. It can include the owner, a security guard, or anyone else who has some written authority to act on behalf of the occupier. Anyone having control over entering a premises can act as an occupier.

2. "Premises" refers to lands and/or structures, and includes water; ships and vessels; trailers and portable structures designed or used for residence, business or shelter; and trains, railway cars, vehicles and aircraft, except while they are in operation.

   It is important to know what constitutes a premises, because many of the offence-related sections deal with access or non-access to premises, failing to leave a premises when directed, or engaging in prohibited activities on these premises.

   Mobile items can also be considered premises; for example, if someone rents a trailer and a private campsite, that person would be the occupier of a premises.

Colour of Right Defence

Your client may be able to use the defence of "colour of right." This defence has been defined in various court decisions to mean "an honest belief in a set of facts that, if they existed, would provide a legal justification or excuse for the act committed." Conducting a proper client interview and establishing the facts are crucial to successfully advancing this defence. The defence operates to excuse behaviour where ownership (or an ownership-like interest), or honest belief of the same, constitutes a valid legal justification or excuse. For example, the property had been recently sold but your client mistakenly believed it was still owned by a relative.

Signage and Notification

Before any entry can be deemed unlawful, there must be some form of notice prohibiting the entry or action:

> 3(1) Entry on premises may be prohibited by notice to that effect and entry is prohibited without any notice on premises,
>
> (a) that is a garden, field or other land that is under cultivation, including a lawn, orchard, vineyard and premises on which trees have been planted and have not attained an average height of more than two metres and woodlots on land used primarily for agricultural purposes; or
>
> (b) that is enclosed in a manner that indicates the occupier's intention to keep persons off the premises or to keep animals on the premises.

Signs that read "No Trespassing" or that contain one large red dot are familiar types of notices. The large red dot marking system is frequently used by farmers or property owners in rural areas.

Notice becomes more complicated where stores or other commercial outlets are involved. Stores often post a sign on the door that reads "No Shoplifting" or "Shoplifters will be prosecuted." If someone steals an item and is caught by store security, there is some jurisprudence, as well as commonly held interpretations, that store security is acting under the authority of both the *Criminal Code* and the *Trespass to Property Act*.

When the police arrive on the scene, they have the option of charging the suspect with engaging in a prohibited activity, in addition to laying a theft charge. But if no notice is posted on any store entrance, this charge is no longer an option. If your client has been charged under these circumstances, you should consider whether the charge has exceeded the legislative intent of the provision. The TPA provides property owners with the ability to restrict persons or activities on their property, but it should not be used as a means for enforcement of other legislative provisions under other statutes.

The different forms of notice can be found in s. 5(1) of the Act. Notice can be provided orally, in writing, or through signage. For example, if hunters are found on a farmer's property, the farmer can ask them to leave. If they do not leave, they can be charged with failing to leave the premises when directed because they have been given oral notice.

Arrest Authority

Under s. 9, a police officer or occupier of the premises has the authority to arrest anyone whom he or she believes, on reasonable and probable grounds, is contravening s. 2. It is important to remember that an occupier who arrests a suspect must immediately turn him or her over to a police officer.

The suspect must still be on the premises when arrested by an occupier. Under s. 10 of the Act, only a police officer can arrest someone who has left the premises.

If the suspect provides a false name or address to the police officer, the officer may arrest the suspect for providing false information. This is in addition to the offence, under s. 129 of the *Criminal Code*, of obstructing a peace officer.

PRACTICE TIP

In reviewing any case that involves an arrest for an offence under the TPA, turn your mind to whether your client's rights under the Charter were preserved throughout the arrest. If your client's rights were violated (no right to counsel, illegal search, or unlawful arrest), successfully bringing a motion before the court alleging the Charter breach may result in a stay of the charges.

Offence Categories and Penalties

Most offences under the TPA are dealt with in s. 2(1). There are three important offence categories:

1. Entering a premises when it is prohibited.
2. Carrying out a prohibited activity.
3. Failing to leave when directed.

It is important to remember these three categories because they each have their own facts in issue that need to be proven. Section 2(1) reads:

> 2(1) Every person who is not acting under a right or authority conferred by law and who,
>
>> (a) without the express permission of the occupier, the proof of which rests on the defendant,
>>
>>> (i) enters on premises when entry is prohibited under this Act, or
>>>
>>> (ii) engages in an activity on premises when the activity is prohibited under this Act; or
>>
>> (b) does not leave the premises immediately after he or she is directed to do so by the occupier of the premises or a person authorized by the occupier,
>
> is guilty of an offence and on conviction is liable to a fine of not more than $2,000.

The maximum fine is $2,000, but in reality, most offences are dealt with using a Part I certificate of offence, because the option of an out-of-court settlement is available.

The chief justice has prescribed the following short-form wordings and corresponding set fines for offences under the Ontario Court of Justice, Schedule 85 to the *Trespass to Property Act*:

	Charge	Section	Set Fine
1.	Enter premises when entry prohibited	2(1)(a)(i)	$50.00
2.	Engage in prohibited activity on premises	2(1)(a)(ii)	$50.00
3.	Fail to leave premises when directed	2(1)(b)	$50.00

BLIND PERSONS' RIGHTS ACT

The intent of the *Blind Persons' Rights Act*, R.S.O. 1990, c. B.7 is to ensure that people who are visually impaired and who use guide dogs receive the same access to accommodation, services, and facilities as sighted people. This legislation is necessary because some facilities restrict access to animals.

Access with a Guide Dog

Many hotels, for example, do not allow patrons to bring their pet dogs. For blind persons, however, their dogs are not merely pets, but are service dogs.

This is why s. 2(1) of the Act clearly stipulates access:

2(1) No person, directly or indirectly, alone or with another, by himself, herself or itself or by the interposition of another, shall,

(a) deny to any person the accommodation, services or facilities available in any place to which the public is customarily admitted; or

(b) discriminate against any person with respect to the accommodation, services or facilities available in any place to which the public is customarily admitted, or the charges for the use thereof,

for the reason that he or she is a blind person accompanied by a guide dog.

The first part of this section states that no one, regardless of the circumstances, may deny access. For example, a person can claim that he or she was merely following directions from an employer in denying access. That is not a defence under this section, and everyone (whether employer or employee) is equally liable.

Paragraphs (a) and (b) state that a person with a guide dog cannot be denied access or be discriminated against when entering a place normally used by the public. This provision includes restaurants, which have often been charged with violating this section of the Act.

Using a White Cane and Carrying an ID Card

Under s. 3, only a person who is visually impaired may use a white cane in public:

(3) No person, other than a blind person, shall carry or use a cane or walking stick, the major part of which is white, in any public place, public thoroughfare or public conveyance.

Section 4 deals with issuing identification cards for any blind person and his or her guide dog. When enforcing any section under this Act, a police officer must prove that the person was visually impaired or blind.

Documentary evidence, such as an identification card, allows an officer to satisfy the fact in issue, which is necessary to form the reasonable grounds that the person was blind.

Penalties

Anyone who is convicted of contravening s. 2 by denying accommodation, services, or facilities to a blind person accompanied by a guide dog faces a maximum fine of $5,000. With a fine of up to $5,000, officers would proceed by way of a Part III summons and information. Otherwise, the fine would be limited to a maximum of $500 under Part I.

Section 6(2) states that any person who falsely identifies themselves as a blind person or who uses a white cane to benefit from the *Blind Persons' Rights Act* is guilty of an offence and if convicted is liable to a fine not exceeding $500.

Because the fine does not exceed $500, a Part I certificate of offence, rather than a Part III summons and information, may be used to charge someone with this offence. It must be proven that the person wanted to appear to be blind and was trying to establish some benefit. It would not be an offence for a person to say that he or she was blind and to use a white cane, unless a benefit was received, such as a discount in transit fares.

DOG OWNERS' LIABILITY ACT

The *Dog Owners' Liability Act* (DOLA) contains provisions for court proceedings against dog owners where violence or "menace" toward "persons or domestic animals" is alleged, or where it is alleged that the owner has committed an offence under the Act.

Section 1(1) of the Act defines a dog owner as "a person who possesses or harbours the dog and, where the owner is a minor, the person responsible for the custody of the minor."

Two "streams" of court orders are set out in the Act—one for biting, attacking, or menacing incidents and the other for general DOLA-related contraventions. If certain criteria are met, court proceedings may result in an order that a dog be destroyed or specific control measures be imposed, under s. 4.

The provisions include mandatory destruction of pit bulls where grounds for a court order are satisfied. It is important to note that court proceedings can be commenced against a dog owner regardless of whether the dog is in the custody of a pound, although dogs in the pound system that are suspected of being pit bulls are subject to much more summary, non-court treatment.

Proceedings under the Act are conducted in the Ontario Court of Justice, and the procedures for court orders are largely the same as those used for Part III prosecutions under the POA. A significant variation from the Part III procedures is that instead of the complainant swearing an information before a justice of the peace alleging the offence, a sworn statement is filed "attesting, on reasonable and probable grounds, to the existence of facts that would justify the order sought" (s. 161(a) of the POA; *Courts of Justice Act*, Regulation 200/90, Form 142).

Further, instead of being asked to enter a plea, the defendant will be asked whether he or she intends to dispute the making of the order, under s. 161(b) of the POA. Under s. 4(1.3) of the DOLA, when hearing an application for such an order, the court will use the civil standard of proof on a balance of probabilities in making findings of fact. This distinguishes such proceedings from typical criminal or regulatory prosecutions, where the higher standard of beyond a reasonable doubt is used. This civil standard applies to a court order proceeding even if it is commenced in conjunction with a prosecution, although the prosecution will be decided using the higher standard.

In such a proceeding, the onus of proof lies with the applicant, or the party commencing the proceeding, but if it is alleged that the dog is a pit bull, the onus rests on the owner to prove otherwise, under s. 4(10).

Under s. 4(1), a proceeding may be commenced in the Ontario Court of Justice for an order against an owner to destroy or control a dog if it is alleged that:

> 4(1) ...
>> (a) the dog has bitten or attacked a person or domestic animal;
>> (b) the dog has behaved in a manner that poses a menace to the safety of persons or domestic animals; or
>> (c) the owner did not exercise reasonable precautions to prevent the dog from,
>>> (i) biting or attacking a person or domestic animal, or
>>> (ii) behaving in a manner that poses a menace to the safety of persons or domestic animals.

PRACTICE TIP

It is important to remember that in a DOLA case your client may be under significant emotional stress. Most dog owners are very attached to their pets and the process is challenging for them. Take extra time to prepare your client for the proceeding and ensure that they are able to control their emotional reactions.

Penalties

Section 18 provides the penalties for violating the Act. Any individual who contravenes any provision of the Act or its regulations or who contravenes an order made under the Act or the regulations is liable upon conviction to a fine of not more than $10,000 or to imprisonment for a term of not more than six months, or both. The fine for a corporation is $60,000. Section 18(3) authorizes additional penalties as determined by the court making the conviction—specifically, in addition to any other penalty, a court may order the person convicted to make compensation or restitution in relation to the offence.

The chief justice has not prescribed short-form wordings or set fines under Part I of the POA for DOLA offences. Most offences are usually commenced under Part III of the POA or, if the municipality has established animal control offences, a ticket may be issued under that bylaw if applicable.

CHARTER ISSUES

It is clear that the *Canadian Charter of Rights and Freedoms* applies to regulatory offences in general. While such offences may not be held to the same stringent standard as criminal matters, the provisions of the Charter still apply and should always be reviewed in the context of any proceeding.

Legal arguments have been made that the Charter applies less to matters commenced under Part I or Part II of the POA than to those under Part III, as the only penalty is economic and the Charter provides no right to economic security. Even so, your client is still entitled to the common-law protection of procedural fairness, and has an inherent right to know the charges and be provided with disclosure.

As a licensed paralegal, it is very important that you be aware of the notice requirements under the *Courts of Justice Act* for bringing an application for a violation of the Charter, which is called a notice of constitutional question:

> 109(1) Notice of a constitutional question shall be served on the Attorney General of Canada and the Attorney General of Ontario in the following circumstances:
>
> 1. The constitutional validity or constitutional applicability of an Act of the Parliament of Canada or the Legislature, of a regulation or by-law made under such an Act or of a rule of common law is in question.
>
> 2. A remedy is claimed under subsection 24(1) of the *Canadian Charter of Rights and Freedoms* in relation to an act or omission of the Government of Canada or the Government of Ontario.
>
> 109(2) If a party fails to give notice in accordance with this section, the Act, regulation, by-law or rule of common law shall not be adjudged to be invalid or inapplicable, or the remedy shall not be granted, as the case may be.

A form has been approved for filing a notice of constitutional question (see Appendix B), but it would be wise to prepare a factum detailing your legal arguments, and the facts and the law upon which you are relying in advancing the constitutional issue.

PRACTICE TIP

Take time to build relationships with other practising paralegals. Rely on the mentoring of more experienced practitioners and seek out opportunities to share information and sample templates on how to best structure a proper factum for a notice of constitutional question.

MUNICIPAL BYLAWS

Municipal bylaws are an area of specialty within provincial law. Every paralegal practising regulatory law in Ontario should have an understanding of the *Municipal Act, 2001*, and its spheres of jurisdiction and enforcement sections. Sections 9, 10, and 11 of the Act, as well as Part IV, should form part of your required knowledge base.

Section 9 of the Act provides a municipality the powers of a natural person for the purpose of exercising its authority under this or any other Act.

Sections 10 and 11 are substantially similar but distinguish between an single-tier municipality and an upper-tier/lower-tier municipality. An example of a single tier municipality would be the City of Barrie in Ontario. An example of a lower-tier/upper-tier municipality is that of the Town of Aurora (lower-tier) being within the Regional Municipality of York (upper-tier).

Regardless of whether a municipality is single, lower or upper tier, the Act provides a broad, general power for municipalities to license businesses and to license, regulate, and govern persons carrying on or engaged in businesses.

Paralegals must have an operational understanding of the legislative requirements and the enabling statutory provisions. Sections 10(2) and 11(3) and Part IV of the Act give municipalities a substantial arsenal to enact bylaws in the public interest, addressing a wide variety of activities and issues:

- governance structure of the municipality and its local boards;
- accountability and transparency of the municipality and its operations and of its local boards and their operations;
- financial management of the municipality and its local boards;
- public assets of the municipality acquired for the purpose of exercising its authority under this or any other Act;
- economic, social and environmental well-being of the municipality;
- health, safety, and well-being of persons;
- services and things that the municipality is authorized to provide under s. 10(1);
- protection of persons and property, including consumer protection;
- animals;
- structures, including fences and signs; and
- business licensing.

Part IV of the Act includes the licensing of adult entertainment establishments, tow trucks, taxicabs, trailers, and motor vehicle racing.

Municipalities are increasingly involved in regulating everyday elements of our lives and have broad legislative authority under the Act. A paralegal needs to understand the links between municipal authority and provincial authority. Municipalities may be responsible for enforcing various provincial statutes, such as the *Building Code*, the *Planning Act*, and various public welfare statutes that are regulatory in nature.

Paralegals may be called on to represent clients in cases involving charges for:

- *Building Code* violations,
- licensing appeal tribunals and hearings,
- animal control offences,
- massage parlour offences,
- property standards concerns, noise bylaw infractions, and health code violations.

PRACTICE TIP

Municipal bylaw and regulatory schemes can be very complex and may involve various procedural streams, such as provincial offences court, the Superior Court of Justice, and administrative tribunals. If you are pursuing a municipal law practice, ensure that you improve your skills with specific training in the areas of municipal law and administrative law. Visit www.amcto.com for training courses and consult the LSUC website for professional development opportunities in these areas.

FEDERAL ACTS

Designated federal statutes may be prosecuted under the POA through a modified procedure authorized by the *Contraventions Act*, S.C. 1992, c. 47.

The *Contraventions Act* provides a procedure to prosecute a failure to comply with federal provisions of a regulatory nature. The Act allows the federal government to make regulations designating federal statutory offences as "contraventions" and to distinguish them from criminal offences. It reflects the distinction between these minor offences and criminal offences, and alters or abolishes the legal consequences of being convicted of a contravention.

The Act also allows Ottawa to establish the fine associated with a federal contravention. That amount is systematically lower than the maximum fine an offender could face should the offence be prosecuted by way of summary conviction.

The following example illustrates this principle. According to the Historic Canals Regulations, SOR/93-220, adopted under the *Department of Transport Act*, "no person shall take off, land or moor an aircraft ... on the navigation channel of a historic canal." The federal government has designated this offence as a contravention. Therefore, an enforcement authority may elect to issue a ticket to someone accused of violating this provision. Should the person be found guilty, he or she will be required to pay a fine of $200.

It is impossible to list all federal statutory offences that have been designated as contraventions. To date, there are close to 3,000 such offences, involving more than 20 federal laws and more than 45 sets of regulations.

Only those offences that have been designated as contraventions by the governor in council may be prosecuted under the *Contraventions Act*. To be designated as a contravention, an offence must be consistent with the underlying philosophy of the

Act, which centres on the prosecution of less serious federal offences. The short-form descriptions of these designated offences and the applicable fines are found in the Contraventions Regulations.

In all provinces and territories, except Ontario and Quebec, the attorney general of Canada is responsible for prosecutions under the Act, either through its regional offices or Crown agents. Ontario and Quebec have chosen to prosecute contraventions under the Act on their own, in part to ensure the integrity of their respective offence schemes.

Although the *Contraventions Act* comprises more than 80 sections, only certain provisions create an adequate legal framework that permits the designated offences to be prosecuted under a modified procedure under the POA. Essentially, once a contravention proceeding has begun under the POA, the procedures and processes are identical to those of a regular POA proceeding. These provisions are listed in s. 65.1(2) of the Act and are the only provisions that apply in this context. They are: ss. 2-5, 7, 42, 54, 55, 58, 59, 63-65, 65.2, 65.3, and 86, as well as s. 8(1)(a), (b), (c), (e), and (f), and ss. 8(1.1) to (7) and 17.

REVIEW QUESTIONS

True/False

_____ 1. The *Trespass to Property Act* has no statutory maximum fine.

_____ 2. If a person is convicted of a contravention, they will have a criminal record.

_____ 3. The *Compulsory Automobile Insurance Act* requires all drivers operating a motor vehicle to have a valid contract of insurance.

_____ 4. It is permissible under the LLA to have an open container of liquor in a vehicle provided it is not being consumed by the driver.

_____ 5. If you are alleging a violation of the *Canadian Charter of Rights and Freedoms*, a "notice of constitutional question" must be served on both the federal and provincial attorneys general.

_____ 6. It is an offence to fail to leave a public mall after being ordered to do so by a security guard.

_____ 7. The *Occupational Health and Safety Act* only places a duty on employers to make the workplace safe.

_____ 8. The *Clean Water Act* requires those in charge of water treatment facilities to notify the Ministry of the Environment if they become aware of any issue with water safety.

Short Answer

1. What was one of the primary reasons the federal government enacted the *Contraventions Act*?

2. How can a property owner or agent give notice that entry is prohibited under the *Trespass to Property Act*?

3. What is the limitation period under the *Compulsory Automobile Insurance Act* and what process would need to be used under the *Provincial Offences Act* to commence a proceeding?

4. Under the LLA, persons may be removed by a licensed establishment or a holder of a permit for three reasons. What are they? Cite the statutory authority.

5. Describe the procedure and standard of proof for orders under the *Dog Owners' Liability Act*.

Exercise

Scenario

Your client has been charged with "failing to leave premises when directed" under the *Trespass to Property Act*. During your client interview he told you that on January 18, 2013 he was walking through the Sunset Mall in the City of Mississauga when he was approached by mall security. He was questioned about why he was in the mall. He advised you that no matter what he said, the security guard continued to "harass" him. Without any further discussion he was told by the security guard that he was under arrest for "failing to leave premises when directed." Your client claims that he was never asked to leave. You request disclosure and learn that Peel Regional Police attended the scene and released your client on a Part III summons for the offence. Upon looking into the disclosure further you believe that your client was never told by the security guard to leave the premises and that there are no notes or evidence to suggest that upon his arrest he was read his rights to counsel or provided with any information other than the summons. He was then told to "get lost" after being served with the summons.

Task

Working alone or with a partner, determine what, if any, violation of your client's Charter rights may have occurred, and prepare an application asserting a violation of your client's rights under the Charter. Go to the Ontario Court Forms website (www.ontariocourtforms.on.ca). Click "English" to enter the site. Click on "Rules of Civil Procedure Forms" and scroll down to Form 4F, Notice of Constitutional Question. Download and complete the Notice of Constitutional Question form. The Law Society of Upper Canada's website (http://rc.lsuc.on.ca) contains additional information on Charter claims in its Practice Resources section (see "Administrative Law" under "How-To Briefs").

Fast Facts to Review

Defendant:	John Doe
Date of Offence:	Friday, January 18, 2013
Court Date:	Wednesday, August 21, 2013
Court:	City of Mississauga, 950 Burnhamthorpe Road West, Mississauga, Ontario L5C 3B4
Time:	1:30 p.m.
Courtroom:	M3
Offence:	Failing to leave premises when directed
Case No.:	C-12345678

- Nothing in the disclosure suggests that he was ever asked to leave.
- There is nothing to support why he would have been asked to leave.
- If he was in fact asked to leave, there is no evidence to suggest that he was provided with any opportunity to comply with that request prior to being arrested.
- He was not advised of the reason for arrest or provided with his rights with respect to retaining and instructing counsel.

Provincial Offences Act

A

PROVINCIAL OFFENCES ACT
R.S.O. 1990, c. P.33

INTERPRETATION

Interpretation

1(1) In this Act,

"certificate" means a certificate of offence issued under Part I or a certificate of parking infraction issued under Part II;

"court" means the Ontario Court of Justice;

"judge" means a provincial judge;

"justice" means a provincial judge or a justice of the peace;

"offence" means an offence under an Act of the Legislature or under a regulation or by-law made under the authority of an Act of the Legislature;

"police officer" means a chief of police or other police officer but does not include a special constable or by-law enforcement officer;

"prescribed" means prescribed by the rules of court;

"prosecutor" means the Attorney General or, where the Attorney General does not intervene, means the person who issues a certificate or lays an information and includes an agent acting on behalf of either of them;

"provincial offences officer" means,

   (a) a police officer,

   (b) a constable appointed pursuant to any Act,

   (c) a municipal law enforcement officer referred to in subsection 101(4) of the *Municipal Act, 2001* or in subsection 79(1) of the *City of Toronto Act, 2006*, while in the discharge of his or her duties,

   (d) a by-law enforcement officer of any municipality or of any local board of any municipality, while in the discharge of his or her duties,

   (e) an officer, employee or agent of any municipality or of any local board of any municipality whose responsibilities include the enforcement of a by-law, an Act or a regulation under an Act, while in the discharge of his or her duties, or

   (f) a person designated under subsection (3);

"representative" means, in respect of a proceeding to which this Act applies, a person authorized under the *Law Society Act* to represent a person in that proceeding;

"set fine" means the amount of fine set by the Chief Justice of the Ontario Court of Justice for an offence for the purpose of proceedings commenced under Part I or II.

   (2) Repealed.

Designation of provincial offences officers

   (3) A minister of the Crown may designate in writing any person or class of persons as a provincial offences officer for the purposes of all or any class of offences.

General

Purpose of Act

2(1) The purpose of this Act is to replace the summary conviction procedure for the prosecution of provincial offences, including the provisions adopted by reference to the *Criminal Code* (Canada), with a procedure that reflects the distinction between provincial offences and criminal offences.

Interpretation

(2) Where, as an aid to the interpretation of provisions of this Act, recourse is had to the judicial interpretation of and practices under corresponding provisions of the *Criminal Code* (Canada), any variation in wording without change in substance shall not, in itself, be construed to intend a change of meaning.

PART I
COMMENCEMENT OF PROCEEDINGS BY CERTIFICATE OF OFFENCE

Certificate of offence and offence notice

3(1) In addition to the procedure set out in Part III for commencing a proceeding by laying an information, a proceeding in respect of an offence may be commenced by filing a certificate of offence alleging the offence in the office of the court.

Issuance and service

(2) A provincial offences officer who believes that one or more persons have committed an offence may issue, by completing and signing in the form prescribed under section 13,

(a) a certificate of offence certifying that an offence has been committed; and

(b) either an offence notice indicating the set fine for the offence or a summons.

Service

(3) The offence notice or summons shall be served personally upon the person charged within thirty days after the alleged offence occurred.

(4) Repealed.

Certificate of service

(5) Where service is made by the provincial offences officer who issued the certificate of offence, the officer shall certify on the certificate of offence that he or she personally served the offence notice or summons on the person charged and the date of service.

Affidavit of service

(6) Where service is made by a person other than the provincial offences officer who issued the certificate of offence, he or she shall complete an affidavit of service in the prescribed form.

Certificate as evidence

(7) A certificate of service of an offence notice or summons purporting to be signed by the provincial offences officer issuing it or an affidavit of service under subsection (6) shall be received in evidence and is proof of personal service in the absence of evidence to the contrary.

Officer not to act as agent

(8) The provincial offences officer who serves an offence notice or summons under this section shall not receive payment of any money in respect of a fine, or receive the offence notice for delivery to the court.

Filing of certificate of offence

4. A certificate of offence shall be filed in the office of the court as soon as is practicable, but no later than seven days after service of the offence notice or summons.

Having a trial

5(1) A defendant who is served with an offence notice may give notice of intention to appear in court for the purpose of entering a plea and having a trial of the matter.

Notice of intention to appear in offence notice

(2) If the offence notice includes a part with a notice of intention to appear, the defendant must give notice of intention to appear by,

(a) completing the notice of intention to appear part of the offence notice; and

(b) delivering the offence notice to the court office specified in it in the manner provided in the offence notice.

Notice of intention to appear to be filed in person

(3) If the offence notice requires the notice of intention to appear to be filed in person, the defendant must give the notice of intention to appear by,

(a) attending in person or by representative at the court office specified in the offence notice at the time or times specified in the offence notice; and

(b) filing a notice of intention to appear in the form prescribed under section 13 with the clerk of the court.

Specified court office

(4) A notice of intention to appear under subsection (3) is not valid if the defendant files the notice of intention to appear at a court office other than the one specified on the offence notice.

Notice of trial

(5) Where a notice of intention to appear is received under subsection (2) or (3), the clerk of the court shall, as soon as is practicable, give notice to the defendant and the prosecutor of the time and place of the trial.

Rescheduling time of trial

(6) The clerk of the court may, for administrative reasons, reschedule the time of the trial by giving a revised notice to the defendant and the prosecutor within 21 days of giving the notice referred to in subsection (5).

Availability of meeting procedure

5.1(1) This section applies where the offence notice requires the notice of intention to appear to be filed in person in the form prescribed under section 13.

Option for meeting with the prosecutor

(2) Instead of filing a notice of intention to appear under subsection 5(3), a defendant may request a meeting with the prosecutor to discuss the resolution of the offence by,

(a) indicating that request on the offence notice; and

(b) delivering the offence notice to the court office specified on it within 15 days after the defendant was served with the offence notice.

Notice of meeting time

(3) Where a defendant requests a meeting with the prosecutor under subsection (2), the clerk of the court shall, as soon as is practicable, give notice to the defendant and the prosecutor of the time and place of their meeting.

Rescheduling the meeting time

(4) If the time for the meeting scheduled in the notice under subsection (3) is not suitable for the defendant, the defendant may, at least two days before the scheduled time of the meeting, deliver to the clerk of the court one written request to reschedule the time for the meeting and the clerk shall arrange a new meeting time to take place within 30 days of the time scheduled in the notice under subsection (3).

Notice of rescheduled meeting time

(5) Where a meeting time is rescheduled under subsection (4), the clerk of the court shall, as soon as is practicable, give notice to the defendant and the prosecutor of the rescheduled time and the place of their meeting.

Meeting by electronic method

(6) The defendant and the prosecutor may, if unable to attend in person because of remoteness, attend their meeting by electronic method in accordance with section 83.1.

Agreement on plea of guilty and submissions

(7) At their meeting, the defendant and the prosecutor may agree that,

(a) the defendant will enter a guilty plea to the offence or a substituted offence; and

(b) the defendant and the prosecutor will make submissions as to penalty, including an extension of time for payment.

Appearance before justice

(8) If an agreement is reached under subsection (7), the defendant shall, as directed by the prosecutor,

(a) appear with the prosecutor before a justice sitting in court and orally enter the plea and make submissions; or

(b) appear without the prosecutor before a justice sitting in court within 10 days, enter the plea orally and make the submissions in the form determined by the regulations.

Conviction

(9) Upon receiving the plea and submissions under subsection (8), the justice may,

(a) require the prosecutor to appear and speak to the submissions, if the submissions were submitted under clause (8)(b); and

(b) enter a conviction and impose the set fine or such other fine as is permitted by law in respect of the offence for which the plea was entered.

If no justice available

(10) If no justice is available after the meeting to conduct the proceeding under clause (8)(a), the clerk of the court shall, as soon as practicable, give notice to the defendant and the prosecutor of the time and place for their joint appearance before a justice.

Notice of trial

(11) The clerk of the court shall, as soon as is practicable, give notice to the defendant and the prosecutor of the time and place of the trial if,

(a) an agreement is not reached under subsection (7); or

(b) the justice does not accept the guilty plea and refers the matter to trial.

Rescheduling time of trial

(12) The clerk of the court may, for administrative reasons, reschedule the time of the trial by giving a revised notice to the defendant and the prosecutor within 21 days of giving the notice referred to subsection (11).

5.1.1 Repealed.

Challenge to officer's evidence

5.2(1) A defendant who gives notice of an intention to appear in court for the purpose of entering a plea and having a trial of the matter shall indicate on the notice of intention to appear or offence notice if the defendant intends to challenge the evidence of the provincial offences officer.

Notifying officer

(2) If the defendant indicates an intention to challenge the officer's evidence, the clerk of the court shall notify the officer.

Note: On a day to be named by proclamation of the Lieutenant Governor, section 5.2 is repealed. See: 2009, c. 33, Sched. 4, ss. 1(9), 5(4).

6. Repealed.

Plea of guilty with submissions

7(1) A defendant who does not have the option of meeting with the prosecutor under section 5.1 and does not wish to dispute the charge in the offence notice, but wishes to make submissions as to penalty, including an extension of time for payment, may attend at the time and place specified in the notice and may appear before a justice sitting in court for the purpose of pleading guilty to the offence and making submissions as to penalty, and the justice may enter a conviction and impose the set fine or such lesser fine as is permitted by law.

Submissions under oath

(2) The justice may require submissions under subsection (1) to be made under oath, orally or by affidavit.

Payment out of court

8(1) A defendant who does not wish to dispute the charge in the offence notice may, in the manner indicated on the offence notice, pay the set fine and all applicable costs and surcharges fixed by the regulations.

Effect of payment

(2) Acceptance by the court office of payment under subsection (1) constitutes,

    (a) a plea of guilty by the defendant;

    (b) conviction of the defendant for the offence; and

    (c) imposition of a fine in the amount of the set fine for the offence.

Deemed not to dispute charge

9(1) A defendant is deemed to not wish to dispute the charge where,

    (a) at least 15 days have elapsed after the defendant was served with the offence notice and the defendant did not give notice of intention to appear under section 5, did not request a meeting with the prosecutor in accordance with section 5.1 and did not plead guilty under section 7 or 8;

    (b) the defendant requested a meeting with the prosecutor in accordance with section 5.1 but did not attend the scheduled meeting with the prosecutor; or

(c) the defendant reached an agreement with the prosecutor under subsection 5.1(7) but did not appear at a sentencing hearing with a justice under subsection 5.1(8).

Action by justice

(2) Where a defendant is deemed to not wish to dispute the charge, a justice shall examine the certificate of offence and shall,

(a) where the certificate of offence is complete and regular on its face, enter a conviction in the defendant's absence and without a hearing and impose the set fine for the offence; or

(b) where the certificate of offence is not complete and regular on its face, quash the proceeding.

Conviction without proof of by-law

(3) Where the offence is in respect of an offence under a by-law of a municipality, the justice shall enter a conviction under clause (2)(a) without proof of the by-law that creates the offence if the certificate of offence is complete and regular on its face.

Failure to appear at trial

9.1(1) A defendant is deemed to not wish to dispute the charge where the defendant has been issued a notice of the time and place of trial and fails to appear at the time and place appointed for the trial.

Examination by justice

(2) If subsection (1) applies, section 54 does not apply, and a justice shall examine the certificate of offence and shall without a hearing enter a conviction in the defendant's absence and impose the set fine for the offence if the certificate is complete and regular on its face.

Quashing proceeding

(3) The justice shall quash the proceeding if he or she is not able to enter a conviction.

Signature on notice

10. A signature on an offence notice or notice of intention to appear purporting to be that of the defendant is proof, in the absence of evidence to the contrary, that it is the signature of the defendant.

Reopening
Application to strike out conviction

11(1) A defendant who was convicted without a hearing may, within 15 days of becoming aware of the conviction, apply to a justice to strike out the conviction.

Striking out the conviction

(2) Upon application under subsection (1), a justice shall strike out a conviction if satisfied by affidavit of the defendant that, through no fault of the defendant, the defendant was unable to appear for a hearing or for a meeting under section 5.1 or the defendant did not receive delivery of a notice or document relating to the offence.

If conviction struck out

(3) If the justice strikes out the conviction, the justice shall,

(a) proceed under section 7, if the offence notice does not require the notice of intention to appear to be filed in person and the defendant wishes to proceed under that section;

(b) direct the clerk of the court to give notice to the defendant and the prosecutor of the time and place of their meeting under subsection 5.1(3), if the offence notice requires the notice of intention to appear to be filed in person and the defendant wishes to proceed under that section; or

(c) direct the clerk of the court to give notice to the defendant and the prosecutor of the time and place of the trial.

Rescheduling time of trial

(4) The clerk of the court may, for administrative reasons, reschedule the time of the trial by giving a revised notice to the defendant and the prosecutor within 21 days of giving the notice referred to clause (3)(c).

Certificate

(5) A justice who strikes out a conviction under subsection (2) shall give the defendant a certificate of the fact in the prescribed form.

Error by municipality

11.1(1) A municipality or other body may apply to a justice requesting that a conviction be struck out if the defendant was convicted because of an error made by the municipality or other body.

Striking out conviction

(2) On an application by a municipality or other body, if a justice is satisfied that an error was made, the justice shall strike out the conviction.

Notice to defendant

(3) If the justice strikes out the conviction, the municipality or other body shall notify the defendant of that fact.

Consequences of conviction
Penalty

12(1) Where the penalty prescribed for an offence includes a fine of more than $1,000 or imprisonment and a proceeding is commenced under this Part, the provision for fine or imprisonment does not apply and in lieu thereof the offence is punishable by a fine of not more than the maximum fine prescribed for the offence or $1,000, whichever is the lesser.

Transitional

(1.1) Subsection (1) applies only to an offence committed on or after the day subsection 1(18) of Schedule 4 to the *Good Government Act, 2009* comes into force.

Other consequences of conviction

(2) Where a person is convicted of an offence in a proceeding initiated by an offence notice,

(a) a provision in or under any other Act that provides for an action or result following upon a conviction of an offence does not apply to the conviction, except,

(i) for the purpose of carrying out the sentence imposed,

(ii) for the purpose of recording and proving the conviction,

(iii) for the purposes of giving effect to any action or result provided for under the *Highway Traffic Act*, and

(iv) Repealed.

(v) for the purposes of section 16 of the *Smoke-Free Ontario Act*; and

(b) any thing seized in connection with the offence after the service of the offence notice is not liable to forfeiture.

Regulations

13(1) The Lieutenant Governor in Council may make regulations,

(a) Repealed.

(b) authorizing the use in a form prescribed under clause (1.1)(a) of any word or expression to designate an offence.

(c) Repealed.

(d) Repealed.

Same, Attorney General

(1.1) The Attorney General may make regulations,

(a) prescribing the form of certificates of offence, offence notices and summonses and such other forms as are considered necessary under this Part;

(b) respecting any matter that is considered necessary to provide for the use of the forms under this Part.

Sufficiency of abbreviated wording

(2) The use on a form prescribed under clause (1.1)(a) of any word or expression authorized by the regulations to designate an offence is sufficient for all purposes to describe the offence designated by such word or expression.

Idem

(3) Where the regulations do not authorize the use of a word or expression to describe an offence in a form prescribed under clause (1.1)(a), the offence may be described in accordance with section 25.

PART II

COMMENCEMENT OF PROCEEDINGS FOR PARKING INFRACTIONS

"Parking infraction," Part II

14. In this Part,

"parking infraction" means any unlawful parking, standing or stopping of a vehicle that constitutes an offence.

Proceeding, parking infraction

14.1 In addition to the procedure set out in Part III for commencing a proceeding by laying an information, a proceeding in respect of a parking infraction may be commenced in accordance with this Part.

Certificate and notice of parking infraction

15(1) A provincial offences officer who believes from his or her personal knowledge that one or more persons have committed a parking infraction may issue,

(a) a certificate of parking infraction certifying that a parking infraction has been committed; and

(b) a parking infraction notice indicating the set fine for the infraction.

Idem

(2) The provincial offences officer shall complete and sign the certificate and notice in the form prescribed under section 20.

Municipal by-laws

(3) If the alleged infraction is under a by-law of a municipality, it is not necessary to include a reference to the number of the by-law on the certificate or notice.

Service on owner

(4) The issuing provincial offences officer may serve the parking infraction notice on the owner of the vehicle identified in the notice,

(a) by affixing it to the vehicle in a conspicuous place at the time of the alleged infraction; or

(b) by delivering it personally to the person having care and control of the vehicle at the time of the alleged infraction.

Service on operator

(5) The issuing provincial offences officer may serve the parking infraction notice on the operator of a vehicle by delivering it to the operator personally at the time of the alleged infraction.

Certificate of service

(6) The issuing provincial offences officer shall certify on the certificate of parking infraction that he or she served the parking infraction notice on the person charged and the date and method of service.

Certificate as evidence

(7) If it appears that the provincial offences officer who issued a certificate of parking infraction has certified service of the parking infraction notice and signed the certificate, the certificate shall be received in evidence and is proof of service unless there is evidence to the contrary.

Payment out of court

16. A defendant who does not wish to dispute the charge may deliver the notice and amount of the set fine to the place shown on the notice.

Intention to appear

17(1) A defendant who is served with a parking infraction notice may give notice of intention to appear in court for the purpose of entering a plea and having a trial of the matter by so indicating on the parking infraction notice and delivering the notice to the place specified in it.

Proceeding commenced

(2) If a defendant gives notice of an intention to appear, a proceeding may be commenced in respect of the charge if it is done within seventy-five days after the day on which the alleged infraction occurred.

Idem

(3) The proceeding shall be commenced by filing in the office of the court,

(a) the certificate of parking infraction; and

(b) if the parking infraction is alleged against the defendant as owner of a vehicle, evidence of the ownership of the vehicle.

Notice of trial

(4) As soon as practicable after the proceeding is commenced, the clerk of the court or a person designated by the regulations shall give notice to the defendant and prosecutor of the time and place of the trial.

Rescheduling time of trial

(4.1) The clerk of the court may, for administrative reasons, reschedule the time of the trial by giving a revised notice to the defendant and the prosecutor within 21 days of giving the notice referred to subsection (4).

Certificate not invalid without by-law number

(5) A certificate of parking infraction issued for an infraction under a by-law of a municipality is not insufficient or irregular by reason only that it does not identify the by-law that creates the offence if the notice of trial given to the defendant identifies the by-law.

Application

17.1(1) This section applies where the parking infraction notice requires the notice of intention to appear to be filed in person at a place specified in the parking infraction notice.

Subss. 17(1), (3) and (4) inapplicable

(2) Subsections 17(1), (3) and (4) do not apply in a municipality in which this section applies.

Filing

(3) A defendant who is served with a parking infraction notice may give notice of intention to appear in court for the purpose of entering a plea and having a trial of the matter by attending in person or by representative at the place specified in the parking infraction notice at the time or times specified in the parking infraction notice and filing a notice of intention to appear with a person designated by the regulations.

Notice

(4) The notice of intention to appear shall be in the form prescribed under section 20.

Proceeding commenced

(5) The proceeding shall be commenced by filing the certificate of parking infraction in the office of the clerk of the court or the person designated by the regulations.

Notice of trial

(6) As soon as practicable after the proceeding is commenced, the clerk of the court or the person designated by the regulations shall give notice to the defendant and the prosecutor of the time and place of the trial.

Rescheduling time of trial

(6.1) The clerk of the court may, for administrative reasons, reschedule the time of the trial by giving a revised notice to the defendant and the prosecutor within 21 days of giving the notice referred to subsection (6).

Evidence required at trial

(7) The court shall not convict the defendant unless the following are presented at the trial:

1. If the parking infraction is alleged against the defendant as owner of a vehicle, evidence of the ownership of the vehicle.
2. A copy of the notice of trial, with the certificate of the person who issued the notice under subsection (6), stating that the notice was given to the defendant and to the prosecutor and stating the date on which this was done.
3. The certificate of parking infraction.

Failure to respond

18(1) The person designated by the regulations may give the defendant a notice of impending conviction if,

(a) at least fifteen days and no more than thirty-five days have elapsed since the alleged infraction occurred;

(b) the defendant has not paid the fine; and

(c) a notice of intention to appear has not been received.

Form of notice

(2) The notice shall be in the form prescribed under section 20.

Contents of notice

(3) The notice shall,

(a) indicate the set fine for the infraction; and

(b) indicate that a conviction will be registered against the defendant unless the defendant pays the set fine or gives notice of an intention to appear in court for the purpose of entering a plea and having a trial of the matter.

Intention to appear

18.1(1) A defendant who receives a notice of impending conviction may give notice of intention to appear in court for the purpose of entering a plea and having a trial of the matter by so indicating on the notice of impending conviction and delivering the notice to the place specified in it.

Proceeding commenced

(2) If a defendant gives notice of an intention to appear after a notice of impending conviction has been given, a proceeding may be commenced in respect of the charge if it is done within seventy-five days after the day on which the alleged infraction occurred.

Idem

(3) The proceeding shall be commenced by filing in the office of the court,

(a) the certificate of parking infraction; and

(b) if the parking infraction is alleged against the defendant as owner of a vehicle, evidence of the ownership of the vehicle.

Notice of trial

(4) As soon as practicable after the proceeding is commenced, the clerk of the court or a person designated by the regulations shall give notice to the defendant and prosecutor of the time and place of the trial.

Rescheduling time of trial

(5) The clerk of the court may, for administrative reasons, reschedule the time of the trial by giving a revised notice to the defendant and the prosecutor within 21 days of giving the notice referred to subsection (4).

Application

18.1.1(1) This section applies where the notice of impending conviction requires the notice of intention to appear to be filed in person at a place specified in the notice of impending conviction.

Subss. 18.1(1), (3) and (4) inapplicable

(2) Subsections 18.1(1), (3) and (4) do not apply in a municipality in which this section applies.

Subss. 17.1(5), (6) and (7) applicable

(2.1) Subsections 17.1(5), (6) and (7) apply to a proceeding begun under this section.

Filing notice of intention to appear

(3) A defendant who receives a notice of impending conviction may give notice of intention to appear in court for the purpose of entering a plea and having a trial of the matter by attending in person or by representative at the place specified in the notice of impending conviction at the time or times specified in the notice of impending conviction and filing a notice of intention to appear with a person designated by the regulations.

Form of notice

(4) The notice of intention to appear shall be in the form prescribed under section 20.

Challenge to officer's evidence

18.1.2(1) A defendant who gives notice of an intention to appear under subsection 17(1), 17.1(3), 18.1(1) or 18.1.1(3) shall indicate on the notice of intention to appear or parking infraction notice if the defendant intends to challenge the evidence of the provincial offences officer who completed the certificate of parking infraction.

Notifying officer

(2) If the defendant indicates an intention to challenge the officer's evidence, the clerk of the court or a person designated by the regulations shall notify the officer.

Note: On a day to be named by proclamation of the Lieutenant Governor, section 18.1.2 is repealed. See: 2009, c. 33, Sched. 4, ss. 1(26), 5(4).

No response to impending conviction notice

18.2(1) A defendant who has been given a notice of impending conviction shall be deemed not to dispute the charge if fifteen days have elapsed since the defendant was given the notice, the fine has not been paid and a notice of intention to appear has not been received.

Request for conviction

(1.1) If subsection (1) applies, the person designated by the regulations may prepare and sign a certificate requesting a conviction in the form prescribed under section 20.

Idem

(2) The certificate requesting a conviction shall state,

(a) that the certificate of parking infraction is complete and regular on its face;

(b) if the defendant is liable as owner, that the person is satisfied that the defendant is the owner;

(c) that there is valid legal authority for charging the defendant with the parking infraction;

(d) that the defendant was given a notice of impending conviction at least fifteen days before the certificate requesting a conviction is filed;

(e) that the alleged infraction occurred less than seventy-five days before the certificate requesting a conviction is filed; and

(f) the prescribed information.

Idem

(3) If the certificate of parking infraction was issued for an infraction under a by-law of a municipality, the certificate requesting a conviction shall also state,

(a) that payment of the set fine has not been made; and

(b) that the defendant has not given notice of intention to appear in court for the purpose of entering a plea and having a trial of the matter.

Idem

(4) A certificate requesting a conviction purporting to be signed by the person authorized to prepare it shall be received in evidence and is proof, in the absence of evidence to the contrary, of the facts contained in it.

Proceeding commenced

(5) A proceeding may be commenced in respect of the charge by filing the certificate requesting a conviction in the office of the court, but only if the certificate is filed within seventy-five days after the alleged infraction occurred.

Recording of conviction

(6) Upon receiving a certificate requesting a conviction, the clerk of the court shall record a conviction and the defendant is then liable to pay the set fine for the offence.

Application where ticket defective

18.3(1) A defendant who is convicted of a parking infraction under section 18.2 may, within fifteen days after becoming aware of the conviction, apply to a justice requesting that the conviction be struck out for the reason that the parking infraction notice is defective on its face.

Idem

(2) On an application by the defendant, if a justice is satisfied that the parking infraction notice is defective on its face, the justice shall strike out the conviction and shall order that the municipality or other body that issued the certificate requesting a conviction pay $25 in costs to the defendant.

Failure to appear at trial

18.4(1) A defendant is deemed to not wish to dispute the charge where the defendant has been issued a notice of the time and place of trial and fails to appear at the time and place appointed for the trial.

Examination by justice

(2) If subsection (1) applies, section 54 does not apply, and a justice shall examine the certificate of parking infraction and shall without a hearing enter a conviction in the defendant's absence and impose the set fine for the offence if the certificate is complete and regular on its face.

Owner liability

(3) Despite subsection (2), if the defendant is alleged to have committed the parking infraction as owner of the vehicle involved in the infraction, the justice shall not enter a conviction and impose the set fine unless he or she is satisfied that the defendant is the owner of the vehicle.

Entering conviction

(4) The justice shall enter a conviction with respect to a parking infraction under a by-law of a municipality without proof of the by-law that creates the offence if the justice is satisfied that the other criteria for entering a conviction have been met.

Quashing proceeding

(5) The justice shall quash the proceeding if he or she is not able to enter a conviction.

Error by municipality

18.5(1) A municipality or other body may apply to a justice requesting that a conviction respecting a parking infraction be struck out if the defendant was convicted because of an error made by the municipality or other body.

Idem

(2) On an application by a municipality or other body, if a justice is satisfied that an error was made, the justice shall strike out the conviction.

Idem

(3) If the justice strikes out the conviction, the municipality or other body shall notify the defendant of that fact.

Authority to collect parking fines

18.6(1) A municipality may collect the fines levied for convictions respecting parking infractions under its by-laws if the municipality,

(a) enters into an agreement with the Attorney General to authorize it; or

(b) enters into a transfer agreement under Part X.

Agreement

(1.1) The Attorney General and a municipality may enter into an agreement for the purpose of clause (1)(a).

Notice to municipality

(2) If a conviction is entered respecting a parking infraction under a by-law of a municipality to which subsection (1) applies, the clerk of the court shall give notice of the conviction to the clerk of the municipality.

Notice of fine

(3) If the clerk of a municipality receives notice of a conviction, the clerk of the municipality or the person designated by the clerk shall give notice to the person against whom the conviction is entered, in the form prescribed under section 20, setting out the date and place of the infraction, the date of the conviction and the amount of the fine.

If default

(4) If the fine is in default, the clerk of the municipality may send notice to the person designated by the regulations certifying that it is in default.

Idem

(5) If a conviction is entered respecting a parking infraction and the parking infraction is not under a by-law of a municipality to which subsection (1) applies, the clerk of the court shall give notice to the person against whom the conviction is entered of the date and place of the infraction, the date of the conviction and the amount of the fine.

Reopening

Application to strike out conviction

19(1) A defendant who was convicted of a parking infraction without a hearing may, within 15 days of becoming aware of the conviction, apply to a justice to strike out the conviction.

Striking out the conviction

(2) Upon application under subsection (1), a justice shall strike out a conviction if satisfied by affidavit of the defendant or otherwise that, through no fault of the defendant, the defendant was unable to appear for a hearing or the defendant never received any notice or document relating to the parking infraction.

If conviction struck out

(3) If the justice strikes out the conviction, the justice shall,

(a) if the defendant enters a plea of guilty, accept the plea and impose the set fine; or

(b) direct the clerk of the court to give notice to the defendant and the prosecutor of the time and place of the trial.

Rescheduling time of trial

(4) The clerk of the court may, for administrative reasons, reschedule the time of the trial by giving a revised notice to the defendant and the prosecutor within 21 days of giving the notice referred to in clause (3)(b).

Regulations

20(1) The Lieutenant Governor in Council may make regulations,

(a) Repealed.

(b) authorizing the use in a form under this Part of any word or expression to designate a parking infraction;

(c), (d) Repealed.

(e) designating the persons or classes of persons who are required to prepare a notice of impending conviction or a certificate requesting a conviction for municipalities and for other bodies on whose behalf parking infraction notices are issued;

(e.1) designating a person or class of persons for the purposes of subsection 17(4), 17.1(3), 17.1(5), 17.1(6), 18.1(4), 18.1.1(3) or 18.1.2(2);

(f) providing that the procedure set out in subsections 18.4(2) to (10) is to apply to all proceedings under this Part;

(g) authorizing Ontario to pay allowances to municipalities and other bodies that issue notices of impending conviction and that collect fines under this Part, providing for the payment of those allowances from the court costs received in connection with the fines levied under this Part and fixing the amount of the allowances;

(h) Repealed.

(i) designating the person to whom a notice certifying that a fine is in default under subsection 18.6(4) is to be sent;

(j) designating municipalities for the purposes of sections 17.1 and 18.1.1.

Same, Attorney General

(1.1) The Attorney General may make regulations,

(a) prescribing the forms that are considered necessary under this Part;

(b) respecting any matter that is considered necessary to provide for the use of the forms under this Part;

(c) prescribing information that is required to be included in a parking infraction notice, a notice of impending conviction or a certificate requesting a conviction;

(d) prescribing the information to be included in a notice certifying that a fine is in default under subsection 18.6(4).

Sufficiency of abbreviations

(2) The use on a form prescribed under clause (1.1)(a) of any word or expression authorized by the regulations to designate a parking infraction is sufficient for all purposes to describe the infraction designated by such word or expression.

Idem

(3) Where the regulations do not authorize the use of a word or expression to describe a parking infraction in a form prescribed under clause (1.1)(a), the offence may be described in accordance with section 25.

Note: Part II of this Act, as it read immediately before September 1, 1993 continues to apply to proceedings that were commenced before September 1, 1993. See: 1992, c. 20, s. 3.

PART III

COMMENCEMENT OF PROCEEDING BY INFORMATION

Commencement of proceeding by information

21(1) In addition to the procedure set out in Parts I and II for commencing a proceeding by the filing of a certificate, a proceeding in respect of an offence may be commenced by laying an information.

Exception

(2) Where a summons or offence notice has been served under Part I, no proceeding shall be commenced under subsection (1) in respect of the same offence except with the consent of the Attorney General or his or her agent.

Summons before information laid

22. Where a provincial offences officer believes, on reasonable and probable grounds, that an offence has been committed by a person whom the officer finds at or near the place where the offence was committed, he or she may, before an information is laid, serve the person with a summons in the prescribed form.

Information

23(1) Any person who, on reasonable and probable grounds, believes that one or more persons have committed an offence, may lay an information in the prescribed form and under oath before a justice alleging the offence and the justice shall receive the information.

Multiple defendants

(1.1) For greater certainty, an information laid under subsection (1) may include one or more persons.

Where information may be laid

(2) An information may be laid anywhere in Ontario.

Procedure on laying of information

24(1) A justice who receives an information laid under section 23 shall consider the information and, where he or she considers it desirable to do so, hear and consider in the absence of the defendant the allegations of the informant and the evidence of witnesses and,

(a) where he or she considers that a case for so doing is made out,

(i) confirm the summons served under section 22, if any,

(ii) issue a summons in the prescribed form, or

(iii) where the arrest is authorized by statute and where the allegations of the informant or the evidence satisfy the justice on reasonable and probable grounds that it is necessary in the public interest to do so, issue a warrant for the arrest of the defendant; or

(b) where he or she considers that a case for issuing process is not made out,

(i) so endorse the information, and

(ii) where a summons was served under section 22, cancel it and cause the defendant to be so notified.

Summons or warrants in blank

(2) A justice shall not sign a summons or warrant in blank.

Counts

25(1) Each offence charged in an information shall be set out in a separate count.

Allegation of offence

(2) Each count in an information shall in general apply to a single transaction and shall contain and is sufficient if it contains in substance a statement that the defendant committed an offence therein specified.

Reference to statutory provision

(3) Where in a count an offence is identified but the count fails to set out one or more of the essential elements of the offence, a reference to the provision creating or defining the offence shall be deemed to incorporate all the essential elements of the offence.

Idem

(4) The statement referred to in subsection (2) may be,

(a) in popular language without technical averments or allegations of matters that are not essential to be proved;

(b) in the words of the enactment that describes the offence; or

(c) in words that are sufficient to give to the defendant notice of the offence with which the defendant is charged.

More than one count

(5) Any number of counts for any number of offences may be joined in the same information.

Particulars of count

(6) A count shall contain sufficient detail of the circumstances of the alleged offence to give to the defendant reasonable information with respect to the act or omission to be proved against the defendant and to identify the transaction referred to.

Sufficiency

(7) No count in an information is insufficient by reason of the absence of details where, in the opinion of the court, the count otherwise fulfils the requirements of this section and, without restricting the generality of the foregoing, no count in an information is insufficient by reason only that,

(a) it does not name the person affected by the offence or intended or attempted to be affected;

(b) it does not name the person who owns or has a special property or interest in property mentioned in the count;

(c) it charges an intent in relation to another person without naming or describing the other person;

(d) it does not set out any writing that is the subject of the charge;

(e) it does not set out the words used where words that are alleged to have been used are the subject of the charge;

(f) it does not specify the means by which the alleged offence was committed;

(g) it does not name or describe with precision any person, place, thing or time; or

(h) it does not, where the consent of a person, official or authority is required before proceedings may be instituted for an offence, state that the consent has been obtained.

Idem

(8) A count is not objectionable for the reason only that,

(a) it charges in the alternative several different matters, acts or omissions that are stated in the alternative in an enactment that describes as an offence the matters, acts or omissions charged in the count; or

(b) it is double or multifarious.

Need to negative exception, etc.

(9) No exception, exemption, proviso, excuse or qualification prescribed by law is required to be set out or negatived, as the case may be, in an information.

Summons

26(1) A summons issued under section 22 or 24 shall,

(a) be directed to the defendant;

(b) set out briefly the offence in respect of which the defendant is charged; and

(c) require the defendant to attend court at a time and place stated therein and to attend thereafter as required by the court in order to be dealt with according to law.

Service

(2) A summons shall be served by a provincial offences officer by delivering it personally to the person to whom it is directed or if that person cannot conveniently be found, by leaving it for the person at the person's last known or usual place of abode with an inmate thereof who appears to be at least sixteen years of age.

Service outside Ontario

(3) Despite subsection (2), where the person to whom a summons is directed does not reside in Ontario, the summons shall be deemed to have been duly served seven days after it has been sent by registered mail to the person's last known or usual place of abode.

Service on corporation

(4) Service of a summons on a corporation may be effected,

(a) in the case of a municipal corporation by,

(i) delivering the summons personally to the mayor, warden, reeve or other chief officer of the corporation or to the clerk of the corporation, or

(ii) mailing the summons by registered mail to the municipal corporation at an address held out by it to be its address;

(b) in the case of any corporation, other than a municipal corporation, incorporated or continued by or under an Act by,

(i) delivering the summons personally to the manager, secretary or other executive officer of the corporation or person apparently in charge of a branch office of the corporation, or

(ii) mailing the summons by registered mail to the corporation at an address held out by it to be its address;

(c) in the case of corporation not incorporated or continued by or under an Act by,

(i) a method provided under clause (b),

(ii) delivering the summons personally to the corporation's resident agent or agent for service or to any other representative of the corporation in Ontario, or

(iii) mailing the summons by registered mail to a person referred to in subclause (ii) or to an address outside Ontario, including outside Canada, held out by the corporation to be its address.

Date of mailed service

(4.1) A summons served by registered mail under subsection (4) is deemed to have been duly served seven days after the day of mailing.

Substitutional service

(5) A justice, upon motion and upon being satisfied that service cannot be made effectively on a corporation in accordance with subsection (4), may by order authorize another method of service that has a reasonable likelihood of coming to the attention of the corporation.

Proof of service

(6) Service of a summons may be proved by statement under oath or affirmation, written or oral, of the person who made the service.

Contents of warrant

27(1) A warrant issued under section 24 shall,

(a) name or describe the defendant;

(b) set out briefly the offence in respect of which the defendant is charged; and

(c) order that the defendant be forthwith arrested and brought before a justice to be dealt with according to law.

Idem

(2) A warrant issued under section 24 remains in force until it is executed and need not be made returnable at any particular time.

PART IV
TRIAL AND SENTENCING

TRIAL

Application of Part

28. This Part applies to a proceeding commenced under this Act.

Territorial jurisdiction

29(1) Subject to subsection (2), a proceeding in respect of an offence shall be heard and determined by the Ontario Court of Justice sitting in the county or district in which the offence occurred or in the area specified in the transfer agreement made under Part X.

Idem

(2) A proceeding in respect of an offence may be heard and determined in a county or district that adjoins that in which the offence occurred if,

(a) the court holds sittings in a place reasonably proximate to the place where the offence occurred; and

(b) the place of sitting referred to in clause (a) is named in the summons or offence notice.

Transfer to proper county

(3) Where a proceeding is taken in a county or district other than one referred to in subsection (1) or (2), the court shall order that the proceeding be transferred to the proper county or district and may where the defendant appears award costs under section 60.

Change of venue

(4) Where, on the motion of a defendant or prosecutor made to the court at the location named in the information or certificate, it appears to the court that,

(a) it would be appropriate in the interests of justice to do so; or

(b) both the defendant and prosecutor consent thereto,

the court may order that the proceeding be heard and determined at another location in Ontario.

Conditions

(5) The court may, in an order made on a motion by the prosecutor under subsection (3) or (4), prescribe conditions that it thinks proper with respect to the payment of additional expenses caused to the defendant as a result of the change of venue.

Time of order for change of venue

(6) An order under subsection (3) or (4) may be made even if a motion preliminary to trial has been disposed of or the plea has been taken and it may be made at any time before evidence has been heard.

Preliminary motions

(7) The court at a location to which a proceeding is transferred under this section may receive and determine any motion preliminary to trial although the same matter was determined by the court at the location from which the proceeding was transferred.

Delivery of papers

(8) Where an order is made under subsection (3) or (4), the clerk of the court at the location where the trial was to be held before the order was made shall deliver any material in his or her possession in connection with the proceeding forthwith to the clerk of the court at the location where the trial is ordered to be held.

Justice presiding at trial

30(1) The justice presiding when evidence is first taken at the trial shall preside over the whole of the trial.

When presiding justice unable to act before adjudication

(2) Where evidence has been taken at a trial and, before making his or her adjudication, the presiding justice dies or in his or her opinion or the opinion of the Chief Justice of the Ontario Court of Justice is for any reason unable to continue, another justice shall conduct the hearing again as a new trial.

When presiding justice unable to act after adjudication

(3) Where evidence has been taken at a trial and, after making his or her adjudication but before making his or her order or imposing sentence, the presiding justice dies or in his or her opinion or the opinion of the Chief Justice of the Ontario Court of Justice is for any reason unable to continue, another justice may make the order or impose the sentence that is authorized by law.

Consent to change presiding justice

(4) A justice presiding at a trial may, at any stage of the trial and upon the consent of the prosecutor and defendant, order that the trial be conducted by another justice and, upon the order being given, subsection (2) applies as if the justice were unable to act.

Retention of jurisdiction

31. The court retains jurisdiction over the information or certificate even if the court fails to exercise its jurisdiction at any particular time or the provisions of this Act respecting adjournments are not complied with.

Stay of proceeding

32(1) In addition to his or her right to withdraw a charge, the Attorney General or his or her agent may stay a proceeding at any time before judgment by direction in court to the clerk of the court and thereupon any recognizance relating to the proceeding is vacated.

Recommencement

(2) A proceeding stayed under subsection (1) may be recommenced by direction of the Attorney General, the Deputy Attorney General or a Crown Attorney to the clerk of the court but a proceeding that is stayed shall not be recommenced,

(a) later than one year after the stay; or

(b) after the expiration of any limitation period applicable, which shall run as if the proceeding had not been commenced until the recommencement,

whichever is the earlier.

Dividing counts

33(1) A defendant may at any stage of the proceeding make a motion to the court to amend or to divide a count that,

(a) charges in the alternative different matters, acts or omissions that are stated in the alternative in the enactment that creates or describes the offence; or

(b) is double or multifarious,

on the ground that, as framed, it prejudices the defendant in the defendant's defence.

Idem

(2) Upon a motion under subsection (1), where the court is satisfied that the ends of justice so require, it may order that a count be amended or divided into two or more counts, and thereupon a formal commencement may be inserted before each of the counts into which it is divided.

Amendment of information or certificate

34(1) The court may, at any stage of the proceeding, amend the information or certificate as may be necessary if it appears that the information or certificate,

(a) fails to state or states defectively anything that is requisite to charge the offence;

(b) does not negative an exception that should be negatived; or

(c) is in any way defective in substance or in form.

Idem

(2) The court may, during the trial, amend the information or certificate as may be necessary if the matters to be alleged in the proposed amendment are disclosed by the evidence taken at the trial.

Variances between charge and evidence

(3) A variance between the information or certificate and the evidence taken on the trial is not material with respect to,

(a) the time when the offence is alleged to have been committed, if it is proved that the information was laid or certificate issued within the prescribed period of limitation; or

(b) the place where the subject-matter of the proceeding is alleged to have arisen, except in an issue as to the jurisdiction of the court.

Considerations on amendment

(4) The court shall, in considering whether or not an amendment should be made, consider,

(a) the evidence taken on the trial, if any;

(b) the circumstances of the case;

(c) whether the defendant has been misled or prejudiced in the defendant's defence by a variance, error or omission; and

(d) whether, having regard to the merits of the case, the proposed amendment can be made without injustice being done.

Amendment, question of law

(5) The question whether an order to amend an information or certificate should be granted or refused is a question of law.

Endorsement of order to amend

(6) An order to amend an information or certificate shall be endorsed on the information or certificate as part of the record and the trial shall proceed as if the information or certificate had been originally laid as amended.

Particulars

35. The court may, before or during trial, if it is satisfied that it is necessary for a fair trial, order that a particular, further describing any matter relevant to the proceeding, be furnished to the defendant.

Motion to quash information or certificate

36(1) An objection to an information or certificate for a defect apparent on its face shall be taken by motion to quash the information or certificate before the defendant has pleaded, and thereafter only by leave of the court.

Grounds for quashing

(2) The court shall not quash an information or certificate unless an amendment or particulars under section 33, 34 or 35 would fail to satisfy the ends of justice.

Costs on amendment or particulars

37. Where the information or certificate is amended or particulars are ordered and an adjournment is necessary as a result thereof, the court may make an order under section 60 for costs resulting from the adjournment.

Joinder of counts or defendants

38(1) The court may, before trial, where it is satisfied that the ends of justice so require, direct that separate counts, informations or certificates be tried together or that persons who are charged separately be tried together.

Separate trials

(2) The court may, before or during the trial, where it is satisfied that the ends of justice so require, direct that separate counts, informations or certificates be tried separately or that persons who are charged jointly or being tried together be tried separately.

Issuance of summons

39(1) Where a justice is satisfied that a person is able to give material evidence in a proceeding under this Act, the justice may issue a summons requiring the person to attend to give evidence and bring with him or her any writings or things referred to in the summons.

Service

(2) A summons shall be served and the service shall be proved in the same manner as a summons under section 26.

Exception

(2.1) Despite subsection (2), a summons served under this section may be served by a person other than a provincial offences officer.

Attendance

(3) A person who is served with a summons shall attend at the time and place stated in the summons to give evidence and, if required by the summons, shall bring with him or her any writing or other thing that the person has in his or her possession or under his or her control relating to the subject-matter of the proceeding.

Remaining in attendance

(4) A person who is served with a summons shall remain in attendance during the hearing and the hearing as resumed after adjournment from time to time unless the person is excused from attendance by the presiding justice.

Arrest of witness

40(1) Where a judge is satisfied upon evidence under oath or affirmation, that a person is able to give material evidence that is necessary in a proceeding under this Act and,

   (a) will not attend if a summons is served; or

   (b) attempts to serve a summons have been made and have failed because the person is evading service,

the judge may issue a warrant in the prescribed form for the arrest of the person.

Idem

(2) Where a person who has been served with a summons to attend to give evidence in a proceeding does not attend or remain in attendance, the court may, if it is established,

   (a) that the summons has been served; and

   (b) that the person is able to give material evidence that is necessary,

issue or cause to be issued a warrant in the prescribed form for the arrest of the person.

Bringing before justice

(3) The police officer who arrests a person under a warrant issued under subsection (1) or (2) shall immediately take the person before a justice.

Release on recognizance

(4) Unless the justice is satisfied that it is necessary to detain a person in custody to ensure his or her attendance to give evidence, the justice shall order the person released upon condition that the person enter into a recognizance in such amount and with such sureties, if any, as are reasonably necessary to ensure his or her attendance.

Bringing before judge

(5) Where a person is not released under subsection (4), the justice of the peace shall cause the person to be brought before a judge within two days of the justice's decision.

Detention

(6) Where the judge is satisfied that it is necessary to detain the person in custody to ensure his or her attendance to give evidence, the judge may order that the person be detained in custody to testify at the trial or to have his or her evidence taken by a commissioner under an order made under subsection (11).

Release on recognizance

(7) Where the judge does not make an order under subsection (6), he or she shall order that the person be released upon condition that the person enter into a recognizance in such amount and with such sureties, if any, as are reasonably necessary to ensure his or her attendance.

Maximum imprisonment

(8) A person who is ordered to be detained in custody under subsection (6) or is not released in fact under subsection (7) shall not be detained in custody for a period longer than ten days.

Release when no longer required

(9) A judge, or the justice presiding at a trial, may at any time order the release of a person in custody under this section where he or she is satisfied that the detention is no longer justified.

Arrest on breach of recognizance

(10) Where a person who is bound by a recognizance to attend to give evidence in any proceeding does not attend or remain in attendance, the court may issue a warrant in the prescribed form for the arrest of that person and,

(a) where the person is brought directly before the court, subsections (6) and (7) apply; and

(b) where the person is not brought directly before the court, subsections (3) to (7) apply.

Commission evidence of witness in custody

(11) A judge or the justice presiding at the trial may order that the evidence of a person held in custody under this section be taken by a commissioner under section 43, which applies thereto in the same manner as to a witness who is unable to attend by reason of illness.

Order for person in a prison to attend

41(1) Where a person whose attendance is required in court to stand trial or to give evidence is confined in a prison, and a judge is satisfied, upon evidence under oath or affirmation orally or by affidavit, that the person's attendance is necessary to satisfy the ends of justice, the judge may issue an order in the prescribed form that the person be brought before the court, from day to day, as may be necessary.

Idem

(2) An order under subsection (1) shall be addressed to the person who has custody of the prisoner and on receipt thereof that person shall,

(a) deliver the prisoner to the police officer or other person who is named in the order to receive the prisoner; or

(b) bring the prisoner before the court upon payment of the person's reasonable charges in respect thereof.

Idem

(3) An order made under subsection (1) shall direct the manner in which the person shall be kept in custody and returned to the prison from which he or she is brought.

Penalty for failure to attend

42(1) Every person who, being required by law to attend or remain in attendance at a hearing, fails without lawful excuse to attend or remain in attendance accordingly is guilty of an offence and on conviction is liable to a fine of not more than $2,000, or to imprisonment for a term of not more than thirty days, or to both.

Proof of failure to attend

(2) In a proceeding under subsection (1), a certificate of the clerk of the court or a justice stating that the defendant failed to attend is admissible in evidence as proof, in the absence of evidence to the contrary, of the fact without proof of the signature or office of the person appearing to have signed the certificate.

Order for evidence by commission

43(1) Upon the motion of the defendant or prosecutor, a judge or, during trial, the court may by order appoint a commissioner to take the evidence of a witness who is out of Ontario or is not likely to be able to attend the trial by reason of illness or physical disability or for some other good and sufficient cause.

Admission of commission evidence

(2) Evidence taken by a commissioner appointed under subsection (1) may be read in evidence in the proceeding if,

(a) it is proved by oral evidence or by affidavit that the witness is unable to attend for a reason set out in subsection (1);

(b) the transcript of the evidence is signed by the commissioner by or before whom it purports to have been taken; and

(c) it is proved to the satisfaction of the court that reasonable notice of the time and place for taking the evidence was given to the other party, and the party had full opportunity to cross-examine the witness.

Attendance of accused

(3) An order under subsection (1) may make provision to enable the defendant to be present or represented by representative when the evidence is taken, but failure of the defendant to be present or to be represented by representative in accordance with

the order does not prevent the reading of the evidence in the proceeding if the evidence has otherwise been taken in accordance with the order and with this section.

Application of rules in civil cases

(4) Except as otherwise provided by this section or by the rules of court, the practice and procedure in connection with the appointment of commissioners under this section, the taking of evidence by commissioners, the certifying and return thereof, and the use of the evidence in the proceeding shall, as far as possible, be the same as those that govern like matters in civil proceedings in the Superior Court of Justice.

Trial of issue as to capacity to conduct defence

44(1) Where at any time before a defendant is sentenced a court has reason to believe, based on,

(a) the evidence of a legally qualified medical practitioner or, with the consent of the parties, a written report of a legally qualified medical practitioner; or

(b) the conduct of the defendant in the courtroom,

that the defendant suffers from mental disorder, the court may,

(c) where the justice presiding is a judge, by order suspend the proceeding and direct the trial of the issue as to whether the defendant is, because of mental disorder, unable to conduct his or her defence; or

(d) where the justice presiding is a justice of the peace, refer the matter to a judge who may make an order referred to in clause (c).

Examination

(2) For the purposes of subsection (1), the court may order the defendant to attend to be examined under subsection (5).

Finding

(3) The trial of the issue shall be presided over by a judge and,

(a) where the judge finds that the defendant is, because of mental disorder, unable to conduct his or her defence, the judge shall order that the proceeding remain suspended;

(b) where the judge finds that the defendant is able to conduct his or her defence, the judge shall order that the suspended proceeding be continued.

Application for rehearing as to capacity

(4) At any time within one year after an order is made under subsection (3), either party may, upon seven days notice to the other, make a motion to a judge to rehear the trial of the issue and where upon the rehearing the judge finds that the defendant is able to conduct his or her defence, the judge may order that the suspended proceeding be continued.

Order for examination

(5) For the purposes of subsection (1) or a hearing or rehearing under subsection (3) or (4), the court or judge may order the defendant to attend at such place or before such person and at or within such time as are specified in the order and submit to an examination for the purpose of determining whether the defendant is, because of mental disorder, unable to conduct his or her defence.

Idem

(6) Where the defendant fails or refuses to comply with an order under subsection (5) without reasonable excuse or where the person conducting the examination satisfies a judge that it is necessary to do so, the judge may by warrant direct that the

defendant be taken into such custody as is necessary for the purpose of the examination and in any event for not longer than seven days and, where it is necessary to detain the defendant in a place, the place shall be, where practicable, a psychiatric facility.

Limitation on suspension of proceeding

(7) Where an order is made under subsection (3) and one year has elapsed and no further order is made under subsection (4), no further proceeding shall be taken in respect of the charge or any other charge arising out of the same circumstance.

Taking of plea

45(1) After being informed of the substance of the information or certificate, the defendant shall be asked whether the defendant pleads guilty or not guilty of the offence charged in it.

Conviction on plea of guilty

(2) Where the defendant pleads guilty, the court may accept the plea and convict the defendant.

Conditions of accepting plea

(3) A court may accept a plea of guilty only if it is satisfied that the defendant,

(a) is making the plea voluntarily;

(b) understands that the plea is an admission of the essential elements of the offence;

(c) understands the nature and consequences of the plea; and

(d) understands that the court is not bound by any agreement made between the defendant and the prosecutor.

Validity of plea not affected

(4) The failure of a court to fully inquire into whether the conditions set out in subsection (3) are met does not affect the validity of the plea.

Refusal to plead

(5) Where the defendant refuses to plead or does not answer directly, the court shall enter a plea of not guilty.

Plea of guilty to another offence

(6) Where the defendant pleads guilty of an offence other than the offence charged, and whether or not it is an included offence and whether or not the defendant has pleaded not guilty to the offence charged, the court may, with the consent of the prosecutor, accept such plea of guilty and accordingly amend the certificate of offence, the certificate of parking infraction or the information, as the case may be, or substitute the offence to which the defendant pleads guilty.

Judicial pre-trial conferences

45.1(1) On application by the prosecutor or the defendant or on his or her own motion, a justice may order that a pre-trial conference be held between the prosecutor and the defendant or a representative of the defendant.

Matters for consideration

(2) The court, or a justice of the court, shall preside over the pre-trial conference, the purpose of which is to,

(a) consider the matters that, to promote a fair and expeditious trial, would be better decided before the start of the proceedings and other similar matters; and

(b) make arrangements for decisions on those matters.

Trial on plea of not guilty

46(1) If the defendant pleads not guilty, the court shall hold the trial.

Right to defend

(2) The defendant is entitled to make full answer and defence.

Right to examine witnesses

(3) The prosecutor or defendant, as the case may be, may examine and cross-examine witnesses.

Agreed facts

(4) The court may receive and act upon any facts agreed upon by the defendant and prosecutor without proof or evidence.

Defendant not compellable

(5) Despite section 8 of the *Evidence Act*, the defendant is not a compellable witness for the prosecution.

Evidence and burden of proof
Evidence taken on another charge

47(1) The court may receive and consider evidence taken before the same justice on a different charge against the same defendant, with the consent of the parties.

Certificate as evidence

(2) Where a certificate as to the content of an official record is, by any Act, made admissible in evidence as proof, in the absence of evidence to the contrary, the court may, for the purpose of deciding whether the defendant is the person referred to in the certificate, receive and base its decision upon information it considers credible or trustworthy in the circumstances of each case.

Burden of proving exception, etc.

(3) The burden of proving that an authorization, exception, exemption or qualification prescribed by law operates in favour of the defendant is on the defendant, and the prosecutor is not required, except by way of rebuttal, to prove that the authorization, exception, exemption or qualification does not operate in favour of the defendant, whether or not it is set out in the information.

Exhibits

48(1) The court may order that an exhibit be kept in such custody and place as, in the opinion of the court, is appropriate for its preservation.

Release of exhibits

(2) Where any thing is filed as an exhibit in a proceeding, the clerk may release the exhibit upon the consent of the parties at any time after the trial or, in the absence of consent, may return the exhibit to the party tendering it after the disposition of any appeal in the proceeding or, where an appeal is not taken, after the expiration of the time for appeal.

Certificate evidence

48.1(1) The certified statements in a certificate of offence or certificate of parking infraction are admissible in evidence as proof, in the absence of evidence to the contrary, of the facts stated therein.

Exception

(2) Subsection (1) does not apply if the defendant has indicated under section 5.2, subsection 11(3), section 18.1.2 or subsection 19(3) that the defendant intends to challenge the evidence of the provincial offences officer who completed the certificate.

Note: On a day to be named by proclamation of the Lieutenant Governor, section 48.1 is repealed and the following substituted:

Certified evidence
Application

48.1(1) This section applies to a hearing, including a hearing in the absence of a defendant under section 54, where,

(a) the proceeding for the offence was commenced by certificate under Part I or II; and

(b) the offence is specified by the regulations.

Admissibility of certified evidence

(2) The following are admissible in evidence as proof of the facts certified in it, in the absence of evidence to the contrary:

1. A certified statement in a certificate of offence.

2. A certified statement in a certificate of parking infraction.

3. Other types of certified evidence specified by the regulations.

Other provisions on admissibility

(3) For greater certainty, subsection (2) does not affect or interfere with the operation of a provision of this Act or any other Act that permits or specifies that a document or type of document be admitted into evidence as proof of the facts certified in it.

Onus

(4) For greater certainty, this section does not remove the onus on the prosecution to prove its case beyond a reasonable doubt.

No oral evidence

(5) A provincial offences officer who provides certified evidence referred to in subsection (2) in respect of a proceeding shall not be required to attend to give evidence at trial, except as provided under subsection 49(4).

Regulations

(6) The Lieutenant Governor in Council may make regulations,

(a) specifying offences for the purposes of clause (1)(b);

(b) respecting other types of certified evidence for the purposes of paragraph 3 of subsection (2);

(c) respecting restrictions or conditions on the admissibility of evidence under subsection (2).

See: 2009, c. 33, Sched. 4, ss. 1(40), 5(4).

Adjournments

49(1) The court may, from time to time, adjourn a trial or hearing but, where the defendant is in custody, an adjournment shall not be for a period longer than eight days without the consent of the defendant.

Early resumption

(2) A trial or hearing that is adjourned for a period may be resumed before the expiration of the period with the consent of the defendant and the prosecutor.

Adjournment

(3) Despite subsection (1), if the trial is being held in respect of a proceeding commenced under Part I or II, the court shall not adjourn the trial for the purpose of having the provincial offences officer who completed the certificate attend to give evidence unless the court is satisfied that the interests of justice require it.

Note: On a day to be named by proclamation of the Lieutenant Governor, subsection (3) is repealed and the following substituted:

Adjournment

(3) Despite subsection (1) and subject to subsection (4), if the trial is being held in respect of a proceeding commenced under Part I or II, the court shall not adjourn the trial for the purpose of having the provincial offences officer who completed the certificate of offence or the certificate of parking infraction, as the case may be, attend to give evidence unless the court is satisfied that the interests of justice require it.

Adjournment where certified evidence

(4) If certified evidence referred to in subsection 48.1(2) is being admitted as evidence in a trial referred to in subsection (1), the court shall not adjourn the trial for the purpose of having any of the following persons attend to give evidence unless the court is satisfied that the oral evidence of the person is necessary in order to ensure a fair trial:

1. The provincial offences officer who completed the certificate of offence or the certificate of parking infraction, as the case may be.

2. Any provincial offences officer who provided certified evidence in respect of the proceeding.

See: 2009, c. 33, Sched. 4, ss. 1(41), 5(4).

Power of clerk to adjourn

(5) The clerk of the court may, on behalf of the court, adjourn,

(a) the first trial date for a proceeding commenced under Part I or Part II to a date agreed to by the defendant and the prosecutor in a written agreement filed with the court; and

(b) any proceeding under this Act or any step in a proceeding under this Act, where no justice is able to attend in person, to a date chosen in accordance with the instructions of a justice.

Appearance by defendant

50(1) A defendant may appear and act personally or by representative.

Appearance by corporation

(2) A defendant that is a corporation shall appear and act by representative.

Exclusion of representatives

(3) The court may bar any person, other than a person who is licensed under the *Law Society Act*, from appearing as a representative if the court finds that the person is not competent properly to represent or advise the person for whom he or she appears, or does not understand and comply with the duties and responsibilities of a representative.

Compelling attendance of defendant

51. Although a defendant appears by representative, the court may order the defendant to attend personally, and, where it appears to be necessary to do so, may issue a summons in the prescribed form.

Restrictions on hearing and publication
Excluding defendant from hearing

52(1) The court may cause the defendant to be removed and to be kept out of court,

(a) when the defendant misconducts himself or herself by interrupting the proceeding so that to continue in the presence of the defendant would not be feasible; or

(b) where, during the trial of an issue as to whether the defendant is, because of mental disorder, unable to conduct his or her defence, the court is satisfied that failure to do so might have an adverse effect on the mental health of the defendant.

Excluding public from hearing

(2) The court may exclude the public or any member of the public from a hearing where, in the opinion of the court, it is necessary to do so,

(a) for the maintenance of order in the courtroom;

(b) to protect the reputation of a minor; or

(c) to remove an influence that might affect the testimony of a witness.

Prohibition of publication of evidence

(3) Where the court considers it necessary to do so to protect the reputation of a minor, the court may make an order prohibiting the publication or broadcast of the identity of the minor or of the evidence or any part of the evidence taken at the hearing.

Failure of prosecutor to appear

53(1) Where the defendant appears for a hearing and the prosecutor, having had due notice, does not appear, the court may dismiss the charge or may adjourn the hearing to another time upon such terms as it considers proper.

Idem

(2) Where the prosecutor does not appear at the time and place appointed for the resumption of an adjourned hearing under subsection (1), the court may dismiss the charge.

Costs

(3) Where a hearing is adjourned under subsection (1) or a charge is dismissed under subsection (2), the court may make an order under section 60 for the payment of costs.

Written order of dismissal

(4) Where a charge is dismissed under subsection (1) or (2), the court may, if requested by the defendant, draw up an order of dismissal stating the grounds therefor and shall give the defendant a certified copy of the order of dismissal which is, without further proof, a bar to any subsequent proceeding against the defendant in respect of the same cause.

Conviction in the absence of the defendant

54(1) Where a defendant does not appear at the time and place appointed for a hearing and it is proved by the prosecutor, having been given a reasonable opportunity to do so, that a summons was served, a notice of trial was given under Part I or II, an undertaking to appear was given or a recognizance to appear was entered into, as the case may be, or where the defendant does not appear upon the resumption of a hearing that has been adjourned, the court may,

(a) proceed to hear and determine the proceeding in the absence of the defendant; or

(b) adjourn the hearing and, if it thinks fit, issue a summons to appear or issue a warrant in the prescribed form for the arrest of the defendant.

Proceeding arising from failure to appear

(2) Where the court proceeds under clause (1)(a) or adjourns the hearing under clause (1)(b) without issuing a summons or warrant, no proceeding arising out of the failure of the defendant to appear at the time and place appointed for the hearing or for the resumption of the hearing shall be instituted, or if instituted shall be proceeded with, except with the consent of the Attorney General or his or her agent.

Included offences

55. Where the offence as charged includes another offence, the defendant may be convicted of an offence so included that is proved, although the whole offence charged is not proved.

SENTENCING

Pre-sentence report

56(1) Where a defendant is convicted of an offence in a proceeding commenced by information, the court may direct a probation officer to prepare and file with the court a report in writing relating to the defendant for the purpose of assisting the court in imposing sentence.

Service

(2) Where a report is filed with the court under subsection (1), the clerk of the court shall cause a copy of the report to be provided to the defendant or the defendant's representative and to the prosecutor.

Other information relevant to sentence
Submissions as to sentence

57(1) Where a defendant who appears is convicted of an offence, the court shall give the prosecutor and the defendant's representative an opportunity to make submissions as to sentence and, where the defendant has no representative, the court shall ask the defendant if he or she has anything to say before sentence is passed.

Omission to comply

(2) The omission to comply with subsection (1) does not affect the validity of the proceeding.

Inquiries by court

(3) Where a defendant is convicted of an offence, the court may make such inquiries, on oath or otherwise, of and concerning the defendant as it considers desirable, including the defendant's economic circumstances, but the defendant shall not be compelled to answer.

Proof of previous conviction

(4) A certificate setting out with reasonable particularity the finding of guilt or acquittal or conviction and sentence in Canada of a person signed by,

(a) the person who made the adjudication; or

(b) the clerk of the court where the adjudication was made,

is, upon the court being satisfied that the defendant is the person referred to in the certificate, admissible in evidence and is proof, in the absence of evidence to the contrary, of the facts stated therein without proof of the signature or the official character of the person appearing to have signed the certificate.

Time spent in custody considered

58. In determining the sentence to be imposed on a person convicted of an offence, the justice may take into account any time spent in custody by the person as a result of the offence.

Provision for minimum penalty

59(1) No penalty prescribed for an offence is a minimum penalty unless it is specifically declared to be a minimum.

Relief against minimum fine

(2) Although the provision that creates the penalty for an offence prescribes a minimum fine, where in the opinion of the court exceptional circumstances exist so that to impose the minimum fine would be unduly oppressive or otherwise not in the interests of justice, the court may impose a fine that is less than the minimum or suspend the sentence.

Idem, re imprisonment

(3) Where a minimum penalty is prescribed for an offence and the minimum penalty includes imprisonment, the court may, despite the prescribed penalty, impose a fine of not more than $5,000 in lieu of imprisonment.

Costs
Fixed costs on conviction

60(1) Upon conviction, the defendant is liable to pay to the court an amount by way of costs that is fixed by the regulations.

Costs respecting witnesses

(2) The court may, in its discretion, order costs towards fees and expenses reasonably incurred by or on behalf of witnesses in amounts not exceeding the maximum fixed by the regulations, to be paid,

(a) to the court or prosecutor by the defendant; or

(b) to the defendant by the person who laid the information or issued the certificate, as the case may be,

but where the proceeding is commenced by means of a certificate, the total of such costs shall not exceed $100.

Costs collectable as a fine

(3) Costs payable under this section shall be deemed to be a fine for the purpose of enforcing payment.

Surcharge

60.1(1) If a person is convicted of an offence in a proceeding commenced under Part I or III and a fine is imposed in respect of that offence, a surcharge is payable by that person in the amount determined by regulations made under this Act.

Collection

(2) The surcharge shall be deemed to be a fine for the purpose of enforcing payment.

Priorities

(3) Any payments made by a defendant shall be credited towards payment of the fine until it is fully paid and then towards payment of the surcharge.

Part X agreements

(3.1) When an agreement made under Part X applies to a fine, payments made by the defendant shall first be credited towards payment of the surcharge, not as described in subsection (3).

Special purpose account

(4) Surcharges paid into the Consolidated Revenue Fund shall be credited to the victims' justice fund account and shall be deemed to be money received by the Crown for a special purpose.

Same

(4.1) Subsection (4) also applies to payments received under clause 165(5)(a).

(5), (6) Repealed.

Regulations

(7) The Lieutenant Governor in Council may make regulations,

(a) prescribing the amount of the surcharges or the method by which they are to be calculated;

(b) Repealed.

(c) exempting any offence or class of offence from the application of subsection (1).

(8) Repealed.

General penalty

61. Except where otherwise expressly provided by law, every person who is convicted of an offence is liable to a fine of not more than $5,000.

Minute of conviction

62. Where a court convicts a defendant or dismisses a charge, a minute of the dismissal or conviction and sentence shall be made by the court, and, upon request by the defendant or the prosecutor or by the Attorney General or his or her agent, the court shall cause a copy thereof certified by the clerk of the court to be delivered to the person making the request.

Time when imprisonment starts

63(1) The term of imprisonment imposed by sentence shall, unless otherwise directed in the sentence, commence on the day on which the convicted person is taken into custody thereunder, but no time during which the convicted person is imprisoned or out on bail before sentence shall be reckoned as part of the term of imprisonment to which he or she is sentenced.

Idem

(2) Where the court imposes imprisonment, the court may order custody to commence on a day not later than thirty days after the day of sentencing.

Sentences consecutive

64. Where a person is subject to more than one term of imprisonment at the same time, the terms shall be served consecutively except in so far as the court has ordered a term to be served concurrently with any other term of imprisonment.

Warrant of committal

65(1) A warrant of committal is sufficient authority,

(a) for the conveyance of the prisoner in custody for the purpose of committal under the warrant; and

(b) for the reception and detention of the prisoner by keepers of prisons in accordance with the terms of the warrant.

Conveyance of prisoner

(2) A person to whom a warrant of committal is directed shall convey the prisoner to the correctional institution named in the warrant.

Prisoner subject to rules of institution

(3) A sentence of imprisonment shall be served in accordance with the enactments and rules that govern the institution to which the prisoner is sentenced.

When fine due

66(1) A fine becomes due and payable fifteen days after its imposition.

Extension of time for payment of a fine

(2) Where the court imposes a fine, the court shall ask the defendant if the defendant wishes an extension of the time for payment of the fine.

Inquiries

(3) Where the defendant requests an extension of the time for payment of the fine, the court may make such inquiries, on oath or affirmation or otherwise, of and concerning the defendant as the court considers desirable, but the defendant shall not be compelled to answer.

Granting of extension

(4) Unless the court finds that the request for extension of time is not made in good faith or that the extension would likely be used to evade payment, the court shall extend the time for payment by ordering periodic payments or otherwise.

Notice where convicted in the absence of the defendant

(5) Where a fine is imposed in the absence of the defendant, the clerk of the court shall give the defendant notice of the fine and its due date and of the defendant's right to make a motion for an extension of the time for payment under subsection (6).

Further motion for extension

(6) The defendant may, at any time by motion in the prescribed form filed in the office of the court, request an extension or further extension of time for payment of a fine and the motion shall be determined by a justice and the justice has the same powers in respect of the motion as the court has under subsections (3) and (4).

Defendant's address

66.1 If a court imposes a fine, grants an extension of time for payment of a fine or deals with a fine under section 69, and the defendant is before the court, the court shall require the defendant to provide the defendant's current address to the clerk of the court.

Fee for refused cheque collectable as a fine

66.2 When a person purports to pay a fine by a cheque that the drawee of the cheque refuses to cash and thereby becomes liable to pay a fee in the amount prescribed for the purpose of section 8.1 of the *Financial Administration Act*, the fee shall be deemed to be a fine for the purpose of enforcing payment.

Regulation for work credits for fines

67. The Lieutenant Governor in Council may make regulations establishing a program to permit the payment of fines by means of credits for work performed, and, for the purpose and without restricting the generality of the foregoing may,

(a) prescribe classes of work and the conditions under which they are to be performed;

(b) prescribe a system of credits;

(c) provide for any matter necessary for the effective administration of the program,

and any regulation may limit its application to any part or parts of Ontario.

Civil enforcement of fines

68(1) When the payment of a fine is in default, the clerk of the court may complete a certificate in the prescribed form as to the imposition of the fine and the amount remaining unpaid and file the certificate in a court of competent jurisdiction and upon filing, the certificate shall be deemed to be an order or judgment of that court for the purposes of enforcement.

(2) Repealed.

Certificate of discharge

(3) Where a certificate has been filed under subsection (1) and the fine is fully paid, the clerk shall file a certificate of payment upon which the certificate of default is discharged and, where a writ of execution has been filed with the sheriff, the clerk shall file a certificate of payment with the sheriff, upon which the writ is cancelled.

Costs of enforcement

(4) Costs incurred in enforcing the deemed court order or judgment shall be added to the order or judgment and form part of it.

More than one fine

(5) The clerk may complete and file one certificate under this section in respect of two or more fines imposed on the same person.

Default

69(1) The payment of a fine is in default if any part of it is due and unpaid for fifteen days or more.

Order on default

(2) A justice of the peace who is satisfied that payment of a fine is in default,

(a) shall order that any permit, licence, registration or privilege in respect of which a suspension is authorized under any Act because of non-payment of the fine be suspended until the fine is paid;

(b) shall order that any permit, licence, registration or privilege in respect of which any Act authorizes a refusal to renew, validate or issue the permit, licence, registration or privilege because of non-payment of the fine not be renewed, validated or issued until the fine is paid; and

(c) may direct the clerk of the court to proceed with civil enforcement under section 68.

Highway Traffic Act permits

(3) If section 7 of the *Highway Traffic Act* authorizes an order or direction under this section that any permit under that Act not be validated or issued because payment

of a fine is in default, a person designated by the regulations who is satisfied that payment of a fine is in default shall direct that until the fine is paid,

(a) validation of any permit held by the person who has defaulted be refused; and

(b) issuance of any permit to the person who has defaulted be refused.

Restriction

(4) If a person holds more than one permit and a direction in respect of that person is made under clause (3)(a), the direction shall not apply so as to prevent validation of any permit in respect of which the numbered plate evidencing validation of the permit had not been displayed on the vehicle involved in the infraction.

Highway Traffic Act licences

(5) If section 46 of the *Highway Traffic Act* authorizes an order or direction under this section that any licence under that Act be suspended or not be issued because payment of a fine is in default, a person designated by the regulations who is satisfied that payment of a fine is in default shall direct that until the fine is paid,

(a) if the person who has defaulted holds a licence, the licence be suspended; or

(b) if the person who has defaulted does not hold a licence, no licence be issued to him or her.

Obtaining convicted person's attendance

(6) A justice may issue a warrant requiring that a person who has defaulted be arrested and brought before a justice as soon as possible if other reasonable methods of collecting the fine have been tried and have failed, or would not appear to be likely to result in payment within a reasonable period of time.

Alternative summons procedure

(7) The clerk of the court that imposed the fine that is in default may issue a summons requiring the person who has defaulted to appear before a justice if the conditions described in subsection (6) exist.

Service of summons

(8) The summons referred to in subsection (7) may be served by regular prepaid mail.

Hearing

(9) If a person who has defaulted in paying a fine is brought before a justice as a result of a warrant issued under subsection (6) or such a person appears before a justice as a result of a summons issued under subsection (7), the justice shall hold a hearing to determine whether the person is unable to pay the fine within a reasonable period of time.

Onus

(10) In a hearing under subsection (9), the onus of proving that the person is unable to pay the fine within a reasonable period of time is on the person who has defaulted.

Adjournment

(11) The justice may adjourn the hearing from time to time at the request of the person who has defaulted.

Warning

(12) When an adjournment is granted, the justice shall warn the person who has defaulted that if the person fails to appear for the resumption of the hearing, the hearing may proceed in the person's absence.

Failure to warn

(13) If a hearing was adjourned and the person who has defaulted does not appear when it is resumed, the hearing may proceed in the person's absence even if the warning required by subsection (12) was not given.

Warrant of committal

(14) If the justice is not satisfied that the person who has defaulted is unable to pay the fine within a reasonable period of time and that incarceration of the person would not be contrary to the public interest, the justice may issue a warrant for the person's committal or may order that such other steps be taken to enforce the fine as appear to him or her to be appropriate.

Note: On a day to be named by proclamation of the Lieutenant Governor, section 69 is amended by adding the following subsection:

Inability to pay

(14.1) Despite subsection 165(3), a defendant may, in accordance with the regulations, apply to a justice to reduce or expunge a defaulted fine under subsection (15) where the defendant meets the criteria for inability to pay defined in the regulations.

See: 2009, c. 33, Sched. 4, ss. 1(45), 5(4).

Inability to pay fine

(15) If the justice is satisfied that the person who has defaulted is unable to pay the fine within a reasonable period of time, the justice may,

(a) grant an extension of the time allowed for payment of the fine;

(b) require the person to pay the fine according to a schedule of payments established by the justice;

(c) in exceptional circumstances, reduce the amount of the fine or order that the fine does not have to be paid.

Term of imprisonment

(16) Subject to subsection (17), the term of imprisonment under a warrant issued under subsection (14) shall be for three days, plus,

(a) if the amount that has not been paid is not greater than $50, one day; or

(b) if the amount that has not been paid is greater than $50, a number of days equal to the sum of one plus the number obtained when the unpaid amount is divided by $50, rounded down to the nearest whole number.

Limit

(17) The term of imprisonment shall not exceed the greater of,

(a) ninety days; and

(b) half of the maximum number of days of imprisonment that may be imposed on conviction of the offence that the person who has defaulted was convicted of.

Effect of payments

(18) Subject to subsection (19), a payment in respect of the fine in default that is made after a warrant is issued under subsection (14) shall result in a reduction of the term of imprisonment by the number of days that is in the same proportion to the term as the payment is to the amount in default.

Restriction

(19) A payment that is less than the amount outstanding on the fine shall not result in a reduction of the term of imprisonment unless it is an amount that would reduce the term by a number of days that is a whole number.

Exceptions

(20) Subsections (6) to (19) do not apply if,

    (a) the person who has defaulted is less than eighteen years old; or

    (b) the fine was imposed on conviction of an offence under subsection 31(2) or (4) of the *Liquor Licence Act*.

Exceptional circumstances

(21) In exceptional circumstances where, in the opinion of the court that imposed the fine, to proceed under subsections (6) to (14) would defeat the ends of justice, the court may order that no warrant be issued under subsection (6) and that no summons be issued under subsection (7).

Regulations

(22) The Lieutenant Governor in Council may make regulations,

    (a) designating a person or class of persons for purposes of subsections (3) and (5);

Note: On a day to be named by proclamation of the Lieutenant Governor, subsection (22) is amended by adding the following clause:

    (a.1) prescribing the form and procedure for an application under subsection (14.1);

See: 2009, c. 33, Sched. 4, ss. 1(46), 5(4).

    (b) prescribing criteria to be considered by a justice in determining whether a person is unable to pay a fine within a reasonable period of time.

Disclosure to consumer reporting agency

69.1(1) When a fine has been in default for at least 90 days, the Ministry of the Attorney General may disclose to a consumer reporting agency the name of the defaulter, the amount of the fine and the date the fine went into default.

Same

(2) When a fine disclosed to a consumer reporting agency has been paid in full, the Ministry of the Attorney General shall inform the agency of this fact as soon as possible after payment.

Fee where fine in default

70(1) Where the payment of a fine is in default and the time for payment is not extended or further extended under subsection 66(6), the defendant shall pay the administrative fee prescribed by the regulations.

Fee collectable as a fine

(2) For the purpose of making and enforcing payment, a fee payable under this section shall be deemed to be part of the fine that is in default.

Suspension of fine on conditions

71. Where an Act provides that a fine may be suspended subject to the performance of a condition,

(a) the period of suspension shall be fixed by the court and shall be for not more than one year;

(b) the court shall provide in its order of suspension the method of proving the performance of the condition;

(c) the suspension is in addition to and not in lieu of any other power of the court in respect of the fine; and

(d) the fine is not in default until fifteen days have elapsed after notice that the period of suspension has expired is given to the defendant.

Probation order

72(1) Where a defendant is convicted of an offence in a proceeding commenced by information, the court may, having regard to the age, character and background of the defendant, the nature of the offence and the circumstances surrounding its commission,

(a) suspend the passing of sentence and direct that the defendant comply with the conditions prescribed in a probation order;

(b) in addition to fining the defendant or sentencing the defendant to imprisonment, whether in default of payment of a fine or otherwise, direct that the defendant comply with the conditions prescribed in a probation order; or

(c) where it imposes a sentence of imprisonment on the defendant, whether in default of payment of a fine or otherwise, that does not exceed ninety days, order that the sentence be served intermittently at such times as are specified in the order and direct that the defendant, at all times when he or she is not in confinement pursuant to such order, comply with the conditions prescribed in a probation order.

Statutory conditions of order

(2) A probation order shall be deemed to contain the conditions that,

(a) the defendant not commit the same or any related or similar offence, or any offence under a statute of Canada or Ontario or any other province of Canada that is punishable by imprisonment;

(b) the defendant appear before the court as and when required; and

(c) the defendant notify the court of any change in the defendant's address.

Conditions imposed by court

(3) In addition to the conditions set out in subsection (2), the court may prescribe as a condition in a probation order,

(a) that the defendant satisfy any compensation or restitution that is required or authorized by an Act;

(b) with the consent of the defendant and where the conviction is of an offence that is punishable by imprisonment, that the defendant perform a community service as set out in the order;

(c) where the conviction is of an offence punishable by imprisonment, such other conditions relating to the circumstances of the offence and of the defendant that contributed to the commission of the offence as the court considers appropriate to prevent similar unlawful conduct or to contribute to the rehabilitation of the defendant; or

(d) where considered necessary for the purpose of implementing the conditions of the probation order, that the defendant report to a responsible person designated by the court and, in addition, where the circumstances warrant it, that the defendant be under the supervision of the person to whom he or she is required to report.

Form of order

(4) A probation order shall be in the prescribed form and the court shall specify therein the period for which it is to remain in force, which shall not be for more than two years from the date when the order takes effect.

Notice of order

(5) Where the court makes a probation order, it shall cause a copy of the order and a copy of section 75 to be given to the defendant.

Regulations for community service orders

(6) The Lieutenant Governor in Council may make regulations governing restitution, compensation and community service orders, including their terms and conditions.

Exception

(7) The court shall not make a probation order when an individual has been convicted of an absolute liability offence, unless the order is made in addition to a sentence of imprisonment imposed under section 69 in default of payment of a fine.

When order comes into force

73(1) A probation order comes into force,

    (a) on the date on which the order is made; or

    (b) where the defendant is sentenced to imprisonment other than a sentence to be served intermittently, upon the expiration of that sentence.

Continuation in force

(2) Subject to section 75, where a defendant who is bound by a probation order is convicted of an offence or is imprisoned in default of payment of a fine, the order continues in force except in so far as the sentence or imprisonment renders it impossible for the defendant to comply for the time being with the order.

Variation of probation order

74. The court may, at any time upon the application of the defendant or prosecutor with notice to the other, after a hearing or, with the consent of the parties, without a hearing,

    (a) make any changes in or additions to the conditions prescribed in the order that in the opinion of the court are rendered desirable by a change in circumstances;

    (b) relieve the defendant, either absolutely or upon such terms or for such period as the court considers desirable, of compliance with any condition described in any of the clauses in subsection 72(3) that is prescribed in the order; or

    (c) terminate the order or decrease the period for which the probation order is to remain in force,

and the court shall thereupon endorse the probation order accordingly and, if it changes or adds to the conditions prescribed in the order, inform the defendant of its action and give the defendant a copy of the order so endorsed.

Breach of probation order

75. Where a defendant who is bound by a probation order is convicted of an offence constituting a breach of condition of the order and,

(a) the time within which the defendant may appeal or make a motion for leave to appeal against that conviction has expired and the defendant has not taken an appeal or made a motion for leave to appeal;

(b) the defendant has taken an appeal or made a motion for leave to appeal against the conviction and the appeal or motion for leave has been dismissed or abandoned; or

(c) the defendant has given written notice to the court that convicted the defendant that the defendant elects not to appeal,

or where the defendant otherwise wilfully fails or refuses to comply with the order, the defendant is guilty of an offence and upon conviction the court may,

(d) impose a fine of not more than $1,000 or imprisonment for a term of not more than thirty days, or both, and in lieu of or in addition to the penalty, continue the probation order with such changes or additions and for such extended term, not exceeding an additional year, as the court considers reasonable; or

(e) where the justice presiding is the justice who made the original order, in lieu of imposing the penalty under clause (d), revoke the probation order and impose the sentence the passing of which was suspended upon the making of the probation order.

PART V
GENERAL PROVISIONS

Limitation
76(1) A proceeding shall not be commenced after the expiration of any limitation period prescribed by or under any Act for the offence or, where no limitation period is prescribed, after six months after the date on which the offence was, or is alleged to have been, committed.

Extension
(2) A limitation period may be extended by a justice with the consent of the defendant.

Electronic format and filing
76.1(1) A document may, in accordance with the regulations, be completed, signed and filed by electronic means in an electronic format.

Electronic copy
(1.1) When a document is filed in paper form, an electronic copy may be retained instead of the paper original if there exists a reliable assurance as to the integrity of the information contained in the electronic copy.

Duty to ensure integrity
(1.2) A person who makes, stores or reproduces an electronic copy of a document for the purposes of subsection (1.1) shall take all reasonable steps to ensure the integrity of the information contained in the electronic copy.

Deemed original
(2) A printed copy of a document filed under subsection (1) or retained under subsection (1.1) shall be deemed to have been filed as the original document if it is printed in accordance with the regulations and for the purpose of disposing of a charge under this Act.

Interpretation

(3) In this section,

"document" includes a certificate of offence, certificate of parking infraction, a certificate requesting a conviction, an offence notice and a parking infraction notice.

Regulations

(4) The Lieutenant Governor in Council may make regulations respecting,

(a) the completion and signing of documents by electronic means;

(b) the filing of documents by direct electronic transmission;

(c) the printing of documents filed by direct electronic transmission.

Parties to offence

77(1) Every person is a party to an offence who,

(a) actually commits it;

(b) does or omits to do anything for the purpose of aiding any person to commit it; or

(c) abets any person in committing it.

Common purpose

(2) Where two or more persons form an intention in common to carry out an unlawful purpose and to assist each other therein and any one of them, in carrying out the common purpose, commits an offence, each of them who knew or ought to have known that the commission of the offence would be a probable consequence of carrying out the common purpose is a party to the offence.

Counselling

78(1) Where a person counsels or procures another person to be a party to an offence and that other person is afterwards a party to the offence, the person who counselled or procured is a party to the offence, even if the offence was committed in a way different from that which was counselled or procured.

Idem

(2) Every person who counsels or procures another person to be a party to an offence is a party to every offence that the other commits in consequence of the counselling or procuring that the person who counselled or procured knew or ought to have known was likely to be committed in consequence of the counselling or procuring.

Computation of age

79. In the absence of other evidence, or by way of corroboration of other evidence, a justice may infer the age of a person from his or her appearance.

Common law defences

80. Every rule and principle of the common law that renders any circumstance a justification or excuse for an act or a defence to a charge continues in force and applies in respect of offences, except in so far as they are altered by or inconsistent with this or any other Act.

Ignorance of the law

81. Ignorance of the law by a person who commits an offence is not an excuse for committing the offence.

Representation

82. A defendant may act by representative.

Evidence, recording and taking

83(1) A proceeding in which evidence is taken shall be recorded.

Evidence under oath or affirmation

(2) Evidence under this Act shall be taken under oath or affirmation, except as otherwise provided by law.

Definition

83.1(1) In this section,

"electronic method" means video conference, audio conference, telephone conference or other method determined by the regulations.

Appearance by electronic method

(2) Subject to this section, in any proceeding under this Act or any step in a proceeding under this Act, if the appropriate equipment is available at the courthouse where the proceeding occurs,

  (a) a witness may give evidence by electronic method;

  (b) a defendant may appear by electronic method;

  (c) a prosecutor may appear and prosecute by electronic method; and

  (d) an interpreter may interpret by electronic method.

Consent required

(3) A witness may appear by electronic method to give evidence in a proceeding commenced by information under Part III only with the consent of both the prosecutor and the defendant.

Attendance by justice

(3.1) A justice may attend and conduct a sentencing hearing under sections 5.1 and 7 and any other proceeding or any step in a proceeding determined by the regulations, by means of electronic method, if the appropriate equipment is available at the courthouse where the proceeding occurs, and the justice may,

  (a) adjourn the sentencing hearing to have the defendant appear in person before the justice for the purpose of ensuring that the defendant understands the plea; and

  (b) adjourn any other proceeding or step in a proceeding determined by the regulations if he or she is satisfied that the interests of justice require it or it is necessary for a fair trial.

Limited use of certain electronic methods

(4) Attendance by audio conference or telephone conference may only be used for the purpose of,

  (a) attending a pre-trial conference;

  (b) attending a meeting between the defendant and the prosecutor under section 5.1; or

  (c) attending or appearing at any other proceeding or step in a proceeding determined by the regulations.

Appearance in person

(5) The court may order any person described in subsection (2) to appear in person if it is satisfied that the interests of justice require it or it is necessary for a fair trial.

Oaths

(6) Despite the *Commissioners for taking Affidavits Act*, where evidence is given under oath by electronic method, the oath may be administered by the same electronic method.

Regulations

(7) The Lieutenant Governor in Council may make regulations,

(a) respecting the conditions for using any electronic method, including the degree of any remoteness required;

(b) determining proceedings where attendance or appearance may be made by electronic method;

(c) requiring the payment of fees for using electronic methods, fixing the amounts of the fees, and prescribing the circumstances in which and the conditions under which a justice or another person designated in the regulations may waive the payment of a fee.

Interpreters

84(1) A justice may authorize a person to act as interpreter in a proceeding before the justice where the person swears the prescribed oath and, in the opinion of the justice, is competent.

Idem

(2) A judge may authorize a person to act as interpreter in proceedings under this Act where the person swears the prescribed oath and, in the opinion of the judge is competent and likely to be readily available.

Extension of time

85(1) Subject to this section, the court may extend any time fixed by this Act, by the regulations made under this Act or the rules of court for doing any thing other than commencing or recommencing a proceeding, whether or not the time has expired.

Limit on number of applications

(2) No more than one application for an extension of the time for filing of an appeal may be made in respect of a conviction.

Exception for commencing parking proceeding

(3) A justice may extend the time for commencing a parking proceeding where the court is unable to obtain proof of ownership of the vehicle or to send a notice of impending conviction to the defendant within that time because of extraordinary circumstances, including labour disputes and disruptions of postal services, power services and technological facilities.

Penalty for false statements

86. Every person who makes an assertion of fact in a statement or entry in a document or form for use under this Act knowing that the assertion is false is guilty of an offence and on conviction is liable to a fine of not more than $2,000.

Delivery

87(1) Any notice or document required or authorized to be given or delivered under this Act or the rules of court is sufficiently given or delivered if,

(a) delivered personally or by mail;

(b) delivered in accordance with a method provided by this Act or the regulations; or

(c) delivered in accordance with a method provided under any other Act or prescribed by the rules of court.

Same

(2) Where a notice or document that is required or authorized to be given or delivered to a person under this Act is mailed to the person at the person's last known

address appearing on the records of the court in the proceeding, there is a rebuttable presumption that the notice or document is delivered to the person.

Regulations

(3) The Lieutenant Governor in Council may make regulations respecting the method of delivery for any notice or document, including additional electronic methods, for the purposes of this Act.

Civil remedies preserved

88. No civil remedy for an act or omission is suspended or affected for the reason that the act or omission is an offence.

Process on holidays

89. Any action authorized or required by this Act is not invalid for the reason only that the action was taken on a non-juridical day.

Irregularities in form

90.(1) The validity of any proceeding is not affected by,

(a) any irregularity or defect in the substance or form of the summons, warrant, offence notice, parking infraction notice, undertaking to appear or recognizance; or

(b) any variance between the charge set out in the summons, warrant, parking infraction notice, offence notice, undertaking to appear or recognizance and the charge set out in the information or certificate.

Adjournment to meet irregularities

(2) Where it appears to the court that the defendant has been misled by any irregularity, defect or variance mentioned in subsection (1), the court may adjourn the hearing and may make such order as the court considers appropriate, including an order under section 60 for the payment of costs.

Contempt

91(1) Except as otherwise provided by an Act, every person who commits contempt in the face of a justice of the peace presiding over the Ontario Court of Justice in a proceeding under this Act is on conviction liable to a fine of not more than $1,000 or to imprisonment for a term of not more than thirty days, or to both.

Statement to offender

(2) Before a proceeding is taken for contempt under subsection (1), the justice of the peace shall inform the offender of the conduct complained of and the nature of the contempt and inform him or her of the right to show cause why he or she should not be punished.

Show cause

(3) A punishment for contempt in the face of the court shall not be imposed without giving the offender an opportunity to show cause why he or she should not be punished.

Adjournment for adjudication

(4) Except where, in the opinion of the justice of the peace, it is necessary to deal with the contempt immediately for the preservation of order and control in the courtroom, the justice of the peace shall adjourn the contempt proceeding to another day.

Adjudication by judge

(5) A contempt proceeding that is adjourned to another day under subsection (4) shall be heard and determined by the court presided over by a provincial judge.

Arrest for immediate adjudication

(6) Where the justice of the peace proceeds to deal with a contempt immediately and without adjournment under subsection (4), the justice of the peace may order the offender arrested and detained in the courtroom for the purpose of the hearing and determination.

Barring representative in contempt

(7) Where the offender is appearing before the court as a representative and the offender is not licensed under the *Law Society Act*, the court may order that he or she be barred from acting as representative in the proceeding in addition to any other punishment to which he or she is liable.

Appeals

(8) An order of punishment for contempt under this section is appealable in the same manner as if it were a conviction in a proceeding commenced by certificate under Part I of this Act.

Enforcement

(9) This Act applies for the purpose of enforcing a punishment by way of a fine or imprisonment under this section.

Regulations for purpose of Act

92. The Lieutenant Governor in Council may make regulations,

(a) prescribing any matter referred to in this Act as prescribed by the regulations;

(b) prescribing the form of certificate as to ownership of a motor vehicle given by the Registrar under subsection 210(7) of the *Highway Traffic Act* for the purpose of proceedings under this Act;

(c) providing for the extension of times prescribed by or under this Act or the rules of court in the event of a disruption in postal services;

(d) requiring the payment of fees upon the filing of anything required or permitted to be filed under this Act or the rules and fixing the amounts thereof, and providing for the waiver of the payment of a fee by a justice, or by a judge under Part VII, in such circumstances and under such conditions as are set out in the regulations;

(e) fixing costs payable upon conviction and referred to in subsection 60(1);

(f) fixing the items in respect of which costs may be awarded under subsection 60(2) and prescribing the maximum amounts that may be awarded in respect of each item;

(g) prescribing administrative fees for the purposes of subsection 70(1) for the late payment of fines or classes of fines, and prescribing the classes.

PART VI
YOUNG PERSONS

Definitions, Part VI

93. In this Part,

"parent," when used with reference to a young person, includes an adult with whom the young person ordinarily resides;

"young person" means a person who is or, in the absence of evidence to the contrary, appears to be,

    (a) twelve years of age or more, but

    (b) under sixteen years of age,

and includes a person sixteen years of age or more charged with having committed an offence while he or she was twelve years of age or more but under sixteen years of age.

Minimum age

94. No person shall be convicted of an offence committed while he or she was under twelve years of age.

Offence notice not to be used

95. A proceeding commenced against a young person by certificate of offence shall not be initiated by an offence notice under clause 3(2)(a).

Notice to parent

96(1) Where a summons is served upon a young person or a young person is released on a recognizance under this Act, the provincial offences officer, in the case of a summons, or the officer in charge, in the case of a recognizance, shall as soon as practicable give notice to a parent of the young person by delivering a copy of the summons or recognizance to the parent.

Where no notice given

(2) Where notice has not been given under subsection (1) and no person to whom notice could have been given appears with the young person, the court may,

    (a) adjourn the hearing to another time to permit notice to be given; or

    (b) dispense with notice.

Saving

(3) Failure to give notice to a parent under subsection (1) does not in itself invalidate the proceeding against the young person.

Sentence where proceeding commenced by certificate

97(1) Despite subsection 12(1), where a young person is found guilty of an offence in a proceeding commenced by certificate, the court may,

    (a) convict the young person and,

        (i) order the young person to pay a fine not exceeding the set fine that would be payable for the offence by an adult, the maximum fine prescribed for the offence, or $300, whichever is the least, or

        (ii) suspend the passing of sentence and direct that the young person comply with the conditions prescribed in a probation order; or

    (b) discharge the young person absolutely.

Term of probation order

(2) Section 72 applies with necessary modifications to a probation order made under subclause (1)(a)(ii), in the same manner as if the proceeding were commenced by information, except that the probation order shall not remain in force for more than ninety days from the date when it takes effect.

s. 12(2) applies where proceeding initiated by summons

(3) Subsection 12(2) applies with necessary modifications where a young person is convicted of an offence in a proceeding initiated by summons, in the same manner as if the proceeding were initiated by offence notice.

Young person to be present at trial

98(1) Subject to subsection 52(1) and subsection (2) of this section, a young person shall be present in court during the whole of his or her trial.

Court may permit absence

(2) The court may permit a young person to be absent during the whole or any part of his or her trial, on such conditions as the court considers proper.

Application of ss. 42, 54

(3) Sections 42 and 54 do not apply to a young person who is a defendant.

Failure of young person to appear

(4) Where a young person who is a defendant does not appear at the time and place appointed for a hearing and it is proved by the prosecutor, having been given a reasonable opportunity to do so, that a summons was served, an undertaking to appear was given or a recognizance to appear was entered into, as the case may be, or where the young person does not appear upon the resumption of a hearing that has been adjourned, the court may adjourn the hearing and issue a summons to appear or issue a warrant in the prescribed form for the arrest of the young person.

Compelling young person's attendance

(5) Where a young person does not attend personally in response to a summons issued under section 51 and it is proved by the prosecutor, having been given a reasonable opportunity to do so, that the summons was served, the court may adjourn the hearing and issue a further summons or issue a warrant in the prescribed form for the arrest of the young person.

Identity of young person not to be published

99(1) No person shall publish by any means a report,

(a) of an offence committed or alleged to have been committed by a young person; or

(b) of a hearing, adjudication, sentence or appeal concerning a young person who committed or is alleged to have committed an offence,

in which the name of or any information serving to identify the young person is disclosed.

Offence

(2) Every person who contravenes subsection (1) and every director, officer or employee of a corporation who authorizes, permits or acquiesces in a contravention of subsection (1) by the corporation is guilty of an offence and is liable on conviction to a fine of not more than $10,000.

Exceptions

(3) Subsection (1) does not prohibit the following:

1. The disclosure of information by the young person concerned.
2. The disclosure of information by the young person's parent or lawyer, for the purpose of protecting the young person's interests.
3. The disclosure of information by a police officer, for the purpose of investigating an offence which the young person is suspected of having committed.
4. The disclosure of information to an insurer, to enable the insurer to investigate a claim arising out of an offence committed or alleged to have been committed by the young person.
5. The disclosure of information in the course of the administration of justice, but not for the purpose of making the information known in the community.

6. The disclosure of information by a person or member of a class of persons prescribed by the regulations, for a purpose prescribed by the regulations.

Pre-sentence report

100(1) Section 56 applies with necessary modifications where a young person is convicted of an offence in a proceeding commenced by certificate of offence, in the same manner as if the proceeding were commenced by information.

Pre-sentence report mandatory where imprisonment considered

(2) Where a young person who is bound by a probation order is convicted of an offence under section 75 and the court is considering imposing a sentence of imprisonment, the court shall direct a probation officer to prepare and file with the court a report in writing relating to the defendant for the purpose of assisting the court in imposing sentence, and the clerk of the court shall cause a copy of the report to be provided to the defendant or his or her representative and to the prosecutor.

Penalties limited

101(1) Despite the provisions of this or any other Act, no young person shall be sentenced,

(a) to be imprisoned, except under clause 75(d); or

(b) to pay a fine exceeding $1,000.

Sentence where proceeding commenced by information

(2) Where a young person is found guilty of an offence in a proceeding commenced by information, the court may,

(a) convict the young person and,

(i) order the young person to pay a fine not exceeding the maximum prescribed for the offence or $1,000, whichever is less, or

(ii) suspend the passing of sentence and direct that the young person comply with the conditions prescribed in a probation order; or

(b) discharge the young person absolutely.

Term of probation order

(3) A probation order made under subclause (2)(a)(ii) shall not remain in force for more than one year from the date when it takes effect.

No imprisonment for non-payment of fine

102(1) No warrant of committal shall be issued against a young person under section 69.

Probation order in lieu of imprisonment

(2) Where it would be appropriate, but for subsection (1), to issue a warrant against a young person under subsection 69(3) or (4), a judge may direct that the young person comply with the conditions prescribed in a probation order, where the young person has been given fifteen days notice of the intent to make a probation order and has had an opportunity to be heard.

Term of probation order

(3) A probation order made under subsection (2) shall not remain in force for more than ninety days from the date when it takes effect.

Open custody

103. Where a young person is sentenced to a term of imprisonment for breach of probation under clause 75(d), the term of imprisonment shall be served in a place of open custody designated under section 24.1 of the *Young Offenders Act* (Canada), whether in accordance with section 88 of the *Youth Criminal Justice Act* (Canada) or otherwise.

Evidence of young person's age

104. In a proceeding under this Act, a parent's testimony as to a young person's age and any other evidence of a young person's age that the court considers credible or trustworthy in the circumstances are admissible.

Appeal

105. Where the defendant is a young person, an appeal under subsection 135(1) shall be to the Superior Court of Justice, but the procedures and the powers of the court and any appeal from the judgment of the court shall be the same as if the appeal were to the Ontario Court of Justice presided over by a provincial judge.

Arrest without warrant limited

106. No person shall exercise an authority under this or any other Act to arrest a young person without warrant unless the person has reasonable and probable grounds to believe that it is necessary in the public interest to do so in order to,

   (a) establish the young person's identity; or

   (b) prevent the continuation or repetition of an offence that constitutes a serious danger to the young person or to the person or property of another.

Release of young persons after arrest by officer

s. 149 does not apply

107(1) Section 149 does not apply to a young person who has been arrested.

Requirement to release

(2) Where a police officer acting under a warrant or other power of arrest arrests a young person, the police officer shall, as soon as is practicable, release the young person from custody unconditionally or after serving him or her with a summons unless the officer has reasonable and probable grounds to believe that it is necessary in the public interest for the young person to be detained in order to,

   (a) establish the young person's identity; or

   (b) prevent the continuation or repetition of an offence that constitutes a serious danger to the young person or the person or property of another.

Release by officer in charge

(3) Where a young person is not released from custody under subsection (2), the police officer shall deliver the young person to the officer in charge who shall, where in his or her opinion the conditions set out in clause (2)(a) or (b) do not or no longer exist, release the young person,

   (a) unconditionally;

   (b) upon serving the young person with a summons; or

   (c) upon the young person entering into a recognizance in the prescribed form without sureties conditioned for his or her appearance in court.

Notice to parent

(4) Where the officer in charge does not release the young person under subsection (3), the officer in charge shall as soon as possible notify a parent of the young person by advising the parent, orally or in writing, of the young person's arrest, the reason for the arrest and the place of detention.

Release after young person brought before justice

(5) Sections 150 and 151 apply with necessary modifications to the release of a young person from custody under this section.

Place of custody

(6) No young person who is detained under section 150 shall be detained in any part of a place in which an adult who has been charged with or convicted of an offence is detained unless a justice so authorizes, on being satisfied that,

(a) the young person cannot, having regard to the young person's own safety or the safety of others, be detained in a place of temporary detention for young persons; or

(b) no place of temporary detention for young persons is available within a reasonable distance.

Idem

(7) Wherever practicable, a young person who is detained in custody shall be detained in a place of temporary detention designated under the *Youth Criminal Justice Act* (Canada).

Functions of a justice of peace limited

108(1) The functions of a justice with respect to a defendant who is a young person shall be performed only by a judge where a defendant is charged with an offence under section 75.

Exception

(2) Subsection (1) does not apply to the functions of a justice under Parts III and VIII.

PART VII
APPEALS AND REVIEW

Definitions, Part VII

109. In this Part,

"court" means the court to which an appeal is or may be taken under this Part;

"judge" means a judge of the court to which an appeal is or may be taken under this Part;

"sentence" includes any order or disposition consequent upon a conviction and an order as to costs.

Custody pending appeal

110. A defendant who appeals shall, if in custody, remain in custody, but a judge may order his or her release upon any of the conditions set out in subsection 150(2).

Payment of fine before appeal

111(1) A notice of appeal by a defendant shall not be accepted for filing if the defendant has not paid in full the fine imposed by the decision appealed from.

Exception with recognizance

(2) A judge may waive compliance with subsection (1) and order that the appellant enter into a recognizance to appear on the appeal, and the recognizance shall be in such amount, with or without sureties, as the judge directs.

Simultaneous applications

(3) A defendant may file an application to waive compliance with subsection (1) at the same time as the notice of appeal.

Role of prosecutor

(4) The defendant shall give the prosecutor notice of any application to waive compliance with subsection (1) and the prosecutor shall have an opportunity to make submissions in the public interest in respect of the application.

Stay

112. The filing of a notice of appeal does not stay the conviction unless a judge so orders.

Fixing of date where appellant in custody

113(1) Where an appellant is in custody pending the hearing of the appeal and the hearing of the appeal has not commenced within thirty days from the day on which notice of the appeal was given, the person having custody of the appellant shall make a motion to a judge to fix a date for the hearing of the appeal.

Idem

(2) Upon receiving a motion under subsection (1), the judge shall, after giving the prosecutor a reasonable opportunity to be heard, fix a date for the hearing of the appeal and give such directions as the judge thinks appropriate for expediting the hearing of the appeal.

Payment of fine not waiver

114. A person does not waive the right of appeal by reason only that the person pays the fine or complies with any order imposed upon conviction.

Transmittal of material

115. Where a notice of appeal has been filed, the clerk or local register of the appeal court shall notify the clerk of the trial court of the appeal and, upon receipt of the notification, the clerk of the trial court shall transmit the order appealed from and transmit or transfer custody of all other material in his or her possession or control relevant to the proceeding to the clerk or local registrar of the appeal court to be kept with the records of the appeal court.

APPEALS UNDER PART III

Appeals, proceedings commenced by information

116(1) Where a proceeding is commenced by information under Part III, the defendant or the prosecutor or the Attorney General by way of intervention may appeal from,

(a) a conviction;

(b) a dismissal;

(c) a finding as to ability, because of mental disorder, to conduct a defence;

(d) a sentence; or

(e) any other order as to costs.

Appeal court

(2) An appeal under subsection (1) shall be,

(a) where the appeal is from the decision of a justice of the peace, to the Ontario Court of Justice presided over by a provincial judge; or

(b) where the appeal is from the decision of a provincial judge, to the Superior Court of Justice.

Notice of appeal

(3) The appellant shall give notice of appeal in such manner and within such period as is provided by the rules of court.

Simultaneous application

(4) Despite subsection (3), the notice of appeal may be filed at the same time as an application under section 85 to extend the time to give notice of appeal.

Conduct of appeal

117(1) The court may, where it considers it to be in the interests of justice,

(a) order the production of any writing, exhibit or other thing relevant to the appeal;

(a.1) amend the information, unless it is of the opinion that the defendant has been misled or prejudiced in his or her defence or appeal;

(b) order any witness who would have been a compellable witness at the trial, whether or not he or she was called at the trial,

(i) to attend and be examined before the court, or

(ii) to be examined in the manner provided by the rules of court before a judge of the court, or before any officer of the court or justice of the peace or other person appointed by the court for the purpose;

(c) admit, as evidence, an examination that is taken under subclause (b)(ii);

(d) receive the evidence, if tendered, of any witness;

(e) order that any question arising on the appeal that,

(i) involves prolonged examination of writings or accounts, or scientific investigation, and

(ii) cannot in the opinion of the court conveniently be inquired into before the court,

be referred for inquiry and report, in the manner provided by the rules of court, to a special commissioner appointed by the court; and

(f) act upon the report of a commissioner who is appointed under clause (e) in so far as the court thinks fit to do so.

Rights of parties

(2) Where the court exercises a power under this section, the parties or their representatives are entitled to examine or cross-examine witnesses and, in an inquiry under clause (1)(e), are entitled to be present during the inquiry and to adduce evidence and to be heard.

Right to representation

118(1) An appellant or respondent may appear and act personally or by representative.

Attendance while in custody

(2) An appellant or respondent who is in custody as a result of the decision appealed from is entitled to be present at the hearing of the appeal.

Sentencing in absence

(3) The power of a court to impose sentence may be exercised although the appellant or respondent is not present.

Written argument

119. An appellant or respondent may present the case on appeal and argument in writing instead of orally, and the court shall consider any case or argument so presented.

Orders on appeal against conviction, etc.

120(1) On the hearing of an appeal against a conviction or against a finding as to the ability, because of mental disorder, to conduct a defence, the court by order,

   (a) may allow the appeal where it is of the opinion that,

      (i) the finding should be set aside on the ground that it is unreasonable or cannot be supported by the evidence,

      (ii) the judgment of the trial court should be set aside on the ground of a wrong decision on a question of law, or

      (iii) on any ground, there was a miscarriage of justice; or

   (b) may dismiss the appeal where,

      (i) the court is of the opinion that the appellant, although the appellant was not properly convicted on a count or part of an information, was properly convicted on another count or part of the information,

      (ii) the appeal is not decided in favour of the appellant on any ground mentioned in clause (a), or

      (iii) although the court is of the opinion that on any ground mentioned in subclause (a)(ii) the appeal might be decided in favour of the appellant, it is of the opinion that no substantial wrong or miscarriage of justice has occurred.

Idem

   (2) Where the court allows an appeal under clause (1)(a), it shall,

   (a) where the appeal is from a conviction,

      (i) direct a finding of acquittal to be entered, or

      (ii) order a new trial; or

   (b) where the appeal is from a finding as to the ability, because of mental disorder, to conduct a defence, order a new trial, subject to section 44.

Idem

   (3) Where the court dismisses an appeal under clause (1)(b), it may substitute the decision that in its opinion should have been made and affirm the sentence passed by the trial court or impose a sentence that is warranted in law.

Orders on appeal against acquittal

121. Where an appeal is from an acquittal, the court may by order,

   (a) dismiss the appeal; or

   (b) allow the appeal, set aside the finding and,

      (i) order a new trial, or

      (ii) enter a finding of guilt with respect to the offence of which, in its opinion, the person who has been accused of the offence should have been found guilty, and pass a sentence that is warranted in law.

Orders on appeal against sentence

122(1) Where an appeal is taken against sentence, the court shall consider the fitness of the sentence appealed from and may, upon such evidence, if any, as it thinks fit to require or receive, by order,

   (a) dismiss the appeal; or

   (b) vary the sentence within the limits prescribed by law for the offence of which the defendant was convicted,

and, in making any order under clause (b), the court may take into account any time spent in custody by the defendant as a result of the offence.

Variance of sentence

(2) A judgment of a court that varies a sentence has the same force and effect as if it were a sentence passed by the trial court.

One sentence on more than one count

123. Where one sentence is passed upon a finding of guilt on two or more counts, the sentence is good if any of the counts would have justified the sentence.

Appeal based on defect in information or process

124(1) Judgment shall not be given in favour of an appellant based on any alleged defect in the substance or form of an information, certificate or process or any variance between the information, certificate or process and the evidence adduced at trial unless it is shown that objection was taken at the trial and that, in the case of a variance, an adjournment of the trial was refused although the variance had misled the appellant.

Idem

(2) Where an appeal is based on a defect in a conviction or an order, judgment shall not be given in favour of the appellant, but the court shall make an order curing the defect.

Additional orders

125. Where a court exercises any of the powers conferred by sections 117 to 124, it may make any order, in addition, that justice requires.

New trial

126(1) Where a court orders a new trial, it shall be held in the Ontario Court of Justice presided over by a justice other than the justice who tried the defendant in the first instance unless the appeal court directs that the new trial be held before the justice who tried the defendant in the first instance.

Order for release

(2) Where a court orders a new trial, it may make such order for the release or detention of the appellant pending such trial as may be made by a justice under subsection 150(2) and the order may be enforced in the same manner as if it had been made by a justice under that subsection.

Appeal by way of new trial

127(1) Where, because of the condition of the record of the trial in the trial court or for any other reason, the court, upon the motion of the appellant or respondent, is of the opinion that the interests of justice would be better served by hearing and determining the appeal by holding a new trial in the court, the court may order that the appeal shall be heard by way of a new trial in the court and for this purpose this Act applies with necessary modifications in the same manner as to a proceeding in the trial court.

Evidence

(2) The court may, for the purpose of hearing and determining an appeal under subsection (1), permit the evidence of any witness taken before the trial court to be read if that evidence has been authenticated and if,

(a) the appellant and respondent consent;

(b) the court is satisfied that the attendance of the witness cannot reasonably be obtained; or

(c) by reason of the formal nature of the evidence or otherwise the court is satisfied that the opposite party will not be prejudiced,

and any evidence that is read under the authority of this subsection has the same force and effect as if the witness had given the evidence before the court.

Dismissal or abandonment

128(1) The court may, upon proof that notice of an appeal has been given and that,

(a) the appellant has failed to comply with any order made under section 110 or 111 or with the conditions of any recognizance entered into under either of those sections; or

(b) the appeal has not been proceeded with or has been abandoned,

order that the appeal be dismissed.

Dismissal by justice

(2) Where the clerk of the court considers that an appeal has not been proceeded with or has been abandoned, the clerk may, after giving notice to the parties to the appeal, have the matter brought before a justice sitting in open court to determine whether the appeal has been abandoned and the appeal should be dismissed.

Motion to restore

(3) A party to an appeal that was dismissed under subsection (2) may apply to have the appeal restored.

Costs

129(1) Where an appeal is heard and determined or is abandoned or is dismissed for want of prosecution, the court may make any order with respect to costs that it considers just and reasonable.

Payment

(2) Where the court orders the appellant or respondent to pay costs, the order shall direct that the costs be paid to the clerk of the trial court, to be paid by the clerk to the person entitled to them, and shall fix the period within which the costs shall be paid.

Enforcement

(3) Costs ordered to be paid under this section by a person other than a prosecutor acting on behalf of the Crown shall be deemed to be a fine for the purpose of enforcing its payment.

Implementation of appeal court order

130. An order or judgment of the appeal court shall be implemented or enforced by the trial court and the clerk or local registrar of the appeal court shall send to the clerk of the trial court the order and all writings relating thereto.

Appeal to Court of Appeal

131(1) A defendant or the prosecutor or the Attorney General by way of intervention may appeal from the judgment of the court to the Court of Appeal, with leave of a judge of the Court of Appeal on special grounds, upon any question of law alone or as to sentence.

Grounds for leave

(2) No leave to appeal shall be granted under subsection (1) unless the judge of the Court of Appeal considers that in the particular circumstances of the case it is essential in the public interest or for the due administration of justice that leave be granted.

Appeal as to leave

(3) No appeal or review lies from a decision on a motion for leave to appeal under subsection (1).

Custody pending appeal

132. A defendant who appeals shall, if the defendant is in custody, remain in custody, but a judge may order his or her release upon any of the conditions set out in subsection 150(2).

Transfer of record

133. Where a motion for leave to appeal is made, the Registrar of the Court of Appeal shall notify the clerk or local registrar of the court appealed from of the motion and, upon receipt of the notification, the clerk or local registrar of the court shall transmit to the Registrar all the material forming the record including any other relevant material requested by a judge of the Court of Appeal.

Application of lower court of appeal procedures, etc.

134. Sections 114, 117, 118, 119, 120, 121, 122, 123, 124, 125 and 126, clause 128(b) and section 129 apply with necessary modifications to appeals to the Court of Appeal under section 131.

APPEALS UNDER PARTS I AND II

Appeals, proceedings commenced by certificate

135(1) A defendant or the prosecutor or the Attorney General by way of intervention is entitled to appeal an acquittal, conviction or sentence in a proceeding commenced by certificate under Part I or II and the appeal shall be to the Ontario Court of Justice presided over by a provincial judge.

Application for appeal

(2) A notice of appeal shall be in the prescribed form and shall state the reasons why the appeal is taken and shall be filed with the clerk of the court within 30 days after the making of the decision appealed from, in accordance with the rules of court.

Simultaneous application

(2.1) Despite subsection (2), the notice of appeal may be filed at the same time as an application under section 85 to extend the time to give notice of appeal.

Notice of hearing

(3) The clerk shall, as soon as is practicable, give a notice to the defendant and prosecutor of the time and place of the hearing of the appeal.

Conduct of appeal

136(1) Upon an appeal, the court shall give the parties an opportunity to be heard for the purpose of determining the issues and may, where the circumstances warrant it, make such inquiries as are necessary to ensure that the issues are fully and effectively defined.

Review

(2) An appeal shall be conducted by means of a review.

Evidence

(3) In determining a review, the court may,

(a) hear or rehear the recorded evidence or any part thereof and may require any party to provide a transcript of the evidence, or any part thereof, or to produce any further exhibit;

(b) receive the evidence of any witness whether or not the witness gave evidence at the trial;

(c) require the justice presiding at the trial to report in writing on any matter specified in the request; or

(d) receive and act upon statements of agreed facts or admissions.

Dismissal on abandonment

137(1) Where an appeal has not been proceeded with or abandoned, the court may order that the appeal be dismissed.

Dismissal by justice

(2) Where the clerk of the court considers that an appeal has not been proceeded with or has been abandoned, the clerk may, after giving notice to the parties to the appeal, have the matter brought before a justice sitting in open court to determine whether the appeal has been abandoned and the appeal should be dismissed.

Motion to restore

(3) A party to an appeal that was dismissed under subsection (2) may apply to have the appeal restored.

Powers of court on appeal

138(1) Upon an appeal, the court may affirm, reverse or vary the decision appealed from or where, in the opinion of the court, it is necessary to do so to satisfy the ends of justice, direct a new trial.

New trial

(2) Where the court directs a new trial, it shall be held in the Ontario Court of Justice presided over by a justice other than the justice who tried the defendant in the first instance, but the appeal court may, with the consent of the parties to the appeal, direct that the new trial be held before the justice who tried the defendant in the first instance or before the judge who directs the new trial.

Costs

(3) Upon an appeal, the court may make an order under section 60 for the payment of costs incurred on the appeal, and subsection (3) thereof applies to the order.

Appeal to Court of Appeal

139(1) An appeal lies from the judgment of the Ontario Court of Justice in an appeal under section 135 to the Court of Appeal, with leave of a judge of the Court of Appeal, on special grounds, upon any question of law alone.

Grounds for leave

(2) No leave to appeal shall be granted under subsection (1) unless the judge of the Court of Appeal considers that in the particular circumstances of the case it is essential in the public interest or for the due administration of justice that leave be granted.

Costs

(3) Upon an appeal under this section, the Court of Appeal may make any order with respect to costs that it considers just and reasonable.

Appeal as to leave

(4) No appeal or review lies from a decision on a motion for leave to appeal under subsection (1).

REVIEW

Mandamus, prohibition, certiorari

140(1) On application, the Superior Court of Justice may by order grant any relief in respect of matters arising under this Act that the applicant would be entitled to in an application for an order in the nature of mandamus, prohibition or certiorari.

Notice of application

(2) Notice of an application under this section shall be served on,

    (a) the person whose act or omission gives rise to the application;

    (b) any person who is a party to a proceeding that gives rise to the application; and

    (c) the Attorney General.

Appeal

(3) An appeal lies to the Court of Appeal from an order made under this section.

Certiorari

141(1) A notice under section 140 in respect of an application for relief in the nature of certiorari shall be given at least seven days and not more than ten days before the date fixed for the hearing of the application and the notice shall be served within thirty days after the occurrence of the act sought to be quashed.

Filing material

(2) Where a notice referred to in subsection (1) is served on the person making the decision, order or warrant or holding the proceeding giving rise to the application, such person shall forthwith file with the Superior Court of Justice for use on the application, all material concerning the subject-matter of the application.

Motion to continue proceeding

(2.1) Where a notice referred to in subsection (1) is served in respect of an application, a person who is entitled to notice of the application under subsection 140(2) may make a motion to the Superior Court of Justice for an order that a trial in the proceeding giving rise to the application may continue despite the application and the Court may make the order if it is satisfied that it is in the interests of justice to do so.

Where appeal available

(3) No application shall be made to quash a conviction, order or ruling from which an appeal is provided by this Act, whether subject to leave or otherwise.

Substantial wrong

(4) On an application for relief in the nature of certiorari, the Superior Court of Justice shall not grant relief unless the court finds that a substantial wrong or miscarriage of justice has occurred, and the court may amend or validate any decision already made, with effect from such time and on such terms as the court considers proper.

(5) Repealed.

Habeas corpus

142(1) On application, the Superior Court of Justice may by order grant any relief in respect of a matter arising under this Act that the applicant would be entitled to in an application for an order in the nature of *habeas corpus*.

Procedure on application for relief in nature of *habeas corpus*

(2) Notice of an application under subsection (1) for relief in the nature of *habeas corpus* shall be served upon the person having custody of the person in respect of whom the application is made and upon the Attorney General and upon the hearing of the application the presence before the court of the person in respect of whom the application was made may be dispensed with by consent, in which event the court may proceed to dispose of the matter forthwith as the justice of the case requires.

Idem

(3) Subject to subsections (1) and (2), the *Habeas Corpus Act* applies to applications under this section, but an application for relief in the nature of certiorari may be brought in aid of an application under this section.

Idem

(4) The *Judicial Review Procedure Act* does not apply to matters in respect of which an application may be made under section 140.

Costs

(5) A court to which an application or appeal is made under section 140 or this section may make any order with respect to costs that it considers just and reasonable.

PART VIII
ARREST, BAIL AND SEARCH WARRANTS

ARREST

Officer in charge, Part VIII

143. In this Part,

"officer in charge" means the police officer who is in charge of the lock-up or other place to which a person is taken after his or her arrest.

Execution of warrant

144(1) A warrant for the arrest of a person shall be executed by a police officer by arresting the person against whom the warrant is directed wherever he or she is found in Ontario.

Idem

(2) A police officer may arrest without warrant a person for whose arrest he or she has reasonable and probable grounds to believe that a warrant is in force in Ontario.

Arrest without warrant

145. Any person may arrest without warrant a person who he or she has reasonable and probable grounds to believe has committed an offence and is escaping from and freshly pursued by a police officer who has lawful authority to arrest that person, and, where the person who makes the arrest is not a police officer, shall forthwith deliver the person arrested to a police officer.

Use of force

146(1) Every police officer is, if he or she acts on reasonable and probable grounds, justified in using as much force as is necessary to do what the officer is required or authorized by law to do.

Use of force by citizen

(2) Every person upon whom a police officer calls for assistance is justified in using as much force as he or she believes on reasonable and probable grounds is necessary to render such assistance.

Immunity from civil liability

147. Where a person is wrongfully arrested, whether with or without a warrant, no action for damages shall be brought,

(a) against the police officer making the arrest if he or she believed in good faith and on reasonable and probable grounds that the person arrested was the person named in the warrant or was subject to arrest without warrant under the authority of an Act;

(b) against any person called upon to assist the police officer if such person believed that the police officer had the right to effect the arrest; or

(c) against any person required to detain the prisoner in custody if such person believed the arrest was lawfully made.

Production of process and giving of reasons

148(1) It is the duty of every one who executes a process or warrant to have it with him or her, where it is feasible to do so, and to produce it when requested to do so.

Notice of reason for arrest

(2) It is the duty of every one who arrests a person, whether with or without warrant, to give notice to that person, where it is feasible to do so, of the reason for the arrest.

BAIL

Release after arrest by officer

149(1) Where a police officer, acting under a warrant or other power of arrest, arrests a person, the police officer shall, as soon as is practicable, release the person from custody after serving him or her with a summons or offence notice unless the officer has reasonable and probable grounds to believe that,

(a) it is necessary in the public interest for the person to be detained, having regard to all the circumstances including the need to,

(i) establish the identity of the person,

(ii) secure or preserve evidence of or relating to the offence, or

(iii) prevent the continuation or repetition of the offence or the commission of another offence; or

(b) the person arrested is ordinarily resident outside Ontario and will not respond to a summons or offence notice.

Release by officer in charge

(2) Where a defendant is not released from custody under subsection (1), the police officer shall deliver him or her to the officer in charge who shall, where in his or her opinion the conditions set out in clauses (1)(a) and (b) do not or no longer exist, release the defendant,

(a) upon serving the defendant with a summons or offence notice;

(b) upon the defendant entering into a recognizance in the prescribed form without sureties conditioned for his or her appearance in court.

Cash bail by non-resident

(3) Where the defendant is held for the reason only that he or she is not ordinarily resident in Ontario and it is believed that the defendant will not respond to a summons or offence notice, the officer in charge may, in addition to anything required under subsection (2), require the defendant to deposit cash or other satisfactory negotiable security in an amount not to exceed,

(a) where the proceeding is commenced by certificate under Part I or II, the amount of the set fine for the offence or, if none, $300; or

(b) where the proceeding is commenced by information under Part III, $500.

Person in custody to be brought before justice

150(1) Where a defendant is not released from custody under section 149, the officer in charge shall, as soon as is practicable but in any event within twenty-four hours, bring the defendant before a justice and the justice shall, unless a plea of guilty is taken, order that the defendant be released upon giving his or her undertaking to appear unless the prosecutor having been given an opportunity to do so shows cause why the detention of the defendant is justified to ensure his or her appearance in court or why an order under subsection (2) is justified for the same purpose.

Order for conditional release

(2) Subject to subsection (1), the justice may order the release of the defendant,

(a) upon the defendant entering into a recognizance to appear with such conditions as are appropriate to ensure his or her appearance in court;

(b) where the offence is one punishable by imprisonment for twelve months or more, conditional upon the defendant entering into a recognizance before a justice with sureties in such amount and with such conditions, if any, as are appropriate to ensure his or her appearance in court or, with the consent of the prosecutor, upon the defendant depositing with the justice such sum of money or other valuable security as the order directs in an amount not exceeding,

(i) where the proceeding is commenced by certificate under Part I or II, the amount of the set fine for the offence or, if none, $300, or

(ii) where the proceeding is commenced by information under Part III, $1,000; or

(c) if the defendant is not ordinarily resident in Ontario, upon the defendant entering into a recognizance before a justice, with or without sureties, in such amount and with such conditions, if any, as are appropriate to ensure his or her appearance in court, and depositing with the justice such sum of money or other valuable security as the order directs in an amount not exceeding,

(i) where the proceeding is commenced by certificate under Part I or II, the amount of the set fine for the offence or, if none, $300, or

(ii) where the proceeding is commenced by information under Part III, $1,000.

Idem

(3) The justice shall not make an order under clause (2)(b) or (c) unless the prosecutor shows cause why an order under the immediately preceding clause should not be made.

Order for detention

(4) Where the prosecutor shows cause why the detention of the defendant in custody is justified to ensure his or her appearance in court, the justice shall order the defendant to be detained in custody until he or she is dealt with according to law.

Reasons

(5) The justice shall include in the record a statement of the reasons for his or her decision under subsection (1), (2) or (4).

Evidence at hearing

(6) Where a person is brought before a justice under subsection (1), the justice may receive and base his or her decision upon information the justice considers credible or trustworthy in the circumstances of each case except that the defendant shall not be examined or cross-examined in respect of the offence with which he or she is charged.

Adjournments

(7) Where a person is brought before a justice under subsection (1), the matter shall not be adjourned for more than three days without the consent of the defendant.

Note: On a day to be named by proclamation of the Lieutenant Governor, section 150 is amended by the Statutes of Ontario, 2002, chapter 18, Schedule A, subsection 15(1) by adding the following subsections:

Alternative to physical presence

(8) Where a defendant is to be brought before a justice under this section, the defendant's actual physical attendance is required, but the justice may, subject to subsection (9), allow the defendant to appear by means of any suitable telecommunication device, including telephone, that is satisfactory to the justice.

Note: On the day the Statutes of Ontario, 2002, chapter 18, Schedule A, subsection 15(1) comes into force, subsection (8) is amended by the Statutes of Ontario, 2006, chapter 19, Schedule B, subsection 15(1) by striking out "subject to subsection (9)" and substituting "despite any other Act and subject to subsection (9)." See: 2006, c. 17, Sched. B, ss. 15(1), 24(2).

Consent required

(9) The consent of the prosecutor and the defendant is required for the purpose of an appearance if,

(a) the evidence of a witness is to be taken at the appearance; and

(b) it is not possible for the defendant to appear by closed-circuit television or any other means that allow the justice and the defendant to engage in simultaneous visual and oral communication.

See: 2002, c. 18, Sched. A, ss. 15(1), 21(3).

Expediting trial of person in custody

151(1) Where a defendant is not released from custody under section 149 or 150, he or she shall be brought before the court forthwith and, in any event, within eight days.

Further orders

(2) The justice presiding upon any appearance of the defendant in court may, upon the motion of the defendant or prosecutor, review any order made under section 150 and make such further or other order under section 150 as to the justice seems appropriate in the circumstances.

Appeal, order re release

152. A defendant or the prosecutor may appeal from an order or refusal to make an order under section 150 or 151 and the appeal shall be to the Superior Court of Justice.

Accounting for deposit, recognizance, etc.
Appointment of agent for appearance

153(1) A person who is released upon deposit under subsection 149(3) or clause 150(2)(c) may appoint the clerk of the court to act as the person's agent, in the event that he or she does not appear to answer to the charge, for the purpose of entering a plea of guilty on the person's behalf and authorizing the clerk to apply the amount so deposited toward payment of the fine and costs imposed by the court upon the conviction, and the clerk shall act as agent under this subsection without fee.

Returns to court

(2) An officer in charge or justice who takes a recognizance, money or security under section 149 or 150 shall make a return thereof to the court.

Returns to sureties

(3) The clerk of the court shall, upon the conclusion of a proceeding, make a financial return to every person who deposited money or security under a recognizance and return the surplus, if any.

Recognizance binding

154(1) The recognizance of a person to appear in a proceeding binds the person and the person's sureties in respect of all appearances required in the proceeding at times and places to which the proceeding is adjourned.

Recognizance binds independently of other charges

(2) A recognizance is binding in respect of appearances for the offence to which it relates and is not vacated upon the arrest, discharge or conviction of the defendant upon another charge.

Liability of principal

(3) The principal to a recognizance is bound for the amount of the recognizance due upon forfeiture.

Liability where sureties

(4) The principal and each surety to a recognizance are bound, jointly and severally, for the amount of the recognizance due upon forfeiture for non-appearance.

Relief of surety

155(1) A surety to a recognizance may, on motion in writing to the court at the location where the defendant is required to appear, ask to be relieved of the surety's obligation under the recognizance and the court shall thereupon issue a warrant for the arrest of the defendant.

Certificate of arrest

(2) When a police officer arrests the defendant under a warrant issued under subsection (1), he or she shall bring the defendant before a justice under section 150 and certify the arrest by certificate in the prescribed form and deliver the certificate to the court.

Vacating of recognizance

(3) The receipt of the certificate by the court under subsection (2) vacates the recognizance and discharges the sureties.

Delivery of defendant by surety

156. A surety to a recognizance may discharge the surety's obligation under the recognizance by delivering the defendant into the custody of the court at the location where he or she is required to appear at any time while it is sitting at or before the trial of the defendant.

Default of recognizance

157(1) Where a person who is bound by recognizance does not comply with a condition of the recognizance, a justice having knowledge of the facts shall endorse on the recognizance a certificate in the prescribed form setting out,

(a) the nature of the default;

(b) the reason for the default, if it is known;

(c) whether the ends of justice have been defeated or delayed by reason of the default; and

(d) the names and addresses of the principal and sureties.

Certificate as evidence

(2) A certificate that has been endorsed on a recognizance under subsection (1) is evidence of the default to which it relates.

Motion for forfeiture

(3) The clerk of the court shall transmit the endorsed recognizance to the local registrar of the Superior Court of Justice and, upon its receipt, the endorsed recognizance constitutes a motion for the forfeiture of the recognizance.

Notice of hearing

(4) A judge of the Superior Court of Justice shall fix a time and place for the hearing of the motion by the court and the local registrar of the court shall, not less than ten days before the time fixed for the hearing, deliver notice to the prosecutor and to each principal and, where the motion is for forfeiture for non-appearance, each surety named in the recognizance, of the time and place fixed for the hearing and requiring each principal and surety to show cause why the recognizance should not be forfeited.

Order as to forfeiture

(5) The Superior Court of Justice may, after giving the parties an opportunity to be heard, in its discretion grant or refuse the motion and make any order in respect of the forfeiture of the recognizance that the court considers proper.

Collection on forfeiture

(6) Where an order for forfeiture is made under subsection (5),

(a) any money or security forfeited shall be paid over by the person who has custody of it to the person who is entitled by law to receive it; and

(b) the principal and surety become judgment debtors of the Crown jointly and severally in the amount forfeited under the recognizance and the amount may be collected in the same manner as money owing under a judgment of the Superior Court of Justice.

SEARCH WARRANTS

Search warrant

158(1) A justice may at any time issue a warrant under his or her hand if the justice is satisfied by information upon oath that there are reasonable grounds to believe that there is in any place,

(a) anything on or in respect of which an offence has been or is suspected to have been committed; or

(b) anything that there are reasonable grounds to believe will afford evidence as to the commission of an offence.

Same

(1.1) The search warrant authorizes a police officer or person named in the warrant,

(a) to search the place named in the information for any thing described in clause (1)(a) or (b); and

(b) to seize the thing and deal with it in accordance with section 158.2.

Expiration

(2) Every search warrant shall name a date upon which it expires, which date shall be not later than fifteen days after its issue.

When to be executed

(3) Every search warrant shall be executed between 6 a.m. and 9 p.m. standard time, unless the justice by the warrant otherwise authorizes.

Definition

(4) In this section and in section 158.1,

"place" includes a building and a receptacle.

Telewarrants
Submission of information

158.1(1) Where a provincial offences officer believes that an offence has been committed and that it would be impracticable to appear personally before a justice to make application for a warrant in accordance with section 158, the provincial offences officer may submit an information on oath, by a means of telecommunication that produces a writing, to a justice designated for the purpose by the Chief Justice of the Ontario Court of Justice.

Filing of information

(2) The justice who receives an information submitted under subsection (1) shall, as soon as practicable, cause the information to be filed with the clerk of the court, certified by the justice as to time and date of receipt.

Same, alternative to oath

(3) A provincial offences officer who submits an information under subsection (1) may, instead of swearing an oath, make a statement in writing stating that all matters contained in the information are true to his or her knowledge and belief, and the statement is deemed to be made under oath.

Contents of information

(4) An information submitted under subsection (1) shall include,

(a) a statement of the circumstances that make it impracticable for the provincial offences officer to appear personally before a justice;

(b) a statement of the alleged offence, the place to be searched and the items alleged to be liable to seizure;

(c) a statement of the provincial offences officer's grounds for believing that items liable to seizure in respect of the alleged offence will be found in the place to be searched; and

(d) a statement as to any prior application for a warrant under this section or any other search warrant, in respect of the same matter, of which the provincial offences officer has knowledge.

Issuing warrant

(5) A justice to whom an information is submitted under subsection (1) may, if the conditions set out in subsection (6) are met,

(a) issue a warrant to a provincial offences officer conferring the same authority respecting search and seizure as may be conferred by a warrant issued by a justice before whom the provincial offences officer appears personally under section 158; and

(b) require that the warrant be executed within such time period as the justice may order.

Conditions

(6) The conditions referred to in subsection (5) are that the justice is satisfied that the information,

(a) is in respect of an offence and complies with subsection (4);

(b) discloses reasonable grounds for dispensing with an information presented personally; and

(c) discloses reasonable grounds, in accordance with section 158, for the issuance of a warrant in respect of an offence.

Application of s. 158(2) and (3)

(7) Subsections 158(2) and (3) apply to a warrant issued under this section.

Form, transmission and filing of warrant

(8) A justice who issues a warrant under this section shall,

(a) complete and sign the warrant, noting on its face the time, date and place of issuance;

(b) transmit the warrant by the means of telecommunication to the provincial offences officer who submitted the information; and

(c) as soon as practicable after the warrant has been issued, cause the warrant to be filed with the clerk of the court.

Copies

(9) The copy of the warrant that is transmitted to the provincial offences officer and any copies that are made from the transmitted copy have the same effect as the original for all purposes.

Providing or affixing copy when executing warrant

(10) When a provincial offences officer executes a warrant issued under this section,

(a) if the place to be searched is occupied, the provincial offences officer shall, before entering or as soon as practicable thereafter, give a copy of the warrant to any person present and ostensibly in control of the place; and

(b) if the place to be searched is unoccupied, the provincial offences officer shall, on entering or as soon as practicable thereafter, cause a copy of the warrant to be suitably and prominently affixed within the place.

Proof of authorization

(11) In any proceeding in which it is material for a court to be satisfied that a search or seizure was authorized by a warrant issued under this section, the warrant or the related information shall be produced and the court shall verify,

(a) in the case of the warrant, that it is signed by the justice and bears on its face a notation of the time, date and place of issuance;

(b) in the case of the related information, that it is certified by the justice as to time and date of receipt.

Presumption

(12) If the warrant or related information is not produced or if the matters set out in clause (11)(a) or (b) cannot be verified, it shall be presumed, in the absence of evidence to the contrary, that the search or seizure was not authorized by a warrant issued under this section.

Duty of person who carries out seizure

158.2(1) Subsection (2) applies when,

(a) a person has, under a warrant issued under this or any other Act or otherwise in the performance of his or her duties under an Act, seized any thing,

(i) upon or in respect of which an offence has been or is suspected to have been committed, or

(ii) that there are reasonable grounds to believe will afford evidence as to the commission of an offence; and

(b) no procedure for dealing with the thing is otherwise provided by law.

Same

(2) The person shall, as soon as is practicable, take the following steps:

1. The person shall determine whether the continued detention of the thing is required for the purposes of an investigation or proceeding.

2. If satisfied that continued detention is not required as mentioned in paragraph 1, the person shall,

    i. return the thing, on being given a receipt for it, to the person lawfully entitled to its possession, and

    ii. report to a justice about the seizure and return of the thing.

3. If paragraph 2 does not apply, the person shall,

    i. bring the thing before a justice, or

    ii. report to a justice about the seizure and detention of the thing.

Order of justice re things seized

159(1) When, under paragraph 3 of subsection 158.2(2), a thing that has been seized is brought before a justice or a report in respect of it is made to a justice, he or she shall, by order,

(a) detain the thing or direct it to be detained in the care of a person named in the order; or

(b) direct it to be returned.

Detention pending appeal, etc.

(1.0.1) A direction to return seized items does not take effect for 30 days and does not take effect during any application made or appeal taken in respect of the thing.

Same

(1.1) The justice may, in the order,

(a) authorize the examination, testing, inspection or reproduction of the thing seized, on the conditions that are reasonably necessary and are directed in the order; and

(b) make any other provision that, in his or her opinion, is necessary for the preservation of the thing.

Time limit for detention

(2) Nothing shall be detained under an order made under subsection (1) for a period of more than three months after the time of seizure unless, before the expiration of that period,

(a) upon motion, a justice is satisfied that having regard to the nature of the investigation, its further detention for a specified period is warranted and he or she so orders; or

(b) a proceeding is instituted in which the thing detained may be required.

Motion for examination and copying

(3) Upon the motion of the defendant, prosecutor or person having an interest in a thing detained under subsection (1), a justice may make an order for the examination, testing, inspection or reproduction of any thing detained upon such conditions as are reasonably necessary and directed in the order.

Motion for release

(4) Upon the motion of a person having an interest in a thing detained under subsection (1), and upon notice to the defendant, the person from whom the thing was seized, the person to whom the search warrant was issued and any other person who has an apparent interest in the thing detained, a justice may make an order for the release of any thing detained to the person from whom the thing was seized where it appears that the thing detained is no longer necessary for the purpose of an investigation or proceeding.

Appeal where order by justice of the peace

(5) Where an order or refusal to make an order under subsection (3) or (4) is made by a justice of the peace, an appeal lies therefrom in the same manner as an appeal from a conviction in a proceeding commenced by means of a certificate.

Claim of privilege

160(1) Where under a search warrant a person is about to examine or seize a document that is in the possession of a lawyer and a solicitor-client privilege is claimed on behalf of a named client in respect of the document, the person shall, without examining or making copies of the document,

(a) seize the document and place it, together with any other document seized in respect of which the same claim is made on behalf of the same client, in a package and seal and identify the package; and

(b) place the package in the custody of the clerk of the court or, with the consent of the person and the client, in the custody of another person.

Opportunity to claim privilege

(2) No person shall examine or seize a document that is in the possession of a lawyer without giving him or her a reasonable opportunity to claim the privilege under subsection (1).

Examination of documents in custody

(3) A judge may, upon the motion made without notice of the lawyer, by order authorize the lawyer to examine or make a copy of the document in the presence of its custodian or the judge, and the order shall contain such provisions as are necessary to ensure that the document is repackaged and resealed without alteration or damage.

Motion to determine privilege

(4) Where a document has been seized and placed in custody under subsection (1), the client by or on whose behalf the claim of solicitor-client privilege is made may make a motion to a judge for an order sustaining the privilege and for the return of the document.

Limitation

(5) A motion under subsection (4) shall be by notice of motion naming a hearing date not later than thirty days after the date on which the document was placed in custody.

Attorney General a party

(6) The person who seized the document and the Attorney General are parties to a motion under subsection (4) and entitled to at least three days notice thereof.

Private hearing and scrutiny by judge

(7) A motion under subsection (4) shall be heard in private and, for the purposes of the hearing, the judge may examine the document and, if he or she does so, shall cause it to be resealed.

Order

(8) The judge may by order,

   (a) declare that the solicitor-client privilege exists or does not exist in respect of the document;

   (b) direct that the document be delivered up to the appropriate person.

Release of document where no motion under subs. (4)

(9) Where it appears to a judge upon the motion of the Attorney General or person who seized the document that no motion has been made under subsection (4) within the time limit prescribed by subsection (5), the judge shall order that the document be delivered to the applicant.

PART IX

ORDERS ON APPLICATION UNDER STATUTES

Orders under statutes

161. Where, by any other Act, a proceeding is authorized to be taken before the Ontario Court of Justice or a justice for an order, including an order for the payment of money, and no other procedure is provided, this Act applies with necessary modifications to the proceeding in the same manner as to a proceeding commenced under Part III, and for the purpose,

   (a) in place of an information, the applicant shall complete a statement in the prescribed form under oath attesting, on reasonable and probable grounds, to the existence of facts that would justify the order sought; and

   (b) in place of a plea, the defendant shall be asked whether or not the defendant wishes to dispute the making of the order.

PART X
AGREEMENTS WITH MUNICIPALITIES CONCERNING ADMINISTRATIVE FUNCTIONS AND PROSECUTIONS

Definition
161.1 In this Part,

"transfer agreement" means an agreement under subsection 162(1).

Agreements
162(1) The Attorney General and a municipality may enter into an agreement with respect to a specified area, authorizing the municipality to,

(a) perform courts administration and court support functions, including the functions of the clerk of the court, for the purposes of this Act and the *Contraventions Act* (Canada); and

(b) conduct prosecutions,

(i) in proceedings under Parts I and II, and

(ii) in proceedings under the *Contraventions Act* (Canada) that are commenced by ticket under Part I or II of this Act.

Application of cl. (1)(a)
(2) Clause (1)(a) also applies to the functions assigned to the clerk of the court by any other Act.

Performance standards and sanctions
(3) Performance standards and sanctions shall be specified in the agreement; the municipality shall meet the standards and is subject to the sanctions for failure to meet them.

Definition
(4) In subsection (3),

"performance standards" includes standards for the conduct of prosecutions, for the administration of the courts and for the provision of court support services.

Area of application
163. A transfer agreement may specify an area that includes territory outside the municipality.

Evidence and effect of agreement
Deposit with clerk
164(1) When the Attorney General and a municipality have entered into a transfer agreement, a copy of the agreement shall be deposited with the clerk of the municipality and with the clerk of any other municipality that has jurisdiction in the specified area.

Judicial notice
(2) Judicial notice shall be taken of the agreement without the agreement or its deposit being specially pleaded or proved.

Non-compliance
(3) No proceeding is invalidated by reason only of a person's failure to comply with the agreement.

Fair hearing

(4) Without limiting the generality of subsection (3), that subsection does not preserve the validity of the proceeding if the failure to comply with the agreement results in prejudice to the defendant's right to a fair hearing.

Collection and enforcement

165(1) When a transfer agreement is in force, the municipality has power to collect fines levied in respect of proceedings under Parts I, II and III, including costs under section 60, surcharges under section 60.1 and fees referred to in section 66.2, and to enforce their payment; collection and enforcement shall be carried out in the manner specified in the agreement.

Contraventions Act (Canada)

(2) Subsection (1) also applies to fines and fees imposed under the *Contraventions Act* (Canada).

Non-application of subss. 69(6-21)

(3) Subsections 69(6) to (21) do not apply to fines that are governed by the agreement.

Fines, etc., payable to municipality

(4) Fines that are governed by the agreement are payable to the municipality and not to the Minister of Finance.

Payments to Minister of Finance

(5) The municipality shall pay to the Minister of Finance, at the times and in the manner specified in the agreement, amounts calculated in accordance with the agreement, in respect of,

(a) surcharges collected by the municipality under section 60.1;

(b) other fine revenues collected by the municipality that constitute money paid to Ontario for a special purpose within the meaning of the *Financial Administration Act*;

(c) costs the Attorney General incurs for adjudication and prosecution, for monitoring the performance of the agreement and for enforcing the agreement; and

(d) fines and fees imposed under the *Contraventions Act* (Canada) and collected by the municipality.

Exception, federal-municipal agreement re parking fines and fees

(6) Despite clause (5)(d), fines and fees imposed under the *Contraventions Act* (Canada) in relation to the unlawful parking, standing or stopping of a vehicle and collected by the municipality shall be paid in accordance with any agreement made under sections 65.2 and 65.3 of that Act.

Payments to another municipality

(7) The municipality acting under a transfer agreement shall pay to another municipality,

(a) the amount of any fine collected by the municipality that was imposed for a contravention of the other municipality's by-law;

(b) the amount of any fine collected by the municipality that was imposed for a contravention of a provincial statute and that would, except for the agreement, be payable to the other municipality; and

(c) the amount of any allowance retained by the municipality that would, except for the agreement, be payable to the other municipality under a regulation made under clause 20(1)(g).

Retention of balance

(8) Despite the *Fines and Forfeitures Act*, the municipality is entitled to retain, as a fee, the balance remaining after payment under subsections (5) and (7).

No other charge

(9) The municipality shall not collect any other charge for acting under a transfer agreement, except in accordance with section 304 of the *Municipal Act, 2001* or section 240 of the *City of Toronto Act, 2006* or with the Attorney General's advance written consent.

Disclosure to consumer reporting agency

(10) When a transfer agreement applies to a fine, section 69.1 applies to the municipality in the same manner as it applies to the Ministry of the Attorney General.

Exception, transitional period

(11) Despite subsection (4), while a regulation made under clause 174(b) is in effect, fines that are governed by the agreement remain payable to the Minister of Finance, who shall,

(a) calculate and retain the appropriate amounts under subsection (5);

(b) make any payments required by subsection (7); and

(c) pay the balance remaining to the municipality in accordance with subsection (8).

Municipal defendants

165.1(1) In this section,

"local board" has the same meaning as in the *Municipal Affairs Act*, but does not include a school board or a hospital board.

Special rules

(2) When a transfer agreement is in effect, the special rules set out in subsection (3) apply to a proceeding if,

(a) the proceeding is under Part I or III; and

(b) the defendant is a municipality or one of its local boards.

Same

(3) The special rules referred to in subsection (2) are:

1. The fine is payable to the Minister of Finance and not to the municipality, despite subsection 165(4).
2. The prosecutor may elect to collect and enforce the fine instead of the municipality, despite subsection 165(1) and the provisions of the agreement relating to collection and enforcement.
3. Notice of the election shall be given to the municipal representative named in the agreement for the purpose, or if none is named, to the clerk of the court.

Fines imposed before effective date

166. A transfer agreement may,

(a) authorize the municipality to collect and enforce the payment of fines that were imposed before the agreement's effective date; and

(b) provide in what proportions and in what manner the amounts collected are to be shared between the municipality and the Minister of Finance.

Rules under agreements

167(1) When a transfer agreement is in effect, the following rules apply:

1. The clerk of the court may be a municipal employee.
2. Subject to section 29, the court may sit in the location designated by the municipality, which need not be in premises operated by the Province of Ontario for court purposes.
3. The court office shall be in the location designated by the municipality.
4. Despite anything else in this Act, the municipality shall not without the Attorney General's written consent, obtained in advance, assign to a person other than its own employee a function that the agreement gives to the municipality.

Definition: "prosecutor," Part X

(2) For the purposes of this Part,

"prosecutor" means the Attorney General or, where the Attorney General does not intervene, means a person acting on behalf of the municipality in accordance with the agreement or, where no such person intervenes, means the person who issues a certificate or lays an information, and includes an agent acting on behalf of any of them.

Attorney General's right to intervene

168. A transfer agreement does not affect the Attorney General's right to intervene in a proceeding and assume the role of prosecutor at any stage, including on appeal.

Municipality not Crown agent

169. A municipality that acts under a transfer agreement does not do so as an agent of the Crown in right of Ontario or of the Attorney General.

Protection from personal liability

170(1) No proceeding shall be commenced against any person for an act done in good faith in the performance or intended performance of a function under a transfer agreement or for an alleged neglect or default in the performance in good faith of such a function.

Municipality not relieved of liability

(2) Subsection (1) does not relieve a municipality of liability in respect of a tort committed by a person referred to in subsection (1) to which the municipality would otherwise be subject.

Revocation or suspension of agreement
Order for compliance

171(1) When a transfer agreement is in effect, the Attorney General may make an order directing the municipality to comply with the agreement within a specified time.

Revocation or suspension

(2) The Attorney General may revoke or suspend the agreement if the municipality does not comply with the order within the specified time.

Protection from personal liability

(3) No proceeding for damages shall be commenced against the Attorney General or an employee of the Ministry of the Attorney General for anything done or omitted in good faith in connection with the revocation or suspension of a transfer agreement.

Review committee

172. A transfer agreement may provide for a review committee whose composition and functions are determined by regulation.

Transition: application to all proceedings

173(1) Unless a transfer agreement provides otherwise, the agreement applies in respect of a proceeding whether it was commenced before or after the agreement's effective date.

Exception

(2) However, if one of the following conditions applies to a proceeding, the trial and disposition, including sentencing, shall be conducted as if there were no agreement:

1. The trial is scheduled to begin within seven calendar days after the effective date.
2. The trial began before the effective date and the disposition, including sentencing, is not yet complete on that date.

Regulations re agreements

174. The Attorney General may, by regulation,

(a) impose obligations in connection with a transfer agreement on a person who is not a party to the agreement;

(b) provide that fines governed by a transfer agreement may, for a transitional period after its effective date, be paid to the Minister of Finance;

(c) determine the composition and functions of a review committee for the purposes of section 172;

(d) provide for the effective implementation of transfer agreements.

Municipal powers

174.1(1) A municipality has power to enter into and to perform a transfer agreement.

Employees and others

(2) The functions given to a municipality by a transfer agreement or by an agreement under subsection (3) or (7) may be performed,

(a) by the municipality's employees;

(b) by a combination of the municipality's employees and the employees of another municipality, if the municipalities have an agreement under subsection (3) or (7); or

(c) by any other person, with the Attorney General's consent, as described in subsection 175(2).

Joint performance agreement between municipalities

(3) A municipality that has entered into a transfer agreement may enter into an agreement with one or more other municipalities for the joint performance, by a joint board of management or otherwise, of the functions given to the first municipality by the transfer agreement.

Attorney General's consent

(4) The joint performance agreement requires the Attorney General's written consent, obtained in advance.

Extra-territorial effect

(5) The power to perform an agreement under subsection (3) may be exercised in an area outside the municipality's territorial limits if that area forms part of the area specified in the agreement.

Intermunicipal agreements

(6) Municipalities may enter into and perform intermunicipal agreements to implement a transfer agreement.

Further agreements

(7) A municipality that has entered into a transfer agreement may enter into an agreement with one or more municipalities for the performance by the other municipality or municipalities of any of the functions given to the first municipality by the transfer agreement and the municipalities have the power to enter into and perform the agreement under this subsection.

Consent

(8) An agreement entered into under subsection (7) requires the Attorney General's written consent.

Extra-territorial effect

(9) The power to perform an agreement under subsection (7) may be exercised in an area outside the municipality's territorial limits.

Delegation

175(1) Subject to subsection (2), a municipality has power to assign to any person a function that a transfer agreement gives to the municipality.

Attorney General's consent

(2) An assignment to a person other than the municipality's employee requires the Attorney General's written consent, obtained in advance.

(3) Repealed.

Group of municipalities

176. A transfer agreement may also be made with two or more municipalities, and in that case sections 162 to 175 apply with necessary modifications.

Common Forms Used for Provincial Offences Matters

B

LIST OF FORMS

NOTICE OF INTENTION TO APPEAR
AVIS D'INTENTION DE COMPARAÎTRE

ONTARIO COURT OF JUSTICE
COUR DE JUSTICE DE L'ONTARIO
PROVINCE OF ONTARIO
PROVINCE DE L'ONTARIO

Form / *Formulaire* **8**
Provincial Offences Act
Loi sur les infractions provinciales

TAKE NOTICE THAT I, _____
VEUILLEZ PRENDRE AVIS QUE JE, SOUSSIGNÉ(E),   (defendant's name / *nom du défendeur/de la défenderesse*)

_____   _____   _____
(current address / *adresse actuelle*)   (street / *rue*)   (apt. / *app.*)

_____   _____   _____
(municipality / *municipalité*)   (province)   (postal code / *code postal*)

_____   _____
(offence number / *numéro de l'infraction*)   (offence date / *date de l'infraction*)

wish to give notice of my intention to appear in court to enter a plea of not guilty at the time and place set for the trial respecting the charge set out in the Offence Notice or Parking Infraction Notice.

désire aviser de mon intention de comparaître devant le tribunal pour inscrire un plaidoyer de non-culpabilité à l'heure et au lieu prévus pour le procès en réponse à l'accusation énoncée dans l'avis d'infraction ou l'avis d'infraction de stationnement.

FOR ANY OFFENCE EXCEPT s.s. 144(18.1) OF THE *HTA*, COMPLETE THIS SECTION: *POUR TOUTE INFRACTION NON VISÉE AU PARAGRAPHE 144 (18.1) DU CODE DE LA ROUTE, REMPLIR CETTE SECTION :*	I intend to challenge the Provincial Offences Officer's evidence. I request that the officer attend the trial. *J'ai l'intention de contester la preuve de l'agent des infractions provinciales. Je demande que l'agent assiste au procès.*	☐ **No** *Non* ☐ **Yes** *Oui*

Note:	If you have been charged with an offence under s.s. 144(18.1) of the *Highway Traffic Act* (red light running/owner), section 205.20 of the *Highway Traffic Act* provides that you must apply to the justice at trial if you wish to compel the attendance of the Provincial Offences Officer who issued the Certificate of Offence or who certified the photographs to be tendered at your trial.	*Remarque :*	*Si vous avez été accusé(e) d'une infraction visée au paragraphe 144 (18.1) du Code de la route (passage au feu rouge/propriétaire), l'article 205.20 du Code de la route prévoit que vous devez vous adresser au juge du procès si vous désirez obtenir la comparution de l'agent des infractions provinciales qui a délivré le procès-verbal d'infraction ou qui a certifié les photos qui seront présentées en preuve lors de votre procès.*

☐ I intend to appear in court to enter a plea at the time and place set for the trial and I wish that it be held in the English language.

☐ *J'ai l'intention de comparaître devant le tribunal pour inscrire un plaidoyer à l'heure et au lieu prévus pour le procès et je désire que le procès se déroule en français.*

I request a _____ language interpreter for the trial.
          (leave blank if inapplicable)

Je demande l'aide d'un interprète de langue _____ *pour le procès.*
          (à remplir, s'il y a lieu)

Note:	If you **fail to notify** the court office of **address changes** you may not receive important notices *e.g.*, your Notice of Trial. You may be convicted in your absence if you do not attend the trial.	*Remarque :*	*Si vous **omettez de prévenir** le greffe du tribunal de **tout changement d'adresse**, vous pourriez ne pas recevoir d'importants avis (par ex., votre avis de procès). Vous pourriez être déclaré(e) coupable en votre absence si vous n'assistez pas au procès.*

_____   _____
Signature of defendant or representative /   (date)
Signature du défendeur/de la défenderesse ou du représentant/de la représentante

_____
(representative's name / *nom du représentant/de la représentante*)

_____   _____   _____
(current address / *adresse actuelle*)   (street / *rue*)   (apt. / *app.*)

_____   _____   _____
(municipality / *municipalité*)   (province)   (postal code / *code postal*)

Form / *Formulaire* 8 (March 17, 2011 / *17 mars 2011*)

NOTICE OF MOTION
AVIS DE MOTION

BETWEEN _____ Prosecutor
ENTRE _____ *Poursuivant*

and
et

_____ Defendant
_____ *Défendeur*

TAKE NOTICE that an application will be made by the _____
SACHEZ QU'UNE requête sera déposée par
(Prosecutor/Defendant) / *(poursuivant/défendeur)*

on _____ , yr. _____ , before the Ontario Court of Justice
le _____ *an* _____ *devant la Cour de justice de l'Ontario*

at _____
á _____

in the following matter:
en ce qui concerne l'affaire suivant :

_____

_____

for an Order as follows:
pour une ordonnance comme suit :

_____

_____

_____

_____

_____

And further take notice that in support of this application will be read the affidavit of _____
Sachez aussi qu'à l'appui de cette requête sera lu l'affidavit de

_____ , and such other and further evidence as may be required.
ainsi que d'autres preuves qui s'avéreront nécessaires.

Dated this _____ day of _____ , yr. _____
Fait le _____ *jour de* _____ *an* _____

at _____
á

Signed _____
Signature

Address _____
Adresse

TO: / *Á :*
Prosecutor (or Defendant) and Clerk of the Court
Poursuivant (ou Défendeur) et au greffier de la Cour

DISTRIBUTION:

☐ Defendant/Prosecutor
   défendeur/poursuivant

☐ Counsel for Defendant/Prosecutor
   avocat du défendeur/poursuivant

☐ Agent for Defendant/Prosecutor
   mandataire du défendeur/poursuivant

FOR INFORMATION ON ACCESS
TO ONTARIO COURTS
FOR PERSONS WITH DISABILITIES, CALL
1-800-387-4456
TORONTO AREA **416-326-0111**

POUR PLUS DE RENSEIGNEMENTS SUR L'ACCÈS
DES PERSONNES HANDICAPÉES
AUX TRIBUNAUX DE L'ONTARIO, COMPOSEZ LE
1-800-387-4456
RÉGION DE TORONTO **416-326-0111**

POA 0007 CSD (rev. 11/03)

FORM 4F

Courts of Justice Act

NOTICE OF CONSTITUTIONAL QUESTION

(General heading)

NOTICE OF CONSTITUTIONAL QUESTION

The *(identify party)* intends to question the constitutional validity *(or* applicability*)* of *(identify the particular legislative provisions or the particular rule of common law) (or* to claim a remedy under subsection 24 (1) of the *Canadian Charter of Rights and Freedoms* in relation to an act or omission of the Government of Canada *(or* Ontario*))*.

The question is to be argued on *(day)*, *(date)*, at *(time)*, at *(address of court house)*.

The following are the material facts giving rise to the constitutional question: *(Set out concisely the material facts that relate to the constitutional question. Where appropriate, attach pleadings or reasons for decision.)*

The following is the legal basis for the constitutional question: *(Set out concisely the legal basis for each question, identifying the nature of the constitutional principles to be argued.)*

(Date)   *(Name, address and telephone number of lawyer or party)*

TO   The Attorney General of Ontario *(as required by section 109 of the Courts of Justice Act)*
         Constitutional Law Branch
         4th floor
         720 Bay Street
         Toronto, Ontario M5G 2K1
         fax: (416) 326-4015

         The Attorney General of Canada *(as required by section 109 of the Courts of Justice Act)*
         Suite 3400, Exchange Tower
         Box 36, First Canadian Place
         Toronto, Ontario M5X 1K6
         fax: (416) 952-0298

         (or Justice Building
         234 Wellington Street
         Ottawa, Ontario K1A 0H8
         fax: (613) 954-1920*)*

         *(Names and addresses of lawyers
         for all other parties and of all
         other parties acting in person)*

(This notice must be served as soon as the circumstances requiring it become known and, in any event, at least 15 days before the question is to be argued, unless the court orders otherwise.)

RCP-E 4F (April 11, 2012)

AFFIDAVIT IN SUPPORT OF A REQUEST FOR REOPENING
AFFIDAVIT À L'APPUI D'UNE DEMANDE DE RÉOUVERTURE

ONTARIO COURT OF JUSTICE
COUR DE JUSTICE DE L'ONTARIO
PROVINCE OF ONTARIO
PROVINCE DE L'ONTARIO

Under Section 11 or Subsection 19(1) of the *Provincial Offences Act,* or Section 205.13 or Section 205.23 of the *Highway Traffic Act*
En vertu de l'article 11 ou du paragraphe 19(1) de la Loi sur les infractions provinciales *ou de l'article 205.13 de l'article 205.23 du* Code de la route

Form / Formule 102
Courts of Justice Act
Loi sur les tribunaux judiciaires
O. Reg. / Règl. de l'Ont. 200

I, _____
Je soussigné(e),   (name / *nom*)

of _____
de   (address / *adresse*)

make oath/affirm and say as follows:
déclare sous serment et affirme ce qui suit :

1. I was convicted without a hearing on the _____ day of _____ , yr. 20 ____ , of the offence of
   J'ai été reconnu(e) coupable sans la tenue d'une audience le jour de an de l'infraction de

   contrary to _____ section _____
   contrairement à la(au)   *article*

2. (a) I was unable to appear at my hearing through no fault of my own because:
   Je n'ai pu comparaître à mon audience, sans faute de ma part, parce que :

   _____
   (state reason / *donner la raison*)
   _____
   _____

   or / ou

   (b) a notice or document relating to the offence was not delivered to me, namely:
   un avis ou un document concernant l'infraction ne m'a pas été livré, notamment :

   _____
   (identify document / *préciser quel document*)
   _____
   _____

3. The conviction first came to my attention on the _____ day of _____ , yr. 20 ____
   J'ai pris connaissance de la déclaration de culpabilité pour la première fois le jour de an

Sworn/Affirmed before me at _____
Fait sous serment/affirmé devant moi à

this _____ day of _____ , yr. 20 ____
le *jour de* *an*

_____
A Commissioner, etc. / *Commissaire, etc.*

_____
Signature of Defendant / *Signature du défendeur/de la défenderesse*

NOTE: Section 86 of the *Provincial Offences Act* provides:

Every person who makes an assertion of fact in a statement or entry in a document or form for use under this Act knowing that the assertion is false is guilty of an offence and on conviction is liable to a fine of not more than $2,000.

REMARQUE : *Selon l'article 86 de la Loi sur les infractions provinciales :*

« Est coupable d'une infraction et passible, sur déclaration de culpabilité, d'une amende d'au plus 2 000 $, quiconque affirme un fit dans une déclaration ou l'inscrit dans un document ou une formule dont la présent loi prévoit l'usage, et sait que cette affirmation est fausse. »

FOR INFORMATION ON ACCESS
TO ONTARIO COURTS
FOR PERSONS WITH DISABILITIES, CALL
1-800-387-4456
TORONTO AREA **416-326-0111**

POUR PLUS DE RENSEIGNEMENTS SUR L'ACCÈS
DES PERSONNES HANDICAPÉES
AUX TRIBUNAUX DE L'ONTARIO, COMPOSEZ LE
1-800-387-4456
RÉGION DE TORONTO **416-326-0111**

NOTICE OF APPEAL
AVIS D'APPEL INTERJETÉ

ONTARIO COURT OF JUSTICE
COUR DE JUSTICE DE L'ONTARIO
PROVINCE OF ONTARIO
PROVINCE DE L'ONTARIO

Parts I and II under Section 135 of the *Provincial Offences Act*
Parties I et II, aux termes de l'article 135 de la
Loi sur les infractions provinciales

Form / *Formule* **1**
Courts of Justice Act
Loi sur les tribunaux judiciaires
O. Reg. / *Règl. de l'Ont.* 722/94

1. Ontario Court of Justice at
   Cour de justice de l'Ontario à

2. Appellant is: / *La partie appelante est :*
   ☐ Defendant
   le défendeur (la défenderesse)
   ☐ Prosecutor
   le poursuivant
   ☐ Attorney General
   le procureur général

3. Name of Appellant:
   Nom de l'appelant(e) :

   Address for service: / *Domicile élu :*

4. Counsel for Appellant: Name:
   Avocat(e) de l'appelant(e) : Nom :

   Address for service: / *Domicile élu :*

5. Name of Respondent *(if known)*:
   Nom de l'intimé(e) (s'il est connu) :

   Address for service: / *Domicile élu :*

6. Counsel for Respondent *(if known)*:
   Nom de l'avocat(e) de l'intimé(e) (s'il est connu) :

   Address for service: / *Domicile élu :*

7. Decision of Ontario Court of Justice: / *Décision rendue par la Cour de justice de l'Ontario :*
   (include name of Judge or Justice of Peace appealed from, if known / *inscrire le nom du juge ou du juge de paix dont la décision est portée en appel, s'il est connu*)

8. Date of decision: / *Date de la décision :*

9. The Appellant appeals against: / *L'appelant(e) interjette appel :*
   ☐ Conviction
   de la déclaration de culpabilité
   ☐ Dismissal
   du rejet de l'accusation
   ☐ Sentence
   de la sentence

10. If Appellant is in custody, place where held:
    Si l'appelant(e) est sous garde, lieu de détention :

11. (a) Description of offence[1]
    Description de l'infraction[1]

    (b) Certificate number *(if known)*:
    Numéro du procès-verbal (s'il est connu) :

FOR INFORMATION ON ACCESS
TO ONTARIO COURTS
FOR PERSONS WITH DISABILITIES, CALL
1-800-387-4456
TORONTO AREA **416-326-0111**

POUR PLUS DE RENSEIGNEMENTS SUR L'ACCÈS
DES PERSONNES HANDICAPÉES
AUX TRIBUNAUX DE L'ONTARIO, COMPOSEZ LE
1-800-387-4456
RÉGION DE TORONTO **416-326-0111**

[1] for example, speeding / *par exemple, excès de vitesse*
POA 0201 CSD (rev.11/03)

12. (1) Statute[2]: _____
         Loi [2]

13. Date of offence: _____
     Date de l'infraction :

14. Plea at trial: _____
     Plaidoyer au procès :

     The plea entered was:
     Le plaidoyer inscrit :
     (check one / *cocher la case appropriée*)

     ☐ guilty   ☐ not guilty   ☐ not known
         coupable   *non coupable*   *non connu*

15. The Appellant wants the appeal court to:
     L'appelant(e) désire que le tribunal d'appel :
     (check one / *cocher la case appropriée*)

     ☐ Find the Defendant not guilty / *Déclare la partie défenderesse non coupable*

     ☐ Find the Defendant guilty / *Déclare la partie défenderesse coupable*

     ☐ Order a new trial / *Ordonne la tenue d'un nouveau procès*

     ☐ Change the sentence / *Modifie la sentence*

     ☐ Other: / *Autre :*
         (specify / *préciser*)

     _____

     _____

     _____

16. The grounds of appeal are: _____
     Les motifs d'appel sont les suivants :

     _____

Complete No. 17 for *Provincial Offences Act*, Part II, parking Offences where the municipality is collecting its own parking fines.
Remplir le N°17 dans le cas des infractions de stationnement visées par la partie II de la Loi sur les infractions provinciales, lorsque la municipalité perçoit ses propres amendes de stationnement.

17. The fine has been paid in full at: _____ on _____
     L'amende a été payée intégralement à   (municipality / *municipalité*)   *le*   (date)

18. Date: _____

19. Signature of Appellant or Counsel or Agent: _____
     Signature de l'appelant(e) ou de son avocat(e) ou représentant(e) :

NOTES:

(1) If Appellant's address for service is that of the Appellant's Counsel, state Counsel's full address and Appellant's own full address.

(2) Please notify the clerk of the court in writing immediately of any change of address. The court will communicate with you by mail at the address shown by you in this notice unless you notify the court of a change in your address.

(3) This notice of appeal must be filed with the local registrar of the Superior Court of Justice or Ontario Court of Justice.

Sections 111 and 112 of the *Provincial Offences Act* are as follows:

111. (1) A notice of appeal by a Defendant shall not be accepted for filing if the Defendant has not paid in full the fine imposed by the decision appealed from.

      (2) A judge may waive compliance with subsection (1) and order that the Appellant enter into a recognizance to appear on the appeal, and the recognizance shall be in such amount, with or without sureties, as the judge directs.

112. The filing of a notice of appeal does not stay the conviction unless a judge so orders.

REMARQUES :

1) *Si le domicile élu de l'appelant(e) est celui de son avocat(e), indiquer l'adresse au complet de l'avocat(e) de même que l'adresse au complet de l'appelant(e) lui-même(elle-même).*

2) *En cas de changement d'adresse, en aviser immédiatement le greffier du tribunal par écrit. Si le tribunal n'est pas avisé, il communiquera avec vous par courrier à l'adresse indiquée au présent avis.*

3) *Le présent avis d'appel doit être déposé auprès du greffier local de la Cour supérieure de justice ou de la Cour de justice de l'Ontario.*

Les articles 111 et 112 de la Loi sur les infractions provinciales se lisent comme suit :

111. 1) *l'avis d'appel d'un défendeur n'est pas accepté pour dépôt s'il n'a pas payé intégralement l'amende imposée par la décision portée en appel.*

      2) *Un juge d'appel peut dispenser l'appelant de se conformer au paragraphe (1) et lui ordonner de consentir un engagement à comparaître en appel. Le juge décide du montant de l'engagement, avec ou sans caution.*

112. *Le dépôt d'un avis d'appel ne suspend pas la déclaration de culpabilité à moins qu'un juge d'appel ne l'ordonne.*

[2] for example *Highway Traffic Act* / *par exemple*, Code de la route

NOTICE OF APPEAL
AVIS D'APPEL INTERJETÉ

Under section 116 of the *Provincial Offences Act*
En vertu de l'article 116 de la Loi sur les infractions provinciales

ONTARIO COURT OF JUSTICE
COUR DE JUSTICE DE L'ONTARIO
PROVINCE OF ONTARIO
PROVINCE DE L'ONTARIO

Form / *Formule* 1
Courts of Justice Act
Loi sur les tribunaux judiciaires
O.Reg. / *Règl. de l'Ont.* 723/94

(Strike out inapplicable words / *Rayer ce qui ne s'applique pas*)

1. Superior Court of Justice or Ontario Court of Justice at _____
   Cour supérieure de justice ou Cour de justice de l'Ontario à

2. Appellant is / *La partie appelante est*

   ☐ Defendant
   le défendeur (la défenderesse)

   ☐ Attorney General
   le procureur général

   ☐ Prosecutor
   le poursuivant

3. Name of Appellant: _____
   Nom de l'appelant(e) :

   Address for service: / *Domicile élu :* _____

4. Counsel for Appellant: Name: _____
   Avocat(e) de l'appelant(e) : Nom :

   Address for service: / *Domicile élu :* _____

5. Name of respondent *(if known)*: _____
   Nom de l'intimé(e) (s'il est connu) *:*

   Address for service: / *Domicile élu :* _____

6. Counsel for respondent *(if known)*: _____
   Nom de l'avocat(e) de l'intimé(e) (s'il est connu) *:*

   Address for service: / *Domicile élu :* _____

7. Decision of Ontario Court of Justice / *Décision rendue par la Cour de justice de l'Ontario* :
   (include name of Judge or Justice of Peace appealed from, if known): / *inscrire le nom du juge ou du juge de paix dont la décision est portée en appel, s'il est connu)* :

8. Date of decision: / *Date de la décision :* _____

9. The Appellant appeals against: / *L'appelant(e) interjette appel :*

   ☐ conviction / *de la déclaration de culpabilité*

   ☐ dismissal / *du rejet de l'accusation*

   ☐ finding as to ability to conduct a defense / *de la conclusion quant à la capacité du défendeur (de la défenderesse) d'assurer sa défense*

   ☐ sentence / *de la sentence*

   ☐ order (s. 161 of the P.O.A.) / *de l'ordonnance (art. 161 de la L.I.P.)*

   by the Ontario Court of Justice / *de la Cour de justice de l'Ontario*

   at _____
   à/au   (address of court / *adresse du tribunal*)

FOR INFORMATION ON ACCESS TO ONTARIO COURTS FOR PERSONS WITH DISABILITIES, CALL
1-800-387-4456
TORONTO AREA **416-326-0111**

POUR PLUS DE RENSEIGNEMENTS SUR L'ACCÈS DES PERSONNES HANDICAPÉES AUX TRIBUNAUX DE L'ONTARIO, COMPOSEZ LE
1-800-387-4456
RÉGION DE TORONTO **416-326-0111**

10. If Defendant is in custody, place where held: _____
    Si l'appelant(e) est sous garde, lieu de détention :
    _____

11. (a) Description of offence[1]: _____
        Description de l'infraction[1]
        _____

    (b) Information number *(if known)*: _____
        Numéro de la dénonciation (s'il est connu) :

12. (1) Statute[2] : / *Loi* [2]: _____

    (2) Section[3] : / *Article* [3] : _____

13. Date of offence: / *Date de l'infraction :* _____

14. Plea at trial: / *Plaidoyer au procès :* _____

15. The grounds for appeal are: / *Moyens d'appel :*
    (specify the question of law or issue where the appeal is from conviction or acquittal or finding as to ability to conduct a defense or specify the ground for appeal against sentence / *préciser la question de droit ou la question en litige lorsqu'il est interjeté appel de la déclaration de culpabilité, de l'acquittement ou de la conclusion quant à la capacité de la partie défenderesse d'assurer sa défense, ou préciser les moyens d'appel contre la sentence*)

    1. _____
    2. _____

16. In support of this appeal, the Appellant relies upon the following:
    À l'appui du présent appel, l'appelant(e) se fonde sur les documents suivants :
    (set out documents such as transcript, etc. upon which the Appellant relies / *indiquer les documents, tels que les transcriptions, sur lesquels se fonde l'appelant(e)*)

    1. _____
    2. _____

17. The relief sought is: _____
    Mesure de redressement demandée :

18. The Appellant intends: / *Intention de l'appelant(e) :*

    ☐ to be present in person or by counsel and to present the issues and the Appellant's arguments orally.
       comparaître en personne ou par l'entremise d'un(e) avocat(e) et débattre les questions en litige et présenter ses arguments oralement.

    ☐ not to be present in person or by counsel and to present the issues and the Appellant's arguments in writing.
       ne comparaître ni en personne ni par l'entremise d'un(e) avocat(e) et débattre les questions en litige et présenter ses arguments par écrit.

19. Does the Appellant intend to make a motion for an order that the appeal be heard by way of a new trial in the appeal court?
    L'appelant(e) a-t-il(elle) l'intention de présenter une motion en vue d'obtenir une ordonnance prévoyant la tenue de l'appel sous forme d'un nouveau procès devant le tribunal d'appel?

    ☐ Yes / *Oui*   ☐ No / *Non*

20. Date: _____

21. Signature of Appellant or Counsel: _____
    Signature de l'appelant(e) ou de son avocat(e) :

NOTES:

(1) If Appellant's address for service is that of the Appellant's Counsel, state Counsel's full address and Appellant's own full address.

(2) Please notify the clerk of the court in writing immediately of any change of address. The court will communicate with you by mail at the address shown by you in this notice unless you notify the court of a change in your address.

(3) This court of appeal must be filed with the local registrar of the Superior Court of Justice or Ontario Court of Justice.

REMARQUES :

1) *Si le domicile élu de l'appelant(e) est celui de son avocat(e), indiquer l'adresse au complet de l'avocat(e) de même que l'adresse au complet de l'appelant lui-même (elle-même).*

2) *En cas de changement d'adresse, en aviser immédiatement le greffier du tribunal par écrit. Si le tribunal n'est pas avisé, il communiquera avec vous par courrier à l'adresse indiquée au présent avis.*

3) *Le présent avis d'appel doit être déposé auprès du greffier local de la Cour supérieure de justice ou de la Cour de justice de l'Ontario.*

[1] for example, careless driving / *par exemple, conduite imprudente*

[2] for example, *Highway Traffic Act* / *par exemple,* Code de la route

[3] for example, Section 130 / *par exemple, article 130*

POA 0301 CSD (rev 11/03)

Set Fines for the Highway Traffic Act

PROVINCIAL OFFENCES ACT
RRO 1990, Regulation 950
Proceedings Commenced by Certificate of Offence
Schedule 43
The Highway Traffic Act

Item	Column 1	Column 2 Section	Set Fine
1.	Drive motor vehicle, no permit	7(1)(a)	$85.00
2.	Drive motor vehicle, no currently validated permit	7(1)(a)	$85.00
3.	Drive motor vehicle, no plates	7(1)(b)(i)	$85.00
4.	Drive motor vehicle, fail to display two plates	7(1)(b)(i)	$85.00
5.	Drive motor vehicle, plate improperly displayed	7(1)(b)(i)	$85.00
6.	Drive motor vehicle, no validation on plate	7(1)(c)(i)	$85.00
7.	Drive motor vehicle, validation improperly affixed	7(1)(c)(i)	$85.00
8.	Draw trailer, no permit	7(4)(a)	$85.00
9.	Draw trailer, no plate	7(4)(b)	$85.00
10.	Draw trailer, plate improperly displayed	7(4)(b)	$85.00
11.	Fail to surrender permit for motor vehicle	7(5)(a)	$85.00
12.	Fail to surrender permit for trailer	7(5)(b)	$85.00
13.	Have more than one permit	7(15)	$85.00
14.	Drive motor vehicle, not in accordance with permit limitations	8	$140.00
15.	Permit driving of motor vehicle, not in accordance with permit limitations	8	$140.00

Item	Column 1	Column 2 Section	Set Fine
16.	REVOKED		
17.	Fail to notify change of address	9(2)	$85.00
18.	Fail to notify change of name	9(2)	$85.00
19.	Fail to notify change of address—lessee	9(3)	$85.00
20.	Fail to notify change of name—lessee	9(3)	$85.00
21.	Drive motor vehicle, no vehicle identification number	10(I)	$85.00
22.	Permit driving of motor vehicle, no vehicle identification number	10(I)	$85.00
23.	Draw trailer, no identification number	10(2)(a)	$85.00
24.	Permit drawing of trailer, no identification number	10(2)(a)	$85.00
25.	Draw conversion unit, no identification number	10(2)(b)	$85.00
26.	Permit drawing of conversion unit, no identification number	10(2)(b)	$85.00
27.	Draw converter dolly, no identification number	10(2)(c)	$85.00
28.	Permit drawing of converter dolly, no identification number	10(2)(c)	$85.00
29.	Fail to remove plates on ceasing to be owner	11(1)(a)	$85.00

Item	Column 1	Column 2 Section	Set Fine
30.	Fail to remove plates on ceasing to be lessee	11(1)(a)	$85.00
31.	Fail to retain plate portion of permit	11(1)(b)	$85.00
32.	Fail to give vehicle portion of permit to new owner	11(1)(c)(i)	$85.00
33.	Fail to give vehicle portion of permit to lessor	11(1)(c)(ii)	$85.00
34.	Fail to apply for permit on becoming owner	11(2)	$85.00
34.1	Fail to provide valid information package for inspection	11.1(1)	$140.00
34.2	Fail to deliver valid information package at time vehicle transfer	11.1(1)	$140.00
35.	Deface plate	12(1)(a)	N.S.F.
36.	Deface validation	12(1)(a)	N.S.F.
37.	Alter plate	12(1)(a)	N.S.F.
38.	Alter validation	12(1)(a)	N.S.F.
39.	Deface permit	12(1)(a)	N.S.F.
40.	Alter permit	12(1)(a)	N.S.F.
41.	Use defaced plate	12(1)(b)	N.S.F.
42.	Use defaced validation	12(1)(b)	N.S.F.
43.	Use altered plate	12(1)(b)	N.S.F.
44.	Use altered validation	12(1)(b)	N.S.F.
45.	Permit use of defaced plate	12(1)(b)	N.S.F.
46.	Permit use of defaced validation	12(1)(b)	N.S.F.
47.	Permit use of altered plate	12(1)(b)	N.S.F.
48.	Permit use of altered validation	12(1)(b)	N.S.F.
49.	Use defaced permit	12(1)(b)	N.S.F.
50.	Permit use of defaced permit	12(1)(b)	N.S.F.

Item	Column 1	Column 2 Section	Set Fine
51.	Remove plate without authority	12(1)(c)	N.S.F.
52.	Use plate not authorized for vehicle	12(1)(d)	140.00
53.	Permit use of plate not authorized for vehicle	12(1)(d)	140.00
54.	Use validation not furnished by Ministry	12(1)(e)	140.00
55.	Use validation not furnished for vehicle	12(1)(e)	140.00
56.	Permit use of validation not furnished by Ministry	12(1)(e)	140.00
57.	Permit use of validation not furnished for vehicle	12(1)(e)	140.00
58.	Use plate not in accordance with Act	12(1)(f)	$140.00
59.	Use plate not in accordance with regulations	12(1)(f)	$140.00
60.	Use validation not in accordance with Act	12(1)(f)	$140.00
61.	Use validation not in accordance with regulations	12(1)(f)	$140.00
62.	Permit use of plate not in accordance with Act	12(1)(f)	$140.00
63.	Permit use of plate not in accordance with regulations	12(1)(f)	$140.00
64.	Permit use of validation not in accordance with Act	12(1)(f)	$140.00
65.	Permit use of validation not in accordance with regulations	12(1)(f)	$140.00
66.	Confuse identity of plate	13(1)	$85.00
67.	Obstruct plate	13(2)	$85.00
68.	Dirty plate	13(2)	$85.00
69.	Entire plate not plainly visible	13(2)	$85.00

Item	Column 1	Column 2 Section	Set Fine
69.0.1	Obstruct plate, preventing accurate photograph by red light camera system	13(3.0.1)	$85.00
69.1	Obstruct plate preventing accurate photograph	13(3)	$85.00
69.2	Obstruct plate preventing identification by toll system	13(3.1)	$85.00
70.	Operate commercial motor vehicle—no valid CVOR certificate	16(2)	$260.00
71.	Drive commercial motor vehicle—no valid CVOR certificate	16(2)	$175.00
72.	Fail to carry fleet limitation certificate	16(3)	$175.00
73.	Fail to carry CVOR certificate	16(3)(a)	$85.00
74.	Fail to carry vehicle lease	16(3)(b)	$85.00
75.	REVOKED		
76.	Fail to surrender CVOR certificate	16(4)	$85.00
77.	Fail to surrender vehicle lease	16(4)	$85.00
78.	REVOKED		
79.	Fail to surrender fleet limitation certificate	16(4)	$175.00
80.	Fail to notify change of officer's name	18	$175.00
81.	Fail to notify change of officer's address	18	$175.00
82.	Fail to notify change of officers	18	$175.00
83.	Fail to retain copy of lease	20(1)	$175.00
83.0.1	Provide fictitious, altered or fraudulently obtained CVOR certificate	21(4)	$400.00

Item	Column 1	Column 2 Section	Set Fine
83.0.2	Use fictitious, altered or fraudulently obtained CVOR certificate	21(4)	$400.00
83.0.3	Permit the use of fictitious, altered or fraudulently obtained CVOR certificate	21(4)	$400.00
83.0.4	Improperly use CVOR certificate	21(4)	$400.00
83.1	Operate commercial motor vehicle—improper insurance	23(1)	N.S.F.
83.2	Driver of commercial motor vehicle—fail to carry proof of insurance	23(3)	$175.00
83.3	Driver of commercial motor vehicle—fail to surrender proof of insurance	23(3)	$175.00
83.4	Inadequate cargo insurance	23.1	$85.00
83.5	No evidence of cargo insurance in vehicle	23.1	$85.00
84.	Drive motor vehicle—no licence	32(1)	$260.00
84.1	Drive commercial motor vehicle—no licence	32(1)	$310.00
85.	Drive motor vehicle—improper licence	32(1)	$260.00
85.1	Drive commercial motor vehicle—improper licence	32(1)	$310.00
86.	Drive street car—no licence	32(2)	$260.00
87.	Drive vehicle with air brakes—no endorsement	32(3)	$200.00
87.1	Drive commercial motor vehicle with air brake—no endorsement	32(3)	$310.00
88.	Drive motor vehicle in contravention of conditions	32(9)	$85.00

Item	Column 1	Column 2 Section	Set Fine
88.1	Drive commercial motor vehicle in contravention of conditions	32(9)	$310.00
89.	Permit unlicensed person to drive motor vehicle	32(10)	$200.00
89.1	Permit unlicensed person to drive commercial motor vehicle	32(10)	$310.00
90.	Permit person with improper licence to drive motor vehicle	32(10)	$200.00
90.1	Permit person with improper licence to drive commercial motor vehicle	32(10)	$310.00
91.	Permit person to drive motor vehicle in contravention of condition	32(10.1)	$200.00
91.0.1	Permit person to drive commercial motor vehicle in contravention of condition	32(10.1)	$310.00
91.1	Permit operation of vehicles with air brakes—no endorsement on licence	32(11)	$200.00
91.2	Permit novice driver to drive in contravention of condition or restriction	32(11.1)	$200.00
92.	Driver fail to surrender licence	33(1)	$85.00
92.1	Accompanying driver fail to surrender licence	33(2)	$85.00
93.	Driver fail to give identification	33(3)	$85.00
93.1	Accompanying driver fail to give identification	33(3)	$85.00
94.	Possess illegal licence	35(1)(a)	N.S.F.
95.	Use illegal licence	35(1)(a)	N.S.F.

Item	Column 1	Column 2 Section	Set Fine
96.	Possess non–Photo Card portion of cancelled, revoked or suspended licence	35(1)(b)	N.S.F.
97.	Use non–Photo Card portion of cancelled, revoked or suspended licence	35(1)	N.S.F.
98.	Permit another person to use all or part of licence	35(1)(c)	N.S.F.
98.1	Use other person's licence	35(1)(d)	N.S.F.
98.2	Apply for more than one licence	35(1)(e)	N.S.F.
98.3	Secure more than one licence	35(1)(e)	N.S.F.
98.4	Possess more than one licence	35(1)(e)	N.S.F.
98.5	Fail to surrender suspended, revoked or cancelled licence	35(1)(f)	N.S.F.
99.	Driving under licence of other jurisdiction while suspended in Ontario	36	N.S.F.
100.	Employ person under 16 to drive	37(2)	N.S.F.
101.	Permit person under 16 to drive	37(2)	N.S.F.
101.1	Permit person under 16 on motor-assisted bicycle	38(2)	N.S.F.
101.2	Permit person under 16 on power-assisted bicycle	38(2)	N.S.F.
102.	Let unlicensed driver hire vehicle	39(1)	N.S.F.
103.	Fail to produce licence when hiring vehicle	39(3)	$85.00
103.1	Pick up passenger for compensation without authority	39.1(1)	$300.00

Item	Column 1	Column 2 Section	Set Fine
103.2	Owner—allow use of vehicle to pick up passenger for compensation without authority	39.1(2)	$300.00
103.3	Arrange for passenger pick-up for compensation without authority	39.1(3)	$300.00
103.4	Offer to arrange for passenger pick-up for compensation without authority	39.1(3)	$300.00
103.5	Fail to carry authority to pick up passengers for compensation	39.1(4)(a)	$300.00
103.6	Fail to surrender authority to pick up passengers for compensation	39.1(4)(b)	$300.00
103.7	Fail to identify self	39.1(6)	N.S.F.
103.8	Novice driver—B.A.C. above zero	44.1(3)	$85.00
103.9	Young driver—B.A.C. above zero	44.1(5)	$85.00
104.	Apply for permit while prohibited	47(5)	N.S.F.
105.	Procure permit while prohibited	47(5)	N.S.F.
106.	Possess permit while prohibited	47(5)	N.S.F.
107.	Apply for licence while prohibited	47(6)	N.S.F.
108.	Procure licence while prohibited	47(6)	N.S.F.
109.	Possess licence while prohibited	47(6)	N.S.F.
110.	Procure CVOR certificate while suspended or cancelled	47(7)	$260.00
111.	Apply for CVOR certificate while suspended or cancelled	47(7)	$260.00

Item	Column 1	Column 2 Section	Set Fine
112.	Operate commercial motor vehicle—fleet limitation certificate not carried	47(8)(a)	N.S.F.
113.	Operate commercial motor vehicle—CVOR certificate suspended	47(8)(b)	N.S.F.
113.1	Novice driver fail to provide breath sample	48.1(3)	$85.00
113.2	Novice driver refuse to provide breath sample	48.1(4)	$85.00
113.3	Novice driver fail to provide breath sample	48.1(4)	$85.00
113.4	Novice driver refuse to provide breath sample	48.1(4)	$85.00
113.5	Novice driver fail to surrender licence	48.1(5)	$85.00
113.6	Accompanying driver fail to provide breath sample	48.2(2)	$85.00
113.7	Accompanying driver refuse to provide breath sample	48.2(2)	$85.00
114.	Operate vehicle for which permit suspended	51	N.S.F.
115.	Operate vehicle for which permit cancelled	51	N.S.F.
116.	Driving while under suspension	53(1)	N.S.F.
116.1	Passenger fail to identify self	57.1.1(1)	$85.00
116.2	Passenger fail to give required information	57.1.1(2)	$85.00
117.	No licence to operate vehicle business	59(1)	N.S.F.
118.	Interfere with officer inspecting vehicle business	59(6)	N.S.F.
119.	Fail to keep records	60(1)	N.S.F.
120.	Deal with vehicle identification number altered	60(2)	N.S.F.

Item	Column 1	Column 2 Section	Set Fine
121.	Deface vehicle identification number	60(3)	N.S.F.
122.	Remove vehicle identification number	60(3)	N.S.F.
123.	Fail to notify re vehicle stored more than 2 weeks	60(4)	$60.00
124.	Fail to report damaged vehicle	60(5)	$140.00
124.1	Give false report	60(6)	N.S.F.
125.	Drive without proper headlights—motor vehicle	62(1)	$85.00
125.1	Drive without proper headlights—commercial motor vehicle	62(1)	$200.00
126.	Drive without proper rear light—motor vehicle	62(1)	$85.00
126.1	Drive without proper rear light—commercial motor vehicle	62(1)	$200.00
127.	Drive without proper headlight—motorcycle	62(2)	$85.00
128.	Drive without proper rear light—motorcycle	62(2)	$85.00
129.	Drive without proper headlights—motorcycle with sidecar	62(3)	$85.00
130.	Drive without proper rear light—motorcycle with side car	62(3)	$85.00
131.	Drive with improper headlights	62(6)	$85.00
131.1	Drive with improper headlights—commercial motor vehicle	62(6)	$200.00
132.	Drive with headlamp coated	62(7)	$85.00

Item	Column 1	Column 2 Section	Set Fine
132.1	Drive with headlight coated—commercial motor vehicle	62(7)	$200.00
133.	Drive with headlamp covered	62(7)	$85.00
133.1	Drive with headlamp covered—commercial motor vehicle	62(7)	$200.00
134.	Drive with headlamp modified	62(7)	$85.00
134.1	Drive with headlamp modified—commercial motor vehicle	62(7)	$200.00
135.	More than 4 lighted headlights	62(9)	$85.00
135.1	More than 4 lighted headlights—commercial motor vehicle	62(9)	$200.00
136.	Improper clearance lights	62(10)	$85.00
136.1	Improper clearance lights—commercial motor vehicle	62(10)	$200.00
137.	Fail to have proper identification lamps	62(11)	$85.00
137.1	Fail to have proper identification lamps—commercial motor vehicle	62(11)	$200.00
138.	Fail to have proper side marker lamps	62(13)	$85.00
138.1	Fail to have proper side marker lamps—commercial motor vehicle	62(13)	$200.00
139.	Use lamp producing intermittent flashes of red light	62(14)	$85.00
139.1	Use lamp producing intermittent flashes of red light—commercial motor vehicle	62(14)	$200.00

Item	Column 1	Column 2 Section	Set Fine
139.2	Unauthorized red and blue lights at front	62(14.1)	$85.00
139.3	Unauthorized red and blue lights at front—commercial motor vehicle	62(14.1)	$200.00
140	Red light at front	62(15)	$85.00
140.1	Red light at front—commercial motor vehicle	62(15)	$200.00
141.	Improper use of green flashing lights	62(16.1)	$85.00
141.1	Improper use of green flashing lights—commercial motor vehicle	62(16.1)	$200.00
142.	Improper bicycle lighting	62(17)	$20.00
143.	Improper lighting on motor assisted bicycle	62(17)	$20.00
144.	Improper number plate light	62(19)	$85.00
145.	Use parking light while vehicle in motion	62(20)	$85.00
146.	Have more than one spotlamp	62(22)	$85.00
146.1	Have more than one spotlamp—commercial motor vehicle	62(22)	$200.00
147.	Improper use of spotlamp	62(22)	$85.00
147.1	Improper use of spotlamp—commercial motor vehicle	62(22)	$200.00
148.	Improper lights on traction engine	62(23)	$85.00
149.	No red light on rear of trailer	62(24)	$85.00
149.1	No red light on rear of trailer—commercial motor vehicle	62(24)	$200.00
150.	No red light on rear of object	62(24)	$85.00

Item	Column 1	Column 2 Section	Set Fine
150.1	No red light on rear of object—commercial motor vehicle	62(24)	$200.00
151.	No proper red lights—object over 2.6 metres	62(25)	$85.00
151.1	No proper red light—object over 2.6 m—commercial motor vehicle	62(25)	$200.00
152.	No lamp on left side	62(26)	$85.00
152.1	No lamp on left side—commercial motor vehicle	62(26)	$200.00
153.	Improper lights on farm vehicle	62(27)	$85.00
154.	No directional signals	62(29)	$85.00
154.1	No directional signals—commercial motor vehicle	62(29)	$200.00
155.	No brake lights	62(29)	$85.00
155.1	No brake lights—commercial motor vehicle	62(29)	$200.00
156.	No blue flashing light on snow removal vehicle	62(31)	$85.00
157.	Improper use of blue flashing light	62(32)	$85.00
157.1	Improper use of red and blue flashing lights	62(32)(b)	$85.00
157.2	Improper use of red and blue flashing lights—commercial motor vehicle	62(32)(b)	$200.00
158.	No sign—"right hand drive vehicle"	63	$85.00
159.	Improper braking system	64(1)	$85.00
159.1	Improper braking system—commercial motor vehicle	64(1)	$400.00
160.	Improper brakes on motorcycle	64(2)	$85.00
161.	Improper brakes on motor-assisted motorcycle	64(2)	$85.00

Item	Column 1	Column 2 Section	Set Fine
161.0.1	Improper brakes on power-assisted bicycle	64(2)	$85.00
161.1	Improper brakes on bicycle	64(3)	$85.00
162.1	Improper brakes on trailer—commercial motor vehicle	64(5)	$400.00
162.	Improper brakes on trailer	64(5)	$85.00
163.	Defective brakes	64(7)	$85.00
163.1	Defective brakes—commercial motor vehicle	64(7)	$400.00
164.	Defective braking system	64(7)	$85.00
164.1	Defective braking system—commercial motor vehicle	64(7)	$400.00
165.	Sell improper brake fluid	65(l)(a)	N.S.F.
166.	Offer to sell improper brake fluid	65(l)(a)	N.S.F.
167.	Install improper brake fluid	65(l)(a)	N.S.F.
168.	Sell improper hydraulic oil	65(l)(b)	N.S.F.
169.	Offer to sell improper hydraulic oil	65(1)(b)	N.S.F.
170.	Install improper hydraulic oil	65(l)(b)	N.S.F.
171.	Improper windshield wiper	66(l)(a)	$85.00
171.1	Improper windshield wiper—commercial motor vehicle	66(1)(a)	$200.00
172.	No windshield wiper	66(l)(a)	$85.00
172.1	No windshield wiper—commercial motor vehicle	66(1)(a)	$200.00
173.	Improper mirror	66(l)(b)	$85.00
173.1	Improper mirror—commercial motor vehicle	66(1)(b)	$200.00
174.	No mirror	66(l)(b)	$85.00
174.1	No mirror—commercial motor vehicle	66(1)(b)	$200.00

Item	Column 1	Column 2 Section	Set Fine
175.	Improper mudguards	66(3)	$85.00
175.1	Improper mudguards—commercial motor vehicle	66(3)	$200.00
176.	No mudguards	66(3)	$85.00
176.1	No mudguards—commercial motor vehicle	66(3)	$200.00
177.	No odometer	66(5)	$85.00
177.1	No odometer—commercial motor vehicle	66(5)	$200.00
178.	Defective odometer	66(5)	$85.00
178.1	Defective odometer—commercial motor vehicle	66(5)	$200.00
179.	Operate motor vehicle—mirrors more than 305 mm	67	$85.00
180.	No speedometer on bus	68	$85.00
181.	Defective speedometer on bus	68	$85.00
181.1	Drive commercial motor vehicle not equipped with working speed-limiting system	68.1(1)	$310.00
181.2	Permit operation of commercial motor vehicle not equipped with working speed-limiting system	68.1(1)	$310.00
181.3	Deactivate speed-limiting system	68.1(2)(a)	$310.00
181.4	Permit person to deactivate speed-limiting system	68.1(2)(a)	$310.00
181.5	Modify speed-limiting system	68.1(2)(b)	$310.00
181.6	Permit person to modify speed-limiting system	68.1(2)(b)	$310.00
181.7	Drive commercial motor vehicle with speed-limiting system tampering device	68.1(3)	$310.00

Item	Column 1	Column 2 Section	Set Fine
181.8	Permit operation of commercial motor vehicle with speed-limiting system tampering device	68.1(3)	$310.00
181.9	Fail to comply with officer's direction re speed-limiting system	68.1(5)	$310.00
181.10	Sell, offer or advertise speed-limiting system tampering device	68.1(7)	$310.00
182.	Improper tire—damage to highway	69(1)	$85.00
183.	Device on wheels—injure highway	69(2)	$85.00
184.	No lock shoe—animal drawn vehicle	69(3)	$85.00
185.	Improper tires	70(3)(a)	$85.00
185.1	Improper tires—commercial motor vehicle	70(3)(a)	$200.00
186.	Improper tires—drawn vehicle	70(3)(a)	$85.00
186.1	Improper tires—drawn vehicle—commercial motor vehicle	70(3)(a)	$200.00
187.	Improperly installed tires	70(3)(b)	$85.00
187.1	Improperly installed tires—commercial motor vehicle	70(3)(b)	$200.00
188.	Improperly installed tires—drawn vehicle	70(3)(b)	$85.00
188.1	Improperly installed tires—drawn vehicle—commercial motor vehicle	70(3)(b)	$200.00
189.	Fail to mark rebuilt tire	71(2)	N.S.F.
190.	Sell unmarked rebuilt tire	71(3)	N.S.F.
191.	Offer to sell unmarked rebuilt tire	71(3)	N.S.F.
192.	Sell new vehicle—no safety glass	72(2)	N.S.F.

Item	Column 1	Column 2 Section	Set Fine
193.	Register new vehicle—no safety glass	72(2)	N.S.F.
194.	Install non-safety glass	72(3)	N.S.F.
195.	Window obstructed	73(l)(a)	$85.00
196.	Windshield obstructed	73(1)(a)	$85.00
197.	Have object obstructing view	73(l)(b)	$85.00
198.	Drive with window coated—view obstructed	73(2)	$85.00
199.	Drive with windshield coated—view obstructed	73(2)	$85.00
200.	Colour coating obscuring interior	73(3)	$85.00
201.	No clear view to front	74(1)(a)	$85.00
202.	No clear view to sides	74(1)(a)	$85.00
203.	No clear view to rear	74(1)(b)	$85.00
204.	No muffler—motor vehicle	75(1)	$85.00
205.	No muffler—motor assisted bicycle	75(1)	$85.00
206.	Improper muffler—motor vehicle	75(1)	$85.00
207.	Improper muffler—motor assisted bicycle	75(1)	$85.00
208.	Excessive fumes	75(3)	$85.00
209.	Unreasonable noise—signalling device	75(4)	$85.00
210.	Unreasonable smoke	75(4)	$85.00
211.	Unnecessary noise	75(4)	$85.00
212.	No horn—motor vehicle	75(5)	$85.00
213.	No horn—motor assisted bicycle	75(5)	$85.00
214.	No horn—bicycle	75(5)	$85.00
215.	Defective horn—motor vehicle	75(5)	$85.00
216.	Defective horn—motor assisted bicycle	75(5)	$85.00

Item	Column 1	Column 2 Section	Set Fine
217.	Defective horn—bicycle	75(5)	$85.00
218.	Have a siren	75(6)	$85.00
219.	No slow moving vehicle sign	76(1)	$85.00
219.1	Slow moving vehicle sign not attached to rear of vehicle or trailer	76(1)	$85.00
219.2	Slow moving vehicle sign not attached in accordance with regulations	76(1)	$85.00
219.3	Slow moving vehicle sign placed on fixed object	76(4)	$85.00
219.4	Prohibited use of slow moving vehicle sign	76(6)	$85.00
219.5	Operate slow moving vehicle over 40 km/h	76(6.1)	$85.00
220.	No sleigh bells	77(1)	$25.00
221.	Drive—display screen visible to driver	78(1)	$125.00
222.	Drive—hand-held communication device	78.1(1)	$125.00
223.	Drive—hand-held entertainment device	78.1(2)	$125.00
224.	REVOKED		
225.	Drive motor vehicle with speed measuring warning device	79(2)	$140.00
225.1	Drive motor vehicle with pre-empting traffic control signal device	79.1(1)	$140.00
226.	Improper means of attachment	80	$85.00
226.1	Improper means of attachment—commercial motor vehicle	80	$200.00
227.	Refuse or fail to stop and move vehicle to a safe location	82(9)	$140.00

Item	Column 1	Column 2 Section	Set Fine
227.1	Refuse or fail to submit vehicle to examinations and tests	82(9)	$140.00
227.2	Refuse or fail to have vehicle repaired and submitted to further examinations and tests	82(9)	$140.00
227.3	Refuse or fail to have vehicle repaired and submit evidence of compliance	82(9)	$140.00
227.4	Refuse or fail to assist with examinations and tests of vehicle	82(9)	$140.00
227.5	Refuse or fail to place vehicle in safe condition	82(9)	$140.00
227.6	Refuse or fail to remove unsafe vehicle from highway	82(9)	$140.00
227.7	Operate unsafe vehicle on highway contrary to officer's prohibition	82(9)	$140.00
227.8	Permit operation of unsafe vehicle on highway contrary to officer's prohibition	82(9)	$140.00
227.9	Refuse or fail to stop and move vehicle to a safe location—commercial motor vehicle	82(10)	$400.00
227.10	Refuse or fail to submit vehicle to examinations and tests—commercial motor vehicle	82(10)	$400.00
227.11	Refuse or fail to have vehicle repaired and submitted to further examinations and tests—commercial motor vehicle	82(10)	$400.00

Item	Column 1	Column 2 Section	Set Fine
227.12	Refuse or fail to have vehicle repaired and submit evidence of compliance—commercial motor vehicle	82(10)	$400.00
227.13	Refuse or fail to assist with examinations and tests of vehicle—commercial motor vehicle	82(10)	$400.00
227.14	Refuse or fail to place vehicle in safe condition—commercial motor vehicle	82(10)	$400.00
227.15	Refuse or fail to remove unsafe vehicle from highway—commercial motor vehicle	82(10)	$400.00
227.16	Operate unsafe vehicle on highway contrary to officer's prohibition—commercial motor vehicle	82(10)	$400.00
227.17	Permit operation of unsafe vehicle on highway contrary to officer's prohibition—commercial motor vehicle	82(10)	$400.00
228.	Operate unsafe vehicle	84	N.S.F.
228.1	Operate unsafe vehicle—commercial motor vehicle	84	N.S.F.
229.	Operate unsafe street car	84	N.S.F.
230.	Operate unsafe combination of vehicles	84	N.S.F.
230.1	Operate unsafe combination of vehicles—commercial motor vehicle	84	N.S.F.
231.	Permit operation of unsafe vehicle	84	N.S.F.
231.1	Permit operation of unsafe vehicle—commercial motor vehicle	84	N.S.F.

Item	Column 1	Column 2 Section	Set Fine
232.	Permit operation of unsafe street car	84	N.S.F.
233.	Permit operation of unsafe combination of vehicles	84	N.S.F.
233.1	Permit operation of unsafe combination of vehicles—commercial motor vehicle	84	N.S.F
234.	Operate vehicle—fail to display device	85(1)	$200.00
235.	Permit operation of vehicle fail to display device	85(1)	$200.00
236.	Issue SSC not provided by Ministry	86	N.S.F.
237.	Affix vehicle inspection sticker not provided by Ministry	86	N.S.F.
238.	Unauthorized person issue SSC	90(1)	N.S.F.
239.	Unauthorized person affix vehicle inspection sticker	90(2)	$200.00
240.	Issue SSC without proper inspection	90(3)(a)	N.S.F.
241.	Affix vehicle inspection certificate without proper inspection	90(3)(a)	N.S.F.
242.	Issue SSC—vehicle not complying	90(3)(a)	N.S.F.
243.	Affix vehicle inspection sticker—vehicle not complying	90(3)(a)	N.S.F.
244.	SSC not made by inspection mechanic	90(3)(b)(i)	N.S.F.
245.	Vehicle inspection record not made by inspection mechanic	90(3)(b)(i)	N.S.F.
246.	SSC not countersigned	90(3)(b)(ii)	N.S.F.
247.	Unlicensed inspection station	91(1)	$400.00

Item	Column 1	Column 2 Section	Set Fine
248.	Corporation fail to notify change of officer or director	91(7)	N.S.F.
249.	Unregistered mechanic certify SSC	92(1)	N.S.F.
250.	Unregistered mechanic sign vehicle inspection record	92(1)	N.S.F.
251.	Obstruct inspector	98(6)	N.S.F.
252.	False statement in SSC	99(2)	N.S.F.
253.	Sell new vehicle not complying with standards	102(3)	N.S.F.
254.	Offer for sale new vehicle not complying with standards	102(3)	N.S.F.
255.	Expose for sale new vehicle not complying with standards	102(3)	N.S.F.
256.	Sell new vehicle not marked or identified	102(3)	N.S.F.
257.	Offer for sale new vehicle not marked or identified	102(3)	N.S.F.
258.	Expose for sale new vehicle not marked or identified	102(3)	N.S.F.
259.	No name on commercial vehicle	103(1)	$85.00
260.	Less than two reflectors—commercial vehicle	103(2)	$85.00
261.	Less than two reflectors—trailer	103(2)	$85.00
262.	Sell new commercial vehicle without two red rear lights	103(3)(a)	N.S.F.
263.	Offer to sell new commercial vehicle without two red rear lights	103(3)(a)	N.S.F.
264.	Sell trailer without two red rear lights	103(3)(a)	N.S.F.

Item	Column 1	Column 2 Section	Set Fine
265.	Offer to sell trailer without two red rear lights	103(3)(a)	N.S.F.
266.	Sell new commercial vehicle without two rear red reflectors	103(3)(b)	N.S.F.
267.	Offer to sell new commercial vehicle without two rear red reflectors	103(3)(b)	N.S.F.
268.	Sell trailer without two rear red reflectors	103(3)(b)	N.S.F.
269.	Offer to sell trailer without two rear red reflectors	103(3)(b)	N.S.F.
270.	No name and address on road-building machine	103(4)	$85.00
270.1	Fail to wear proper helmet on power-assisted bicycle	103.1(2)	$85.00
271.	Fail to wear proper helmet on motorcycle	104(1)	$85.00
272.	Fail to wear proper helmet on motor assisted bicycle	104(1)	$85.00
273.	Carry passenger under 16 not wearing proper helmet	104(2)	$85.00
273.1	Fail to wear proper helmet on bicycle	104(2.1)	$60.00
273.2	Permit person under 16 not wearing proper helmet on bicycle	104(2.2)	$60.00
273.3	Equestrian rider—fail to use proper equipment	104.1(1)	$60.00
273.4	Authorize or permit equestrian rider under 16 to ride without proper equipment	104.1(3)	$60.00
274.	Dealing with vehicle not conforming to standard	105(1)	N.S.F.
275.	Dealing with motor assisted bicycle—no document of compliance	105(2)	N.S.F.

Item	Column 1	Column 2 Section	Set Fine
276.	Drive with seat belt removed	106(1)	$200.00
277.	Drive with seat belt inoperative	106(1)	$200.00
278	Drive with seat belt modified	106(1)	$200.00
279.	Driver—fail to properly wear seat belt	106(2)	$200.00
280.	Passenger—fail to occupy position with seat belt	106(3)(a)	$200.00
281.	Passenger—fail to properly wear seat belt	106(3)(b)	$200.00
282.	Drive while passenger under 16 fails to occupy position with seat belt	106(4)(a)(i)	$200.00
283.	Drive while passenger under 16 fails to properly wear seat belt	106(4)(a)(ii)	$200.00
284.	Drive while child passenger not properly secured	106(4)(b)	$200.00
285.	REVOKED		
286.	REVOKED		
287.	REVOKED		
287.1	REVOKED		
288.	Fail to establish system to periodically inspect and maintain commercial motor vehicles and drawn vehicles	107(1)	$310.00
289.	Fail to keep written record of system to periodically inspect and maintain commercial motor vehicles and drawn vehicles	107(1)	$310.00
290.	Fail to ensure periodic inspections and maintenance are carried out	107(2)	$310.00
291.	Fail to ensure performance standards are met	107(3)	$310.00

Item	Column 1	Column 2 Section	Set Fine
292.	Fail to supply driver with daily inspection schedule	107(4)(a)	$310.00
293.	Fail to ensure daily inspection is conducted properly	107(4)(b)	$310.00
294.	Fail to ensure under-vehicle inspection is conducted properly	107(4)(c)	$310.00
295.	Fail to ensure daily inspection report is accurately completed	107(4)(d)	$310.00
296.	Fail to ensure under-vehicle inspection report is accurately completed	107(4)(d)	$310.00
297.	Fail to complete daily inspection report forthwith after inspection	107(5)	$200.00
298.	Fail to accurately complete daily inspection report	107(5)	$200.00
299.	Fail to complete under-vehicle inspection report forthwith after inspection	107(5)	$200.00
300.	Fail to accurately complete under-vehicle inspection report	107(5)	$200.00
301.	Fail to carry inspection schedule	107(6)	$85.00
302.	Fail to carry completed daily inspection report	107(6)	$85.00
303.	Fail to carry completed under-vehicle inspection report	107(6)	$85.00
303.1	Fail to surrender inspection schedule	107(7)	$85.00
303.2	Fail to surrender completed daily inspection report	107(7)	$85.00
303.3	Fail to surrender completed under-vehicle inspection report	107(7)	$85.00

Item	Column 1	Column 2 Section	Set Fine
303.4	Fail to enter defect in daily inspection report	107(8)(a)	$85.00
303.5	Fail to report defect to operator	107(8)(b)	$200.00
303.6	Fail to submit completed daily inspection report to operator	107(8)(c)	$85.00
303.7	Fail to submit completed under-vehicle inspection report to operator	107(8)(c)	$85.00
303.8	Drive commercial motor vehicle without required inspection	107(9)	$200.00
303.9	Drive commercial motor vehicle with a major defect in it or in drawn vehicle	107(11)	$310.00
303.10	Improperly drive commercial motor vehicle with a minor defect in it or in drawn vehicle	107(12)	$200.00
303.11	Fail to maintain books and records	107(13)	$310.00
303.12	Fail to produce books and records	107(13)	$310.00
304.	Overwidth vehicle	109(1)	$310.00
305.	Overwidth load	109(2)	$310.00
306.	Overlength vehicle	109(6)	$310.00
306.1	Overlength full trailer	109(6.2)	$310.00
307.	Overlength combination of vehicles	109(7)	$310.00
307.1	Operate overlength combination of vehicles	109(8)	$310.00
308.	Overlength semi-trailer	109(10)	$310.00
309.	Overlength bus	109(11)	$310.00
309.1	Overlength recreational vehicle	109(11)	$310.00
310.	Overheight vehicle	109(14)	$310.00

Item	Column 1	Column 2 Section	Set Fine
311.	Fail to carry permit in vehicle	110(6)	$310.00
312.	Fail to produce permit	110(6)	$310.00
313.	Oversize vehicle—violate permit	110(7)	$310.00
314.	Overweight vehicle—violate permit	110(7)	$200.00 + Schedule A
314.1	Fail to comply with condition of permit	110(7)	$310.00
314.2	Violate non-weight condition of special permit	110.2(3)(a)	$310.00
314.3	Violate weight condition of special permit	110.2(3)(b)	Schedule A
314.4	Violate weight condition of special permit—liftable axle lifted	110.2(3)(b)	$200.00 + Schedule A
314.5	Violate weight condition of special permit—liftable axle deployed improperly	110.2(3)(b)	$200.00 + Schedule A
314.6	Violate more than one condition, including a weight condition, of special permit	110.2(3)(c)	$200.00 + Schedule A
314.7	Violate more than one condition, including a weight condition, of special permit—liftable axle lifted	110.2(3)(c)	$400.00 + Schedule A
314.8	Violate more than one condition, including a weight condition, of special permit—liftable axle deployed improperly	110.2(3)(c)	$400.00 + Schedule A
315.	Fail to mark overhanging load	111(1)	$130.00
315.1	Fail to mark overhanging load—commercial motor vehicle	111(1)	$200.00
316.	Insecure load	111(2)	$130.00

Item	Column 1	Column 2 Section	Set Fine
316.1	Insecure load—commercial motor vehicle	111(2)	$310.00
316.2	Operate vehicle with load not secured as prescribed	111(2.1)	$130.00
316.3	Operate commercial motor vehicle with load not secured as prescribed	111(2.1)	$310.00
316.4	Permit operation of vehicle with load not secured as prescribed	111(2.1)	$130.00
316.5	Permit operation of commercial motor vehicle with load not secured as prescribed	111(2.1)	$310.00
316.6	Drive commercial motor vehicle without conducting inspections	111(2.2)	$310.00
317.	Overweight on tires …kg. … less than 150 mm	115(1)(a)	Schedule A
317.1	Overweight on tires …kg. liftable axle lifted	115(1)(a)	$200.00 + Schedule A
317.2	Overweight on tires …kg.—liftable axle deployed improperly	115(1)(a)	$200.00 + Schedule A
318.	Overweight on tires …kg. … 150 mm or over	115(1)(b)	Schedule A
318.1	Overweight on tires …kg.—liftable axle lifted	115(1)(b)	$200.00 + Schedule A
318.2	Overweight on tires …kg.—liftable axle deployed improperly	115(1)(b)	$200.00 + Schedule A
319.	Overweight single axle (single tires) …kg. Class A Highway	116(1)(a)	Schedule A
319.1	Overweight single axle (single tires) …kg. Class A Highway—liftable axle lifted	116(1)(a)	$200.00 + Schedule A

Item	Column 1	Column 2 Section	Set Fine
319.2	Overweight single axle (single tires) …kg. Class A Highway—liftable axle deployed improperly	116(1)(a)	$200.00 + Schedule A
320.	Overweight single axle (dual tires) …kg. Class A Highway	116(1)(a)	Schedule A
320.1	Overweight single axle (dual tires) …kg. Class A Highway—liftable axle lifted	116(1)(b)	$200.00 + Schedule A
320.2	Overweight single axle (dual tires) …kg. Class A Highway—liftable axle deployed improperly	116(1)(b)	$200.00 + Schedule A
321.	Overweight dual axle …kg. Class A Highway	116(1)(c)	Schedule A
321.1	Overweight dual axle …kg. Class A Highway —liftable axle lifted	116(1)(c)	$200.00 + Schedule A
321.2	Overweight dual axle …kg. Class A Highway —liftable axle deployed improperly	116(1)(c)	$200.00 + Schedule A
322.	Overweight triple axle …kg. Class A Highway	116(1)(d)	Schedule A
322.1	Overweight triple axle …kg. Class A Highway —liftable axle lifted	116(1)(d)	$200.00 + Schedule A
322.2	Overweight triple axle …kg. Class A Highway —liftable axle deployed improperly	116(1)(d)	$200.00 + Schedule A
323.	Overweight dual axle (single tires) …kg. Class A Highway	116(2)	Schedule A
323.1	Overweight dual axle (single tires) …kg. Class A Highway—liftable axle lifted	116(2)	$200.00 + Schedule A

Item	Column 1	Column 2 Section	Set Fine
323.2	Overweight dual axle (single tires) …kg. Class A Highway—liftable axle deployed improperly	116(2)	$200.00 + Schedule A
324.	Overweight triple axle (single tires) …kg. Class A Highway	116(3)	Schedule A
324.1	Overweight triple axle (single tires) …kg. Class A Highway—liftable axle lifted	116(3)	$200.00 + Schedule A
324.2	Overweight triple axle (single tires) …kg. Class A Highway—liftable axle deployed improperly	116(3)	$200.00 + Schedule A
325.	Overweight single front axle …kg. No verification. Class A Highway	116(4)	Schedule A
325.1	Overweight single front axle …kg. No verification. Class A Highway —liftable axle lifted	116(4)	$200.00 + Schedule A
325.2	Overweight single front axle …kg. No verification. Class A Highway —liftable axle deployed improperly	116(4)	$200.00 + Schedule A
326.	Overweight single front axle …kg. Exceed rating. Class A Highway	116(4)	Schedule A
326.1	Overweight single front axle …kg. Exceed rating. Class A Highway— liftable axle lifted	116(6)	$200.00 + Schedule A
326.2	Overweight single front axle …kg. Exceed rating. Class A Highway— liftable axle deployed improperly	116(6)	$200.00 + Schedule A
327.	Overweight two axle group …kg. Class A Highway	117(a)	Schedule A
327.1	Overweight two axle group …kg. Class A Highway—liftable axle lifted	117(1)(a)	$200.00 + Schedule A
327.2	Overweight two axle group …kg. Class A Highway—liftable axle deployed improperly	117(1)(a)	$200.00 + Schedule A
328.	Overweight three axle group …kg. Class A Highway	117(1)(b)	Schedule A
328.1	Overweight three axle group …kg. Class A Highway—liftable axle lifted	117(1)(b)	$200.00 + Schedule A
328.2	Overweight three axle group …kg. Class A Highway—liftable axle deployed improperly	117(1)(b)	$200.00 + Schedule A
329.	Overweight four axle group …kg. Class A Highway	117(1)(c)	Schedule A
329.1	Overweight four axle group …kg. Class A Highway—liftable axle lifted	117(1)(c)	$200.00 + Schedule A
329.2	Overweight four axle group …kg. Class A Highway—liftable axle deployed improperly	117(1)(c)	$200.00 + Schedule A
330.	Overweight vehicle …kg. Class A Highway	118	Schedule A
330.1	Overweight vehicle …kg. Class A Highway— liftable axle lifted	118	$200.00 + Schedule A
330.2	Overweight vehicle …kg. Class A Highway— liftable axle deployed improperly	118	$200.00 + Schedule A
331.	Overweight during freeze-up …kg.	119(4)	Schedule A

Item	Column 1	Column 2 Section	Set Fine
331.1	Overweight vehicle during freeze-up ...kg.—liftable axle lifted	119(4)	$200.00 + Schedule A
331.2	Overweight vehicle during freeze-up ...kg.—liftable axle deployed improperly	119(4)	$200.00 + Schedule A
332.	Overweight on axle ...kg. Class B Highway	120	Schedule A
332.1	Overweight on axle ...kg. Class B Highway —liftable axle lifted	120	$200.00 + Schedule A
332.2	Overweight on axle ...kg. Class B Highway— liftable axle deployed improperly	120	$200.00 + Schedule A
333.	Overweight vehicle— violate permit ...kg.	121(1)	Schedule A
334.	Fail to have receipt in vehicle	121(3)	$75.00
335.	Fail to produce receipt	121(3)	$75.00
335.1	Overweight on axle ...kg.—reduced load period	122(1)	Schedule A
335.2	Overweight on axle ...kg.—reduced load period—liftable axle lifted	122(1)	$200.00 + Schedule A
335.3	Overweight on axle ...kg.—reduced load period—liftable axle deployed improperly	122(1)	$200.00 + Schedule A
335.4	Overweight on tire ...kg.—reduced load period	122(3)	Schedule A
335.5	Overweight on tire ...kg.—reduced load period—liftable axle lifted	122(3)	$200.00 + Schedule A

Item	Column 1	Column 2 Section	Set Fine
335.6	Overweight on tire ...kg.—reduced load period—liftable axle deployed improperly	122(3)	$200.00 + Schedule A
336.	Fail or refuse to stop	124(3)	$200.00
337.	Fail or refuse to drive vehicle to scale	124(3)	$200.00
338.	Fail or refuse to redistribute or remove load	124(4)(a)	$100.00
338.1	Fail or refuse to stop— commercial motor vehicle	124(5)	$310.00
338.2	Fail or refuse to drive vehicle to scale— commercial motor vehicle subsection 124(5)	124(5)	$310.00
338.3	Fail or refuse to redistribute or remove load—commercial motor vehicle	124(6)(a)	$310.00
339.	Cause vehicle to be overloaded	126	Schedule A
340.	Speeding	128	Schedule B
340.1	Speeding—liability of owner where evidence obtained through photo-radar	128	Schedule C
340.2	Speeding—community safety zone	128	Schedule D
340.3	Owner—speeding pursuant to section 207 community safety zone	128	Schedule D
340.4	Speeding—construction zone	128	Schedule E
340.5	Speeding—construction zone—worker present	128	Schedule F
341.	Careless driving	130	$400.00
341.1	REVOKED		
342.	Unnecessary slow driving	132	$85.00

Item	Column 1	Column 2 Section	Set Fine
342.1	Unnecessary slow driving—community safety zone	132	$120.00
343.	Disobey officer directing traffic	134(1)	$85.00
343.1	Disobey officer directing traffic—community safety zone	134(1)	$120.00
344.	Drive on closed highway	134(3)	$85.00
344.1	Drive on closed highway—community safety zone	134(3)	$120.00
345.	Fail to yield—uncontrolled intersection	135(2)	$85.00
345.1	Fail to yield—uncontrolled intersection—community safety zone	135(2)	$150.00
346.	Fail to yield to vehicle on right	135(3)	$85.00
346.1	Fail to yield to vehicle on right—community safety zone	135(3)	$150.00
347.	Disobey stop sign—stop wrong place	136(1)(a)	$85.00
347.1	Disobey stop sign—stop wrong place—community safety zone	136(1)(a)	$120.00
348.	Disobey stop sign—fail to stop	136(l)(a)	$85.00
348.1	Disobey stop sign—fail to stop—community safety zone	136(1)(a)	$150.00
349.	Fail to yield to traffic on through highway	136(1)(b)	$85.00
349.1	Fail to yield to traffic on through highway—community safety zone	136(1)(b)	$150.00
350.	Traffic on through highway—fail to yield	136(2)	$85.00
350.1	Traffic on through highway—fail to yield—community safety zone	136(2)	$150.00
351.	Fail to yield—yield sign	138(1)	$85.00
351.1	Fail to yield—yield sign—community safety zone	138(1)	$150.00
352.	Fail to yield from private road	139(1)	$85.00
352.1	Fail to yield from private road—community safety zone	139(1)	$150.00
353.	Fail to yield from driveway	139(1)	$85.00
353.1	Fail to yield from driveway— community safety zone	139(1)	$150.00
354.	Fail to yield to pedestrian	140(1)(a)	$150.00
354.1	Fail to yield to pedestrian—community safety zone	140(1)(a)	$300.00
355.	Fail to yield to pedestrian approaching	140(1)(b)	$150.00
355.1	Fail to yield to pedestrian approaching—community safety zone	140(1)(b)	$300.00
356.	Fail to yield to person in wheelchair	140(1)(a)	$150.00
356.1	Fail to yield to person in wheelchair—community safety zone	140(1)(a)	$300.00
357.	Fail to yield to person in wheelchair approaching	140(1)(b)	$150.00
357.1	Fail to yield to person in wheelchair approaching—community safety zone	140(1)(b)	$300.00
358.	Pass stopped vehicle at crossover	140(2)	$150.00

Item	Column 1	Column 2 Section	Set Fine
358.1	Pass stopped vehicle at crossover—community safety zone	140(2)	$300.00
359.	Pass stopped street car at crossover	140(2)	$150.00
359.1	Pass stopped street car at crossover—community safety zone	140(2)	$300.00
360.	Stopped vehicle at crossover—fail to yield to pedestrian	140(2)(a)	$150.00
360.1	Stopped vehicle at crossover—fail to yield to pedestrian—community safety zone	140(2)(a)	$300.00
361.	Stopped street car at crossover—fail to yield to pedestrian	140(2)(a)	$150.00
361.1	Stopped street car at crossover—fail to yield to pedestrian—community safety zone	140(2)(a)	$300.00
362.	Stopped vehicle at crossover—fail to yield to person in wheelchair	140(2)(a)	$150.00
362.1	Stopped vehicle at crossover—fail to yield to person in wheelchair—community safety zone	140(2)(a)	$300.00
363.	Stopped street car at crossover—fail to yield to person in wheelchair	140(2)	$150.00
363.1	Stopped street car at crossover—fail to yield to person in wheelchair—community safety zone	140(2)(a)	$300.00
364.	Stopped vehicle at crossover—fail to yield to pedestrian approaching	140(2)(b)	$150.00

Item	Column 1	Column 2 Section	Set Fine
364.1	Stopped vehicle at crossover—fail to yield to pedestrian approaching—community safety zone	140(2)(b)	$300.00
365.	Stopped street car at crossover fail to yield to pedestrian approaching	140(2)(b)	$150.00
365.1	Stopped street car at crossover—fail to yield to pedestrian approaching community safety zone	140(2)(b)	$300.00
366.	Stopped vehicle at crossover—fail to yield to person in wheelchair approaching	140(2)(b)	$150.00
366.1	Stopped vehicle at crossover—fail to yield to person in wheelchair approaching—community safety zone	140(2)(b)	$300.00
367.	Stopped street car at crossover—fail to yield to person in wheelchair approaching	140(2)(b)	$150.00
367.1	Stopped street car at crossover—fail to yield to person in wheelchair approaching—community safety zone	140(2)(b)	$300.00
368.	Pass front of vehicle within 30 m of crossover	140(3)	$150.00
368.1	Pass front of vehicle within 30 m of crossover—community safety zone	140(3)	$300.00
369.	Pass front of street car within 30 m of crossover	140(3)	$150.00
369.1	Pass front of street car within 30 m of crossover—community safety zone	140(3)	$300.00
370.	Pedestrian fail to yield at crossover	140(4)	$35.00

Item	Column 1	Column 2 Section	Set Fine
371.	Person in wheelchair—fail to yield at crossover	140(4)	$35.00
371.1	Cyclist—ride in crossover	140(6)	$85.00
372.	Improper right turn	141(2)	$85.00
372.1	Improper right turn—community safety zone	141(2)	$120.00
373.	Improper right turn—multi-lane highway	141(3)	$85.00
373.1	Improper right turn—multi-lane highway—community safety zone	141(3)	$120.00
374.	Left turn—fail to afford reasonable opportunity to avoid collision	141(5)	$85.00
374.1	Left turn—fail to afford reasonable opportunity to avoid collision—community safety zone	141(5)	$150.00
375.	Improper left turn	141(6)	$85.00
375.1	1mproper left turn—community safety zone	141(6)	$120.00
376.	Improper left turn—multi-lane highway	141(7)	$85.00
376.1	Improper left turn—multi-lane highway—community safety zone	141(7)	$120.00
377.	Turn—not in safety	142(1)	$85.00
377.1	Turn—not in safety—community safety zone	142(1)	$150.00
378.	Change lane—not in safety	142(1)	$85.00
378.1	Change lane—not in safety—community safety zone	142(1)	$150.00
379.	Fail to signal for turn	142(1)	$85.00
379.1	Fail to signal for turn—community safety zone	142(1)	$120.00
380.	Fail to signal—lane change	142(1)	$85.00
380.1	Fail to signal—lane change—community safety zone	142(1)	$120.00
381.	Start from parked position—not in safety	142(2)	$85.00
381.1	Start from parked position—not in safety—community safety zone	142(2)	$150.00
382.	Start from stopped position—not in safety	142(2)	$85.00
382.1	Start from stopped position—not in safety—community safety zone	142(2)	$150.00
383.	Start from parked position—fail to signal	142(2)	$85.00
383.1	Start from parked position—fail to signal—community safety zone	142(2)	$120.00
384.	Start from stopped position—fail to signal	142(2)	$85.00
384.1	Start from stopped position—fail to signal—community safety zone	142(2)	$120.00
385.	Improper arm signal	142(4)	$85.00
385.1	Improper arm signal—community safety zone	142(4)	$120.00
386.	Improper signal device	142(6)	$85.00
386.1	Improper signal device—community safety zone	142(6)	$120.00
387.	Use turn signals improperly	142(7)	$85.00
387.1	Use turn signals improperly—community safety zone	142(7)	$120.00
388.	Fail to signal stop	142(8)	$85.00
388.1	Fail to signal stop—community safety zone	142(8)	$120.00
389.	Fail to signal decrease in speed	142(8)	$85.00

Item	Column 1	Column 2 Section	Set Fine
389.1	Fail to signal decrease in speed community safety zone	142(8)	$120.00
390.	Improper signal to stop	142(8)	$85.00
390.1	Improper signal to stop—community safety zone	142(8)	$120.00
391.	Improper signal to decrease in speed	142(8)	$85.00
391.1	Improper signal to decrease in speed community safety zone	142(8)	$120.00
392.	Brake lights—improper colour	142(8)(b)	$85.00
392.1	Brake lights—improper colour—community safety zone	142(8)(b)	$120.00
392.2	Fail to yield to bus re-entering lane from bus bay	142.1(1)	$85.00
392.3	Fail to yield to bus re-entering lane from bus bay—community safety zone	142.1(1)	$120.00
393.	U-turn on a curve—no clear view	143(a)	$85.00
393.1	U-turn on a curve—no clear view community safety zone	143(a)	$150.00
394.	U-turn—railway crossing	143(b)	$85.00
394.1	U-turn—railway crossing—community safety zone	143(b)	$150.00
395.	U-turn near crest of grade—no clear view	143(c)	$85.00
395.1	U-turn near crest of grade—no clear view—community safety zone	143(c)	$150.00
396.	U-turn—bridge—no clear view	143(d)	$85.00

Item	Column 1	Column 2 Section	Set Fine
396.1	U-turn—bridge—no clear view—community safety zone	143(d)	$150.00
397.	U-turn—viaduct—no clear view	143(d)	$85.00
397.1	U-turn—viaduct—no clear view—community safety zone	143(d)	$150.00
398.	U-turn—tunnel—no clear view	143(d)	$85.00
398.1	U-turn—tunnel—no clear view—community safety zone	143(d)	$150.00
399.	Improper stop—traffic signal at intersection	144(5)	$85.00
399.1	Improper stop—traffic signal at intersection community safety zone	144(5)	$120.00
400.	Improper stop—traffic signal not at intersection	144(6)	$85.00
400.1	Improper stop—traffic signal not at intersection—community safety zone	144(6)	$120.00
401.	Fail to yield to pedestrian	144(7)	$150.00
401.1	Fail to yield to pedestrian—community safety zone	144(7)	$300.00
402.	Fail to yield to traffic	144(8)	$85.00
402.1	Fail to yield to traffic—community safety zone	144(8)	$150.00
403.	Proceed contrary to sign at intersection	144(9)	$85.00
403.1	Proceed contrary to sign at intersection—community safety zone	144(9)	$120.00
404.	Disobey lane light	144(10)	$85.00
404.1	Disobey lane light—community safety zone	144(10)	$120.00

Item	Column 1	Column 2 Section	Set Fine
405.	Green light—fail to proceed as directed	144(12)	$85.00
405.1	Green light—fail to proceed as directed—community safety zone	144(12)	$120.00
406.	Flashing green light—fail to proceed as directed	144(13)	$85.00
406.1	Flashing green light—fail to proceed as directed—community safety zone	144(13)	$120.00
407.	Green arrow—fail to proceed as directed	144(14)	$85.00
407.1	Green arrow—fail to proceed as directed—community safety zone	144(14)	$120.00
408.	Amber light—fail to stop	144(15)	$150.00
408.1	Amber light—fail to stop—community safety zone	144(15)	$300.00
409.	Amber arrow—fail to stop	144(16)	$85.00
409.1	Amber arrow—fail to stop—community safety zone	144(16)	$120.00
410.	Amber arrow—fail to proceed as directed	144(16)	$85.00
410.1	Amber arrow—fail to proceed as directed—community safety zone	144(16)	$120.00
411.	Flashing amber light—fail to proceed with caution	144(17)	$85.00
411.1	Flashing amber light—fail to proceed with caution—community safety zone	144(17)	$120.00
412.	Red light—fail to stop	144(18)	$260.00
412.1	Red light—fail to stop—community safety zone	144(18)	$400.00
413.	Red light—proceed before green	144(18)	$260.00

Item	Column 1	Column 2 Section	Set Fine
413.1	Red light—proceed before green—community safety zone	144(18)	$400.00
413.2	Red light—vehicle owner fails to stop pursuant to section 207	144(18.1)	$260.00
414.	Turn on red light—fail to yield	144(19)	$85.00
414.1	Turn on red light—fail to yield—community safety zone	144(19)	$150.00
415.	REVOKED		
416.	Flashing red light—fail to stop	144(21)	$85.00
416.1	Flashing red light—fail to stop community safety zone	144(21)	$150.00
417.	Flashing red light—fail to yield	144(21)	$85.00
417.1	Flashing red light—fail to yield—community safety zone	144(21)	$150.00
418.	Pedestrian fail to use crosswalk	144(22)	$35.00
419.	Pedestrian disobey flashing green light	144(24)	$35.00
420.	Pedestrian disobey red light	144(25)	$35.00
421.	Pedestrian disobey amber light	144(25)	$35.00
422.	Pedestrian disobey "don't walk" signal	144(27)	$35.00
422.1	Cyclist—ride in or along crosswalk	144(29)	$85.00
423.	Disobey portable amber light—fail to stop	146(3)	$150.00
423.1	Disobey portable amber light—fail to stop—community safety zone	146(3)	$300.00

Item	Column 1	Column 2 Section	Set Fine
424.	Disobey portable red light—fail to stop	146(4)	$260.00
424.1	Disobey portable red light—fail to stop—community safety zone	146(4)	$400.00
425.	Disobey portable red light—proceed before green	146(4)	$260.00
425.1	Disobey portable red light—proceed before green—community safety zone	146(4)	$400.00
426.	Disobey portable red light—stop wrong place	146(5)	$85.00
426.1	Disobey portable red light—stop wrong place—community safety zone	146(5)	$120.00
427.	Disobey portable amber light—stop wrong place	146(5)	$85.00
427.1	Disobey portable amber light—stop wrong place—community safety zone	146(5)	$120.00
428.	Remove portable lane control signal system	146(6)	$85.00
428.1	Remove portable lane control signal system community safety zone	146(6)	$150.00
429.	Deface portable lane control signal system	146(6)	$85.00
429.1	Deface portable lane control signal system community safety zone	146(6)	$120.00
430.	Interfere with portable lane signal system	146(6)	$85.00
430.1	Interfere with portable lane control signal system—community safety zone	146(6)	$120.00

Item	Column 1	Column 2 Section	Set Fine
430.2	Fail to obey traffic control stop sign	146.1(3)	$85.00
430.3	Fail to obey traffic control stop sign—community safety zone	146.1(3)	$120.00
430.4	Fail to obey traffic control slow sign	146.1(4)	$85.00
430.5	Fail to obey traffic control slow sign—Community safety zone	146.1(4)	$120.00
430.6	Display traffic control sign—unauthorized person	146.1(5)	$85.00
431.	Fail to keep right when driving at less than normal speed	147(1)	$85.00
431.1	Fail to keep right when driving at less than normal speed—community safety zone	147(1)	$120.00
432.	Fail to share half road-way—meeting vehicle	148(1)	$85.00
432.1	Fail to share half roadway—meeting vehicle—community safety zone	148(1)	$120.00
433.	Fail to turn out to right when overtaken	148(2)	$85.00
433.1	Fail to turn out to right when overtaken—community safety zone	148(2)	$120.00
434.	Fail to share roadway—meeting bicycle	148(4)	$85.00
434.1	Fail to share roadway—meeting bicycle—community safety zone	148(4)	$120.00
435.	Fail to turn out to left to avoid collision	148(5)	$85.00

Item	Column 1	Column 2 Section	Set Fine
435.1	Fail to turn out to left to avoid collision community safety zone	148(5)	$120.00
436.	Bicycle—fail to turn out to right when overtaken	148(6)	$85.00
436.1	Bicycle—fail to turn out to right when overtaken—community safety zone	148(6)	$120.00
437.	Fail to turn out to left to avoid collision with bicycle	148(6)	$85.00
437.1	Fail to turn out to left to avoid collision with bicycle—community safety zone	148(6)	$120.00
438.	Motor assisted bicycle—fail to turn out to right when overtaken	148(6)	$85.00
438.1	Motor assisted bicycle—fail to turn out to right when overtaken—community safety zone	148(6)	$120.00
439.	Fail to turn out to left to avoid collision with motor assisted bicycle	148(6)	$85.00
439.1	Fail to turn out to left to avoid collision with motor assisted bicycle—community safety zone	148(6)	$120.00
440.	Fail to stop to facilitate passing	148(7)	$85.00
440.1	Fail to stop to facilitate passing—community safety zone	148(7)	$120.00
441.	Fail to assist in passing	148(7)	$85.00
441.1	Fail to assist in passing—community safety zone	148(7)	$120.00
442.	Pass—roadway not clear—approaching traffic	148(8)(a)	$85.00

Item	Column 1	Column 2 Section	Set Fine
442.1	Pass—roadway not clear—approaching traffic—community safety zone	148(8)(a)	$150.00
443.	Attempt to pass—roadway not clear—approaching traffic	148(8)(a)	$85.00
443.1	Attempt to pass—roadway not clear—approaching traffic—community safety zone	148(8)(a)	$150.00
444.	Pass—roadway not clear—overtaking traffic	148(8)(b)	$85.00
444.1	Pass—roadway not clear—overtaking traffic—community safety zone	148(8)(b)	$150.00
445.	Attempt to pass—roadway not clear—overtaking traffic	148(8)(b)	$85.00
445.1	Attempt to pass—roadway not clear—overtaking traffic—community safety zone	148(8)(b)	$150.00
446.	Drive left of centre—approaching crest of grade	149(1)(a)	$85.00
446.1	Drive left of centre—approaching crest of grade—community safety zone	149(1)(a)	$150.00
447.	Drive left of centre—on a curve	149(1)(a)	$85.00
447.1	Drive left of centre—on a curve—community safety zone	149(1)(a)	$150.00
448.	Drive left of centre within 30 m of bridge—no clear view	149(1)(a)	$85.00

Item	Column 1	Column 2 Section	Set Fine
448.1	Drive left of centre within 30 m of bridge—no clear view—community safety zone	149(1)(a)	$150.00
449.	Drive left of centre within 30 m of viaduct—no clear view	149(1)(a)	$85.00
449.1	Drive left of centre within 30 m of viaduct—no clear view—community safety zone	149(1)(a)	$150.00
450.	Drive left of centre within 30 m of tunnel—no clear view	149(1)(a)	$85.00
450.1	Drive left of centre within 30 m of tunnel—no clear view—community safety zone	149(1)(a)	$150.00
451.	Drive left of centre within 30 m of level railway crossing	149(1)(b)	$85.00
452.	Drive left of centre within 30 m of level railway crossing—community safety zone	149(1)(b)	$150.00
453.	Pass on right—not in safety	150(1)	$85.00
453.1	Pass on right—not in safety—community safety zone	150(1)	$150.00
454.	Pass—off roadway	150(2)	$85.00
454.1	Pass—off roadway—community safety zone	150(2)	$150.00
455.	Non-authorized driving on paved shoulder	151(5)	$85.00
455.1	Non-authorized driving on paved shoulder—community safety zone	151(5)	$120.00
456.	Drive wrong way—one way traffic	153	$85.00

Item	Column 1	Column 2 Section	Set Fine
456.1	Drive wrong way—one way traffic—community safety zone	153	$150.00
457.	Fail to drive in marked lane	154(1)(a)	$85.00
457.1	Fail to drive in marked lane—community safety zone	154(1)(a)	$120.00
458.	Unsafe lane change	154(1)(a)	$85.00
458.1	Unsafe lane change—community safety zone	154(1)(a)	$150.00
459.	Use centre lane improperly	154(1)(b)	$85.00
459.1	Use centre lane improperly—community safety zone	154(1)(b)	$120.00
460.	Fail to obey lane sign	154(1)(c)	$85.00
460.1	Fail to obey lane sign—community safety zone	154(1)(c)	$120.00
460.2	Improper use of high occupancy vehicle lane	154.1(3)	$85.00
460.3	Improper use of border approach lane	154.2(2)	$85.00
460.4	Driver in border approach lane—fail to stop	154.2(4)	$150.00
460.5	Fail to provide required document—driver	154.2(4)	$85.00
460.6	Fail to provide required document—occupant	154.2(4)	$85.00
461.	Drive wrong way—divided highway	156(1)(a)	$85.00
461.1	Drive wrong way—divided highway—community safety zone	156(1)(a)	$150.00
462.	Cross divided highway—no proper crossing provided	156(1)(b)	$85.00
462.0.1	Cross divided highway—no proper crossing provided—community safety zone	156(1)(b)	$120.00

Item	Column 1	Column 2 Section	Set Fine
462.1	Backing on roadway—divided highway	157(1)	$85.00
462.1.1	Backing on roadway—divided highway—community safety zone	157(1)	$120.00
462.2	Backing on shoulder—divided highway	157(1)	$85.00
462.3	Backing on shoulder—divided highway—community safety zone	157(1)	$120.00
463.	Follow too closely	158(1)	$85.00
463.1	Follow too closely—community safety zone	158(1)	$120.00
464.	Commercial vehicle—follow too closely	158(2)	$85.00
464.1	Commercial vehicle—follow too closely—community safety zone	158(2)	$120.00
465.	Fail to stop on right for emergency vehicle	159(1)(a)	$400.00
465.1	REVOKED		
466.	Fail to stop—nearest curb—for emergency vehicle	159(1)(b)	$400.00
466.1	REVOKED		
467.	Fail to stop—nearest edge of roadway—for emergency vehicle	159(1)(b)	$400.00
467.1	REVOKED		
468.	Fail to slow down and proceed with caution for emergency vehicle	159(2)	$400.00
468.1	Fail to move into another lane for emergency vehicle—if safe to do	159(3)	$400.00
468.2	Follow fire department vehicle too closely	159(4)	$400.00
468.3	REVOKED		

Item	Column 1	Column 2 Section	Set Fine
469.	Permit attachment to vehicle	160	$85.00
469.1	Permit attachment to vehicle—community safety zone	160	$120.00
470.	Permit attachment to street car	160	$85.00
470.1	Permit attachment to street car community safety zone	160	$120.00
471.	Draw more than one vehicle	161	$85.00
471.1	Draw more than one vehicle—community safety zone	161	$120.00
472.	Drive while crowded	162	$85.00
472.1	Drive while crowded—community safety zone	162	$120.00
473.	Disobey railway crossing signal—stop wrong place	163(1)	$85.00
473.1	Disobey railway crossing signal—stop at wrong place—community safety zone	163(1)	$150.00
474.	Disobey railway crossing signal—fail to stop	163(1)	$85.00
474.1	Disobey railway crossing signal—fail to stop—community safety zone	163(1)	$150.00
475.	Disobey railway crossing signal—proceed unsafely	163(1)	$85.00
475.1	Disobey railway crossing signal—proceed unsafely—community safety zone	163(1)	$150.00
475.2	Disobey stop sign at railway crossing—stop at wrong place	163(2)	$85.00

Item	Column 1	Column 2 Section	Set Fine
475.3	Disobey stop sign at railway crossing—stop at wrong place—community safety zone	163(2)	$150.00
475.4	Disobey stop sign at railway crossing—fail to stop	163(2)	$85.00
475.5	Disobey stop sign at railway crossing—fail to stop—community safety zone	163(2)	$150.00
475.6	Disobey stop sign at railway crossing—proceed unsafely	163(2)	$85.00
475.7	Disobey stop sign at railway crossing—proceed unsafely—community safety zone	163(2)	$150.00
476.	Disobey crossing gate	164	$85.00
476.1	Disobey crossing gate—community safety zone	164	$150.00
477.	Open vehicle door improperly	165(a)	$85.00
478.	Leave vehicle door open	165(b)	$85.00
479.	Pass street car improperly	166(1)	$85.00
479.1	Pass street car improperly—community safety zone	166(1)	$150.00
480.	Approach open street car door too closely	166(1)	$85.00
480.1	Approach open street car door too closely—community safety zone	166(1)	$150.00
481.	Pass street car on the left side	166(2)	$85.00
481.1	Pass street car on the left side—community safety zone	166(2)	$120.00

Item	Column 1	Column 2 Section	Set Fine
482.	Frighten animal	167	$85.00
482.1	Frighten animal—community safety zone	167	$120.00
483.	Fail to ensure safety of person in charge of animal	167	$85.00
483.1	Fail to ensure safety of person in charge of animal—community safety zone	167	$120.00
484.	Fail to use lower beam—oncoming	168(a)	$85.00
484.1	Fail to use lower beam—oncoming—community safety zone	168(a)	$120.00
485.	Fail to use lower beam—following	168(b)	$85.00
485.0.1	Fail to use lower beam—following—community safety zone	168(b)	$120.00
485.1	Prohibited use of alternating highbeam headlights	169(2)	$85.00
485.2	Prohibited use of alternating highbeam headlights—community safety zone	169(2)	$120.00
486.	Fail to take precaution against vehicle being set in motion	170(9)	$50.00
487.	Fail to have warning lights	170(10)(a)	$50.00
488.	Fail to use warning lights	170(11)	$50.00
489.	Interfere with traffic	170(12)	$50.00
490.	Interfere with snow removal	170(12)	$50.00
490.1	Offer tow truck services in King's Highway within 200 m of accident or apparent accident	171(1)(a)	$200.00

Item	Column 1	Column 2 Section	Set Fine
490.2	Offer tow truck services on King's Highway within 200 m of vehicle involved in accident	171(1)(b)	$200.00
490.3	Park tow truck on King's Highway within 200 m of accident or apparent accident—sufficient tow trucks available	171(2)(a)	$200.00
490.4	Stop tow truck on King's Highway within 200 m of accident or apparent accident—sufficient tow trucks available	171(2)(a)	$200.00
490.5	Park tow truck on King's Highway within 200 m of vehicle involved in accident—sufficient tow trucks available	171(2)(b)	$200.00
490.6	Stop tow trucks on King's Highway within 200 m of vehicle involved in accident—sufficient tow trucks available	171(2)(b)	$200.00
491.	Race a motor vehicle	172(1)	N.S.F.
491.1	Race a motor vehicle—community safety zone	172(1)	N.S.F.
492.	Race an animal	173	$85.00
493.	Fail to stop at railway crossing—public vehicle	174(1)	$85.00
494.	Stop wrong place at railway crossing—public vehicle	174(1)(a)	$85.00
495.	Fail to look both ways at railway crossing—public vehicle	174(1)(b)	$85.00
496.	Fail to open door at railway crossing—public vehicle	174(1)(c)	$85.00
497.	Cross tracks using gear requiring change—public vehicle	174(1)(d)	$85.00
497.1	Change gears while crossing railway track—public vehicle	174(1)(e)	$85.00
497.2	Fail to stop at railway crossing—school bus	174(2)	$85.00
497.3	Stop wrong place at railway crossing—school bus	174(2)(a)	$85.00
497.4	Fail to look both ways at railway crossing—school bus	174(2)(b)	$85.00
497.5	Fail to open door at railway crossing—school bus	174(2)(c)	$85.00
497.6	Cross tracks using gear requiring change—school bus	174(2)(d)	$85.00
497.7	Change gears while crossing railway track—school bus	174(2)(e)	$85.00
498.	Bus not used to transport adults with developmental handicaps or children, painted chrome yellow	175(3)	$85.00
499.	Prohibited markings	175(4)	$85.00
499.1	Prohibited equipment—school bus stop arm	175(4)	$85.00
500.	Drive chrome yellow vehicle, not used to transport adults with developmental handicaps or children	175(5)	$85.00
501.	Drive vehicle with prohibited school bus markings	175(5)	$85.00
502.	Drive vehicle with prohibited school bus stop arm	175(5)	$85.00
503.	Fail to actuate school bus signals	175(6)	$85.00

Item	Column 1	Column 2 Section	Set Fine
504.	Improperly actuate school bus signals	175(8)	$85.00
505.	Improperly actuate school bus signals at intersection controlled by operating traffic control system	175(9)(a)	$85.00
506.	Improperly actuate school bus signals at location, other than an intersection, controlled by operating traffic control system—at sign or roadway marking indicating stop to be made	175(9)(b)(i)	$85.00
507.	Improperly actuate school bus signals at location, other than an intersection, controlled by operating traffic control system—in area immediately before entering crosswalk	175(9)(b)(ii)	$85.00
507.1	Improperly actuate school bus signals at location, other than an intersection, controlled by operating traffic control system—within 5 m of traffic control system	175(9)(b)(iii)	$85.00
507.2	Improperly actuate school bus signals within 60 m of location controlled by operating traffic control system	175(9)(c)	$85.00
507.3	Stop school bus opposite loading zone	175(10)(a)	$85.00
507.5	Fail to stop for school bus—meeting	175(11)	$400.00
507.6	Fail to stop for school bus—overtaking	175(12)	$400.00
507.7	Fail to stop for school bus—owner	175(19)	$400.00

Item	Column 1	Column 2 Section	Set Fine
507.8	Fail to stop for school bus—owner	175(20)	$400.00
508.	Guard fail to properly display school crossing stop sign	176(2)	$85.00
509.	Fail to obey school crossing stop sign	176(3)	$150.00
509.1	Fail to obey school crossing stop sign community safety zone	176(3)	$300.00
510.	Improper use of school crossing stop sign	176(4)	$85.00
511.	Unauthorized person display school crossing stop sign	176(5)	$85.00
512.	Solicit a ride	177(1)	$50.00
513.	Solicit business	177(2)	$50.00
514.	Attach to vehicle	178(1)	$85.00
515.	Attach to street car	178(1)	$85.00
516.	Ride 2 on a bicycle	178(2)	$85.00
517.	Ride another person on a motor assisted bicycle	178(3)	$85.00
518.	Person—attach to vehicle	178(4)	$35.00
519.	Person—attach to street car	178(4)	$35.00
520.	Pedestrian fail to walk on left side of highway	179	$35.00
521.	Pedestrian on roadway fail to keep to left edge	179	$35.00
522.	Litter highway	180	$85.00
523.	Deposit snow or ice on roadway	181	$85.00
524.	Disobey sign	182(2)	$85.00
524.1	Disobey sign—community safety zone	182(2)	$120.00
525.	Disobey sign at tunnel	183(2)	$85.00
526.	Deface notice	184	N.S.F.

Item	Column 1	Column 2 Section	Set Fine
527.	Remove notice	184	N.S.F.
528.	Interfere with notice	184	N.S.F.
529.	Deface obstruction	184	N.S.F.
530.	Remove obstruction	184	N.S.F.
531.	Interfere with obstruction	184	N.S.F.
532.	Fail to remove aircraft	187(1)	N.S.F.
533.	Move aircraft improperly	187(2)	N.S.F.
534.	Aircraft unlawfully take off	187(3)	N.S.F.
535.	Draw occupied trailer	188	$85.00
536.	Operate air cushioned vehicle	189	$85.00
537.	Fail to maintain daily log	190(3)	$320.00
538.	Fail to carry daily log	190(3)	$320.00
539.	Fail to surrender daily log	190(4)	$320.00
540.	Driver in possession of more than one daily log	190(5)	$320.00
540.1	Permit person to drive commercial motor vehicle not in accordance with the regulations	190(6)	$320.00
540.2	Fail to produce proof of exemption	191(7)	$85.00
540.3	Drive motor vehicle—toll device improperly affixed	191.2(1)	$85.00
540.4	Drive motor vehicle—no toll device	191.2(1)	$85.00
540.5	Drive motor vehicle— invalid toll device	191.2(1)	$85.00
540.6	Engage in activity to evade toll system	191.3(1)	$85.00
540.7	Engage in activity to obstruct toll system	191.3(1)	$85.00
540.8	Engage in activity to interfere with toll system	191.3(1)	$85.00
540.9	Use device to evade toll system	191.3(1)	$85.00

Item	Column 1	Column 2 Section	Set Fine
540.10	Use device to obstruct toll system	191.3(1)	$85.00
540.11	Use device to interfere with toll system	191.3(1)	$85.00
540.12	Sell device designed to interfere with toll system	191.3(4)	$85.00
540.13	Offer to sell device designed to interfere with toll system	191.3(4)	$85.00
540.14	Advertise for sale device designed to interfere with toll system	191.3(4)	$85.00
540.15	Sell device intended to interfere with toll system	191.3(4)	$85.00
540.16	Offer to sell device intended to interfere with toll system	191.3(4)	$85.00
540.17	Advertise for sale device intended to interfere with toll system	191.3(4)	$85.00
541.	Fail to report accident	199(1)	$85.00
542.	Fail to furnish required information	199(1)	$85.00
542.1	Fail to report accident —specified location	199(1.1)	$85.00
542.2	Fail to furnish required information	199(1.1)	$85.00
543.	Occupant fail to report accident	199(2)	$85.00
544.	Police officer fail to report accident	199(3)	$85.00
544.1	Insurer fail to notify Registrar as prescribed re irreparable or salvage vehicle	199.1(4)	$400.00
544.2	Specified person ail to notify Registrar as prescribed re irreparable or salvage vehicle	199.1(5)	$400.00

Item	Column 1	Column 2 Section	Set Fine
544.3	Misclassify vehicle as irreparable or salvage in notice to Registrar	199.1(7)	$400.00
544.4	Fail to notify permit holder as prescribed re irreparable or salvage vehicle	199.1(8)	$400.00
544.5	Fail to return permit or portion of permit for irreparable or salvage vehicle to Registrar as prescribed	199.1(19)	$400.00
544.6	Drive or draw irreparable or salvage vehicle	199.1(19)	$140.00
544.7	Permit irreparable or salvage vehicle to be driven or drawn	199.1(19)	$140.00
545.	Fail to remain	200(1)(a)	N.S.F.
546.	Fail to render assistance	200(1)(b)	N.S.F.
547.	Fail to give required information	200(1)(c)	N.S.F.
548.	Fail to report damage to property on highway	201	$85.00
549.	Fail to report damage to fence bordering highway	201	$85.00
550.	Medical practitioner—fail to report	203(1)	$85.00

Item	Column 1	Column 2 Section	Set Fine
551.	Optometrist—fail to report	204(1)	$85.00
552.	Failing to forward suspended licence to Registrar	211(2)	$85.00
553.	Fail to surrender suspended driver's licence	212(2)	$60.00
554.	Refuse to surrender suspended driver's licence	212(2)	$60.00
554.0.1	Fail to assist in examination of commercial vehicle	216.1(1)	$310.00
554.0.2	Fail to stop commercial vehicle for examination	216.1(2)	$310.00
554.0.3	Fail to surrender documents	216.1(3)	$310.00
554.0.4	Fail to furnish information	216.1(3)	$310.00
554.0.5	Fail to comply with direction of officer	216.1(7)	$310.00
554.1	Cyclist—fail to stop	218(2)	$85.00
554.2	Cyclist—fail to identify self	218(2)	$85.00
555.	Obstruct officer	225(5)	$260.00
556.	Withhold record	225(5)	$260.00
557.	Conceal record	225(5)	$260.00
558.	Destroy record	225(5)	$260.00

SCHEDULE	OVERWEIGHT	PENALTY
Schedule A	0-2,499 kg.	$4.00 per 100 kg. or part kg.*
Highway Traffic Act	2,500-4,999 kg.	$5.00 per 100 kg. or part kg.
Set Fine	5,000-7,499 kg.	$6.00 per 100 kg. or part kg.
	Over 7,500 kg.	No Set Fine

* Regardless of the overweight, the penalty will not be less than $100.00

SCHEDULE	SPEED OVER THE MAXIMUM LIMIT	SET FINES
Schedule B	a) 1-19 kilometres per hour	$2.50 per kilometre
Highway Traffic Act	b) 20-29 kilometres per hour	$3.75 per kilometre
Speeding	c) 30-49 kilometres per hour	$6.00 per kilometre
	d) 50 kilometres per hour or more	No out of court settlement
Schedule C	a) 1-19 kilometres per hour	$2.50 per kilometre
Highway Traffic Act	b) 20-34 kilometres per hour	$3.75 per kilometre
Speeding—Photo Radar	c) 35-49 kilometres per hour	$6.00 per kilometre
	d) 50-60 kilometres per hour	$8.00 per kilometre
	e) 61+ kilometres per hour	No Set Fine
Schedule D	a) 1-19 kilometres per hour	$5.00 per kilometre
Highway Traffic Act	b) 20-29 kilometres per hour	$7.50 per kilometre
Speeding—Community Safety Zone	c) 30-49 kilometres per hour	No out of court settlement
Schedule E	a) 1-19 kilometres per hour	$2.50 per kilometre
Highway Traffic Act	b) 20-29 kilometres per hour	$3.75 per kilometre
Speeding—Construction Zone	c) 30-49 kilometres per hour	$6.00 per kilometre
	d) 50 kilometres per hour or more	No out of court settlement
Schedule F	a) 1-19 kilometres per hour	$5.00 per kilometre
Highway Traffic Act	b) 20-29 kilometres per hour	$7.50 per kilometre
Speeding—Construction Zone Worker Present	c) 30-49 kilometres per hour	No out of court settlement

Highway Traffic Act
Demerit Point System

ONTARIO REGULATION 339/94
Demerit Point System

INTERPRETATION

1.(1) In this Regulation,

"accumulated demerit points" means the total demerit points in a person's record acquired as a result of offences committed within any period of two years, less any points deducted for that period under this Regulation.

(2) A reference in this Regulation to a class of driver's licence is a reference to the class of licence as prescribed in Ontario Regulation 340/94.

(3) A reference in this Regulation to "fully licensed driver," "level 1 exit test," "level 2 exit test," "novice driver" and "valid driver's licence" is a reference to those expressions as defined in Ontario Regulation 340/94.

(4) A reference in this Regulation to the surrender of a licence does not include the surrender of a licence card that has been marked by the Ministry as valid only to show the driver's photograph.

(5) The short descriptions in Column 3 of the Table to this Regulation indicate, for convenience of reference only, the general nature of the offences under the provisions in Column 1 of the Table and shall not be construed to limit the offences for which demerit points are imposed.

GENERAL

2. If a person is convicted of an offence under a provision of an Act, regulation or municipal by-law set out in Column 1 of the Table to this Regulation and the penalty imposed by the court for the conviction does not include a period of licence suspension, the Registrar shall record in respect of the person, as of the date of commission of the offence, the number of demerit points set out opposite thereto in Column 2.

3(1) If a person is convicted of an offence or two or more offences arising out of the same circumstances and the penalty imposed by the court includes a period of licence suspension, no demerit points shall be recorded.

(2) If a person is convicted of two or more offences arising out of the same circumstances and the penalty imposed by the court does not include a period of licence suspension, demerit points shall only be recorded for the conviction carrying the greatest number of points.

4(1) If a resident of Ontario is convicted or forfeits bail in another province or territory of Canada or in one of the states of the United States of America for an offence that, in the opinion of the Registrar, is in substance and effect equivalent to an offence for which demerit points would be recorded upon conviction in Ontario, the Registrar may record the demerit points for the conviction as if the conviction had been entered or the bail forfeited in Ontario for the equivalent offence.

(2) For the purposes of subsection (1),

"conviction" includes a plea of guilty or a finding of guilt.

(3) Any accumulated demerit points of a new Ontario resident who becomes a fully licensed driver or a novice driver here, including a person classed as a novice

driver under subsection 28(1) of Ontario Regulation 340/94 shall be reduced, from the day on which he or she becomes a fully licensed driver or a novice driver,

(a) to seven, if the driver becomes a fully licensed driver and his or her accumulated demerit points total eight or more;

(b) to four, if the driver becomes a novice driver and his or her accumulated demerit points total five or more.

(4) After a reduction under subsection (3), the accumulated demerit points that remain shall be those recorded for the most recently committed offences.

5(1) If a person convicted of an offence set out in Column 1 of the Table appeals the conviction and notice of the appeal is served on the Registrar, the conviction and the demerit points related to it shall not be entered on the person's record unless the conviction is sustained on appeal.

(2) If a conviction referred to in subsection (1) and related demerit points have been recorded prior to service of notice of an appeal on the Registrar, the conviction and demerit points shall be removed from the record, and any suspension imposed as a result of the conviction shall be stayed, as of the date notice is served on the Registrar, unless the conviction is sustained on appeal.

6(1) The notice of suspension sent to a person in respect of a suspension under this Regulation shall state the effective date of the suspension.

(2) Revoked.

(3) The period of licence suspension is concurrent with the unexpired portion of any other licence suspension under this or any other authority.

DEMERIT POINTS: FULLY LICENSED DRIVERS

7(1) If a person who is a fully licensed driver in Ontario in one or more licence classes or a person who is not a resident of Ontario has six, seven or eight accumulated demerit points, the Registrar shall mail a notice setting out the number of points to the person at his or her latest address appearing on the records of the Ministry.

(2) A failure to give notice under subsection (1) does not render any further proceeding under this Regulation ineffective.

8(1) If a person who is a fully licensed driver in Ontario in one or more licence classes or a person who is not a resident of Ontario has 9, 10, 11, 12, 13 or 14 accumulated demerit points, the Registrar may require the person to attend an interview before a Ministry official and to provide information or other evidence to show cause why his or her driver's licence should not be suspended.

(2) The Minister may suspend or cancel the person's driver's licence,

(a) if the person fails to attend the required interview; or

(b) if the person does not comply with the Ministry's requirements as a result of the interview; or

(c) if, in the Minister's opinion, the person has not shown cause at the interview why the licence should not be suspended.

(3) A licence suspended under subsection (2) shall not be reinstated until such period as the Minister considers advisable has elapsed from the date the licence was surrendered on account of the suspension or two years have elapsed from the date of the suspension, whichever occurs first.

9(1) If a person who is a fully licensed driver in Ontario in one or more licence classes or a person who is not a resident of Ontario has 15 or more accumulated demerit points, the Registrar shall, after giving notice, suspend the person's driver's licence.

(2) A licence suspended under subsection (1) shall not be reinstated until,

(a) in the case of a first suspension, 30 days have elapsed from the date the licence was surrendered on account of the suspension or two years have elapsed from the date of the suspension, whichever occurs first; or

(b) in the case of a subsequent suspension, six months have elapsed from the date the licence was surrendered on account of the suspension or two years have elapsed from the date of the suspension, whichever occurs first.

(3) For the purpose of clause (2)(b), a suspension is a subsequent suspension only if it occurs as a result of a conviction for an offence committed within two years after the expiry of a prior suspension under this section.

(4) If a suspension is imposed on a person who, at the time of the suspension, is a fully licensed driver in Ontario in one or more licence classes or a person who is not a resident of Ontario, the person's accumulated demerit points for convictions for offences that occurred prior to the effective date of the suspension shall be reduced to seven on that date and the remaining points shall be those recorded for the most recently committed offences.

10.–14. Revoked.

DEMERIT POINTS: NOVICE DRIVERS

15(1) The Registrar shall mail a notice to a novice driver at his or her latest address on the records of the Ministry setting out the reason for the notice, the circumstances under which his or her licence may be suspended and any other action the Ministry may take if, within any two-year period, the novice driver accumulates two, three, four or five demerit points.

(2) A failure to give notice under subsection (1) does not render any further proceeding under this Regulation ineffective.

16(1) The Registrar may require a novice driver to attend an interview before a Ministry official at a designated time and place if, within any two-year period, the novice driver accumulates six, seven or eight demerit points.

(2) The Minister may suspend or cancel the person's driver's licence,

(a) if the person does not attend the required interview;

(b) if the person does not comply with the Ministry's requirements as a result of the interview; or

(c) if, in the Minister's opinion, the person has not shown cause at the interview why the licence should not be suspended.

(3) A licence suspended under subsection (2) shall not be reinstated until such period as the Registrar considers advisable has elapsed from the date the licence was surrendered on account of the suspension or two years have elapsed from the date of the suspension, whichever occurs first.

17(1) If a novice driver has nine or more accumulated demerit points, the Registrar shall, after giving notice, suspend his or her driver's licence.

(2) A licence suspended under subsection (1) shall not be reinstated until,

(a) in the case of a first suspension, 60 days have elapsed from the date the licence was surrendered on account of the suspension or two years have elapsed from the date of the suspension, whichever occurs first; or

(b) in the case of a subsequent suspension, six months have elapsed from the date the licence was surrendered on account of the suspension or two years have elapsed from the date of the suspension, whichever occurs first.

(3) For the purpose of clause (2)(b), a suspension is a subsequent suspension only if it occurs as a result of a conviction for an offence committed within two years after the expiry of a prior suspension under this section.

(4) If a suspension is imposed on a person who, at the time of the suspension, is a novice driver, the person's accumulated demerit points for convictions for offences that occurred prior to the effective date of the suspension shall be reduced to four on that date and the remaining points shall be those recorded in respect of the most recently committed offences.

(5) If a suspension is imposed on a person who, at the time of the suspension, is no longer a novice driver, the person's accumulated demerit points for convictions for offences that occurred prior to the effective date of the suspension shall be reduced to seven on that date and the remaining points shall be those recorded in respect of the most recently committed offences.

18(1) Sections 7 to 9 apply, and not sections 15, 16 and 17, to a driver who holds a licence that includes more than one licence class, only one of which is novice class, if he or she is a fully licensed driver in the other licence class or classes.

(2) Revoked.

19. Omitted (revokes other Regulations).

20. Omitted (provides for coming into force of provisions of this Regulation).

TABLE

Item	Column 1 Provisions for Offences	Column 2 Number of Demerit Points	Column 3 Short Description of Offences for Convenience of Reference Only
1	Section 200 of the *Highway Traffic Act*	7	Failing to remain at scene of accident
1.1	Section 216 of the *Highway Traffic Act*, except where a suspension order is made under subsection 216(3)	7	Driver failing to stop when signalled or requested to stop by a police officer
2	Section 130 of the *Highway Traffic Act*	6	Careless driving
3	Section 172 of the *Highway Traffic Act*	6	Racing
4	Section 128 of the *Highway Traffic Act*; subsection 13(3) of Regulation 829 of the Revised Regulations of Ontario, 1990; any provision of the National Capital Commission Traffic and Property Regulations CRC 1978, c. 1044 made under the *National Capital Act* (Canada) fixing maximum rates of speed and any municipal by-law fixing maximum rates of speed where the rate of speed is exceeded by,		
	(a) 50 km/h or more	6	Exceeding speed limit by 50 km/h or more
	(b) 30 km/h or more and less than 50 km/h	4	Exceeding speed limit by 30 to 49 km/h
	(c) more than 15 km/h and less than 30 km/h	3	Exceeding speed limit by 16 to 29 km/h
5	Subsections 174(1) and (2) of the *Highway Traffic Act*	5	Driver of public vehicle or school bus failing to stop at railway crossings
6	Section 164 of the *Highway Traffic Act*	3	Driving through, around or under railway crossing barrier
7	Subsections 135(2) and (3), clause 136(1) (b), subsection 136(2), subsection 138(1), subsection 139(1), subsection 141(5) and subsections 144(7), (8) and (21) of the *Highway Traffic Act*	3	Failing to yield right of way

Item	Column 1 Provisions for Offences	Column 2 Number of Demerit Points	Column 3 Short Description of Offences for Convenience of Reference Only
8	Clause 136(1)(a), subsections 144(14), (15), (16), (17), (18) and (21), subsections 146 (3) and (4) and section 163 of the *Highway Traffic Act*, any municipal by-law requiring a driver to stop for a stop sign or signal light, and the National Capital Commission Traffic and Property Regulations CRC 1978, c. 1044 made under the *National Capital Act* (Canada) requiring a driver to stop for a stop sign	3	Failing to obey a stop sign, signal light or railway crossing signal
9	Subsection 134(1) of the *Highway Traffic Act*	3	Failing to obey directions of police constable
10	Subsection 134(3) of the *Highway Traffic Act*	3	Driving or operating a vehicle on a closed highway
11	Subsections 199(1) and (1.1) of the *Highway Traffic Act*	3	Failing to report an accident
12	Subsection 148(8), sections 149, 150 and 166 of the *Highway Traffic Act*	3	Improper passing
13	Section 154 of the *Highway Traffic Act*	3	Improper driving where highway divided into lanes
14	Subsections 175(11) and (12) of the *Highway Traffic Act*	6	Failing to stop for school bus
15	Section 158 of the *Highway Traffic Act*	4	Following too closely
16	Section 162 of the *Highway Traffic Act*	3	Crowding driver's seat
17	Clause 156(1)(a) of the *Highway Traffic Act*	3	Drive wrong way—divided highway
18	Clause 156(1)(b) of the *Highway Traffic Act*	3	Cross divided highway—no proper crossing provided
19	Section 153 of the *Highway Traffic Act*	3	Wrong way in one way street or highway
20	Subsection 157(1) of the *Highway Traffic Act*	2	Backing on highway
21	Subsections 140(1), (2) and (3) of the *Highway Traffic Act*	3	Pedestrian crossover

Item	Column 1 Provisions for Offences	Column 2 Number of Demerit Points	Column 3 Short Description of Offences for Convenience of Reference Only
22	Subsections 148(1), (2), (4), (5), (6) and (7) of the *Highway Traffic Act*	2	Failing to share road
23	Subsections 141(2) and (3) of the *Highway Traffic Act*	2	Improper right turn
24	Subsections 141(6) and (7) of the *Highway Traffic Act*	2	Improper left turn
25	Subsections 142(1), (2) and (8) of the *Highway Traffic Act*	2	Failing to signal
26	Section 132 of the *Highway Traffic Act*	2	Unnecessary slow driving
27	Section 168 of the *Highway Traffic Act*	2	Failing to lower headlamp beam
28	Section 165 of the *Highway Traffic Act*	2	Improper opening of vehicle door
29	Section 143 and subsection 144(9) of the *Highway Traffic Act* and any municipal by-law prohibiting turns	2	Prohibited turns
30	Section 160 of the *Highway Traffic Act*	2	Towing of persons on toboggans, bicycles, skis, etc., prohibited
31	Subsection 182(2) of the *Highway Traffic Act*	2	Failing to obey signs prescribed by regulation under subsection 182 (1)
32	Subsection 106(2) of the *Highway Traffic Act*	2	Driver failing to properly wear seat belt
33	Subclause 106(4)(a)(i) of the *Highway Traffic Act*	2	Driving while passenger under 16 fails to occupy position with seat belt
33.1	Subclause 106 (4)(a)(ii) of the *Highway Traffic Act*	2	Driving while passenger under 16 fails to properly wear seat belt
33.2	Clause 106(4)(b) of the *Highway Traffic Act*	2	Driving while child passenger not properly secured
34	Subsection 8(2) of Regulation 613 of the Revised Regulations of Ontario, 1990	2	Driver failing to ensure infant passenger is secured as prescribed

Item	Column 1 Provisions for Offences	Column 2 Number of Demerit Points	Column 3 Short Description of Offences for Convenience of Reference Only
34.1	Subsection 8(3) of Regulation 613 of the Revised Regulations of Ontario, 1990	2	Driver failing to ensure toddler passenger is secured as prescribed
34.2	Subsection 8(4) of Regulation 613 of the Revised Regulations of Ontario, 1990	2	Driver failing to ensure child passenger is secured as prescribed
35	Clause 159(1)(a) of the *Highway Traffic Act*	3	Failing to stop on right for emergency vehicle
36	Clause 159(1)(b) of the *Highway Traffic Act*	3	Failing to stop—nearest curb—for emergency vehicle
36.1	Clause 159(1)(b) of the *Highway Traffic Act*	3	Failing to stop—nearest edge of roadway—for emergency vehicle
36.2	Subsection 159(2) of the *Highway Traffic Act*	3	Failing to slow down and proceed with caution for emergency vehicle
36.3	Subsection 159(3) of the *Highway Traffic Act*	3	Failing to move into another lane for emergency vehicle—if safe to do so
36.4	Subsection 159(4) of the *Highway Traffic Act*	3	Following fire department vehicle too closely
37	Subsection 79(2) of the *Highway Traffic Act*	3	Motor vehicle equipped with or carrying a speed measuring warning device
38	Subsection 154.1(3) of the *Highway Traffic Act*	3	Improper use of high occupancy vehicle lane
39	Subsection 146.1(3) of the *Highway Traffic Act*	3	Failing to obey traffic control stop sign
40	Subsection 146.1(4) of the *Highway Traffic Act*	3	Failing to obey traffic control slow sign
41	Subsection 176(3) of the *Highway Traffic Act*	3	Failing to obey school crossing stop sign

Modernization of the Provincial Offences Act

E

The Executive Summary on the following pages is reproduced by kind permission of the Law Commission of Ontario from their *Modernization of the Provincial Offences Act: Final Report* (Toronto: August 2011). To view the full report, go to the Law Commission's website at www.lco-cdo.org.

EXECUTIVE SUMMARY

I. INTRODUCTION

Regulatory law dictates how we drive our vehicles, the safety of our places of work, the food and beverages we consume and how we treat our pets, among many other areas that affect Ontarians on a daily basis. The *Provincial Offences Act* mandates the process to deal with the millions of charges that are brought under regulatory statutes each year. The vast majority involve "less serious" offences for which defendants are most likely to be unrepresented. It is important that the process governing these offences is fair, efficient, accessible and proportionate to the interests at stake.

The POA was enacted more than 30 years ago, establishing a procedure for the prosecution of offences under Ontario statutes, regulations and municipal by-laws. A comprehensive review of the POA has not been undertaken since then to assess whether it continues to meet its original objectives and whether those objectives remain current today. Nor has there been a review to consider the impact of significant developments such as the enactment of the *Charter of Rights and Freedoms*, the transfer of prosecution and court administration of POA matters from the Province to municipalities, significantly increased penalties for many offences, and the increased use of administrative monetary penalties to enforce regulatory standards.

The Board of Governors of the Law Commission of Ontario (LCO) therefore approved a project on Modernization of the *Provincial Offences Act* on April 2, 2009. We have examined specific procedural issues, and have proposed structural improvements and a mechanism whereby procedural improvements in the future can be more easily achieved. This Final Report provides an analytical framework for modernizing and reforming the *Provincial Offences Act* (POA).

II. STRUCTURAL REFORMS TO THE POA

Provincial Offences and the POA

Prior to the POA's coming into force, the *Summary Convictions Act* governed the procedure for enforcing and prosecuting provincial offences. It largely adopted the federal *Criminal Code*'s provisions for the prosecution of summary conviction offences. The new POA was intended to establish a speedy, efficient, simple and appropriate method of dealing with, for the most part, minor offences by the provincial offences court. This objective remains current today.

The POA sets out three distinct streams for commencing prosecutions of provincial offences before a judge or justice of the peace (justice) in the Ontario Court of Justice. It contains ten parts described in detail in the Report. Parts I, II and III address the three different ways a POA proceeding may be commenced; Part IV provides for the trial process for all offences; Part V addresses general matters; Part VI describes procedures for young persons; Part VII deals with appeals and reviews; Part VIII is concerned with arrest, bail and search warrants; Part IX concerns the application of the POA to statutes that provide for orders but does not provide for a procedure; and Part X provides for agreements between the Attorney General and municipalities.

Seven regulations apply to POA proceedings, governing such matters as costs, fees for late payment of fines, forms and notices for various types of proceedings and fine surcharges. In addition, four different sets of procedural rules dictate the practice and procedure for POA proceedings and appeals.

To give some context to the type of provincial offences that would be governed by the POA, we describe key areas of regulatory law in Ontario. They include motor vehicle regulation, occupational health and safety laws, environmental protection, the regulation of controlled substances such as liquor and tobacco, safety regulation such as fire protection and restraining orders, general public order and safety regulation such as soliciting in certain public locations and consumer protection regulation.

A separate statute addressing procedural matters reflects the view that there is a clear distinction between regulatory offences and true crimes. Criminal conduct under the federal *Criminal Code* is said to constitute conduct that is inherently contrary to basic human values and is therefore prohibited completely through criminal enactments. There is usually stigma associated with a conviction of a crime. Regulatory offences, on the other hand, most often involve conduct that is prohibited not because it is inherently wrongful but because dangerous conditions and risks to society at large would result if that conduct was not regulated. There is little or no stigma associated with most provincial offence convictions. Unlike criminal activity, there is usually an expectation that people will continue to engage in the regulated activity after a prosecution, but that they will do so lawfully. It is not always easy to make the distinction, particularly for provincial offences that have significant penalties and the possibility of imprisonment. Nevertheless, the vast majority of POA charges relate to matters that are clearly regulatory and are minor in nature and warrant distinctive treatment, including sentencing.

We therefore recommend maintaining a distinct procedural code in relation to provincial offences. (Recommendation 1)

POA Reform Framework
Certain principles ought to guide the reform of POA procedure now and in the future.

They are:

Fairness. Fairness must remain a paramount consideration when reforming the POA, although not necessarily as broad in scope as in the criminal context.

Access to Justice. Given the volume of minor provincial offences, the POA system is the "face of the justice system" for most Ontarians. Most defendants are believed to be unrepresented. The POA must therefore provide for simple, easily understood and accessible procedures for the most common offences.

Proportionality. The procedure governing the prosecution of an offence must be proportionate to the interests at stake.

Efficiency and the Administration of Justice. Any procedural system must be efficient to handle the millions of minor charges as well as the less common, but increasingly complex, cases under Part III.

We have also applied the concept of responsive regulation to POA reform. Responsive regulation is most applicable when deciding how best to enforce regulatory standards, but it also has relevance to sentencing of regulatory offences. In this regard we briefly discuss "the regulatory pyramid", under which regulators proceed with modest strategies to encourage parties to comply with regulatory standards, and if unsuccessful, resort to successively more punitive mechanisms, as an alternative to regulatory prosecutions and fines as a first response. We discuss alternative sentencing tools in Part III of this Final Report.

The Purpose of the POA and a Proposed New Structure
Section 2 of the POA states that the statute's purpose is "to replace the summary conviction procedure for the prosecution of provincial offences...with a procedure that reflects the distinction between provincial offences and criminal offences." The POA's underlying objectives were to establish a fair and efficient method of resolving provincial offences proportionate to the complexity or seriousness of the offence, but different from the process governing criminal cases. Given the numbers of unrepresented litigants today, accessibility is an increasingly important objective. It is also important that the POA, as a procedural code, further the objectives of the offence-creating statute to which it applies.

We therefore recommend that the purpose section be amended to incorporate these concepts in order to guide parties and the court when interpreting the POA, and to inform the development of any rules, forms or other subordinate authority. (Recommendation 2)

We believe the POA and its four sets of rules and seven regulations must be simplified. The POA contains 10 parts and

176 sections, with internal exceptions and frequent cross-references to other sections, regulations or forms. The trial provisions apply to the most serious and less serious offences without distinction.

We therefore recommend that the POA be restructured to remove the detailed procedural code to regulation, leaving only those matters that are properly left within a statute. While it should continue to prescribe different streams for less serious and more serious matters, the bulk of the procedural code should appear in a single rule, regulation or other subordinate authority, with streamlined procedures for less serious offences, and more detailed procedures for more complex cases, consistent with the principle of proportionality. Simple, plain language guides for defendants would make the POA more readily accessible. We further recommend that the Attorney General and the Chief Justice (Ontario Court of Justice), in consultation with others, jointly determine the most appropriate body to develop the new procedural code. (Recommendations 3 to 9)

Administrative Monetary Penalties as an Alternative to the Court Process

Justices of the peace preside over virtually all provincial offence trials, with nearly 60% of their time spent presiding over Part I and Part II trials. Given the relatively minor nature of many of these offences, we assess whether the relevant POA provisions be replaced by an administrative monetary penalty system that is less expensive and more efficient.

An administrative monetary penalty (AMP or AMPS) is a penalty imposed that is due once an infraction has been detected, unlike a fine, which is imposed only once a party has pleaded guilty to an offence or the court has convicted the defendant. AMP systems are already in place in Ontario for certain regulatory breaches. They are said to be an effective and efficient tool to enforce compliance with regulatory standards, while respecting principles of fairness since they typically provide an opportunity to dispute the AMP before an independent, administrative decision-maker (rather than the court).

The *Municipal Act, 2001* (which does not apply to the City of Toronto) authorizes municipalities to establish systems of administrative penalties for parking infractions which are then no longer subject to the POA, but so far, only the City of Vaughan and the City of Oshawa have done so (although the City of Oshawa approved the adoption of an AMPS parking regime on January 31, 2011 which came into effect on March 1, 2011). The experience of the City of Vaughan has been that matters are heard much more quickly; defendants are given a firm hearing date; less time is wasted by the public; there are cost savings by using administrative hearing officers; hearings are streamlined without the need for a prosecutor; and it frees up time on the court's dockets to hear more serious matters.

While cost arguments support a move to an AMPS regime, they are not determinative. Proportionality is a major consideration. Non-judicial adjudicators in Ontario deal with matters of fundamental importance to us, such as our human rights, our rights as tenants, our entitlement to social assistance and our ability to work and be licensed in a chosen profession. Yet, under our current POA regime, it is possible to get a trial before a justice to adjudicate upon a disputed $30 parking ticket. We believe greater respect for the rule of law and the administration of justice would be achieved if court and judicial resources were reserved for more serious matters.

In light of the challenges arising for each municipality, we recommend a three year delay before any provincial legislation providing for mandatory AMPS systems for parking infractions comes into force. (Recommendations 10 and 14)

We provide a constitutional analysis under sections 7 and 11 of the *Canadian Charter of Rights and Freedoms* in relation to the AMPS system under the *Municipal Act, 2001*, based on Supreme Court of Canada jurisprudence and cases examining AMPS in other contexts. We conclude that given the maximum permissible penalty and that penalties cannot be punitive, the system we endorse is constitutional. We further conclude that higher penalties for improperly using disabled parking spaces would be constitutionally permissible under AMPS and therefore *we recommend that the AMPS regulation under the Municipal Act, 2001 be appropriately amended to include the improper use of disabled parking spaces in an AMPS regime.* (Recommendations 11 to 13)

The vast majority (80%) of Part I offences arise under the *Highway Traffic Act* and are heard by justices of the peace. We considered whether they should also be subject to an AMPS system. We concluded, however, that the nature of these offences raises more complicated issues than do parking infractions and therefore *we recommend that the Ontario government review Part I offences to determine which, if any, would be better addressed through AMPS.* (Recommendation 15)

Under Part IV, we briefly discuss the used AMPS for parking enforcement by First Nation communities

Sentencing Reform

The maximum fine for a Part I offence is $1,000. For Part III offences, the maximum fine is $5,000, unless a statute directs otherwise, and imprisonment is possible where authorized by the offence-creating statute. Certain other sentencing tools, such as probation, are available, but only for Part III offences and their use is limited.

The POA lacks a statement of sentencing principles and only a few decisions from appellate courts are available to guide lower courts, including a leading decision now a quarter century old. As a result, there has been marked variation in sentences and a call for consistent sentencing principles. Sentencing principles adopted under the *Criminal Code* may serve as a model, although these principles have been criticized as failing to give sufficient guidance to the court on their application or interrelationship.

If sentencing is to be legitimate, it should be based on a consistent and principled approach that aligns that part of the regulatory process with the underlying regulatory objectives. *We therefore recommend that the POA be amended to provide a statement of sentencing principles for general application within the POA, subject to different or additional principles being prescribed in the offence-creating statute.* (Recommendations 16 to 17)

Sentencing would promote the remedying of harm, rehabilitation, deterrence and where there are aggravating factors, a denunciatory or punitive penalty.

For many offences, the sentencing principles may have little or no impact. Fines for certain regulatory offences may well remain the most effective means of promoting compliance with regulatory standards. However, where fines are issued, it will only be after a court has first considered whether remediation and rehabilitation sentencing orders can best achieve regulatory objectives.

The adoption of sentencing principles represents a shift away from the traditional deterrence-fine paradigm and will be most helpful and appropriate for Part III offences. Given the principle of proportionality and the objective of maintaining simple, streamlined processes for Part I offences, the LCO is not persuaded that the new sentencing principles *must* apply when sentencing Part I offences, but rather where the unusual circumstances of the case warrant it.

The proposed sentencing principles cannot be realized with the penalties currently available. *We therefore recommend that the POA be amended to give the court authority to (a) make probation orders for all provincial offences in order to achieve the remedial and rehabilitative sentencing principles, including broad authority to order terms of probation (although for less serious offences only under certain circumstances); (b) make express, freestanding restitution or compensatory orders outside of probationary terms that may be enforced in civil courts; (c) use victim impact statements; and (d) impose an embedded auditor to monitor compliance with regulatory standards. We defer to the Ministry of the Attorney General consideration of whether alternative measure programs should also be available for less serious offences, after further consultation with municipalities.* (Recommendations 18 to 23)

When corporations and other business enterprises breach regulatory standards, it can have significant deleterious effects on communities and potentially thousands of consumers. Fines may not be the most effective sentencing tool since they can often be passed on to consumers.

We therefore recommend that the POA adopt a provision similar to that under the Criminal Code expressly giving the court the power to include remedial and rehabilitative terms within a probation order against a corporation or other business enterprise, whether incorporated or not, as well as clear authority for the court to impose a punitive or denunciatory penalty where appropriate. We further recommend that the Ministry of the Attorney General, in consultation with others, develop a non-exhaustive list of aggravating factors that may justify such a penalty for inclusion within the POA sentencing provisions. (Recommendations 24 and 25)

Bail Reform

Although very few people are arrested for the commission of provincial offences, and even fewer are held or released on bail, the principles of fundamental justice require that a fair and effective mechanism be in place for pre-trial release from custody.

The presumption under the POA is that a defendant who is arrested be released pending the disposition of the charge, unless the detention is necessary to ensure the defendant's attendance in court. There does not appear to be authority to deny bail for the protection and safety of the public, leading to the anomaly that a police officer has the authority to detain a defendant to prevent the continuation or repetition of an offence or the commission of another offence, but a justice does not have the authority to deny bail where there is evidence of a real threat to the safety of the public, including a victim or witness.

We therefore recommend the POA bail provisions be amended to add the protection and safety of the public as a ground for denying bail, but only where there is a real and substantial likelihood that the defendant will commit a serious offence that will harm the public. (Recommendation 26)

Generally speaking, the only justification under the POA to impose bail conditions is to ensure the defendant's appearance in court. There may be other appropriate bail conditions within the limits imposed by the *Charter* and case law, in addition to the safety of the public. However, given the nature of most provincial offences, we are concerned that bail conditions may be overused or unnecessarily imposed. *We therefore recommend that the Ministry of the Attorney General, in consultation with the judiciary, municipal prosecutors, defence bar, paralegals and relevant legal and community organizations review and consider any further bail conditions that ought to be added to the POA. We further recommend the development of judicial guidelines to promote the use of any new bail conditions and review of their use to ensure they are not abused or overused.* (Recommendation 27)

Finally, the bail procedure in the POA has not kept up with recent bail procedural amendments in the *Criminal Code. We recommend that the POA bail procedure be reviewed to assess whether it would benefit from process improvements after considering the Criminal Code bail amendments and other relevant considerations.* (Recommendation 28)

III. OTHER PROCEDURAL REFORMS TO THE POA AND ITS RULES AND REGULATIONS

This Report focuses primarily on structural and major process reforms to the POA, but several discrete procedural issues were raised during our consultations and we make recommendations on several of them.

The POA allows for search warrants to be executed on particular "things", but it fails to appreciate searches of electronic data on computerized systems or devices. While we believe that it would be appropriate to amend the POA accordingly, we recognize the highly intrusive nature of searches of personal computers and other electronic sources of information. Also, section 160 of the POA, which seeks to protect searches that uncover documents subject to solicitor-client privilege, may not be lawful because it does not require that the client – the privilege holder – to be advised that the document has been seized.

We therefore recommend that the Ministry of the Attorney General or body responsible for developing the new POA procedural code consider these search warrant issues, so that appropriate amendments may be made. (Recommendations 29 and 30)

With the licensing of paralegals in Ontario, more paralegals appear on POA matters, raising the appropriateness of paralegal-client privilege. *We recommend that the Ministry of the Attorney General further consider this in consultation with the Law Society of Upper Canada, paralegals and others.* (Recommendation 31)

At least one Ontario regulator relies on the POA's search warrant provisions to obtain bank records in order to investigate and prosecute certain offences, although it is not clear that banks have the authority to disclose bank records in response to a search warrant without first giving notice to the account holder. It appears that what is truly sought is a production order from a non-party (e.g., a bank), rather than a search warrant. At this time, we do not recommend that production orders be authorized under the POA because there are outstanding policy and operational issues that must first be considered. *We therefore recommend that the Ministry of the Attorney General or body responsible for developing the new POA procedural code consider this issue further.* (Recommendation 32)

The POA states that common law defences are applicable in POA proceedings. It was proposed that common law defences be codified within the POA; however, we do not recommend the implementation of this proposal given the difficulty of codifying common law defences and the risk of freezing them under the POA while the common law would develop in the criminal context. However, *we do recommend that the Ministry of the Attorney General include a summary of common defences in its guides on POA proceedings.* (Recommendations 33 and 34)

Section 109 of the *Courts of Justice Act*, requiring that Notice of Constitutional Question (NCQ) be served on the federal and provincial Attorneys General under certain circumstances, was drafted prior to municipalities taking over the prosecution and courts administration of POA offences. *We therefore recommend that the Court of Justice Act be amended to: require that prosecutors in all POA matters be served with NCQ; and require that that a NCQ be served on a municipal prosecutor when relief is sought arising from an act or omission of a municipality.* (Recommendation 35)

The POA allows for convictions of Parts I and II offences to be "reopened" if a defendant has been convicted without a hearing and seeks to have the case reopened within 15 days of becoming aware of the conviction. There have been concerns that this rule has been abused and it has been proposed that limits on its use be introduced. *We therefore recommend that the Ministry of the Attorney General or body responsible for developing the new POA procedural code consider this issue further.* (Recommendation 36)

Section 124 of the POA references when an appeal of a Part III matter should not be allowed, but it refers to a "certificate" which suggests a proceeding commenced under Parts I or II. *We recommend that the Ministry of the Attorney General or body responsible for developing the new POA procedural code consider this issue further.* (Recommendation 37)

Media reports suggest that there are over $1 billion in unpaid fines in Ontario, although this may not be completely accurate. New enforcement tools have recently been introduced, but they may be of limited assistance. Other provinces have agreements with the Canada Revenue Agency whereby unpaid fines are deducted from income tax refunds and GST rebates. However, for some low-income Ontarians, tax refunds and GST rebates may represent a significant source of income needed for basic necessities. *We recommend that the Government of Ontario, in consultation with municipalities and others, assess whether this tax diversion is an effective and fair fine enforcement tool, with due policy consideration given to its potential impact on low-income Ontarians.* (Recommendation 38)

The POA contains various provisions to allow for certain hearings to be heard by telephone or videoconference, although some have not yet been proclaimed. *We recommend that the Ministry of the Attorney General or body responsible for developing the new POA procedural code consider the effectiveness of these provisions (once proclaimed) and recommend any improvements it may deem appropriate.* (Recommendation 39)

The POA permits the Superior Court of Justice to review POA decisions, but the Superior Court does not have the authority to review cost decisions which must be appealed, leading to unnecessarily fractured proceedings. *We therefore recommend that the POA be amended to provide jurisdiction to the Superior Court of Justice to review a cost award when a review to that court has been brought.* (Recommendation 40)

The ability to identify the French language needs of Francophones is not reflected in current POA procedures. *We recommend the development of proactive procedures for early identification of French Language needs.* (Recommendation 41)

The fair and equitable treatment of persons with disabilities requires that their needs be given particular attention when developing any court process, including the newly updated POA procedural code. *We recommend that these needs be identified so that the newly updated POA procedural code can respond to them early and effectively.* (Recommendation 42)

We were also told of concerns with having to physically attend a courthouse to file a notice of intention to appear in response to a Part I certificate of offence or Part II parking infraction notice. This can be particularly burdensome where a defendant (or defendant's representative) does not reside near the courthouse where the offence is filed. *We recommend that options be developed to reduce the cost and burden of attending courthouses to file notices of intention to appear.* (Recommendation 43)

The Ministry of the Attorney General's POA Streamlining Review of 2006 developed a list of proposals for POA reform, but only some of them have been implemented. *We recommend that body responsible for developing the newly updated POA procedural code review the recommendations of the POA Streamlining Review Working Group to assess whether any recommended amendments not yet implemented should be adopted by way of rule, regulation or statutory amendment.* (Recommendation 44)

IV. FUTURE LAW REFORM INITIATIVES

We also identify three issues that were brought to our attention but which we are unable to address in this report: the treatment of young persons charged with provincial offences; the application of the POA to Aboriginal people; and the possible application of AMPS to First Nation communities. In each case, *we recommend that the Ontario government review these matters, in consultation with affected groups.* (Recommendations 45 to 47)

Legislative References

A

Access to Justice Act, 2006, S.O. 2006, c. 21 (Bill 14)

B

Blind Persons' Rights Act, R.S.O. 1990, c. B.7

Building Code Act, 1992, S.O. 1992, c. 23

C

Canada Shipping Act, 2001, S.C. 2001, c. 26

Canadian Charter of Rights and Freedoms, part I of the *Constitution Act, 1982*, RSC 1985, app. II, no. 44

Canadian Environmental Protection Act, S.C. 1999, c. 33

Clean Water Act, 2006, S.O. 2006, c. 22

Compulsory Automobile Insurance Act, R.S.O. 1990, c. C.25

Constitution Act, 1982, RSC 1985, app. II, no. 44

Contraventions Act, S.C. 1992, c. 47

Courts of Justice Act, R.S.O. 1990, c. C.43

Criminal Code, R.S.C. 1985, c. C-46

D

Department of Transport Act, R.S.C. 1985, c. T-18
    Historic Canals Regulations, SOR/93-220

Dog Owners' Liability Act, R.S.O. 1990, c. D.16

E

Environmental Protection Act, R.S.O. 1990, c. E.19

Evidence Act, R.S.O. 1990, c. E.23

F

Fisheries Act, R.S.C. 1985, c. F-14

G

Gaming Control Act, S.O. 1992, c. 24

H

Highway Traffic Act, R.S.O. 1990, c. H.8

L

Law Society Act, R.S.O. 1990, c. L.8

Liquor Licence Act, R.R.O. 1990,

Liquor Licence Act, R.S.O. 1990, c. L.19
    Regulation 719, Licences to Sell Liquor

M

Municipal Act, 2001, S.O. 2001, c. 25

O

Occupational Health and Safety Act, R.S.O. 1990, c. O.1

P

Paralegal Professional Conduct Guidelines (Toronto: Law Society of Upper Canada, 2008)

Paralegal Rules of Conduct (Toronto: Law Society of Upper Canada, 2007)

Pesticides Act, R.S.O. 1990, c. P.11

Planning Act, R.S.O. 1990, c. P.13

Police Services Act, R.S.O. 1990, c. P.15

Practice Management Guidelines (Toronto: Law Society of Upper Canada, 2011)

Provincial Offences Act, R.S.O. 1990, c. P.33

R

Rules of Professional Conduct (Toronto: Law Society of Upper Canada, 2000)

T

Trespass to Property Act, R.S.O. 1990, c. T.21

Glossary

absolute liability offence an offence for which the prosecution must prove that the defendant committed the illegal act; the defendant has no opportunity to argue reasonableness or due diligence

adjourn put the trial over to a new date

amending up the practice of having the defendant tried on the actual rate of speed instead of the reduced rate of speed specified by the officer when the charges were laid

appellant the party bringing an appeal, either the defence or the prosecution

arraignment the formal reading of the charges to the defendant or the defendant's representative in anticipation of a plea

balance of probabilities a standard of proof where an illegal act must be proven to be more likely than not to have occurred

beyond a reasonable doubt a standard of proof where the prosecution must fully prove that the defendant committed the illegal act (to the extent that a reasonable person would not doubt that the act was committed)

burden of proof the responsibility for proving guilt or innocence; rests with either the prosecution or the defence, depending on the circumstances

certificate of offence a certificate of a violation prepared by an officer under Part I of the POA

certificate of parking infraction a notice of a violation issued by an officer under Part II of the POA

charging act a piece of legislation under which a person is charged (e.g., the *Highway Traffic Act*)

charging documents used to initiate charges against a defendant

conviction a final decision by a justice that there is proof that the defendant committed the offence for which he or she was charged

costs a fee added to a court-imposed penalty

court the Ontario Court of Justice, which includes the provincial offences court

court administration staff work within the courthouse providing information and performing various administrative duties

court clerk ensures POA proceedings run smoothly by providing assistance to the judge or justice

court interpreter provides translation services to defendants who do not speak English

court security officer special constables who have been appointed to assist with courthouse security and attend to specific incidents that may arise

cross-examination the prosecution or defence questions the opposing side's witnesses, following examination-in-chief

defence of due diligence the defendant must show that he or she took all reasonable steps to avoid committing the act in question

defence of necessity the defendant must show that it was necessary to commit the act in question, that no reasonable alternative existed, and that the harm caused by the act was outweighed by the harm that was avoided

defendant has been charged with an offence under a statute governed by the *Provincial Offences Act*

demerit points a penalty administered by the Ministry of Transportation for driving offences

deterrence a principle of sentencing intended to discourage a defendant from reoffending; specific and general are the two types of deterrence

disclosure documentation that the prosecutor will be relying on to prove the charges against the defendant

dismissed a final decision by a justice that there is not enough evidence to support a conviction against the defendant

docket the list of defendants scheduled for trial

driving record a record of convictions against a driver maintained by the Ministry of Transportation

due diligence the standard of care that a reasonable person would be expected to apply to a specific situation

elements of the offence the items that have to be proven by the prosecutor to secure a conviction

***ex parte* trial** a trial held without the defendant or the defendant's representative

examination-in-chief the prosecution or defence questions its own witnesses at the trial

fatal error a serious mistake on a charging document that will result in the charges being withdrawn, dismissed, or stayed

guilty with submissions pleading guilty, but providing additional information on why the penalty should be reduced or the time for payment should be extended

held down hearing a matter at a later time

institutional delay the amount of time it takes for a matter to get to trial, minus any delay that was caused by the defendant

justice of the peace a magistrate who presides over proceedings in provincial offences court

limitation period the time allowed for an officer to lay a charge against a defendant

mens rea offence an offence for which the prosecution must prove that the defendant committed the illegal act and had a guilty mind (i.e., the knowledge, intent, or willingness to commit the act)

mitigating factor information about a defendant that is presented to a justice after conviction and may lead to a lesser penalty

monetary retainer a sum of money paid up front for legal services to be provided in the future

non-fatal error a mistake on a charging document that is not serious and will likely be amended in court

Notice of Intention to Appear Form 8, used for the defendant to request a trial

offence a violation of a piece of legislation, or of a regulation or a bylaw made under a piece of legislation

offence notice a yellow copy attached to a certificate of offence that is served on the defendant, commonly called a "ticket"

onus the responsibility on the part of the prosecution for proving an allegation, or on the part of the defendant for bringing forward and proving a defence

police officer has the authority to lay charges against a defendant

probation order a court order that places conditions on a defendant after conviction, often to control the defendant's movements and require certain action

prohibition order a court order that prohibits a defendant from engaging in activities that could lead to a repetition of the offence

prosecutor an agent of the attorney general who prosecutes the charges against the defendant

provincial court judge a lawyer who has been appointed a judge and typically presides over more serious provincial offences cases and appeals

provincial offences officer has the authority to lay charges against a defendant for specific types of provincial offences (includes a police officer)

quash to nullify or invalidate charges against a defendant

quasi-criminal offences offences that bear a resemblance to criminal matters because the procedure for dealing with them is similar to the criminal process (also known as provincial offences)

recognizance an acknowledgment and agreement by the defendant that he or she will attend the next scheduled court appearance

regulations legislation that contains the rules or principles that are enacted under the authority of a statute

regulatory offences laws that have been enacted to regulate behaviour in society (also known as provincial offences)

representative a lawyer or a paralegal who is authorized to represent a defendant in a proceeding under the POA

retainer agreement an agreement for legal services between a licensee and a client

set fine the amount of monetary penalty determined by the chief justice of the Ontario Court of Justice for an offence under Part I or Part II

standard of proof the level of certainty needed for the prosecution to convict, or for a defendant to exonerate himself or herself; can be beyond a reasonable doubt or on a balance of probabilities

staying the proceedings the prosecution of the offence has been halted and a conviction will not be entered against the defendant

strict liability offence an offence for which the prosecution must prove that the defendant committed the illegal act; the defendant then has an opportunity to prove reasonableness or due diligence

summons a document issued to a defendant requiring attendance in court

surety a person who agrees to be responsible for the defendant's appearance in court

tier a court session over a specific period of time

uncontested adjournment moving a trial to a new date after a request by either the prosecution or the defence is agreed to by the other side

verdict the decision or ruling of the justice

victim fine surcharge a fee added to a court-imposed penalty that is then transferred to a special fund to assist victims of crime

waive arraignment a legal representative tells the court clerk that it is not necessary to read the charges

withdrawn a decision by the prosecution to remove the charges against the defendant

witness has first-hand knowledge about the matter being prosecuted

Index

A

absolute liability offence, 34–35

adjourn, 63

adjournment request, 63

Affidavit in Support of a Request for Reopening, 124, 255

aggravating factors, 112

amending up, 140

appeals
- notice of appeal, 126–127
- overview, 125–126
- procedure
  - Parts I and II, 127–128
  - Part III, 128–129

appellant, 126

arraignment, 92

arrest with a warrant, 48

arrest without a warrant, 48, 162

B

bail hearing, 49

balance of probabilities, 33

beyond a reasonable doubt, 32

Blind Persons' Rights Act, 163–164

burden of proof, 97–98

C

Canadian Charter of Rights and Freedoms
- s. 7, 35, 79, 141
- s. 11, 42, 62, 79, 82–83
- s. 14, 14
- s. 24, 166

careless driving, 147

certificate of offence, 18, 19

certificate of parking infraction, 20, 21, 22

charging act
- defined, 2
- review by paralegal, 68–70

charging documents
- certificate of offence, 18, 19
- certificate of parking infraction, 20, 22
- defined, 41
- information, 24, 26
- review of, 41, 71–72
- summons, 24, 25

client communication
- closing letter, 121

final account, 121–122

follow up, 120–122

importance of, 75

closing statements, 103

colour of right defence, 97, 160–161

Compulsory Automobile Insurance Act, 154–156

conviction
- consequences of, 56, 121
- defined, 120

costs, 56, 110–112

court, *see also* trial
- defined, 18

court administration staff, 11

court clerk, 12

court interpreter
- defined, 14
- need for, 74–75

court orders, 114–116

court security officer, 12

courtroom
- layout, 90
- rules and etiquette, *see* rules and etiquette in courtroom

Courts of Justice Act
- Regulation 200, 21, 42, 48, 81, 82, 124, 125
- Regulation 722/94, 126
- Regulation 723/94, 127
- s. 38, 6
- s. 39, 6
- s. 42, 14
- s. 125, 14, 60, 74
- s. 136, 89

cross-examination, 101

Crown, *see* prosecutor

D

defence of due diligence, 98–99

defence of necessity, 99

defences, 98–100

defendant, 10

demerit points, 55, 137, 296–303

deterrence, 109

disclosure
- defined, 61
- request for, 72–74

dismissed charge, 120

display screen offences, 150